Landscape and resource management in Bronze Age Nubia

Contributions to the Archaeology of Egypt, Nubia and the Levant

CAENL

Edited by
Manfred Bietak, Robert Rollinger, Rahim Shayegan
and Willeke Wendrich

Volume 17

2024
Harrassowitz Verlag · Wiesbaden

Landscape and resource management in Bronze Age Nubia:

Archaeological perspectives on the exploitation of natural resources and the circulation of commodities in the Middle Nile

Edited by
Julia Budka and Rennan Lemos

2024
Harrassowitz Verlag · Wiesbaden

Cover photo: C. Geiger, © MUAFS Project, LMU.

The research leading to these results has received funding from the European Research Council (ERC) under the European Union's Horizon 2020 research and innovation programme (grant agreement No. 865463).

This publication has undergone the process of international blind peer review.

Bibliografische Information der Deutschen Nationalbibliothek
Die Deutsche Nationalbibliothek verzeichnet diese Publikation in der Deutschen Nationalbibliografie; detaillierte bibliografische Daten sind im Internet über https://dnb.de abrufbar.

Bibliographic information published by the Deutsche Nationalbibliothek
The Deutsche Nationalbibliothek lists this publication in the Deutsche Nationalbibliografie; detailed bibliographic data are available in the Internet at https://dnb.de

For further information about our publishing program consult our website https://www.harrassowitz-verlag.de

Printed on permanent/durable paper.
Typesetting and layout: Kim-Denise Uhe, u.ni medienservice, Hönze
Printing and binding: Hubert & Co., Göttingen
Printed in Germany

ISSN 2627-8022 | e ISSN 2701-5831
ISBN 978-3-447-12137-8 | Ebook ISBN 978-3-447-39498-7

Table of Contents

Part IV: Circulating products, society and ritual landscapes

Foreword by the Editorial Board

Following the UNESCO Campaign to Save the Monuments of Nubia, which faced the threat of submersion in the vast reservoir of the Gamal 'Abd-el-Nasser Lake shared by Egypt and Sudan, there was a surge in research and publications on the ancient cultures of Lower Nubia. This momentum, however, has dwindled, leaving unresolved questions about the development of Nubian communities and their over seven millennia-long contributions to the prehistory and history of Egypt and Africa. Currently, field research on ancient Nubia is possible only to a limited extent in southern Upper Egypt. For a broader understanding, one must turn to research conducted in northern Sudan. In this region, a series of Sudanese and foreign expeditions have found a very promising field for in-depth exploration of Nubia's past—a land aptly dubbed "The Corridor to Africa."

This volume focuses on the resources and crafts of the Middle Nile and its adjoining steppe and desert regions. It presents the initial results of the ERC DiverseNile Project at LMU Munich, incorporating contributions from the online DiverseNile Seminars held in 2021 and 2022 as well as studies by expert researchers. The volume aims to provide a deeper understanding of the economic background of communities in Nubia. The ongoing seminar series in 2023 and 2024 holds the promise of a follow-up volume.

The primary focus of this volume is on the exploitation of gold, which captured the interest of the Egyptians and contributed to the success stories of Egypt and Napata. Additionally, the presentations and discussions encompass other equally important resources and products of the country, highlighting their contributions to shaping history.

The editors of this volume are Julia Budka from Ludwig-Maximilians University Munich (LMU), who served as Principal Investigator of the ERC-funded DiverseNile Project at the University of Munich, and Rennan Lemos from the University of Cambridge. Lemos was part of the LMU team working on the DiverseNile Project from 2020 to 2022 and continues to be affiliated with it. Both Budka and Lemos possess extensive experience in the archaeology of Egypt and Sudan, exemplifying the collaborative nature of international research involving a diverse range of experts in science and archaeology.

This book aims to spark interest in the history of a captivating country. It is sincerely hoped that Sudan's current turmoil will soon cease, paving the way for the restoration of the economy and the well-being of its people. The welfare of this nation, deserving of a brighter future, plays a pivotal role in supporting archaeological research, a key element in shaping national consciousness.

Manfred Bietak
On behalf of the Editorial Board

Preface

This volume first stems from our collective interest in the diachronic exploration of gold extraction, processing and consumption in the Middle Nile within the ERC-funded DiverseNile Project. More specifically, the volume is the direct result of an initial idea for a paper in collaboration with various colleagues focusing on the agency of local inhabitants of Nubia and their input to the gold industry that marked the experiences of communities in Nubia for centuries. This volume is also a direct result of many discussions held in the first DiverseNile seminar series organised by Rennan Lemos in 2021 as well as the second one in 2022, partly co-organised by Chloë Ward. The input of various colleagues working on several aspects of research extraction and management in ancient Nubia provided an opportunity to further develop an idea originally focused on gold into a collective effort to understand Nubian resource management in the Bronze Age. We are deeply grateful to all contributors to this volume, whose work illustrates the rich potential for a better understanding of how resources were extracted, managed, and utilised in complex ways in Nubia by various groups, including both Egyptians and indigenous communities, but also desert nomads.

Fieldwork in Sudan carried out within the framework of the DiverseNile and MUAFS Projects form much of the basis for the discussions introduced here. Our sincere gratitude goes to all authorities of the National Corporation for Antiquities and Museums, Sudan (NCAM), especially Ghalia Garelnabi (Acting Director General during our season in 2022; Director of the Museum), Ibrahim Musa Hamdoon (Director General since 2022) and Abdel Hai Abdel Sawy (Director of Fieldwork). We are also extremely grateful to our inspector Huda Magzoub Elbashir for all her contributions to the projects.

We are grateful to Manfred Bietak and the CAENL Editorial Board for accepting this volume for publication in their series. Julia Budka would like to acknowledge the role of Chloë Ward in improving the written English of her contributions to this book and for taking over the task of organising the DiverseNile Seminars from September 2022. Chloë Ward was also responsible for improving the written English of all contributions by non-native authors in this volume after the peer-reviewing process. Julia Budka would furthermore like to thank Patrizia Heindl who helped with some of the editing of this publication. We are also grateful to the two anonymous reviewers and their productive feedback which helped to strengthen some of the arguments throughout this book.

This volume was finalised in a difficult time for Sudan as a result of the conflict between the Sudanese Armed Forces and the Rapid Support Forces. As much as we are delighted to offer a further contribution to the investigation of ancient Sudan, we are also deeply concerned about the risks the people and the cultural heritage of Sudan are facing. We fully support all our friends and colleagues in Sudan and would like to express our appreciation for their commitment to the preservation of the Sudanese cultural heritage in these extremely difficult times.

Funding statement

This volume is a result of the DiverseNile Project. The project received funding from the European Research Council (ERC) under the European Union's Horizon 2020 research and innovation programme (grant agreement No. 865463).

Munich and Cambridge, December 2023
Julia Budka and Rennan Lemos

<table>
<tr><th>BC</th><th colspan="2">Egypt</th><th>Lower Nubia</th><th>Upper Nubia</th><th>Desert</th></tr>
<tr><td>2500</td><td rowspan="2">Old Kingdom</td><td>4th Dynasty
5th Dynasty</td><td></td><td rowspan="4">Kerma ancien
(Old Kush I)</td><td rowspan="7"></td></tr>
<tr><td>2150</td><td>6th Dynasty</td><td rowspan="2">C-Group Ia</td></tr>
<tr><td rowspan="3"></td><td rowspan="3">First Intermediate Period</td><td>7th/8th Dynasty</td></tr>
<tr><td>9th Dynasty</td><td rowspan="3">C-Group Ib</td></tr>
<tr><td>10th Dynasty</td><td rowspan="4">Kerma moyen
(Old Kush II)</td></tr>
<tr><td rowspan="3">1950</td><td rowspan="3">Middle Kingdom</td><td>11th Dynasty</td></tr>
<tr><td>12th Dynasty</td><td>C-Group IIa
C-Group IIb</td></tr>
<tr><td>13th Dynasty</td><td rowspan="2"></td><td rowspan="2">Pan-Grave</td></tr>
<tr><td>1700</td><td>Second Intermediate Period</td><td>15th/17th Dynasty</td><td>Kerma Classique
(Old Kush III)</td></tr>
<tr><td>1550</td><td rowspan="2">New Kingdom</td><td>18th Dynasty</td><td colspan="2" rowspan="2">Colonial Nubia</td><td rowspan="3"></td></tr>
<tr><td>c. 1290</td><td>19th & 20th Dynasties</td></tr>
<tr><td>1070</td><td colspan="2">Third Intermediate Period
(c. until 750 BC)</td><td colspan="2">Pre-Napatan Period
(c. until 900 BC)</td></tr>
</table>

Fig. 1 Time table of Bronze Age Sudan in correlation to Egypt.

General introduction

Julia Budka and Rennan Lemos

Bronze Age[1] Nubia[2] (Fig. 1) especially during the colonial New Kingdom Period,[3] has often been considered as little more than the source of Egypt's wealth. As such, the Kerma Kingdom's engagement with Nubia's natural landscape has been largely ignored, despite considerable archaeological evidence for the Nubian extraction of natural resources and the use of a large variety of materials in the production of objects.

This volume brings together scholars working across Sudan (Fig. 2) to consider the management of resources in Bronze Age Nubia; though a few contributions focus on earlier and later periods, providing a diachronic perspective (see, e.g., Chapters 2 and 3). Proper consideration of the situation before and after the Bronze Age is, of course, crucial to address questions of regionality, landscape use and access to natural resources, as well as how this may have changed over time.

The collected papers cover a wide range of topics, including, among others, the extraction and processing of gold from the Nubian deserts and its use in objects of consumption and tribute, the production and consumption of pottery, the role of materials and products in the shaping of mortuary landscapes, and connectivity – through materials – between the Nile Valley and other areas of Nubia.

As Dietrich Klemm and colleagues have stressed: "[t]he main natural resource necessary for human life is water, and its availability within an arid climate zone is a basic necessity. In addition, arable soil areas are indispensable for sedentary cultures."[4] The crucial role of the river Nile and Nile mud as an important building material – as well as raw material for pottery and other objects – are key elements to understand the development of Nubian cultures. Despite the important role of the Nile, Nubia was rich in many other natural resources and there is still a limited understanding of how these were utilised by different Nubian communities over time.

Our hope is that the present volume will help fill a gap in our knowledge of how natural resources were extracted, managed and utilised in complex ways, with a primary focus on the time between the Kerma Period and the end of the New Kingdom colonial Period in Nubia. We also hope that these chapters open up new research beyond Egyptocentric perspectives which focus on the colonial exploration/exploitation of Nubia.

The contributions gathered here are significant for various reasons. Firstly, research has often been biased in its investigation of the Middle Nile – with Nubia traditionally viewed from an Egyptian perspective[5] –resulting in several shortcomings in assessing African cultures in Sudan.[6] In reality, complex multi-directional cultural encounters are traceable between the Lower and Middle Nile over time, which resulted in cultural mixing, intermingling and entanglement, as well as blurred cultural and geographic boundaries.[7] Recent research in the region more appropriately integrates postcolonial theories and avoids Egyptocentric perspectives. The effectiveness of such research is nicely illustrated by Andrea Manzo's recent publication, which addresses Egypt and Africa with new approaches towards the study of technology, networks and trade.[8] These approaches are the backbone on which this volume is built, see especially the contributions by Schrader and Buzon (Chapter 8) and Smith (Chapter 9).

Secondly, the procurement of materials and management of resources are topics which have recently gained in popularity, and increasingly refined multidisciplinary approaches enable us to investigate objects' complete *chaîne opératoire* (see also D'Ercole, Chapter 10).[9] An excellent example for these new advances is the study of copper in Egypt and Nubia[10] and copper production at Kerma.[11] From the New Kingdom town of Amara West, a recent study has provided important insights into the complexity of production chains, the availability of material and

1 Bronze Age for Sudan is a disputed term, see most recently de Souza 2023. We use it, however, to correlate the periods of the Middle and Late Bronze Age with the ones in Egypt (for details see Fig. 1).

2 Nubia has been defined in various ways; we refer to it in this volume in a broad geographical sense as the region extending from the First to the Sixth Cataract, see Auenmüller 2019, 39.

3 See, e.g., Vercoutter 1959, 120–153; Müller 2013, 74–79; Morris 2018, 130.

4 Klemm, Klemm and Murr 2019, 25.

5 As stressed, e.g., by Edwards 2004, 7–9; van Pelt 2013; Lemos and Tipper 2021.

6 See, e.g., Bonnet 2019.

7 See, e.g., Smith 2003. See also van Pelt 2013; Smith 2015; Spencer, Stevens and Binder 2017, 42; Howley 2018; Smith and Buzon 2018; Lemos 2020a; Smith 2020.

8 Manzo 2022; see also a review of this study: Smith 2023. Another recent perspective is Moreno García 2023.

9 For a recent detailed reconstruction of ancient activities connected to paint and painting at Amara West see Fulcher 2022, 75–87.

10 Odler 2023.

11 Rademakers et al. 2022.

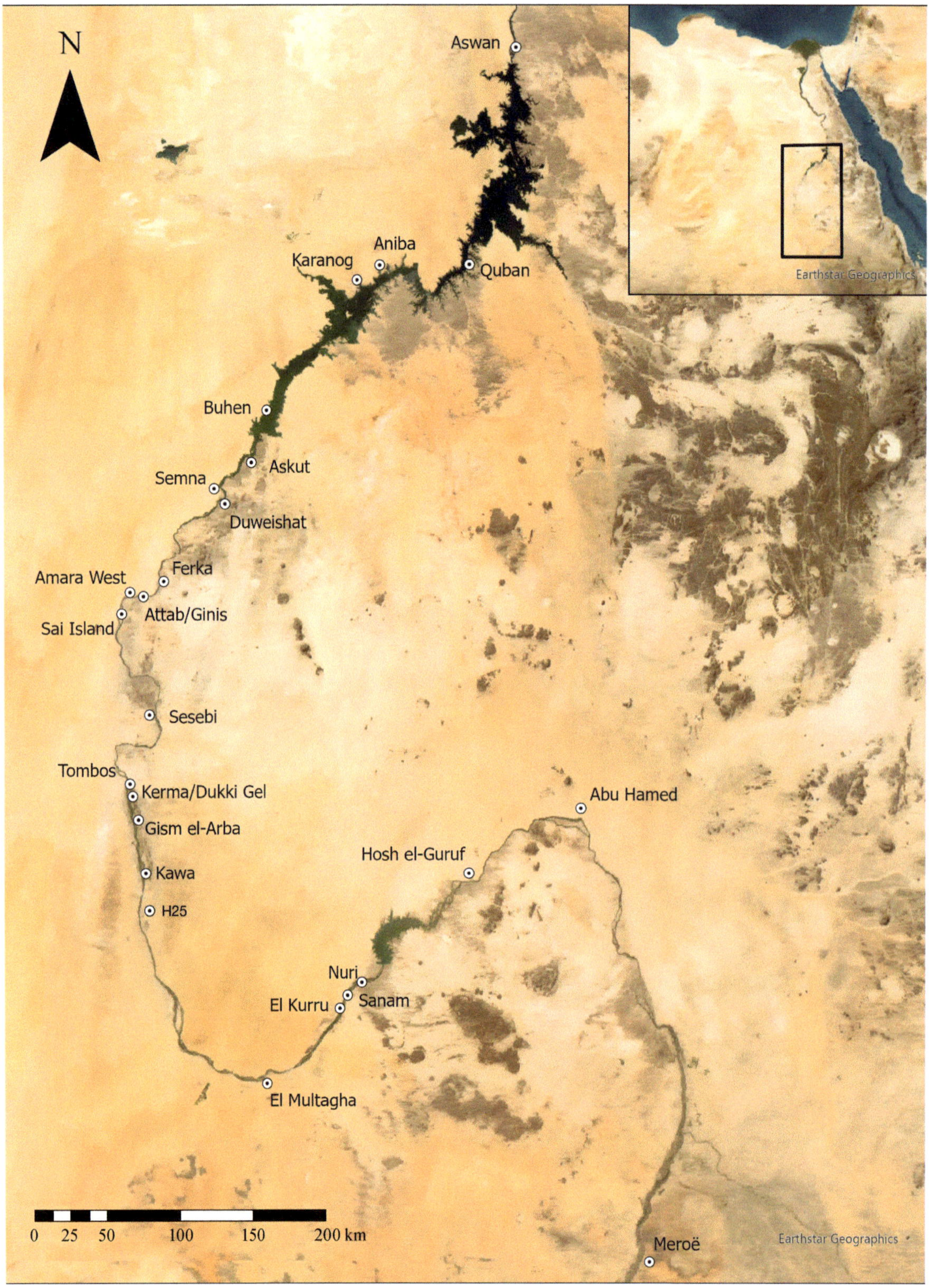

Fig. 2 Map with the sites mentioned in this volume (map by K. Rose, ©DiverseNile Project).

supply in colonial Nubia through a direct comparison with Egypt.[12] Recycling of metal and long-time circulation are crucial topics to understand the import of products and materials from Egypt into Nubia and the related complex interactions. Current research is beginning to ask crucial questions about the co-option and co-operation of various groups inhabiting the Nile Valley, as well as the deserts and oases, especially regarding technologies like metal working, pottery (see D'Ercole, Chapter 10) and faience production (see Lacovara, Chapter 2).[13] The social organisation of raw material procurement is still unclear and requires further research, as will be outlined throughout this volume.

The DiverseNile Project and DiverseNile Seminar Series

Over the last few years, considerable progress has been made in the assessment of cultural diversity in Egyptian and Sudanese archaeology.[14] Cultural diversity encompasses a large variety of topics (e.g., intersocial aspects like gender, age, ethnicity, origin; social complexity and settlement patterns; subsistence strategies; cooking practice/nutrition; religious practices; health and shape; technologies and technology transfer; trade and contacts) and allows us to consider concepts beyond identity, including external factors (e.g. geographic location, educational background, religious practices and religion etc.) and organisational dimensions (e.g. work location, group and unit, administration etc.) wherever possible.[15]

This volume is the result of ideas, discussions and questions that arose primarily during the DiverseNile Seminar Series in 2021 and 2022 – a series of lectures dedicated to cultural diversity in the Bronze Age Middle Nile organised within the framework of the ERC DiverseNile Project.[16] The main hypothesis of this project is that regional studies, such as the one focusing on the hinterland of the Kerma Kingdom's northern stronghold at Sai, hold great potential for achieving a more realistic understanding of complex social dynamics and cultural interactions in the Bronze Age (focusing on c. 1800–1200 BC). Considering earlier and later phases can also contribute to new reconstructions of social practices embedded in the use of landscape (see, e.g., Garcea, Chapter 5).

There is a need to expedite such integrative research which focuses on the periphery and hinterland of principal urban centres, considers both landscape and people and permits us to address the cultural dynamics and diversity of ancient Nilotic groups. The ERC DiverseNile Project aims to do just that with the concept of 'contact spaces'.[17] The primary objective of the DiverseNile Project is to reconstruct Middle Nile landscape biographies beyond established cultural categories, enabling new insights into the ancient dynamics of social spaces.[18] The geographic focus of the study is the research concession area of the Munich University Attab to Ferka Survey Project (MUAFS) which covers a stretch of the Nile, including various islands, between Attab and Ferka in northern Sudan (see below, Introduction to Part I).

Since 2020, the ERC DiverseNile Project has been evaluating specific living conditions in the Attab to Ferka region during the Bronze Age in direct comparison to urban centres, such as Amara West and Sai Island. One of the aims is also to construct landscape biographies shaped by humans, human activities, technologies, materiality, and animals.[19] The project has adopted an objectscapes approach[20] and has already demonstrated that an effective integration of the range of evidence available – rather than focusing primarily on textual sources – means that more suitable alternative narratives can be established.[21]

Outlook

This volume will hopefully illustrate the fundamental necessity of including social practices, communities, and subsistence strategies of both central sites and regions, as well as so-called peripheries in ancient Nubia in order to understand the complexities of cultural processes and encounters. Fundamentally, we must diversify our approach to the study of Bronze Age Nubia to move away from inherent regional biases which have influenced almost all aspects of our existing interpretations of life and death in Nubia,[22] including resource management and production techniques. Future work in marginal regions like the area between Attab and Ferka has much potential to address further aspects of cultural diversity in various social settings and will enable us to write new, more inclusive narratives. As the chapters in this volume demonstrate, new scientific data and analyses can be effectively integrated into interdisciplinary approaches to help establish these new narratives.

12 Rademakers et al. 2023.

13 See most recently Minor 2023 for a case study.

14 See, e.g., for Egypt: Maynart, Velloza and Lemos 2018; for Sudan: Raue 2019; Lemos and Tipper 2021 with references, cf. also Budka 2021.

15 Following the modern concept "4 Layers of Diversity" (personality, internal dimensions, external dimensions and organisational dimensions) after Gardenswartz and Rowe 2003.

16 See https://www.sudansurvey.gwi.uni-muenchen.de/index.php/erc-project-diversenile/.

17 Following the concept of 'contact spaces' by Stockhammer and Athanassov 2018. See Budka in press.

18 Budka 2019; Budka 2020.

19 Kolen and Renes 2015.

20 E.g., Lemos 2020b. See also below, Introduction to Part I and Chapter 10 (D'Ercole this volume).

21 See Lemos and Budka 2021.

22 See, e.g., Näser 2017; Lemos 2020b; Smith 2020.

Bibliography

Auenmüller, J.
2019 Topography and regional geography of Nubia: river, cataract and desert landscapes, in: D. Raue (ed.), *Handbook of Ancient Nubia, Vol. 1*, Berlin; Boston, 39–61.

Bonnet, C.
2019 *The Black Kingdom of the Nile*, Cambridge, MA; London.

Budka, J.
2019 Towards Middle Nile biographies: The Munich University Attab to Ferka survey project 2018/2019, *Sudan & Nubia* 23, 13–26.
2020 Kerma presence at Ginis East: the 2020 season of the Munich University Attab to Ferka survey project, *Sudan & Nubia* 24, 57–71.
2021 *Tomb 26 on Sai Island: A New Kingdom Elite Tomb and Its Relevance for Sai and Beyond*, Leiden.
in press New approaches to landscape archaeology: towards contact space biographies in the Middle Nile, in: *FS NN*, in press.

Edwards, D.N.
2004 *The Nubian Past. An Archaeology of the Sudan*, London.

Fulcher, K.
2022 *Painting Amara West: The Technology and Experience of Colour in New Kingdom Nubia*, British Museum Publications on Egypt and Sudan 13; Amara West Research Publications 1, Leuven.

Gardenswartz, L. and Rowe, A.
2003 *Diverse Teams at Work. Capitalzing on the Power of Diversity*, 2nd edition, Alexandria, Virgina.

Howley, K.
2018 Power relations and the adoption of foreign material culture: a different perspective from first-millennium BCE Nubia, *Journal of Ancient Egyptian Interconnections* 17, 18–36.

Klemm, D., Klemm, R. and Murr, A.
2019 Geologically induced raw materials stimulating the development of Nubian culture, in: D. Raue (ed.), *Handbook of Ancient Nubia, Vol. 1*, Berlin; Boston, 15–38.

Kolen, J. and Renes, J.
2015 Landscape biographies: key issues, in: J. Kolen, J. Renes and R. Hermans (eds.), *Landscape Biographies: Geographical, Historical and Archaeological Perspectives on the Production and Transmission of Landscapes*, Amsterdam, 21–47.

Lemos, R.
2020a Material culture and colonization in ancient Nubia: Evidence from the New Kingdom cemeteries, in: C. Smith (ed.), *Encyclopedia of Global Archaeology*, Cham, https://doi.org/10.1007/978-3-319-51726-1_3307-1.
2020b *Foreign Objects in Local Contexts: Mortuary Objectscapes in Late Colonial Nubia (16th–11th centuries BCE)*, PhD thesis, University of Cambridge, https://doi.org/10.17863/CAM.71911.

Lemos, R. and Budka, J.
2021 Alternatives to colonization and marginal identities in New Kingdom colonial Nubia (1550–1070 BCE), *World Archaeology* 53/3, 401–418, https://doi.org/10.1080/00438243.2021.1999853.

Lemos, R. and Tipper, S.
2021 Sudanese and Nubian Archaeology: Scholarship past and present, in: R. Lemos and S. Tipper (eds.), *Current Research in Sudanese and Nubian Archaeology: A Collection of Papers Presented at the Second Sudan Studies Research Conference, Cambridge*, Oxford, 1–12.

Manzo, A.
2022 *Ancient Egypt in its African Context: Economic Networks, Social and Cultural Interactions*, Cambridge Elements: Ancient Egypt in Context, Cambridge.

Maynart, É., Velloza, C. and Lemos, R. (eds.)
2018 *Perspectives on Materiality in Ancient Egypt: Agency, Cultural Reproduction and Change*, Access Archaeology, Oxford.

Minor, E.
2023 Faience tiles from Deir el-Ballas and Kerma: new evidence of Egyptian-Nubian relations at the foundation of the New Kingdom, in: D. Kiser-Go and C.A. Redmount (eds.), *Weseretkau "Mighty of Kas": Papers in Memory of Cathleen A. Keller*, Columbus, GA, 103–116.

Moreno García, J.C.
2023 Egyptology and African history, in: *Oxford Research Encyclopedia of African History*, https://doi.org/10.1093/acrefore/9780190277734.013.1280.

Morris, E.
2018 *Ancient Egyptian Imperialism*, Hoboken, NJ; Chichester.

Müller, I.
2013 *Die Verwaltung Nubiens im Neuen Reich*, Meroitica, Schriften zur altsudanesischen Geschichte und Archäologie 18, Wiesbaden.

Näser, C.
2017 Structures and realities of the Egyptian presence in Lower Nubia from the Middle Kingdom to the New Kingdom: the Egyptian cemetery S/SA at Aniba, in: N. Spencer, A. Stevens and M. Binder (eds.), *Nubia in the New Kingdom: Lived Experience, Pharaonic Control and Indigenous Traditions*, British Museum Publications on Egypt and Sudan 3, Leuven, 557–574.

Odler, M.
2023 *Copper in Ancient Egypt: Before, During and After the Pyramid Age (c. 4000–1600 BC)*, Culture and History of the Ancient Near East 132, Leiden; Boston.

van Pelt, W.P.
2013 Revising Egypto-Nubian relations in New Kingdom Lower Nubia: From Egyptianization to cultural entanglement, *Cambridge Archaeological Journal* 23.3, 523–550.

Rademakers, F.W., Verly, G., Degryse, P., Vanhaecke, F., Marchi, S. and Bonnet, C.
2022 Copper at ancient Kerma: a diachronic investigation of alloys and raw materials, *Advances in Archaeomaterials* 3 (1), 1–18.

Rademakers, F., Auenmüller, J., Spencer, N., Fulcher, K., Lehmann, M., Vanhaecke, F. and Degryse, P.
2023 Metals and pigments at Amara West: Cross-craft perspectives on practices and provisioning in New Kingdom Nubia, *Journal of Archaeological Science* 153, 105766, https://doi.org/10.1016/j.jas.2023.105766.

Raue, D.
2019 Cultural diversity of Nubia in the later 3rd – mid 2nd millennium BC, in: D. Raue (ed.), *Handbook of Ancient Nubia, Vol. 1*, Berlin; Boston, 293–333.

Smith, S.T.
2003 *Wretched Kush. Ethnic Identities and Boundaries in Egypt's Nubian Empire*, London; New York.
2015 Hekanefer and the Lower Nubian Princes. Entanglement, double identity or topos and mimesis?, in: H. Amstutz, A. Dorn, M. Müller, M. Ronsdorf and S. Uljas (eds.), *Fuzzy Boundaries (Festschrift Loprieno) II*, Hamburg, 767–779.
2020 The Nubian experience of Egyptian domination during the New Kingdom, in: G. Emberling and B.B. Williams (eds.), *The Oxford Handbook of Ancient Nubia*, Oxford, 369–394.
2023 Andrea Manzo: Ancient Egypt in its African Context: Economic Networks, Social and Cultural Interactions, *African Archaeological Review* 40, 589–591, https://doi.org/10.1007/s10437-023-09538-5.

Smith, S.T. and Buzon, M.R.
2018 The fortified settlement at Tombos and Egyptian colonial strategy in New Kingdom Nubia, in: J. Budka and J. Auenmüller (eds.), *From Microcosm to Macrocosm: Individual Households and Cities in Ancient Egypt and Nubia*, Leiden, 205–225.

Spencer, N., Stevens, A. and Binder, M.
2017 Introduction: History and historiography of a colonial entanglement, and the shaping of new archaeologies for Nubia in the New Kingdom, in: N. Spencer, A. Stevens and M. Binder (eds.), *Nubia in the New Kingdom: Lived Experience, Pharaonic Control and Indigenous Traditions*, British Museum Publications on Egypt and Sudan 3, Leuven, 1–61.

de Souza, A.
2023 The "Bronze Age" concept and Nubia during the second Millennium BCE: does one size fit all?, *Old World: Journal of Ancient Africa and Eurasia* 3, https://doi.org/10.1163/26670755-20230005.

Stockhammer, P.W. and Athanassov, B.
2018 Conceptualising contact zones and contact spaces: An archaeological perspective, in: S. Gimatzidis, M. Pieniążek and S. Mangaloğlu-Votruba (eds.), *Archaeology Across Frontiers and Borderlands. Fragmentation and Connectivity in the North Aegean and the Central Balkans from the Bronze Age to the Iron Age*, Oriental and European Archaeology (OREA) 9, Vienna, 93–112.

Vercoutter, J.
1959 The gold of Kush, *Kush* 7, 120–153.

Part I

Regional perspectives on resource management in the Middle Nile

Introduction

Regionality of resource management in Bronze Age Sudan: An overview and case studies

Julia Budka

In the past decade, there has been an increase in archaeological research in Sudanese regions typically regarded as marginal, such as the Fourth Cataract,[1] Eastern Sudan,[2] the Eastern Desert[3] and the Bayuda Desert.[4] The following part of this volume provides case studies which demonstrate the need to address questions of regionality in the study of resource management in Bronze Age Sudan, not least in order to emphasise "the dynamic nature of society and space."[5]

Jana Eger-Karberg and Tim Karberg use the Bayuda Desert and the region of Kordofan as specific examples (Chapter 1), following the broad theme of this volume. As the authors show, peripheries on the fringes of Nubia, like the Bayuda and Northern Kordofan, are characterised by specific land use strategies adapted to the limited resources available. Understanding these specific strategies can help to reconstruct patterns of regionality in other parts of ancient Sudan.

Peter Lacovara presents an updated perspective on the faience industry in Nubia (Chapter 2) – stressing evidence of both Egyptian and local production of the faience found at Kerma. The topic of the regionality of resource management is closely tied to the next part of this volume, the gold industry. There are also several links with Part IV – which focuses on circulating products, society, and ritual landscapes – where the contributions by Giulia D'Ercole on pottery production in northern Sudan (Chapter 10) and by Loretta Kilroe (Chapter 12) on site H25 close to Kawa as a potential indigenous distribution place, primarily based on ceramic evidence, are especially relevant.

The following provides a short overview of regional aspects of resource management in Bronze Age Sudan, as well as selected case studies to set the scene for the next chapters. Furthermore, stone as a resource in Nubia is also addressed with a particular focus on possible cultural implications for stone quarrying and mining.

Regional complexity in archaeology with a focus on ancient Egypt and Sudan

"Reimagining regional analysis as a multi-scalar, multi-disciplinary practice, inclusive of both natural and cultural landscapes (or inclusive of a landscape that is both cultural and natural), as well as avoiding the errorsnow associated with equating styles or production methods with 'cultures' or 'peoples'"[6]

The last decade has seen regional cultural variation revived as an important topic in archaeology in general[7], and specifically in Northeast African archaeology, including in Egyptian and Sudanese archaeology. This is connected to an increased interest in identity, migration, and mobility, as well as recent advances in spatial analysis, such as GIS based studies.[8]

For ancient Egypt, David Jeffreys has raised the importance of tracing regional differences at the landscape-level.[9] Joan Carlos Moreno García and others have convincingly argued[10] against the monolithic illusion of "the ancient Egypt"[11] – with local and temporal differences highlighted in the last few years in both settlement and funerary archaeology.[12] This has resulted in the recent understanding that there was not a single, static ancient Egypt, but several "Egypts" shaped by local and super-regional dynamics which we need to address with multidisciplinary methods.[13]

Moreno García has addressed, in particular, long neglected collaborations and rivalries between local powers, central authorities and "marginal" populations in Egypt, especially in relation to the flow of objects and resources, and, therefore, wealth. Trade, trade routes, markets, and the control of the circulation of goods hold significant information about power strategies and actors on the political

1 See the summary by Drzewiecki and Cedro 2019, 992–1001; for specific sites see, e.g., Näser 2008; Emberling and Williams 2010; Weschenfelder 2015.
2 Manzo 2017.
3 Davies and Welsby 2020.
4 Lohwasser, Karberg and Auenmüller 2018; Obłuski, Paner and Masojć 2021.
5 Salisbury 2009, 9.
6 Salisbury 2009, 3.
7 Studies of regionality increased in archaeology during the 1960s and 1970s, see, e.g., Johnson 1977. For more recent studies see, e.g., Salisbury 2009 with references.
8 See, e.g., Osman Abdollah 2022; Devesa et al. 2023.
9 Jeffreys 2010.
10 See, e.g., Schneider 2003, 161.
11 Moreno García 2019.
12 See, e.g., Smith and Buzon 2017; Spencer, Stevens and Binder 2017; Budka 2020a.
13 Budka 2021a; see also Moers 2015.

level (see also Lemos in this volume, Introduction to Part IV).[14]

The recent archaeological concept of objectscapes is highly relevant to the study of material culture within the context of cultural encounters because "an objectscape comprises a dynamic repertoire of objects in motion."[15] With the objectscape approach, phenomena within material culture become traceable which offer new insights into various social realities, reflecting lived experiences and local choices. For Bronze Age Sudan, flows of objects and their impact in establishing objectscapes, as well as regional patterns, have been investigated by Rennan Lemos.[16] Building on these results, the ERC DiverseNile Project investigates regionality in the Middle Nile from a multidisciplinary perspective (see also, the Main Introduction to this volume). We combine the objectscape approach with our understanding of contact space as a fluid space shaped by actors and objects within a certain region, in conjunction with the spatial and temporal dimensions of the landscape.[17] As an important outcome, the complexity of cultural dynamics within the Middle Nile and in the adjacent deserts indicates that there was no such entity such as "Ancient Nubia" (or Lower and Upper Nubia) in the New Kingdom, or in any other period, but rather multiple "Nubias".[18] Although this is a similar result to what has recently been proposed for Egypt, one can argue that the impact of regionality in ancient Sudan was perhaps more significant than in the Lower Nile, reflected in the more diverse physiographic subdivision of the region and the long tradition of landscape archaeology in Sudanese archaeology, as opposed to Egyptian archaeology.[19] We can trace similar patterns in different parts of Nubia through ongoing investigations of regional developments of which we still have an only limited understanding.[20]

Regionality on a meso- and microlevel: the Kerma age in Ginis

In the following, some case studies from my own research in northern Sudan will be discussed, illustrating the importance of regional archaeology, specifically in the study of resource management in Bronze Age Nubia.

The Munich University Attab to Ferka Survey Project (MUAFS) started in 2018 in the Attab to Ferka region in northern Sudan.[21] Next to the Dal Cataract region and the natural frontier of the Batn el-Hagar rocky outcrop, the MUAFS research concession (see Fig. 1) – previously documented by the Sudan Antiquities Service, in conjunction with the French Archaeological Unit, with a preliminary survey directed by André Vila in the 1970s – is both a geological boundary zone and a cultural frontier zone. The area has a long history as a contact zone between cultural groups from either the northernmost realm (e.g., for the Kerma Kingdom) or the southernmost region of influence (e.g., for C-Group communities). The aim is to study cultural encounters in this peripheral borderscape, focusing on the period of the Middle and Late Bronze Age. Based on evidence from Hannek and Abu Fatima in the neighbourhood of Tombos, it was appropriately argued that "individual Kerma communities experienced disparate effects of Nubian-Egyptian interaction throughout the Nubian Bronze Age and beyond."[22]

Kerma cemetery GiE 003

Within the MUAFS concession, the Kerma cemetery GiE 003 in Ginis East, on the outskirts of Attab East, was excavated in 2022 and 2023.[23] Five trenches with eroded circular tumuli structures on their surfaces yielded a total of 58 burial pits (Fig. 2). The oldest burials were unearthed in the southern part of the cemetery, Trenches 2 and 5. Whereas Trench 2 only had circular pits associated with the Middle Kerma Period (c. 2000–1750 BC), Trench 5 also revealed Pan-Grave style burials (the Pan-Grave tradition dating to 1800–1550 BC). The burials in Trenches 1, 3 and 4 are all associated with the Classic Kerma Period (c. 1750–1500 BC). It therefore seems likely that Trench 5 shows a transition between the Middle Kerma and the Classic Kerma Period, probably between 1800–1700 BC.

The burial pit types of the Middle and Classic Kerma Period have close parallels at other cemeteries, for example at Akasha, Ukma and Sai.[24] Kerma funerary practices and identities are evident in the ceramics, as well as in the primary grave goods. Strong Kerma cultural expressions are unmistakable for the Classic Kerma burials through the position of the interments on wooden beds/bedframes, animal sacrifices and Black-topped fine ware. The use of funerary beds at GiE 003 is restricted to pits datable to the Classic Kerma Period.[25]

14 Moreno García 2023. For studies on case studies from Sudan with a similar theoretical framework see, e.g., Lemos 2020; Walsh 2022.
15 Pitts and Versluys 2021.
16 Lemos 2020.
17 Budka in press.
18 Cf. Lemos 2020.
19 See Edwards 2020 with references.
20 For a recent case study see Dalton et al. 2023.
21 Budka 2019; Budka 2020b.
22 Akmenkalns 2018, xiv. Cf. also Walsh 2022; Budka 2023.
23 Labelled by Vila 1977, 80 as 2-T-39; see Budka 2023; Budka, Rose and Ward 2023, 20–24.
24 See Budka 2023.
25 Budka 2023.

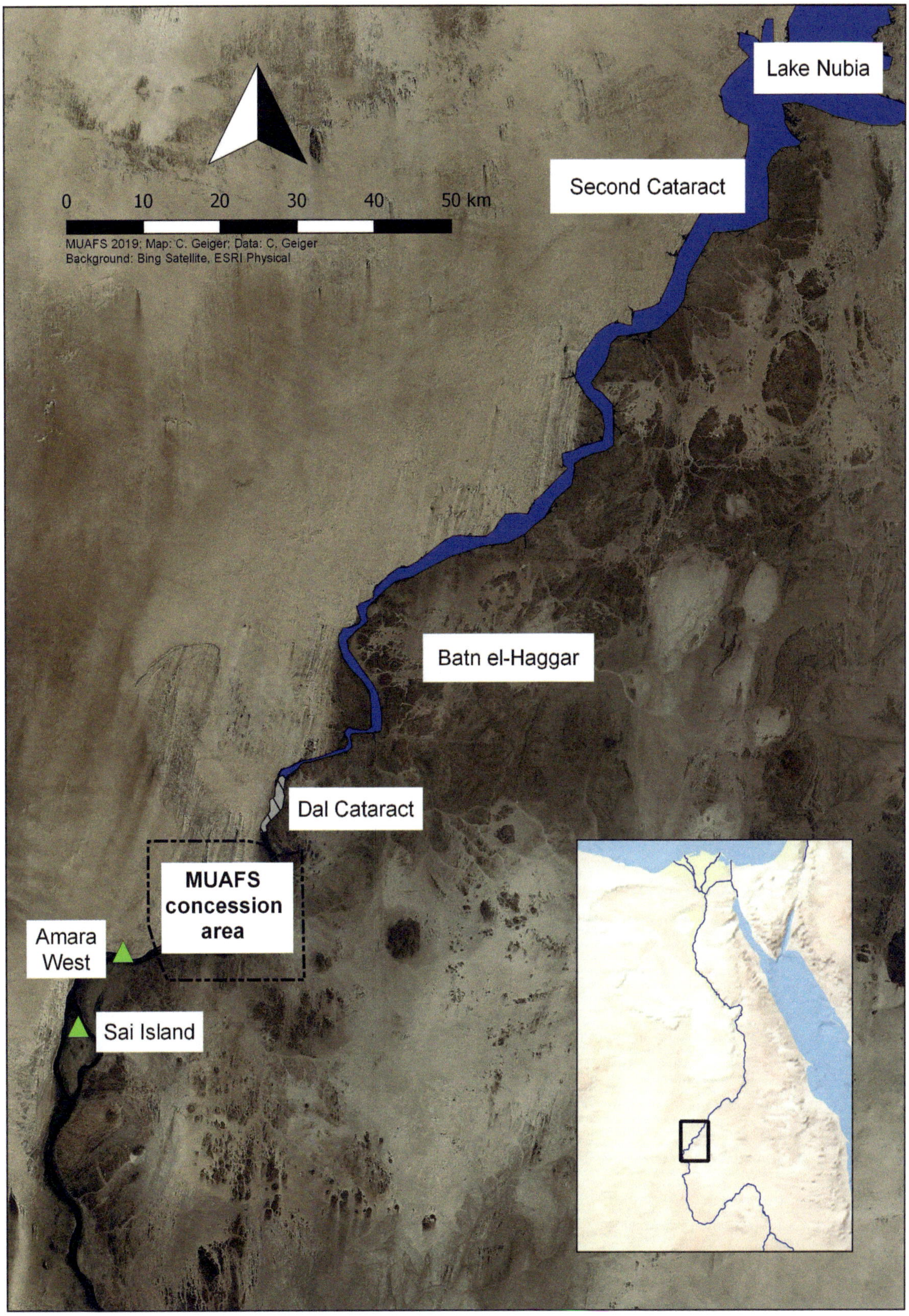

Fig. 1 Location of the MUAFS concession area in Sudan (map by C. Geiger, © DiverseNile Project).

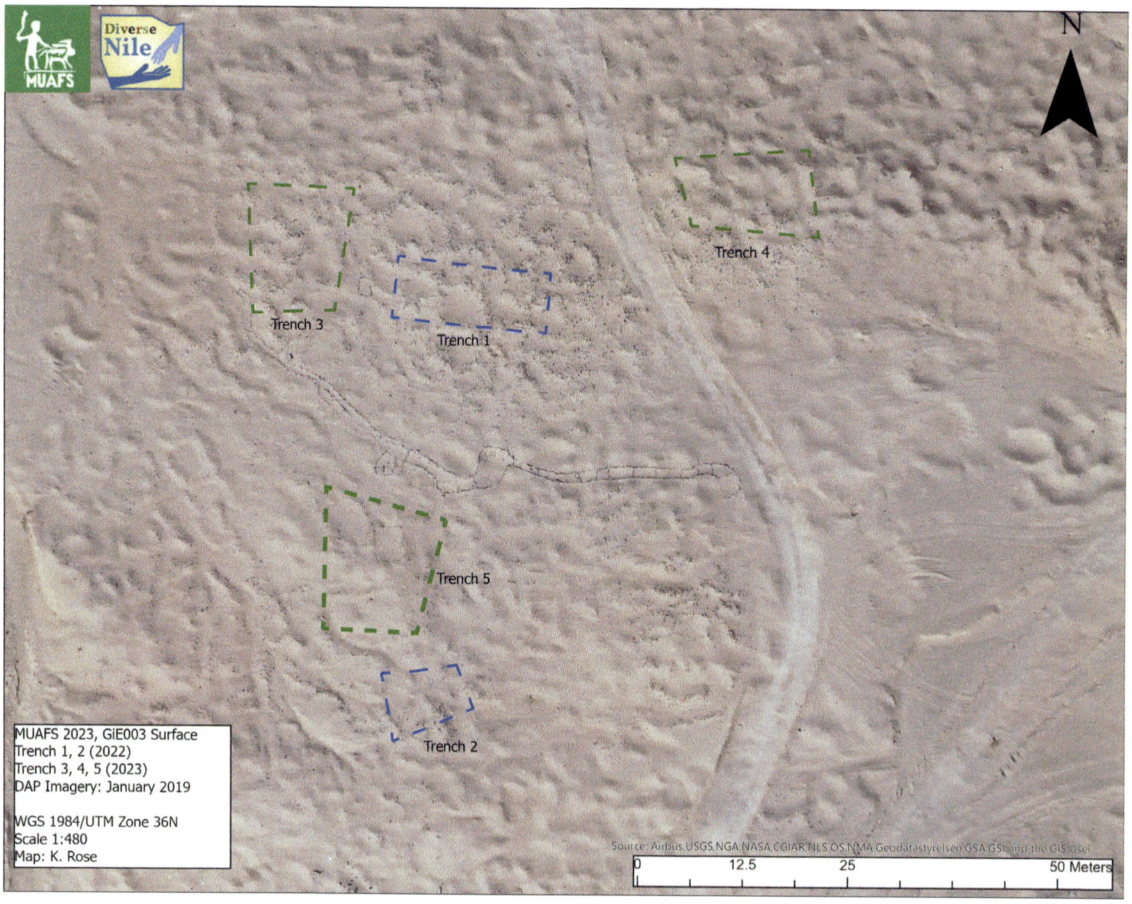

Fig. 2 Surface of Kerma cemetery GiE 003 showing the outline of the trenches and remains of the superstructures (map by K. Rose, © DiverseNile Project).

To understand the impact of different cultural contacts on those buried at GiE 003, ceramics and jewellery seem the most relevant types of finds. Some of the ceramics are not typical of the Kerma culture but associated with the Pan-Grave horizon.[26] Feature 50, a large Pan-Grave style burial in Trench 5 (Fig. 3), provides clear evidence for the combination of Kerma style and Pan-Grave style material culture in one tomb, reflecting findings from the Fourth Cataract region.[27]

Feature 50 contained the remains of a wooden bed frame, partial remains of a contracted burial, several goat offerings (one with what seems to be a horn protector made with various types of beads) and a considerable number of intact pottery vessels, comprising Black-topped fine wares, as well as incised and impressed decorated vessels and a few fragments of Egyptian wheel-made Nile clay vessels. Among the Black-topped fine wares, one typical Pan-Grave style beaker is especially interesting because it shows several repair holes (Fig. 4), suggesting it was particularly valued by the owner. Unlike the repairs made to vessels by desert nomads travelling with their herds far from the Nile – which would make sense for practical reasons – the fact that such repairs occurred in the riverine region of Ginis – where there is evidence for a local manufacture of Kerma Black-topped beakers[28] – is significant. The repaired beaker from cemetery GiE 003 was most likely an "imported" vessel which could not be replaced by a Kerma product, as it held a specific marker of regionality and/or identity. Another complete vessel from Feature 50 is also significant, a globular pot with a pronounced lip and impressed decoration (Fig. 5). There are no known parallels for this vessel which might suggest a regional or local design and emphasises our still limited knowledge of Pan-Grave ceramics.[29]

26 Budka 2023.

27 Emberling and Williams 2010, 27, 29 and 33. The finds in El-Widay I were dated to the Classic Kerma Period. For the local characteristics of the Pan-Grave pottery from the site see most recently Walsh 2022, 14 with references.

28 For the likelihood of several production centres for Kerma Black-topped fine ware see also Knoblauch 2020.

29 Despite of the seminal work of de Souza 2019.

Fig. 3 Pan-Grave style burial pit, Feature 50 in cemetery GiE 003 (photo by J. Budka).

Fig. 4 Pan-Grave style Black-topped beaker from Feature 50 with repair holes (photo by J. Budka, photo edits by C. Ward, © DiverseNile Project).

Fig. 5 Pan-Grave style pot from Feature 50 with incised decoration (photo by J. Budka, photo edits by C. Ward, © DiverseNile Project).

Prior to the discoveries at GiE 003, Pan-Grave material in the Nile Valley south of the Second Cataract was only known from the Fourth Cataract.[30] This stresses that there is a need for a more regional-based approach when investigating the Pan-Grave horizon in Upper Nubia, especially its association with the Kerma culture. For now, it seems likely that Pan-Grave people were part of the social structure of the Attab to Ferka region between c. 1800–1700 BC.[31]

Imported Marl clay vessels from Egypt, as well as Levantine amphorae were found on the surfaces of Trenches 1, 3 and 4 and reflect the cultural contacts and trade routes used during the Classic Kerma Period. One particularly interesting example is a Hyksos scarab found in Trench 1, bearing the name of king Y'amu (MUAFS 005, Fig. 6). Royal Hyksos scarabs are known from Ukma, Akasha, Sai and Kerma, as well as several Lower Nubian sites.[32] The reign of King Y'amu, not attested to in Nubia before the discovery of MUAFS 005, is difficult to date and it remains unclear whether his scarab at Ginis is an "out of place" artefact or is evidence of continuous exchange between Kerma communities and the Hyksos.[33]

In conclusion, GiE 003 is a provincial cemetery in the Kerma Kingdom's northern reaches, with evidence of continuous use from the Middle Kerma to Classic Kerma Period and an intriguing presence of the Pan-Grave tradition. The latter has no published parallels in the region south of the Second Cataract. The Kerma burials in GiE 003 are similar to those from cemeteries in the Batn el-Hagar, such as Ukma and Akasha, as well as from the Kerma cemeteries in Sai and Ferka. However, no evidence for the use of bucrania was found in Ginis, Ferka, Ukma or Akasha, which may be a way of differentiating central Kerma cemeteries, such as Sai and Kerma, from those in more marginal regions.[34]

It seems likely that the impact of interactions with the Hyksos, Egyptians and Eastern Nomadic groups, such as the Pan-Grave people, on Kerma culture varied significantly. In part, this would

30 See de Souza 2019, 82–89.

31 Cf. de Souza 2022, 189.

32 Ahrens and Kopetzky 2021, 295 with references and discussion.

33 Ward 1984, 164 placed Y'amu in the second half of the 15th Dynasty; this sequence was discussed by Ryholt and is not archaeologically confirmed, see Ben-Tor 2007, 108 with references. See Budka 2023 for a more detailed discussion.

34 Budka 2023.

have been determined by the responses of different communities, shaping what can be called marginal communities in the Kerma state.[35] Excavations at Kerma cemeteries (and of course settlements) in rural regions such as the MUAFS concession are therefore crucial to answering questions on regionality, both on the micro- and meso-level.

Regionality on a macrolevel: the case study of New Kingdom Nubia

Recent fieldwork in Egyptian colonial towns, so-called temple towns, in the Nubian Nile Valley has revealed new information about material culture and complex cultural interactions.[36] Most of these projects, including the ERC AcrossBorders Project explored cultural diversity and connectivity in the region.[37] The data gathered so far illustrate the need to look beyond state-built foundations in the Nile Valley, and to challenge existing, but biased, narratives on the Kerma Kingdom and New Kingdom Nubia which are based, almost exclusively, on evidence from large central sites.

Site AtW 001 in Attab West

The investigation of a domestic site in the hinterland of the urban site on Sai Island was carried out by the ERC DiverseNile Project in 2022 and 2023 with the excavation of AtW 001 (see also below, Introduction to Part II).[38] Substantial layers of mud brick collapse were found, as well as rubbish deposits which included a large amount of animal bone, charcoal and pottery sherds, as well as a surprising number of intact and almost intact vessels. The ceramics from AtW 001 are comparable to material from other New Kingdom sites in Nubia and can be dated to the early 18th Dynasty and Thutmoside Period. The majority of the sherds are wheel-made Nile clay variants, predominantly a Nile clay B2 variant.

There was a remarkable mix of Nubian and Egyptian traditions in the cooking pots found at AtW 001. Egyptian wheel-made cooking pots – likely, both imported from regional centres like Aniba and Sai, and also locally produced – are used side-by-side with Nubian-style products (including hand-made pots with basketry impression or incised decoration, some with notched rim decoration or Black-topped rims). This mix of traditions is exemplified by vessel MUAFS 082/2023 produced using a Nubian surface treatment (incised wavy-line decoration and pinched rim notches) with an Egyptian production technique and style Nile clay, on a traditionally Egyptian shape.[39] Interestingly, pinched rims on Nubian cooking pots are very common at AtW 001, whereas this style of decoration is rare in the New Kingdom town of Sai. MUAFS 082/2023 is thus an innovative product deeply embedded in local traditions, as well as a cross-cultural piece.[40]

Fig. 6 Hyksos scarab of king Y'amu, MUAFS 005, from cemetery GiE 003 (photo by R. Lemos, photo edits by M. Devigne, © DiverseNile Project).

35 See Lemos and Budka 2021; Walsh 2022.
36 Spencer, Stevens and Binder 2017 with references.
37 See Budka 2020a.
38 Budka 2022; Budka, Rose and Ward 2023, 26–30.
39 For this vessel see Budka, Rose and Ward 2023, 28, fig. 16.
40 For cross-over ceramics at New Kingdom sites in Nubia see Rose 2017, 466; Stevens and Garnett 2017; cf. Budka 2020a, 410. See also Kilroe this volume.

Overall, the Egyptian-style ceramic assemblage from AtW 001 is directly comparable to material from early levels at Sai. The vessels are associated with storage, cooking, serving and drinking. Thanks to Organic Residue Analysis, the hybrid cooking pot MUAFS 082/2023 can be associated with the processing of dairy products (see below, Introduction to Part III). The presence of imported amphorae and Marl clay vessels is significant and the quantity, similar to the main urban site of Sai, might suggest a close relation between the sites or at least a re-distribution of vessels into the hinterland.[41] Typical domestic types, such as pot stands, are common and a small number of functional vessels, including crucibles, spinning bowls, fire dogs, bread plates and bread moulds, were also found (see also Chapter 9).

One striking difference between AtW 001 and the city of Sai is the amount of Nubian material – in the earliest phase of the former this makes up to as much as 45.6% of the material and averages at 20% in the later phase, whereas the average amount of Nubian style vessels in New Kingdom sectors of Sai is of only 2.1%. This suggests a stronger preference for handmade indigenous ceramic vessels at AtW 001 which might be related to its rural character, to its occupants and/or to its function.

Another notable contrast to Sai is the abundance of painted Nile clay carinated bowls and dishes with white slip and wavy-line decoration (Fig. 7). This decoration is also known from Sai, but usually with a red slip.[42] Similar white-slipped painted vessels have been found at Askut (see also Chapter 9),[43] which could suggest that networks between AtW 001 and Lower Nubia differed from Sai city's connections. In any case, this style of decoration, combining wheel-made Egyptian style vessel types with Nubian style decoration patterns, could be significant in studying the effects that material culture has on creating communities, similar to the hybrid cooking pot discussed above.[44] Scientific analyses of ceramic samples collected from AtW 001 is ongoing and will include instrumental neutron activation analysis to specify the provenience of the Nile clay vessels, after which a more detailed assessment of the assemblage from AtW001 will be possible.[45]

In conclusion, there is growing evidence that New Kingdom Nubia must be considered as much more diverse than previously thought and that regional preferences are notable in almost every aspect of life, as well as death.[46] Future work in marginal regions, such as the Attab to Ferka area, has considerable potential in addressing further aspects of cultural diversity across different social settings, and in writing new, more inclusive narratives of Bronze Age Sudan.

Regionality of a resource material: stone quarrying in Nubia

Stone is a natural resource which has typically been associated with Egypt[47] and has led, in recent years, to the development of a new, holistic approach towards quarrying sites in Egypt.[48] While stone was not an important raw material for Nubian cultures, it still had a role in the complex framework of cultural exchange with Egypt: "Due to progressive cultural exchange with Nubia's great northern neighbour, the use of natural building blocks, here primarily of sandstone, gained prominence in Nubian architecture. This was especially employed for the construction of sacral buildings and progressively for the construction of pyramids."[49] Whereas Nubian sandstone (quartz sandstone) only started to be used as building material in the Middle Nile during the Middle Kingdom, mostly for Egyptian fortresses, there is evidence for a much earlier use of natural- and dry-stone architecture, in both settlement architecture and funerary buildings.[50] It is important to stress that sandstone architectural pieces were well integrated within Nubian monumental architecture (e.g., the columns and stelae at the eastern *Deffufa* in Kerma).[51] Charles Bonnet has interpreted this, together with other elements, as evidence for cultural entanglement (labelled by him as "Egyptianising" features) during the Classic Kerma Period.[52]

In the Napatan and Meroitic Kingdoms Nubian sandstone was widely used, especially for temples and pyramids.[53] While Nubian sandstone is found almost everywhere in ancient Sudan, though in varying qualities, other stones, such as, limestone are not present.[54] Because of its occurrence as bedrock, quartz sandstone was favoured in Egyptian architecture from Esna in Upper Egypt to Gebel Barkal in Upper Nubia .[55]

41 Note, however, that Rose 2017 has proposed a different scenario for Sesebi; she interpreted the small number of imported amphorae as private pieces, not as part of the official provision of the temple town. This interpretation was also favoured by Stevens and Garnett 2017 for 2-R-18, a site comparable to AtW 001 located close to Amara West. I imagine that both private and official trade could apply, maybe in combination with each other.

42 Miélle 2014, 387–389, fig. 4.

43 Smith 2003, fig. 3.7; Budka 2018, 153. See also Rose 2018, 136.

44 Budka 2022, 58.

45 Analysis for the DiverseNile Project by Johannes Sterba, Atominstitut Wien and Giulia D'Ercole (see also her contribution in this volume, Chapter 10).

46 See, e.g., Näser 2017; Lemos 2020; Smith 2020.

47 See, e.g., Reader 2022.

48 See Bloxam 2010 with references. Cf. also Harrell 2016.

49 Klemm, Klemm and Murr 2019, 15. For geology in Nubia see also Harrell 2020.

50 Cf. Liszka 2017. For the early indigenous tradition of stone tumuli in Nubia see Welsby 1996, 100.

51 Bonnet 1994, especially figs. 2 and 4.

52 Bonnet 1994.

53 See, e.g., Welsby 1996, 103–113; 115–122.

54 Klemm, Klemm and Murr 2019, 24, fig. 3, 29; Harrell 2020.

55 Harrell 2016, 11. Meroitic sandstone quarries are attested to further south, near the city of Meroe and Hamadab, see Klemm, Klemm and Murr 2019, 29.

Fig. 7 White-slipped monochrome painted wheel-made carinated vessel from AtW 001 (MUAFS 222/2023), presumably a local style of New Kingdom Nubia (photo by J. Budka, photo edits by C. Ward, © DiverseNile Project).

Sandstone and the case study of Sai Island

18th Dynasty evidence from Sai Island can help us understand regional patterns in the use of sandstone in northern Sudan during the Late Bronze Age. As one of the largest islands in the Nile, Sai lies just south of the Batn el-Hagar and the granite outcrops of the Dal Cataract (see Fig. 1) and is situated between the Second and Third Nile Cataracts. Both cataracts are the results of a large-scale east-west tectonic uplift zone that caused the Nile to cut into the uplifted Neoproterozoic crystalline basement and its sedimentary cover.[56] The geology of Sai includes several types of metamorphic Precambrian rock and Nubian sandstone, largely covered by thin layers of, by comparison, much younger Nile sediments.[57]

In general, the rock types used in the New Kingdom town of Sai reflect the natural geology of the island and are predominantly locally available. By far the most common rock types are quartz sandstone and amphibolite (or schist), while vein quartz, calcrete, biotite gneiss and calcite marble are comparatively rare. Rock types which were probably imported to the island include granite,[58] diorite,[59] gabbro[60] and gypsum.[61]

Several variants of Nubian sandstone – the most common rock identified on Sai Island – were documented by the ERC AcrossBorders Project.[62] One of the main achievements of the project was locating the source of the stone used for the New Kingdom stone buildings on Sai, particularly for the 18th Dynasty sanctuary, Temple A.[63] Thanks to preparatory research (especially with lithologically processed Landsat-TM images), as well as on site research by Dietrich and Rosemarie Klemm, seven sandstone quarries were

56 Thurmond et al. 2004; Anonymous 2005.

57 See Budka 2020a, 29 with references.

58 For various types of granite from the area of Aswan see Klemm and Klemm 2008, 233–267. Cf. also Aston, Harrell and Shaw 2000, 35–37.

59 Also from the area of Aswan, see Klemm and Klemm 2008, 21

60 See Klemm and Klemm 2008, 13. See also Aston, Harrell and Shaw 2000, 32–34.

61 See Klemm and Klemm 2008, 14–15. This sedimentary rock was used for producing plaster at Sai, see Budka 2020a, 269–270.

62 Budka 2020a, 42–52.

63 Sandstone quarries on Sai were already mentioned as being located north and south of the fortress by Vercoutter 1958, 147, note 24; Vercoutter 1986, 8–10.

identified adjacent to the New Kingdom town.[64] Two of these sandstone quarries (quarry sites 1 & 2) are located just east of the town wall and would be the most convenient for building material used in the town.

Based on both petrographic analysis and observations of the chisel marks, the Klemms could propose that the builders of Temple A on Sai made a clear choice between the aesthetic appeal and the durability of the sandstones available on the island. Aesthetics were noticeably prioritised for temple buildings, and this might have also influenced the choice of sandstone from Sai in other building projects in Nubia, as is suggested by textual sources from a Nubian temple outside the island. Specifically, the contemporary toponym for Sai Island, *Š3ʿ.t*, is repeated five times in the inscriptions of the 18th Dynasty temple of Kumma (Semna East) as a source of building material for the temple.[65] Kumma is located 112 km north of Sai, and the Dal Cataract and the Batn el-Hagar act as considerable natural obstacles between the sites. Based on this and the logistics of transporting stone, Didier Devauchelle and Florence Doyen have expressed doubts that Sai Island could be a source of building material used at Kumma.[66] As one building inscription in Kumma mentions stone from *T3-Stj* for "Nubia", instead of *Š3ʿ.t* for "Sai", they proposed that both toponyms, in this context, refer to a large, mostly metaphorical, region.[67] Although this remains a possibility, Martina Ullmann has shown that there are more arguments in favour of taking the reference to *Š3ʿ.t* (as part of *T3-Stj*) more literally.[68] She also considered the geology and landscape of the Second Cataract and the Batn el-Hagar region, in which no sandstone formation can be found. The temples of Kumma and Semna were necessarily built with stone brought from elsewhere – be this from the north, the region of Wadi Halfa, or from the south, the region of Sai Island. Ullmann pointed out that transportation northward, with the current of the Nile, seems less difficult than navigation upstream, making the origin of the Kumma blocks from Sai more likely.[69] The petrographic investigation of samples from the temples at Kumma and Semna and their comparative analysis with samples from Sai could be the solution to solving the provenience of the "fine white stone from Sai" mentioned in the 18th Dynasty texts. For now, the example of sandstone from Sai can be regarded as reflecting regional patterns in the exploitation of Nubian sandstone during the New Kingdom.

A final noteworthy aspect of the local quarrying of Nubian sandstone on Sai are the chisel marks documented both in quarries and on the foundation blocks of Temple A. These marks are characteristic of the early New Kingdom,[70] which corresponds to the dating of the temple on Sai. Flat chisel traces of about 1 to 1.5 cm width have parallels in Egyptian sandstone quarries, for example at Gebel el-Silsileh.[71] The herringbone patterns commonly found on Sai are caused by bronze chisels, and are also well-known from almost all early New Kingdom sandstone quarries, up to and including the Amarna Period.[72]

However, there also seem to be some local characteristics in the quarry marks on Sai. On some of the stone blocks of Temple A, two types of chisel marks have been identified, sometimes on the same block of stone. While the first type is a systematic and regular linear parallel mark, characteristic of the Thutmoside Period,[73] the other type is slightly haphazard and considerably wider, presumably resulting from relatively broad flat chisels, whose lines are less parallel and occasionally completely discordant. These two distinct marks could reflect different stages of the *chaîne opératoire* for the rendering of stone to building blocks. However, another possibility, of which Dietrich and Rosemarie Klemm were in favour, is to interpret these two different sets of marks as evidence for the involvement of different groups of workmen.[74] Whereas the typical Thutmoside regular chisel marks clearly mirror the presence of Egyptian stone masons – specialised craftsmen – the unusual second type of chisel marks might attest to local workmen, trained by Egyptians but with their own idiosyncrasies. This remains hypothetical and would have to be investigated on a broader scale through comparisons with other 18th Dynasty Egyptian stone temples in New Kingdom Nubia. As will be stressed below, this possible cooperation of Egyptian and Nubian workmen teams in New Kingdom stone quarries would nicely parallel new ideas pertaining to goldworking during this period in Nubia (see Chapter 4).

Nubian quarry sites for granite

The most well-known granite quarry used for building projects and objects in ancient Egypt, not only during the Bronze Age, but over millennia, is in Aswan.[75] However, there are also a number of granite quarry sites in the Middle Nile, although these seem to have been used for a considerably shorter amount of time.

The site of Tombos close to the Third Nile Cataract is particularly well known and includes a large quarry of magmatic rocks, principally granite and granitic

64 Budka 2020a, 44, pls. 15–16.
65 For details see Ullmann 2020.
66 Devauchelle and Doyen 2009, 36.
67 Devauchelle and Doyen 2009, 36; Ullmann 2020, 56.
68 Ullmann 2020, 56–58.
69 Ullmann 2020, 57.
70 On dating of chisel marks in Egyptian quarries, see Klemm and Klemm 2008, 194–201.
71 Klemm and Klemm 2008, 196.
72 See Klemm and Klemm 2008, 196–197.
73 Klemm and Klemm 2008, 196.
74 See Budka 2020a, 45.
75 See Storemyr et al. 2013. Cf. also Klemm and Klemm 2008, 233–267.

Fig. 8 Traces of quarrying in the northern part of the granite quarry site, 3-L-6 N, at Jebel Kitfoggo (photo by J. Budka).

gneisses, with known activity from the 18th Dynasty until Napatan and Meroitic times (particularly for statues and steale).[76] There is no clear evidence that the quarry site was used prior to the New Kingdom.[77]

Another type of granite, pink granite, is available just south of the Dal Cataract in the MUAFS concession (see Fig. 1). Here, site 3-L-6 is a large red granite quarry at the foot of Jebel Kitfoggo in Ferka West (Fig. 8).[78] Fragments of unfinished columns testify to an intensive use in Medieval times for architectural pieces.[79] This is supported by evidence from settlement site 3-G-30, just to the north of 3-L-6, where Medieval ceramics were found on the surface. The building technique and general layout of these stone-built huts are also typical of the Medieval era. Although several Kerma sites are also identifiable in the surroundings of 3-L-6, there is no evidence for Bronze Age or Iron Age use of the granite quarry at Jebel Kitfoggo.

Both Tombos and Jebel Kitfoggo were used for a relatively limited time span, compared to other quarry sites. In addition to regional patterns, these examples also illustrate the need to consider political and historical circumstances when investigating the management of raw material and resources.

Stone as resource for objects

As well as building material, stone can also be used for objects (as attested to at Tombos, see above; for the use of carnelian by Kerma people see Lemos, Introduction to Part IV). Of particular interest are stone statues and stone sarcophagi which seem to illustrate restricted access to the material in New Kingdom Nubia[80] – stone sarcophagi are at present known only from Soleb.[81] The case of one of the two stone sarcophagi found in Soleb Tomb 5 made in local sandstone is particularly interesting. It belonged to the *'quarryman'* Wabset, an official engaged in the building activities related to the royal temple at Soleb.[82] This clearly put him in a privileged position to secure material for his coffin which was not widely available. This could be comparable to the "personalised" access to raw materials proposed for Tomb 26 on Sai Island, although for gold rather than stone (see also Chapter 4).[83] Furthermore, it is at present impossible to know whether Wabset was one of the co-opted Nubian officials working in the colonial administration,

76 Harrell 1999; Harrell 2000; Klemm, Klemm and Murr 2019, 27.

77 Klemm, Klemm and Murr 2019, 28.

78 Vila 1976, 72–73.

79 See Welsby 2002, 173.

80 For a case study of stone shabtis and their specific distribution in New Kingdom Nubia see Auenmüller and Lemos 2021.

81 See Lemos 2020.

82 Leclant 1963.

83 See Budka 2021b, passim.

or an official from Egypt proper and buried in his new home in Nubia.[84] Ingeborg Müller lists for the colonial administration in New Kingdom Nubia only two more quarrymen besides Wabset, one of them, Hornakht, is given the title *ḫrtj-nṯr* with an additional epithet of "the one who reached *Tꜣ-Stj*", implying he came from Egypt to work with stone in Nubia.[85]

Quarrying and Nubian agency

Stone quarrying in Nubia is an activity with strong regional character and with a specific cultural connotation. Prior to the Napatan Period, there seems to have been a strong Egyptian influence on stone exploitation, particularly for building material. However, the examples of Wabset's stone sarcophagus and the use of sandstone at colonial Sai suggest that Nubians also had an important role in the stone quarrying industry from as early as the Late Bronze Age. Studies of the gold industry (see Chapters 3 and 4) warn us against oversimplification and continued use of outdated narratives – such as the association of monumental stone architecture with "high culture" and being brought to Nubia from Egypt. Although sources are, at present very limited, it seems beyond doubt that Nubians were involved in stone quarrying in the Middle Nile prior to Napatan and Meroitic times (see the chisel marks from Sai mentioned above). Initially, this may have been primarily as simple workmen but given the highly sophisticated stone work reached during Napatan times, it is very likely that indigenous persons were being expertly trained and participated in a collaborative strategy of stone exploitation over a considerable time span, presumably starting during the Kerma Period.

Towards a better understanding of resource management in ancient Sudan

The focus in much previous research on central sites like Kerma and New Kingdom temple towns, as well as on Egyptian textual references has led to a bias in the understanding of resource management in Bronze Age Sudan. Complex dynamics and changing patterns are traceable through archaeological evidence. Furthermore, since many of the raw materials and other resources are found in desert regions, there is a clear need to look beyond the Nile Valley and to consider the contribution of groups living and working in the desert, especially in relation to that of the permanent, as well as seasonal, occupants of settlements along the river.

So-called marginal regions in ancient Sudan hold much potential for understanding trade networks in their entirety, as well as dynamics of contact spaces on different regional scales. Finally, trade and exchange are always embedded in their historical framework. Therefore, we need an approach which considers the macro picture, while also taking into account what was happening at the local scale in different regions as will be specified throughout this volume and especially in Part I.

84 For questions of biological and cultural identities in New Kingdom Nubia see Budka 2021b, passim with references, as well as Schrader and Buzon this volume; Smith this volume.

85 Müller 2013, 183, Table 2.3.2, nos. 14–16.

Bibliography

Ahrens, A. and Kopetzky, K.

2021 Difficult times and drastic solutions: the diffusion of looted Middle Kingdom objects found in the northern Levant, Egypt and Nubia, in: M. Bietak and S. Prell (eds.), *The Enigma of the Hyksos, Volume IV: Changing Clusters and Migration in the Near Eastern Bronze Age. Collected Papers of a Workshop held in Vienna 4th–6th of December 2019*, Contributions to the Archaeology of Egypt, Nubia and the Levant 12, Wiesbaden, 253–313.

Akmenkalns, J.

2018 *Cultural continuity and change in the wake of ancient Nubian-Egyptian interactions*, PhD thesis, University of California Santa Barbara.

Anonymous

2005 *Geological map of Sudan. 1:3,500,000*, Geological Research Authority of the Sudan, Khartoum.

Aston, B., Harrell, J.A. and Shaw, I.

2000 Stone, in: P.T. Nicholson and I. Shaw (eds.), *Ancient Egyptian Materials and Technology*, Cambridge, 5–77.

Auenmüller, J. and Lemos, R.

2021 Khnummose and a group of New Kingdom serpentinite shabtis: insights into colonial society in 18th Dynasty Nubia, in: J. Budka, *Tomb 26 on Sai Island: A New Kingdom Elite Tomb and Its Relevance for Sai and Beyond*, Leiden, 305–349.

Ben-Tor, D.

2007 *Scarabs, Chronology, and Interconnections: Egypt and Palestine in the Second Intermediate Period*, Fribourg; Göttingen.

Bloxam, E.

2010 Quarrying and mining (stone), *UCLA Encyclopedia of Egyptology*, 1(1). Retrieved from https://escholarship.org/uc/item/9bb918sd.

Bonnet, C.

1994 La deffufa orientale à Kerma: nouvelle analyse archéologique, in: C. Berger, G. Clerc and N. Grimal (eds.), *Hommages à Jean Leclant, Vol. II*, Bibliothèque d'Étude 106.2, Cairo, 55–60.

Budka, J.

2019 Towards Middle Nile biographies: The Munich University Attab to Ferka survey project 2018/2019, *Sudan & Nubia* 23, 13–26.

2020a *AcrossBorders 2. Living in New Kingdom Sai*. With contributions by Johannes Auenmüller, Annette M. Hansen, Frits Heinrich, Veronica Hinterhuber, Ptolemaios Paxinos, Nadja Pöllath, Helmut Sattmann, Sara Schnedl and Martina Ullmann, Archaeology of Egypt, Sudan and the Levant 1, Vienna.

2020b Kerma presence at Ginis East: the 2020 season of the Munich University Attab to Ferka survey project, *Sudan & Nubia* 24, 57–71.

2021a Commentary: Winnerman, Jonathan 2021. Forum – Egyptology and political theology: an examination of the ethics of scholarship, *Journal of Near Eastern Studies* 80 (1), 167–193, 186–187.

2021b *Tomb 26 on Sai Island: A New Kingdom Elite Tomb and Its Relevance for Sai and Beyond*. With contributions by Johannes Auenmüller, Cajetan Geiger, Rennan Lemos, Andrea Stadlmayr and Marlies Wohlschlager, Leiden.

2022 Early New Kingdom settlement activities in the periphery of Sai Island: towards a contextualisation of fresh evidence from Attab West, *Der antike Sudan. Mitteilungen der Sudanarchäologischen Gesellschaft zu Berlin e.V.* 33, 45–61.

2023 Investigating Nubian funerary practices of marginal communities: new evidence from a Kerma cemetery at Ginis, *Egitto e Vicino Oriente* 45 (2022), 37–62.

in press New approaches to landscape archaeology: towards contact space biographies in the Middle Nile, in: *Festschrift NN*, in press.

Budka, J., Rose, K. and Ward, C.

2023 Cultural diversity in the Bronze Age in the Attab to Ferka region: new results based on excavations in 2023, *Der antike Sudan. Mitteilungen der Sudanarchäologischen Gesellschaft zu Berlin e.V.* 34, 19–35.

Dalton, M., Spencer, N., Macklin, M.G., Woodward, J.C. and Ryan, P.

2023 Three thousand years of river channel engineering in the Nile Valley, *Geoarchaeology* 38/5, 565–587 https://doi.org/10.1002/gea.21965

Davies, W.V. and Welsby, D.A. (eds.)

2020 *Travelling the Korosko Road: Archaeological Exploration in Sudan's Eastern Desert* Sudan Archaeological Research Society Publication 24, Oxford.

Devauchelle, D. and Doyen, F.

2009 Retour à l'Île de Saï (Soudan, 2006–2009), *Bulletin de la société française d'égyptologie* 175, 29–49.

Devesa, A.L., Campmany Jiménez, J., Marzo Pallàs, M. and Morillas Samaniego, O. (eds.)

2023 *(Not) All Roads Lead to Rome: Interdisciplinary Approaches to Mobility in the Ancient World,* Access Archaeology, Oxford.

Drzewiecki, M. and Cedro, A.

2019 Archaeological surveys at the Third, Fourth and Fifth Cataract regions, in: D. Raue (ed.), *Handbook of Ancient Nubia, Vol. 2*, Berlin; Boston, 987–1018.

Emberling, G. and Williams, B.

2010 The Kingdom of Kush in the 4th Cataract: Archaeological Salvage of the Oriental Institute Nubian Expedition 2007 season, Part 1: Preliminary report on the sites of Hosh el-Guruf and El-Widay, *Gdańsk Archaeological Museum African Reports* 7, 17–38.

Edwards, D.N.

2020 Landscape archaeologies in Nubia and the Middle Nile, in: G. Emberling and B.B. Williams (eds.), *The Oxford Handbook of Ancient Nubia*, Oxford, 1071–1089.

Harrell, J.A.
1999 Ancient stone quarries at the Third and Fourth Nile Cataracts, Northern Sudan, *Sudan & Nubia* 3, 21–27.
2000 Granite gneiss and granite from Tumbos, in: P.T. Nicholson and I. Shaw (eds.), *Ancient Egyptian Materials and Technology*, Cambridge, 34.
2016 Mapping the Tura-Masara limestone quarries, *Journal of the American Research Center in Egypt* 52, 199–214.
2020 Geology of Nubia and surrounding regions, in: G. Emberling and B.B. Williams (eds.), *The Oxford Handbook of Ancient Nubia*, Oxford, 49–62.

Jeffreys, D.
2010 Regionality, cultural and cultic landscapes, in: W. Wendrich (ed.), *Egyptian Archaeology*, Chichester, 102–118.

Johnson, G.A.
1977 Aspects of regional analysis in archaeology, *Annual Review of Anthropology* 6, 479–508.

Klemm, R. and Klemm, D.
2008 *Stones and Quarries in Ancient Egypt*, London.

Klemm, D., Klemm, R. and Murr, A.
2019 Geologically induced raw materials stimulating the development of Nubian culture, in: D. Raue (ed.), *Handbook of Ancient Nubia, Vol. 1*, Berlin; Boston, 15–38.

Knoblauch, C.
2020 Between Egypt and Kerma: a strange tulip-beaker from Mirgissa, in: A.R. Warfe, J.C.R. Gill, C.R. Hamilton, A.J. Pettman and D.A. Stewart (eds.), *Dust, Demons and Pots: Studies in Honour of Colin A. Hope*, Leuven, 415–424.

Leclant, J.
1963 Le sarcophage de Ouabset de la nécropole de Soleb, *Kush* 11, 141–158.

Lemos, R.
2020 Material culture and colonization in ancient Nubia: Evidence from the New Kingdom cemeteries, in: C. Smith (ed.), *Encyclopedia of Global Archaeology*, Cham, https://doi.org/10.1007/978-3-319-51726-1_3307-1.

Lemos, R. and Budka, J.
2021 Alternatives to colonization and marginal identities in New Kingdom colonial Nubia (1550–1070 BCE), *World Archaeology* 53/3, 401–418.

Lohwasser, A., Karberg, T. and Auenmüller, J. (eds.)
2018 *Bayuda Studies: Proceedings of the First International Conference on the Archaeology of the Bayuda Desert in Sudan*, Meroitica, Schriften zur altsudanesischen Geschichte und Archäologie 27, Wiesbaden.

Manzo, A.
2017 *Eastern Sudan in Its Setting: The Archaeology of a Region Far From the Nile Valley*, Access Archaeology; Cambridge Monographs in African Archaeology 94, Oxford.

Miellé, L.
2014 Nubian traditions on the ceramics found in the pharaonic town on Sai Island, in: J.R. Anderson and D.A. Welsby (eds.), *The Fourth Cataract and Beyond: Proceedings of the 12th International Conference for Nubian Studies*, British Museum Publications on Egypt and Sudan 1, Leuven, 387–392.

Moreno García, J.C.
2019 *The State in Ancient Egypt: Power, Challenges and Dynamics*, Debates in Archaeology, London; New York.
2023 Trade, statehood, and configurations of power in ancient Egypt (early-middle Bronze Age), in: D. Candelora, N. Ben-Marzouk and K.M. Cooney (eds.), *Ancient Egyptian Society: Challenging Assumptions, Exploring Approaches*, London; New York, 49–61.

Moers, G.
2015 "Egyptian identity"? Unlikely, and never national, in: H. Amstutz, A. Dorn, M. Müller, M. Ronsdorf and S. Uljas (eds.), *Fuzzy Boundaries: Festschrift für Antonio Loprieno 2*, Hamburg, 693–704.

Müller, I.
2013 *Die Verwaltung Nubiens im Neuen Reich*, Meroitica, Schriften zur altsudanesischen Geschichte und Archäologie 18, Wiesbaden.

Näser, C.
2008 Die *Humboldt University Nubian Expedition* 2008: Arbeiten auf der Insel Mograt, *Der antike Sudan. Mitteilungen der Sudanarchäologischen Gesellschaft zu Berlin e.V.* 19, 47–51.
2017 Structures and realities of the Egyptian presence in Lower Nubia from the Middle Kingdom to the New Kingdom: the Egyptian cemetery S/SA at Aniba, in: N. Spencer, A. Stevens and M. Binder (eds.), *Nubia in the New Kingdom: Lived Experience, Pharaonic Control and Indigenous Traditions*, British Museum Publications on Egypt and Sudan 3, Leuven, 557–574.

Obłuski, A., Paner, H. and Masojć, M. (eds.)
2021 *Bayuda and Its Neighbours*, Nubia: Studies in the Archaeology and History of Northeast Africa 1, Turnhout.

Osman Abdollah, M.
2022 *Trade Centers and Trade Routes in Upper Egypt, During the Old and Middle Kingdoms*, Golden House Publications Egyptology 36, London:

Pitts, M. and Versluys, M.J.
2021 Objectscapes: A manifesto for investigating the impacts of object flows on past societies, *Antiquity* 95(380), 367–381, https://doi.org/10.15184/aqy.2020.148.

Reader, C.D.
2022 *A Gift of Geology: Ancient Egyptian Landscapes and Monuments*, Cairo; New York.

Rose, P.
2017 Sesebi: Ceramics, chronology and society, in: N. Spencer, A. Stevens and M. Binder (eds.), *Nubia in the New Kingdom: Lived Experience, Pharaonic Control and Indigenous Traditions*, British Museum Publications on Egypt and Sudan 3, Leuven, 465–473.
2018 Egyptian pottery from the site of Sesebi, in: R. David (ed.), *Egyptian Pottery in Ancient Sudan: Imports, Imitations and Influences*, Cahiers de la céramique égyptienne 11, Cairo, 135–149.

Salisbury, R.B.
2009 Introduction – reimagining regional analysis in archaeology, in: T.L. Thurston and R.B. Salisbury, *Reimagining Regional Analyses – the Archaeology of Spatial and Social Dynamics*, Cambridge, 2–15.

Schneider, T.
2003 Foreign Egypt: Egyptology and the concept of cultural appropriation, *Ägypten & Levante* 13, 155–161.

Smith, S.T.
2003 *Wretched Kush. Ethnic Identities and Boundaries in Egypt's Nubian Empire*, London; New York.
2020 The Nubian experience of Egyptian domination during the New Kingdom, in: G. Emberling and B.B. Williams (eds), *The Oxford Handbook of Ancient Nubia*, Oxford, 369–394.

Smith, S.T. and Buzon, M.
2017 Colonial encounters at New Kingdom Tombos: Cultural entanglements and hybrid identity, in: N. Spencer, A. Stevens and M. Binder (eds.), *Nubia in the New Kingdom: Lived Experience, Pharaonic Control and Indigenous Traditions*, British Museum Publications on Egypt and Sudan 3, Leuven, 615–630.

de Souza, A.
2019 *New Horizons: The Pan-Grave Ceramic Tradition in Context*, Middle Kingdom Studies 9, London.
2022 Not marginal, but marginalised: the "Pan-Grave" archaeological culture, pharaonic Egypt, and Egyptology, *Journal of Ancient Near Eastern History* 9 (2), 173–194.

Spencer, N., Stevens, A. and Binder, M.
2017 Introduction: History and historiography of a colonial entanglement, and the shaping of new archaeologies for Nubia in the New Kingdom, in: N. Spencer, A. Stevens and M. Binder (eds.), *Nubia in the New Kingdom: Lived Experience, Pharaonic Control and Indigenous Traditions*, British Museum Publications on Egypt and Sudan 3, Leuven, 1–61.

Stevens, A. and Garnett, A.
2017 Surveying the Pharaonic desert hinterland of Amara West, in: N. Spencer, A. Stevens and M. Binder (eds.), *Nubia in the New Kingdom: Lived Experience, Pharaonic Control and Indigenous Traditions*, British Museum Publications on Egypt and Sudan 3, Leuven, 227–306.

Storemyr, P., Bloxam, E., Heldal, T. and Kelany, A.
2013 The Aswan west bank ancient quarry landscape: stone procurement, hunting, desert travel and rock-art from the palaeolithic to the Roman period, in: D. Raue, S.J. Seidlmayer and P. Speiser (eds.), *The First Cataract of the Nile: One Region - Diverse Perspectives*, Sonderschriften des Deutschen Archäologischen Instituts, Abteilung Kairo 36, Berlin; Boston, 223–240.

Thurmond, A.K., Stern, R.J., Abdelsalam, M.G., Nielsen, K.C., Abdeen, M.M. and Hinz, E.
2004 The Nubian swell, *Journal of African Earth Sciences* 39, 401–407.

Ullmann, M.
2020 2.4 Textual sources for sandstone from Sai, in: J. Budka, *AcrossBorders 2. Living in New Kingdom Sai*, Archaeology of Egypt, Sudan and the Levant 1, Vienna, 52–58.

Vercoutter, J.
1958 Excavations at Sai 1955–7: a preliminary report, *Kush* 6, 144–169.
1986 Préface: l'archéologie de l'île de Saï, in: B. Gratien (ed.), *Saï I. La nécropole Kerma*, Paris, 7–17.

Vila, A.
1976 *La prospection archéologique de la Vallée du Nil, au Sud de la Cataracte de Dal (Nubie Soudanaise). Fascicule 3: District de Ferka (Est et Ouest)*, Paris.
1977 *La prospection archéologique de la Vallée du Nil, au Sud de la Cataracte de Dal (Nubie Soudanaise). Fascicule 5: District de Ginis (Est et Ouest)*, Paris.

Walsh, C.
2022 Marginal communities and cooperative strategies in the Kerma pastoral state, *Journal of Ancient Near Eastern History* 9 (2), 195–220.

Ward, W.A.
1984 Royal-name scarabs, in: O. Tufnell, *Scarab Seals and Their Contribution to the History in the Early Second Millennium BC*, Warminster, 151–192.

Welsby, D.A.
1996 *The Kingdom of Kush: The Napatan and Meroitic Empires*, London.
2002 *The Medieval Kingdoms of Nubia: Pagans, Christians and Muslims Along the Middle Nile*, London.

Weschenfelder, J.
2015 Preliminary report of the second and third field seasons at the Bronze Age cemetery MOG034 on Mograt Island, Sudan, *Der antike Sudan. Mitteilungen der Sudanarchäologischen Gesellschaft zu Berlin e.V.* 26, 153–168.

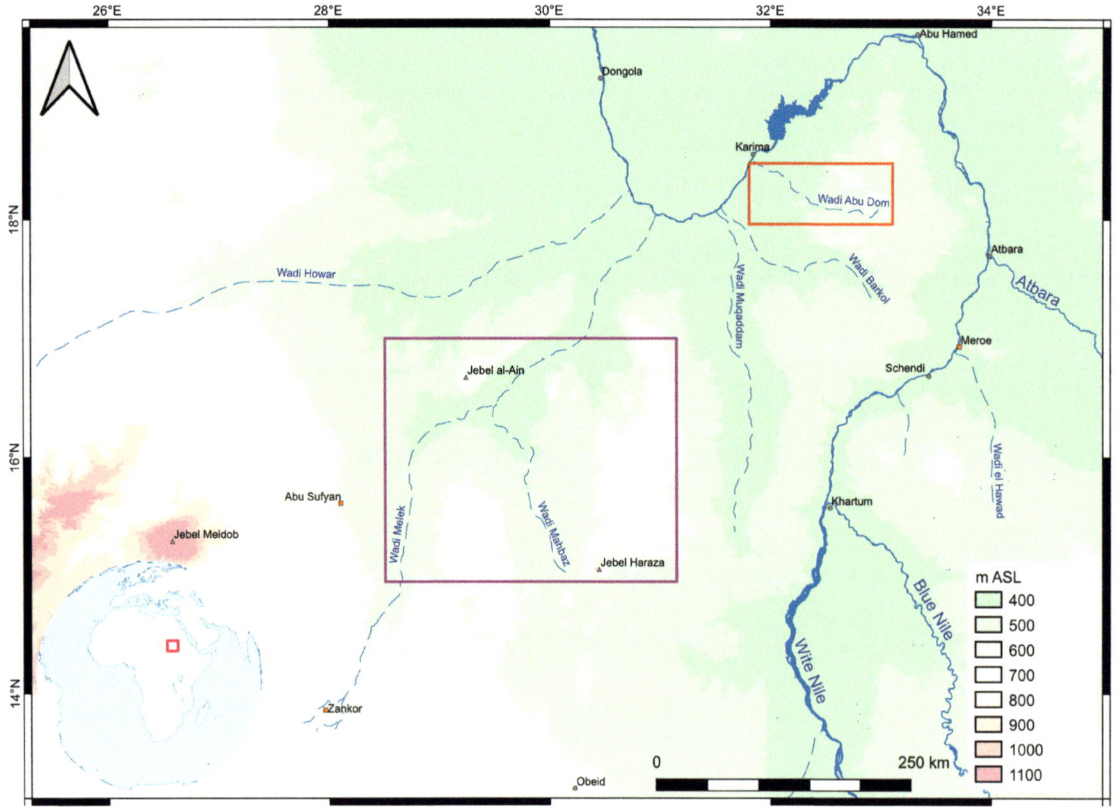

Fig. 1 Areas in the Bayuda (orange) and Northern Kordofan (purple) discussed in this chapter. Elevation data: ALOS DEM © JAXA.

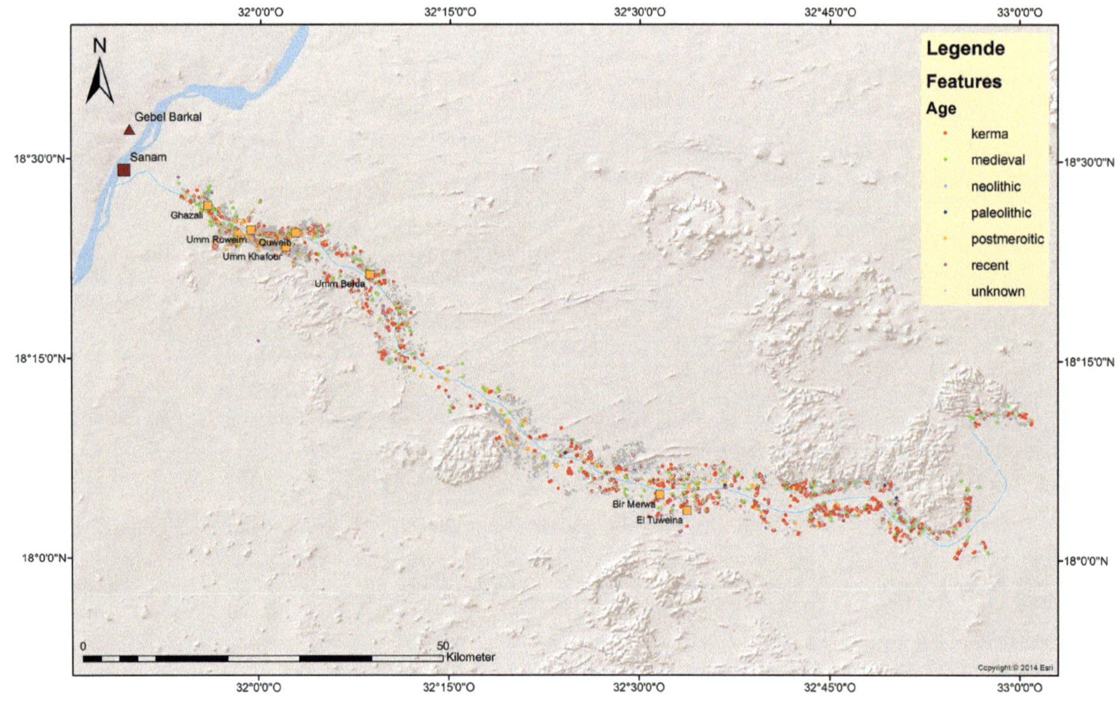

Fig. 2 Wadi Abu Dom with archaeological features discovered during the Wadi Abu Dom Itinerary (W.A.D.I.) survey project 2009–2016.

Chapter 1

The management of resources in remote desert areas: Bayuda and North Kordofan

Jana Eger-Karberg and Tim Karberg[1]

Abstract

This chapter deals with different economic systems and the management of limited resources at the fringes of ancient Nubia. Northern Kordofan and the Bayuda are peripheries of the ancient Kushite and Nubian realm. On the one hand, they are semi-desertic rangelands mainly used by pastoralists as natural pasture, on the other they are desert lands which allow subsistence agriculture only at specific oasis-like ecologically favoured zones where irrigation from groundwater aquifers is possible.

Keywords:

Resource management, hinterland, Bayuda, North Kordofan

Introduction

Despite being in most aspects a primarily riverine culture and economy, use of the rangelands in the hinterland also played an important role for the Kushite and Nubian states. As such, archaeological research in and about ancient Nubia still focuses on the riverine landscapes to a great extent. The "desert" in the hinterlands of the river course is – if at all – often investigated and interpreted in relation to trade and caravan routes, or, especially in the east, as regions exploited for mining activities.

Comparably little attention has been paid to the specific forms and basic principles of agricultural productivity of hinterlands which are not reached by river water. Different soil types and the availability of water in several forms, especially the use of direct rainfall, as well as irrigation from groundwater sources, are the major limiting factors for agricultural production in rangeland conditions. Therefore, different modes of production correlate with specific water and soil management, as well as land use strategies – mainly divided along general socio-economic concepts like extensive rangeland economies with a focus on pastoralism, and intensified sedentary, but nevertheless often topographically fluctuating, agricultural strategies. Longstanding traditional resource management systems provide a sustainable way of sharing these natural resources between different and often competing, but nevertheless highly entangled socio-economic and socio-cultural groups.

The landscapes of the Central Bayuda and Northern Kordofan (Fig. 1)

The Bayuda Desert is situated between the Great Nile Bend and the Nubian Desert (in its southwestern part, it directly merges into Northern Kordofan), and is bordered by the towns of El Multagha, Abu Hamed, Atbara, and Omdurman. It is characterised by a vast expanse of arid, rugged terrain with sparse vegetation and a topography ranging from flat plains to rocky hills, especially around the eponymous volcano field situated in its central part around the catchment area of the upper Wadi Abu Dom and some of its tributaries (Fig. 2).[2]

The landscape is dominated by rocky outcrops and plateaux (especially in the northern and central parts), gravel plains, and sand dunes (predominantly in the southern Bayuda). Between the dunes and rocky outcrops, there are vast stretches of gravel plains with scattered scrub vegetation. Vegetation in the Bayuda Desert is adapted to the arid conditions and typically consists of tundub and other thorny shrubs, acacia trees, and seasonal grass vegetation.

One of the most notable features of the Bayuda Desert is the presence of larger wadis (such as the Muqqatam, Barkol, and Abu Dom wadis), which are seasonal riverbeds that occasionally fill with water during sparse rainfall events. These wadis can create a striking contrast to the surrounding arid landscape with pockets of greenery and diverse plant and animal life congregating around these temporary water sources.

The Central Bayuda is dominated by two major landscape features: the volcanic field with its adjacent basement rock complexes, and the Wadi Abu Dom, including its catchment area within the volcanic field, streaming down towards the Nile, flowing into it near the modern town of Merowe (and the ancient site of Sanam). The volcanic field

1 Universität Münster; jana.eger@uni-muenster.de; timkarberg@uni-muenster.de.

2 Cf. i.e. Lohwasser, Karberg and Auenmüller 2018, VIII.

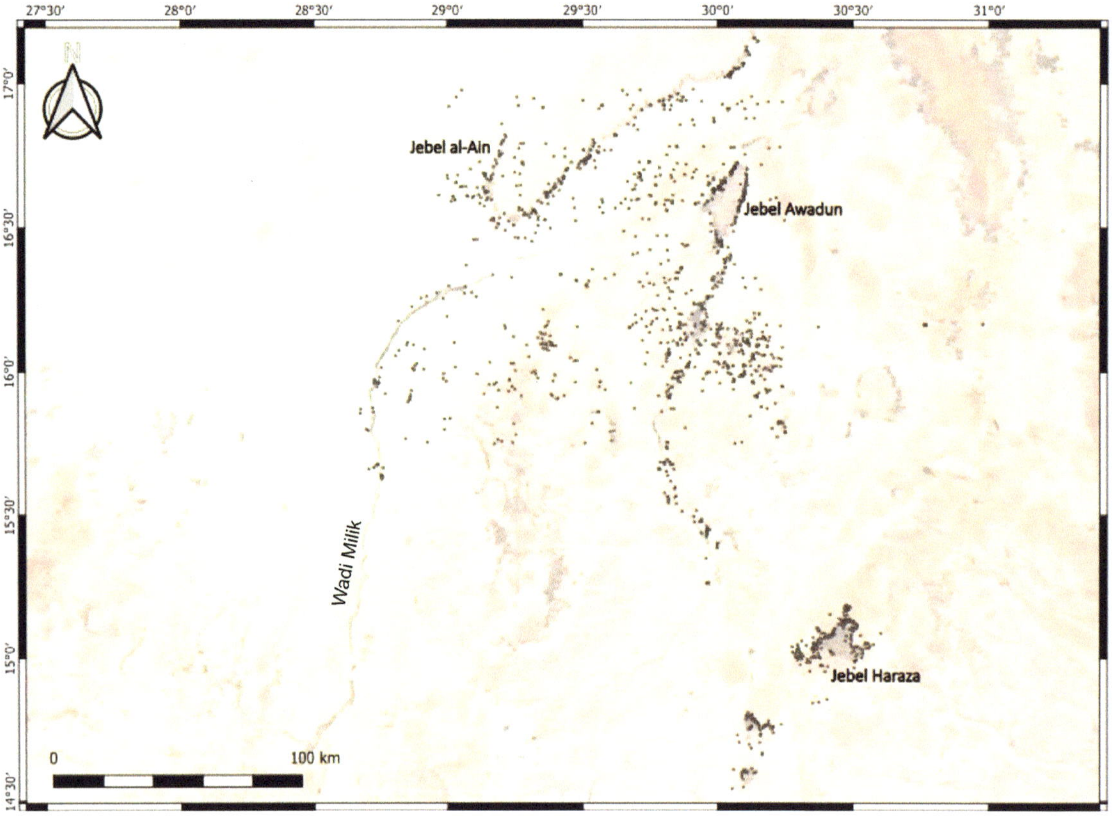

Fig. 3 Northern Kordofan with archaeological sites discovered during the Interregional Linkage Investigations in Northern Kordofan (map by InterLINK Project).

covers an area of approximately 600 km^2,[3] and is characterised by a series of volcanic features, including volcanic cones, maars, and lava flows. Most volcanic activity in this region took place relatively recently in geological terms, with eruptions occurring predominantly during the Pleistocene era within the last few tens of thousands of years.[4] There are even some, albeit disputed, indications for sporadic eruptions until the Medieval Period around AD 850.[5]

One of the prominent features of the Bayuda volcanic field is its scoria cones, which are small steep-sided volcanoes built primarily of loose fragmented volcanic rock known as scoria.[6] These scoria cones are created by the accumulation of ejected volcanic material during relatively mild and intermittent eruptions, presumably under, in general, more humid ecological circumstances.[7] They can vary in size and shape and often have a crater at their summit. Maars are another common volcanic feature in the Bayuda volcanic field. Maars are large, shallow volcanic craters formed by explosive eruptions resulting from the interaction of magma with groundwater or surface water. They are often filled with water, forming shallow lakes or ponds known as maar lakes. The lava flows in the Bayuda volcanic field are generally basaltic (formed of a type of dark, fine-grained volcanic rock that is low in silica content). Basaltic lava flows can cover large areas and create vast fields of solidified lava.[8]

The volcanic activity in the Bayuda volcanic field has had a significant impact on the local landscape, has contributed to the diverse geological formations in the region, and has influenced the regional climate. The volcanic soil and ash have also enriched the land,[9] supporting natural vegetation, as well as local clusters of rain-fed agriculture.[10]

3 The area was measured using ALOS World 3D – 30m digital surface model, Tile ALPSMLC30 DSM 018E032 (JAXA 2016). The area of the volcanic field is estimated as smaller in the geological literature – e.g., Lenhardt et al. give an area of 476 km^2 (Lenhardt et al. 2018, 212).

4 Almond, Kheir and Poole 1984, 234–235; Lenhardt et al. 2018, 212.

5 Almond, Kheir and Poole 1984, 235.

6 Grabham 1920.

7 Almond, Ahmed and Khalil 1969, 562–563.

8 Almond, Kheir and Poole 1984, 237–238.

9 Cf. the distribution of Eutric Fluvisol soils downstream of the volcano field (Jones et al. 2013, 94–95, Plate 8).

10 Karberg and Lohwasser 2018a, 101–102.

The second major landscape feature in the central Bayuda is the Wadi Abu Dom. The course of the Wadi Abu Dom reaches from its catchment area in the volcano field, described above, and its adjacent basement outcrops, and extends in a generally north-eastward direction towards the Nile River. The wadi is characterised by its sandy riverbed, which is mostly dry but occasionally shows some significant surface water.[11] At both banks of the actual wadi bed, different steps of low and high flood terraces were formed by surface water. The low flood terraces are, in some cases, still subject to geomorphological formation, while the high flood terraces are the result of significantly higher surface water levels during the Holocene pluvial periods.[12]

The Wadi Abu Dom, like other wadis in the region, serves as a vital lifeline for mobile, as well as sedentary communities, making different use of surface and groundwater resources. Interestingly, the use of different sources of water for specific purposes differs along the course of the wadi. In its upper and central part, sparse agriculture is fed by surface water from the wadi course itself, as well as from rainwater, and wells are exclusively used for watering livestock. In the lower Wadi Abu Dom, however, most of the groundwater accessed via wells is used for irrigation purposes.[13] The reasons for these differing strategies in the use of soil and water resources are highlighted in this chapter.

In Northern Kordofan, the landscape features are, generally, similar to the Bayuda, but differ from each other in specific aspects which are highly significant and result in different specific land use strategies (Fig. 3).

In general, like the Bayuda, Northern Kordofan has an arid climate and an absence of permanent natural water bodies. The threefold division of landscape surface elements – rocky hills, gravel plains, and areas dominated by sand dunes – are also present here, but the rocky areas are in most cases not formed by volcanic activities or the basement complex (with the Jebel Haraza being one of the few exceptions), but are merely cuestas of the Nubian Sandstone formation.[14] This limits their role as sources for minerals enriching the natural soil.

Like the Bayuda, the natural surface water bodies of Northern Kordofan are limited to large seasonal wadis. In Northern Kordofan, only one large wadi system, the Wadi Milik and its tributaries, dominate the geo-hydrology of the region. While most larger wadis in the Bayuda are directed, more or less, in an east-western direction, the Wadi Milik is oriented predominantly from south to north. This fact, in combination with its length of around 700 km (covering almost 4.5 degrees of latitude), characterises the Wadi Milik as a diarrheic water body, projecting the eco-hydrological circumstances of an area with significant rainfall into a more arid area.

Therefore, more intensive rainfall in the more southern areas directly affects the water resources of the lower Wadi Milik, and therefore the arid and partly hyper arid areas of Northern Kordofan. During earlier periods, there are indications for more rainfall, including, at and around the surface of the Jebel al-Ain cuesta.[15] At the pediment of the Jebel al-Ain, sediments containing significant quantities of calcium carbonate – which indicates the presence of surface water over a longer period – are present.[16] While some of them date to the late African Humid Period,[17] there are indications that, at least, some of them may date to younger periods with significant temporary increases in rainfall, which can be assumed as the regional equivalents of the Roman Warm Period, as well as the Medieval Climate Anomaly.[18] But even if there were periods with a significant northern shift of isohyets during the past 2000 years, they might have only had a local impact. As such, they, presumably, did not contribute to major changes in the surface water regime of the Wadi Milik, since the catchment areas of the Jebel al-Ain, as well as the Jebel Nagashush draining towards the Wadi Milik, are rather small, and most of any possible rainfall in this area might have drained – either as surface water or via sub-surface aquifers – northwards to the Wadi Howar.[19]

Concerning the major soils, relatively fertile eutric Fluvisols occur in the immediate vicinity of the Wadi Milik and in an area west of the Jebel Awadun, while most of the area is dominated by sandy Arenosols.[20] They are in general less fertile, but their greater water permeability makes them more suitable for climatic conditions with sporadic rainfalls, where durrha, or other crops with low requirements on soil fertility, can be grown.[21] Jebel Haraza, whose soils are characterised as Leptosol,[22] occupies a special position, as its mineral-rich rocks – some of which are of volcanic origin[23] – form fertile micro-soils through erosion.

11 Karberg 2021, 75–78.
12 Pflaumbaum 1987.
13 Karberg and Lohwasser 2018a, 12–17.
14 Geological and Mineral Resources Department (Sudan) 1981.
15 Eger-Karberg and Karberg 2021.
16 Eger and Karberg 2020, 90–92; Pachur and Altmann 2006, 254.
17 Pachur and Altmann 2006, 257–258.
18 Eger and Karberg 2020, 92–96.
19 This drainage modelling is derived from TerraSAR/TanDEM-SAR-X DEM data provided to the authors by the German Aerospace Center (DLR) and analysed using the *Deterministic 8 Drainage Model* developed by John O'Callaghan and David Mark (O'Callaghan and Mark 1984). For the historical significance of sub-surface draining from the Jebel al-Ain area towards the Wadi Howar, cf. Eger-Karberg and Karberg 2021.
20 Jones et al. 2013, 94–95, Plate 8.
21 Born 1965, 15.
22 Jones et al. 2013, 94–95, Plate 8.
23 Müller-Sohnius and Horn 1994, 608–609.

Fig. 4 Well used for irrigation purposes in the oasis of El Rum in the lower Wadi Abu Dom (photo by H. Berkahn).

Land use patterns

As stated in the description of the different landscapes of the Bayuda and Northern Kordofan, the two major limiting resources for the local economies are water and soil. Different combinations of their respective availabilities result in considerably different land use strategies which is reflected in the archaeological record.

Within the central part of the Bayuda, especially along the Wadi Abu Dom, the availability of water plays a more important role than the fertility of the soil. The distribution of different soil types (and subtypes) and their different suitability for agricultural use does not correspond topographically with peaks in density and productivity of arable land. While the eutric fluvisol soil is estimated as the most fertile in the direct vicinity of the Bayuda volcanic field (i.e. in and around the alluvial fans at the offspring of the Wadi Dejamon, one of the major tributaries of the Wadi Abu Dom), indicators for highly productive agriculture are lacking in the archaeological record, as well as in the written historical record covering roughly the last 150 years,[24] and in the analysis of land use patterns from satellite imagery covering roughly the last 50 years.[25]

This seems significant as the alluvial fans around the offspring area of the Wadi Dejamon, as well as the Wadi Abu Dom itself, indicate the presence of significant amounts of surface water, at least during periods with higher rainfall. Nevertheless, small-scale seasonal agriculture of durrha in this part of the wadi seems to rely completely on direct rainfall,[26] without any indicators for an intensification of agricultural production by means of irrigation from wells or surface water management. Wells in this part of the wadi are specifically designed and used for watering animals, and not for the provision of water to agricultural irrigation schemes (Fig. 4).[27] Areas like the alluvial fans – despite their role as small-scale ecologically favoured zones – were obviously used, predominantly, as areas for extensive, mostly pastoral, land use strategies[28] with a peak in activity during the Medieval Period, which most likely offered more favourable ecological circumstances during the so-called Medieval Climate Anomaly than in other periods.[29]

In the middle Wadi Abu Dom, even less indicators for agricultural production schemes are found

24 Gleichen 1905, Vol. I, 208–209; Vol. II, 186–187.
25 Karberg 2021, 74–78.
26 Karberg and Lohwasser 2018a, 101–102.
27 Karberg and Lohwasser 2018a, 83–85.
28 Karberg and Lohwasser 2018a, 10.
29 Karberg and Lohwasser 2018a, 43–47; 101.

Fig. 5 Hafir, west of the Jebel al-Ain (photo by J. Eger-Karberg).

archaeologically, as well as for sub-recent periods. From the archaeological record, there are indications that, at least for the past 2500 years, the population of the middle Wadi Abu Dom was highly mobile and practiced pastoral land use strategies.[30] Even in the direct vicinity of geological lineaments forming natural sub-terranean barrages across the groundwater aquifers along the Wadi Abu Dom – resulting in relatively high local levels of groundwater – there are no traces for its use in intensified agriculture until very recently.[31] There are a small number of small-scale water management installations – such as small dams across tributary khors – the date and function of which are still somewhat enigmatic. They are not clearly dated and due to their position within rocky areas not suitable for any agricultural purposes. As such these installations are clearly not connected with water harvesting for agricultural use.[32] Larger water harvesting installations like hafirs were not documented in the Wadi Abu Dom at all – the only example from the central Bayuda is a single hafir in the Wadi Barkol, which has yet to be investigated archaeologically and, as such, still of unknown date.

In the lower Wadi Abu Dom, the traces of agricultural production in the archaeological record, as well as observations on recent and sub-recent developments are completely different. Here, until today, two micro-oases dominate the landscape. The density and distribution patterns of archaeological evidence indicates that the modern micro-oasis of El Rum was an exceptionally ecologically favoured zone for, at least, the last 2000 years.[33] It is still not known how old its well-fed irrigation schemes are but they can be dated back to, at least, the Medieval Period.[34] In earlier times, it is possible that the oasis was fed by natural surface water. Because the groundwater aquifers along the course of the Wadi Abu Dom are highly dependent on rainfall in the arid area of the Bayuda volcano field, the level of groundwater in the wells of the lower Wadi Abu Dom would have been rather unpredictable over longer periods. Therefore, planning of stable long-term horticultures like date

30 Karberg and Lohwasser 2018a, 109–112; cf. also Karberg and Lohwasser 2018b, 7–9.

31 Karberg and Lohwasser 2018a, 12–15; 100–101; cf. also Cantauw 2023, 25–26.

32 Karberg and Lohwasser 2018a, 87–89.

33 Karberg 2021, 78–81.

34 Karberg and Lohwasser 2018a, 83–85; 97–99; nevertheless, this is only a terminus post quem, while the question of possible older traces of well-fed irrigation at El Rum is still subject to investigation.

palm plantations became rather difficult, which in turn made the oases of El Rum and Ghazali cyclically fluctuating cultural landscapes with a considerable range of productivity in the long term.

In Northern Kordofan, along the course of the Wadi Milik, as well as in the hills around Jebel Haraza, the situation is considerably different. As in the Bayuda, there are general indicators for an entangled economy with extensive rain-fed agriculture, comparatively small areas with intensified agriculture, and areas used for various – overlapping and interacting – pastoral economic strategies.

One of the most significant differences between the archaeological evidence for resource management in the Bayuda and Northern Kordofan is the presence of hafirs. Unlike the central Bayuda, hafirs occur in considerable quantities in Northern Kordofan along the banks of the Wadi Milik, as well as around the Jebel al-Ain and the Jebel Nagashush (Fig. 5). During our research for the InterLINK survey project, we were able to document 67 hafir structures,[35] which were previously unknown.[36] Kernel density analysis of the distribution pattern of these hafirs show significant concentrations of these structures in the middle of the Wadi Melek, at the adjacent Jebel al-Ain, and in the immediate vicinity of the ruined site of Zankor in the headwaters of the Wadi Milik (Fig. 6).[37] The general construction patterns of these hafirs closely resemble known examples from the Butana and Keraba.[38] Pottery recovered from these hafirs during fieldwork proved to be too unspecific for dating the installations. However, there are at least indications that they are of significant age: their structural similarity to examples from the Keraba and Butana dated to the Meroitic Period; the severe erosion and sedimentation of the sites; and, most importantly, the fact that at least the hafirs around the Jebel al-Ain and the Jebel Nagashush are located in areas where regularly flowing surface water or significant rainfall was not present for the last centuries, obviously indicating wetter climatic episodes.[39]

In order to understand the function of these hafirs, a multidirectional landscape archaeological approach proved useful. At the southern pediment of the Jebel Nagashush, as well as at the western pediment of Jebel al-Ain this involved the analysis of recent vegetation concentrations from multispectral satellite data combined with information provided by drainage khors – today partly below the surface – derived from radar data, and drainage modelling using Digtial Elevation Models (DEMs).[40] At the Jebel Nagashush, the placement of hafirs corresponds to recent, partly sub-terranean, drainage during extreme rains (such as those in September 2020), but under normal circumstances not enough water is available for a significant filling of these hafirs. West and north-west of the Jebel al-Ain, the situation is even clearer: here, some hafirs are situated along palaeo-khors which are now heavily covered by aeolic sand accumulations and, therefore, long since inactive.

These qualitative observations associate the hafirs, at least of the lower Wadi Milik and the area around Jebel al-Ain and Jebel Nagashush with significantly wetter climatic episodes. The results can be further quantified using data from satellite imagery and field research on the ground. Based on diameter and capacity, there are both significantly smaller hafirs in the north, and significantly larger ones in the south.[41] Some outliers of smaller hafirs than expected from this simplified, linear model are found in the south, but no outliers of larger hafirs than expected in the north.[42] The common dependent variable underlying this statistical correlation may explain the smaller hafirs in the South, but not the larger ones in the North. One probable variable explaining the distribution patterns of the hafirs is local rainfall during their planning and construction. However, flowing surface water from south to north over longer distances can be ruled out as a common dependent variable.

Agricultural cultivation terraces are also indicative of intensified agricultural production and have been documented in Kordofan in the hills of Jebel Haraza and Jebel Abu Hadid.[43] Comparable constructions

35 Most of these hafirs were discovered using satellite imagery. Some of them were also investigated on the ground (Eger and Karberg 2019, 133–135).

36 For example to Marion Hinkel, whose posthumously published standard work "Die Hafire im Sudan" essentially reflects the state of research of the 1980s (Hinkel 2015).

37 For general remarks on the site of Zankor, cf. Gratien et al. 2013. Geo-hydrological aspects and water harvesting strategies around Zankor are subject to investigation by Cécilia Populaire, the results are still unpublished.

38 Eger and Karberg 2019, 134–135; cf. also Scheibner 2014; Weschenfelder 2014.

39 Cf. Eger-Karberg and Karberg 2021.

40 O'Callaghan and Mark 1984.

41 This distribution is therefore not clearly linear, but statistically highly significant. A Moran's I analysis of the spatial correlation of the distribution of the hafirs along the Wadi Milik according to their diameters and capacities (carried out using ArcGIS 10.2.1 spatial statistics toolbox) results in a spatial correlation index of 0,7525049, indicating a strong positive spatial correlation with a p value of 0,000007.

42 A focus on low value clustering using the Getis Ord-G analysis method (also done with the ArcGIS 10.2.1 spatial statistics toolbox) results in an p value of 0,037, less significant than the general Moran's I index of spatial correlation, but still estimated as statistically significant (< 0,05). This means a higher degree of spatial correlation of larger hafirs with smaller ones than *vice versa*. In other words, there are area where large hafirs are correlated with smaller ones, and areas where smaller hafirs occur alone, but no areas where larger hafirs occur alone without any smaller counterparts.

43 Eger and Karberg 2019, 137–143.

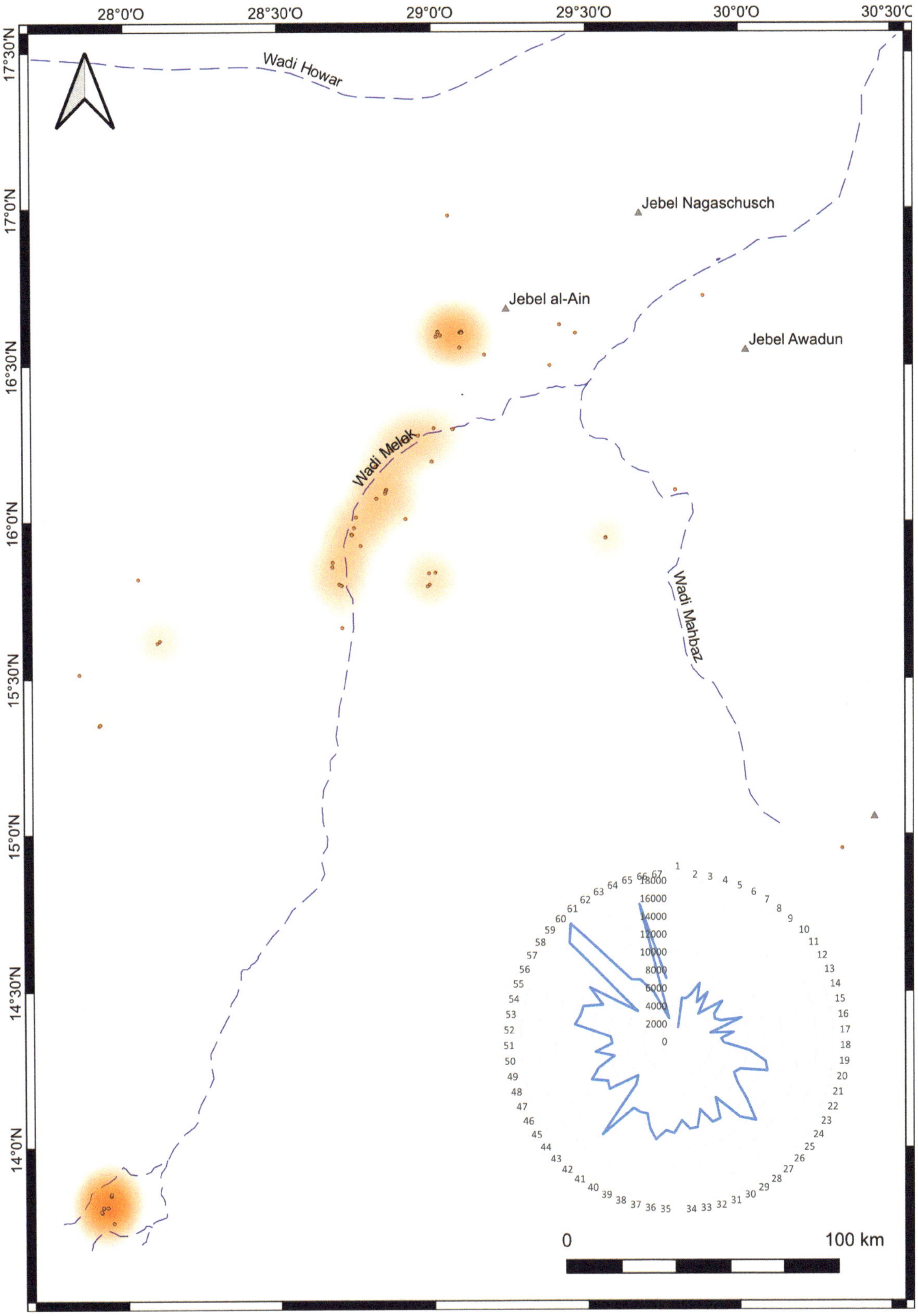

Fig. 6 Kernel density map and diagram of the distribution of the diameters of hafirs in Northern Kordofan.

were previously documented in some detail in Darfur around the settlement concentrations in the vicinity of Jebel Marra.[44] The dating of these installations remains unclear so far. Interestingly, comparable installations are so far unknown in the settlement concentrations around Jebel Midob or in the vicinity of Zankor, although the terrain, as well as the local landscape and ecology, would be quite suitable for this type of cultivation. It remains equally unclear whether this cultivation technique is associated with similar systems in the Ethiopian highlands and in eastern and southern Africa, or whether they are independent developments.

Socio-economic strategies

The different land use patterns in the central Bayuda and Northern Kordofan outlined in the previous section can be interpreted as the result of different socio-economic strategies associated with different modes of production. Along the Wadi Abu Dom, intensified agricultural production based on irrigation schemes is only present in the lower Wadi Abu Dom. Other parts of the central Bayuda (for example, the alluvial fans of the headwaters of the Wadi Dejamon or the ecologically favoured zones connected with the natural lineaments across the middle Wadi Abu Dom) which are, at least, comparatively suitable for an intensification of agricultural production based on the availability of water and soil fertility, do not show any indicators of such intensified agriculture. At first glance this seems somewhat paradoxical as, combined with the highly fluctuating character of the oases in the lower Wadi Abu Dom, this suggests a closer entanglement of the oases of the lower Wadi Abu Dom with the Nile Valley than would have been possible in more remote areas. A complex cultural and socio-economic land use model for the oases of El Rum and Ghazali has to incorporate factors other than natural conditions and resource use strategies, especially the need for exchange of workforces between the riverine and the oasis economies.[45] Both pull and push factors come into play. Pull factors, from the point of view of the oasis economy indicate – in addition to the natural resources considered above – technical progress in irrigation methods,[46] population pressure in the agriculturally more productive Nile valley, and possible administrative pressure (e.g., taxation and regulations) in core territories that are more strongly characterised by statehood.[47] Push factors would include price declines for agricultural products, labour shortages in the more productive Nile Valley agriculture, and economic shifts toward earning opportunities outside of the agricultural sector. The fact that the intensification of agricultural production only covered the lower Wadi Abu Dom might indicate that entanglement processes with the Nile Valley – including occasional exchange of population and therefore workforces, as can still be observed today – was a more important factor for the specific development of the lower Wadi Abu Dom than the adaptation to different ecological resources.

In Northern Kordofan, similar irrigation-based micro-oases did not emerge, maybe due to a lesser degree of entanglement with densely populated areas like the Nile valley. On the other hand, other strategies of agricultural production intensification – like the terraces at Jebel Haraza and Jebel Abu Hadid – might have required a similar amount of human labour than irrigation schemes of similar size. Since both jebels are partly covered by (micro) soil relatively rich in mineralisation, while the wider vicinity is dominated by relatively unfertile Arenosol soils, the strategy of constructing agricultural terraces might be an adaptation to the small amount of available land reached by the erosion of highly mineralised material of volcanic origin, especially if crops with higher demands on soil fertility were cultivated. Nevertheless, as stated above, the less fertile Arenosols of the plains in the wider vicinity of the jebels are not as unsuitable for agriculture as might be estimated when solely evaluating their fertility, since they can deal better with sporadic rainfalls. Another reason for the construction of the agricultural terraces, therefore, could be a better delimitation of areas for high-demanding crops and areas where extensive sporadic agriculture and pastoralism was practiced in order to manage conflicts over land use strategies.[48] Comparable conflicts between groups practicing different land use strategies can be observed in Kordofan and Darfur today.

The construction of a large number of hafirs as installations for harvesting and managing surface water can be another aspect of managing conflicting land use strategies. As in the Keraba and the Butana, it can be assumed that – due to their water storage capacity in relation to the much lower grazing capacity of natural grasslands, which can be reached from the hafir by different species of livestock –[49] hafirs were in fact, not only used for pastoral purposes, but served a highly integrated economy with pastoral, as well as extensive agricultural aspects. The entanglement of these different modes of production enabled the more economical use of surface water available sporadically but in large quantities, and mitigated risks by diversifying production in marginal conditions.[50]

44 Hale 1966.
45 Karberg 2021, 81.
46 Cf. Oleson 1984, 363–370.
47 Cf. Shaw 1929, 64, who describes taxation as a push factor towards remote areas for long-ranged trading routes.
48 Schinkel 1970, 161.
49 Karberg 2017, 112–115.
50 Akhtar-Schuster 1995, 67.

Conclusions

As shown in this chapter, peripheries at the fringes of Nubia, like the Bayuda and Northern Kordofan, are characterised by specific land use strategies adapted to limited resources. Factors limiting production in these areas are the availability of water and the fertility of the soil, which is often subject to erosion and Aeolic deformation. Nevertheless, analysis of the contextualisation of different forms of production with the geo- and eco-factors they are based on, shows that the availability of water is a stronger limiting factor than soil. Different strategies to improve access and management of water resources – like irrigations schemes fed by wells or systems of hafirs – were constructed in order to maximise productivity and, often more importantly, to minimise risks in areas where rainfall is not only rare, but also lacking a homogenous distribution. Climatic regimes where rainfall seldom occurs other than as short intense episodes mean reliable rain and surface water management is crucial. Hafir constructions can be used to harvest water during such rainy episodes, as well as canalise surface water in order to minimise the effects of local floodings. Fluctuating oasis agriculture, on the other hand, is a more flexible way of making use of temporary episodes of rising groundwater. Their embedding into highly integrated economic systems characterised by close entanglement of agricultural and pastoral production strategies demonstrates their resilience in climatic and ecological shifts.

Acknowledgements

This contribution is based on data from the research projects "Wadi Abu Dom Itinerary (W.A.D.I.)", "El Rum Oasis", and "Interregional Linkage Investigations in Northern Kordofan (InterLINK)". All projects are affiliated with the Research Unit "Old Sudan" at the Institute for Egyptology and Coptic Studies at the University of Münster under the supervision of Angelika Lohwasser and funded by the German Research Foundation (DFG). Additionally, the InterLINK project is part of the DFG Priority Program (SPP) 2143 "Entangled Africa". The authors express their gratitude to Angelika Lohwasser, Jörg Linstädter, Torsten Prinz, Judith Verstegen, Patricia Göbel, Loai Shamsalola, Mohammed el-Toum, Ibrahim Musa, and Huweida Mohammed Adam for their collegial support.

Bibliography

Akhtar-Schuster, M.
1995 *Degradationsprozesse und Desertifikation im semiariden randtropischen Gebiet der Butana, Republik Sudan*, Göttingen.

Almond, D.C., Ahmed, F. and Khalil, B.E.
1969 An excursion to the Bayuda volcanic field of Northern Sudan, *Bulletin Volcanologique* 33, 549–565.

Almond, D.C., Kheir, O.M. and Poole, S.
1984 Alkaline basalt volcanism in northeastern Sudan: a comparison of the Bayuda and Gedaref areas, *Journal of African Earth Sciences* 2 (3), 233–245.

Born, M.
1965 *Zentralkordofan. Bauern und Nomaden in Savannengebieten des Sudan*, Marburg.

Cantauw, P.
2023 *Identification of Potential Groundwater Storage Areas in Wadi Abu Dom, Sudan, Using Remote Sensing Mapping Techniques and GIS. A Conceptual Hydrogeological Approach in Context of Historical Land Use*, MA Thesis, University of Münster.

Eger, J. and Karberg, T.
2019 Neue Forschungen in Nord-Kordofan. Vorbericht über die Feldkampagnen des InterLINK-Projektes der Jahre 2017 und 2018, *Der antike Sudan, Mitteilungen der Sudanarchäologischen Gesellschaft zu Berlin e.V.* 30, 131–146.
2020 Nord-Kordofan im Satellitenbild. Vorbericht über die Forschungen des InterLINK-Projektes 2020, *Der antike Sudan, Mitteilungen der Sudanarchäologischen Gesellschaft zu Berlin e.V.* 31, 87–98.

Eger-Karberg, J. and Karberg, T.
2021 Wasser für Gala Abu Ahmed. Ein Paläo-Drainagesystem zwischen Jebel Nagaschusch und Wadi Howar (Sudan) im Radar-Satellitenbild, *Der antike Sudan, Mitteilungen der Sudanarchäologischen Gesellschaft zu Berlin e.V.* 32, 99–108.

Geological and Mineral Resources Department (Sudan)
1981 *Geological Map of the Sudan*, Paris.

Gleichen, E.
1905 *The Anglo-Egyptian Sudan: A Compendium Prepared by Officers of the Sudan Government*, London.

Grabham, C.W.
1920 The Bayuda volcanic field, *Sudan Notes and Records* 3 (2), 133–136.

Gratien, B., Dissaux, R.-P., Evrard, J., Marchi, S., Nogara, G. and Usai, D.
2013 *Abou Sofyan et Zankor. Prospections dans le Kordofan occidental (Soudan)*, Villeneuve d'Ascq.

Hale, G.A.
1966 *Cultivation Terraces in Western Darfur, Sudan: A Study in an Agricultural Form and Practice*, Los Angeles.

Hinkel, M.
2015 *Die Hafire im Sudan*, The Archaeological Map of the Sudan Supplement 2, Bonn.

Jones, A., Breuning-Madsen, H., Brossard, M., Dampha, A., Deckers, J., Dewitte, O. and Zougmoré, R. (eds.)
2013 *Soil Atlas of Africa*, Luxemburg.

Karberg, T.
2017 Cattle in the Meroitic hinterland exemplified by archaeological record from Musawwarat es Sufra, in: E. Fantusani and M. Baldi (eds.), *The Fifth Day for Nubian Studies*, Rome, 105–116.
2021 Landnutzungsentwicklung und -modelle der Oase El Rum –Analyse multispektraler und SAR-Satellitenaufnahmen im Kontext raumbezogener Surveydaten, *Der antike Sudan, Mitteilungen der Sudanarchäologischen Gesellschaft zu Berlin e.V.* 32, 69–82.

Karberg, T. and Lohwasser, A.
2018a The Wadi Abu Dom Itinerary Survey Project, in: A. Lohwasser, T. Karberg and J. Auenmüller (eds.), *Bayuda Studies. Proceedings of the First International Conference on the Archaeology of the Bayuda Desert in Sudan, 10.-12. September 2015 in Münster*, Meroitica, Schriften zur altsudanesischen Geschichte und Archäologie 27, Wiesbaden, 1–120.
2018b Pastoralism in the Wadi Abu Dom. Non-Sedentary Economical Strategies in the Central Bayuda, *Ādāb al-Neelain* 3 (2), 1–15.
2021 Wadi Abu Dom investigations: El Rum Oasis, *Sudan & Nubia* 25, 108–120.

Lenhardt, N., Borah, S.B., Lenhardt, S.Z., Bumby, A.J., Ibinoof, M.A. and Salih, A.S.
2018 The monogenetic Bayuda volcanic field, Sudan – new insights into geology and volcanic morphology, *Journal of Volcanology and Geothermal Research* 356, 211–224.

Lohwasser, A., Karberg, T. and Auenmüller, J.
2018 *Bayuda Studies. Proceedings of the First International Conference on the Archaeology of the Bayuda Desert in Sudan, 10.-12. September 2015 in Münster*, Meroitica, Schriften zur altsudanesischen Geschichte und Archäologie 27, Wiesbaden.

Müller-Sohnius, D. and Horn, P.
1994 K-Ar dating of ring complexes and fault systems in Northern Kordofan, Sudan: evidence for independent magmatic and tectonic activity, *Geologische Rundschau* 83, 604–613.

O'Callaghan, J.F. and Mark, D.M.
1984 The extraction of drainage networks from digital elevation data, *Computer Vision, Graphics and Image Processing* 28, 323–344.

Oleson, J.
1984 *Greek and Roman Mechanical Water-Lifting Devices*, Toronto.

PACHUR, H.-J. and ALTMANN, N.
2006 *Die Ostsahara im Spätquartär. Ökosystemwandel im größten hyperariden Raum der Erde*, Berlin.

PFLAUMBAUM, H.
1987 *Waditerrassen- und Fußflächengenese in der Bayuda-Wüste (Republik Sudan). Ein Beitrag zur „Morphogenetischen Sequenz" eines randtropischen Raumes*, Hamburg.

SCHEIBNER, T.
2014 Entstehung, Ursprung und Nutzung – Die Hafire in Musawwarat es-Sufra und in der Keraba als Wirtschaftsbauten, in: A. LOHWASSER and P. WOLF (eds.), *Ein Forscherleben zwischen den Welten. Zum 80. Geburtstag von Steffen Wenig*, Berlin, 299–322.

SCHINKEL, H.-G.
1970 *Haltung, Zucht und Pflege des Viehs bei den Nomaden Ost- und Nordostafrikas*, Veröffentlichungen des Museums für Völkerkunde Leipzig, Berlin.

SHAW, W.B.
1929 Darb el Arba'in. The Forty Days' road, *Sudan Notes and Records* 12 (1), 63–71.

WESCHENFELDER, P.
2014 Who gets the lion's share? Thoughts on Meroitic water management and its role in royal legitimization, in: A. LOHWASSER and P. WOLF (eds.), *Ein Forscherleben zwischen den Welten. Zum 80. Geburtstag von Steffen Wenig*, Berlin, 335–350.

Chapter 2

Nubian faience

Peter Lacovara[1]

Abstract

The complex interactions between Egypt and its Nubian neighbours are reflected in the most telling way in the artefactual materials left by these distinct yet interconnected cultures. One can see this in particular within the medium of what is known as "Egyptian faience", a sintered-quartz, non-clay ceramic.[2] Analysis has revealed that the material from the site of Kerma, the centre of a Bronze Age Nubian civilization, is both of Egyptian manufacture and local production.[3] Further investigation of both the composition and context of the faience has revealed a distinct and dramatic difference in the use and production of the material that references the political dynamic that developed between the two cultures, and which appears to be echoed in the succeeding Nubian Napatan and Meroitic Periods in Nubia.

Keywords:

Faience production, Kerma, cultural development, Napatan Period, Meroitic Period

Bronze Age Nubia

Although faience seems to have been largely restricted to beads found in prehistoric and A-Group contexts and may have been Egyptian imports,[4] no comprehensive analysis has been done on this material to date. However, it appears that Nubian craftsmen were producing objects with a faience glaze applied to milky quartz, which would become a hallmark of the later Kerma Culture.[5] A blue-glazed quartz lion's head was discovered in an unusually rich grave at Sayala during the First Archaeological Survey of Nubia,[6] and a similar example was also discovered in an A-Group grave by the Joint Scandinavian Expedition during the Aswan Dam Salvage campaign.[7]

Faience has also been found associated with the Middle Kingdom occupation of Lower Nubia. Bowls, cups, scarabs, amulets, beads, and figurines have all been found in both graves and habitations associated with the Egyptian frontier fortifications.[8] Whether this material was all shipped upriver from Egypt or made within the forts remains an unanswered question. Certainly, there appears to have been local production of pottery by Egyptian artisans in the area,[9] so faience manufacture may also have taken place.

The Kerma culture

For much of the Bronze Age, the most important state in the Middle Nile was the First Kingdom of Kush in the area of the Third Cataract in Sudan. Located in the Dongola Reach the site was first excavated by George A. Reisner in 1913–1916, who discovered there, both a vast cemetery site and a large settlement.[10] An abundance of faience was noted by Reisner, who reported that, "I have never seen a site where there was so much broken faience littering the surface as at Kerma. Every traveller has been struck by that fact; for the bright bits of blue against the grey desert catch and hold the eye."[11] The character and nature of the abundant remains of this material has been a matter of much speculation. As Reisner noted, they are typical of many of the faiences found in Middle Kingdom Egypt.[12] In particular, there are close parallels to those found by the Metropolitan Museum Expedition at Lisht;[13] and Geneviève Pierrat has postulated that the similarity of the material at Lisht and at Kerma suggested that the artisans of Lisht, for which she has proposed an Eastern identity,[14] were somehow also in service to the ruler of Kerma, simultaneously or successively.[15] However, the correspondence of the material is perhaps explained more logically by the importation of similar faiences from Egypt. This would be confirmed by the fact that they occur in contexts at Kerma that are later than the date of the Lisht material,[16] and that a large percentage of the faience found at the site derived from broken vessels.

1 The Ancient Egyptian Archaeology and Heritage Fund; lacovara.peter@gmail.com.

2 Cf. Tite, Manti and Shortland 2007, 1568–1583.

3 Lacovara 2021, 32–38.

4 Then-Obłuska 2022, 20–22.

5 Hardwick and Lacovara 2020/2021, 129–140.

6 Firth 1927, 38, pl. 18.

7 Nordström 1972, 124.

8 Dunham and Janssen 1960, pl. 119; Dunham 1967, pls. LXVI a–b, LXVII a, LXXXVId.

9 Knoblauch 2011, 167–184.

10 Reisner 1923a.

11 Reisner1923b, 134.

12 Reisner1923b, 135.

13 Hayes 1990, 224–227.

14 Pierrat-Bonnefois 2016–2017, 103–118.

15 Pierrat-Bonnefois 2016–2017, 114–115.

16 Miniaci 2019, 13–32.

Fig. 1 Ceiling slab from K XI, Classic Kerma Period, c. 1750–1480 BC. Sandstone, gypsum plaster and faience, H. 49.0 x W. 79.2 x Depth 10.5 cm. Harvard University – Boston Museum of Fine Arts Expedition, 13.4360.2 (photograph courtesy of the Museum of Fine Arts, Boston).

Fig. 2 Detail of faience inlay set into ceiling slab from K XI (photo by the author).

The importation of vast quantities of faience in the form of fragments, including wasters, might seem puzzling, however, just as with the fragments of Egyptian sculpture found at Kerma,[17] these faience sherds seem to have been acquired for use as raw materials. This is certainly the case with a ceiling tile from the funerary chapel K XI[18] (Fig. 1). Here, a sandstone slab was inlaid with a rosette decoration in a pattern similar to that found as ceiling decoration in Egyptian tombs.[19] The petals of the rosettes were formed of fragments of faience vessels ground down and fitted together with dowels and then cemented into place (Fig. 2). Plain and patterned tiles were often found and used together again, suggesting that disparate, fragmentary pieces were being sourced.

The number of Egyptian imports seems to decline towards the end of the Classic Kerma Period, suggesting the beginning of hostilities between the Theban, Hyksos and Kerma Kingdoms.[20] In response to this loss of material, local production of faience suddenly appears. The extensive use of distinctly different faience tile inlays in the funerary chapel, K II, also known as the Upper, or Eastern *Defuffa*,[21] indicates the emergence of indigenous production. The tiles used in K II themselves are visually different from the earlier, imported material, having largely undecorated surfaces and also a less uniform glaze coat, both in colour and thickness. The tiles bear imprints of textile patterns on the back, a rough linen[22] rather than vegetal matting, from their placement in the sun to dry prior to firing.[23] Both the exterior façade and the interior spaces of the *Defuffa* were decorated with faience tiles.[24] On the façade, the doorway was flanked by two opposing figures of lions (Fig. 3),[25] and perhaps standing above a row of bound captives.[26] Additionally, the structure was embellished with local interpretations in faience of a cavetto cornice, torus moulding and *kheker* frieze. The utilization of such 'Egyptianising' elements in the mortuary architecture of the rulers of Kerma mirrors the same pattern that would be seen in the Second Kingdom of Kush beginning with the 25th Dynasty.[27]

17 Lacovara 1991, 118–128.
18 Reisner 1923a, 266–267.
19 Cf. Prisse D'Avennes 2014, 172–173.
20 Cf. Davies 2003.

21 Reisner 1923b, 147–153.
22 Possibly from reused sail cloth (Sheila Shear, personal communication).
23 Reisner 1923b, 149–150.
24 Bonnet 2000, 126–132.
25 Bonnet 1990, 209, no. 251.
26 Friedman, Borromeo and Leveque 1998, 253, no. 137.
27 van Pelt 2013.

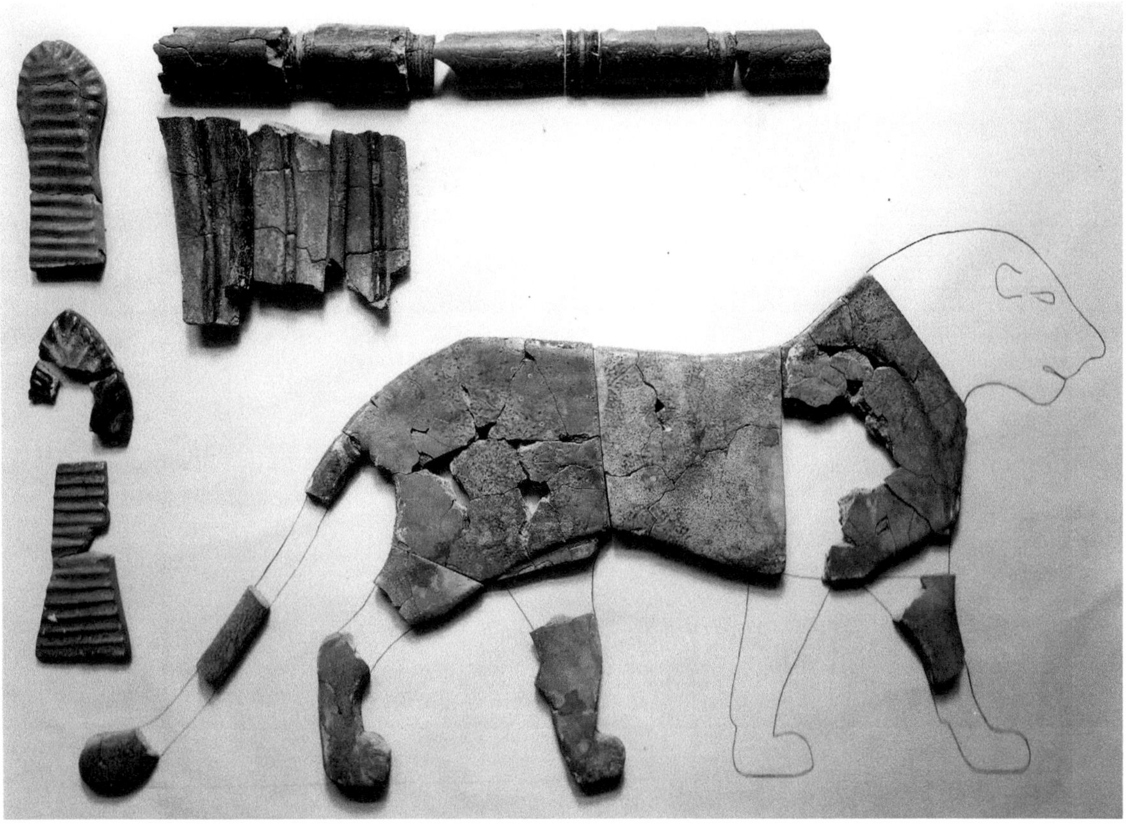

Fig. 3 Tiles from K II, Classic Kerma Period, c. 1750–1480 BC. Faience, H. 55.0 x 120.0 cm (lion only).
Harvard University—Boston Museum of Fine Arts Expedition, 20.1224
(photograph courtesy of the Museum of Fine Arts, Boston).

Analysis undertaken by Pamela Vandiver and Alex Kaczmarczyk of a variety of samples from Kerma, shows a distinctly different composition in the glaze and bodies of these later tiles from Egyptian faiences. In particular, the material produced at Kerma displays a much higher percentage of potassium that has been suggested to be the result of using plant ash as a substitute for the natron employed as an alkali in Egypt.[28] It is clear that with the commencement of the conflict with Egypt, access to faience was cut off and the ingredients of its traditional composition, and so, as a result, the material needed to be re-engineered by the Nubian artisans in much the same way as the attempts of European artists to recreate Chinese porcelain at the beginning of the Eighteenth Century.[29]

The faience objects created at this point at Kerma included both local creations and imitations of Egyptian goods, such as basket weave vessels,[30] a large hippopotamus figure[31] and a boat model similar to that of the gold example from the tomb of Ahhotep.[32] In addition to faience, experimentation with applying a vitreous glaze to quartz crystal, milky quartz, and even carnelian,[33] appears to be a local innovation carrying on a tradition of glazed stone that we have already seen going back to the A-Group. This remarkable transition from imported to locally produced faience at Kerma[34] underscores the inventiveness and resourcefulness of the Nubian cultures and the way in which Egyptian material culture was reinterpreted and utilized in the ideology of these early states.[35]

28 Analysis carried out by Hatcher, Henderson, Kaczmarczyk, Lacovara and Vandiver.

29 Kingery and Vandiver 1986, 163–177.

30 Cf. Brovarski, Doll and Freed 1982, 142, no. 138; 151, no. 157.

31 Lacovara 1992.

32 Salah and Sourouzian 1987, 123.

33 Reisner 1923b, 49–54.

34 While there is a significant distinction between the composition of the Egyptian and Kerma faiences, there is a small overlap which may be due to the reprocessing of Egyptian faience. This would account for the importation of a Middle Kingdom faience waster (BMFA SU 494). It should be noted that the local production of faience does not appear until the very end of the Classic Period and the suggestion that some amulets were made earlier (see D'Itria 2018) is not correct and rather they are clearly Egyptian imports.

35 Minor 2023.

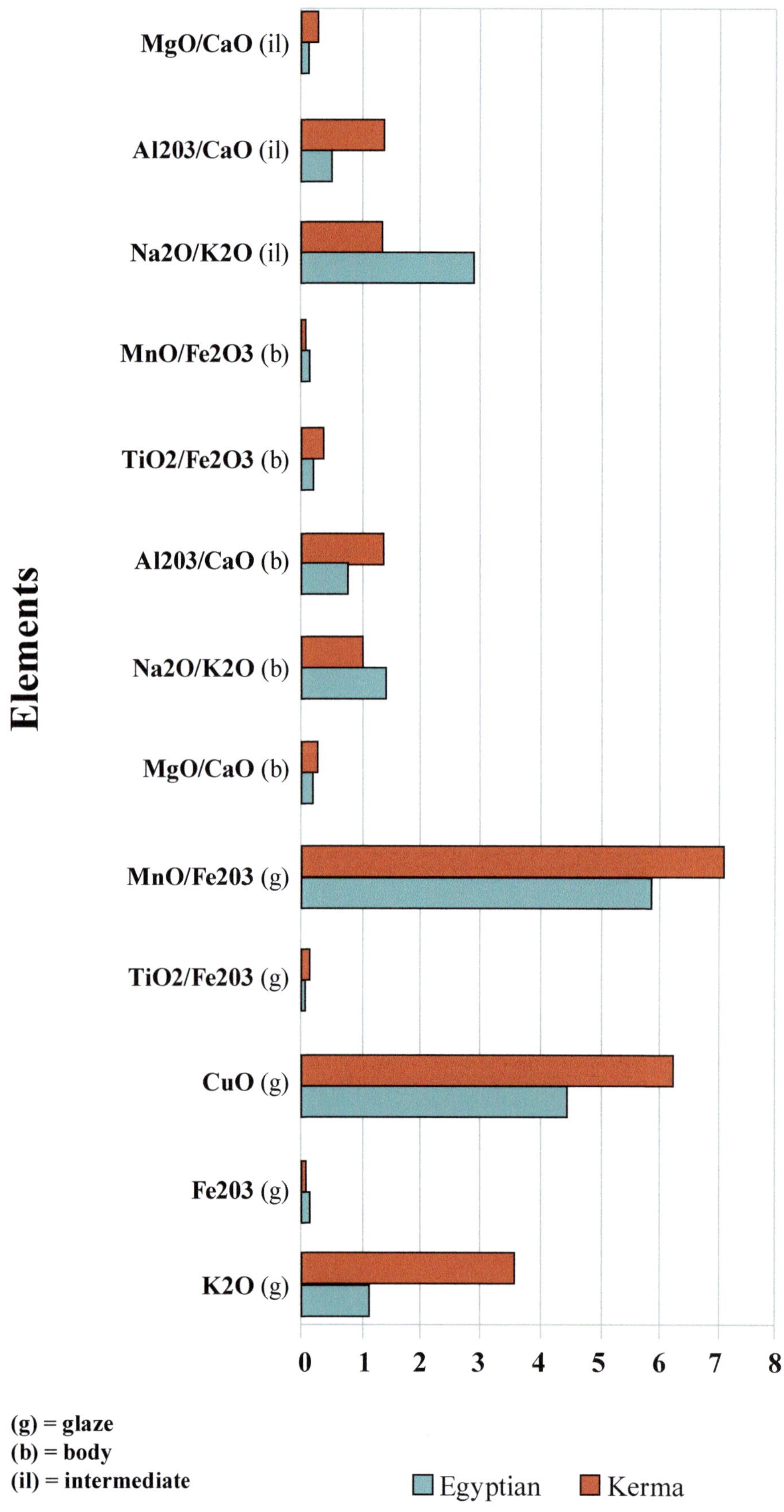

Table 1 Comparison of the constituent elements in samples of faience from Kerma and Egypt.

Fig. 4 Ankh inscribed for Malonaqan, Napatan, reign of Malonaqan, c. 555–542 BC. Faience, H. 21. 3 cm x W. 9.3 cm, British Museum EA 65274 (photo by Alamy Photo Services).

Fig. 5 Vase, Napatan Period, c. 712–664 BC. Faience. Vase: H. 8.0 x Diam. 6.5 cm; lid: H. 2 cm; Diam. 3.1 cm. From Tombos, Khartoum, Sudan National Museum, SNM 34671–34672 (photo Wikimedia Commons).

Napatan Nubia

With the Egyptian re-conquest of Nubia in the 18th Dynasty (c. 1539–1075 BC), faience manufacture appears to have returned to Egyptian traditions as with much of the material culture of the New Kingdom forts, fortified towns and temples in New Kingdom Nubia which appears largely indistinguishable from that of contemporary Egypt.[36] This may however be due in part to a lack of analytical investigation as there has been no comprehensive study of New Kingdom Nubian faience. Recent work on paint samples from Amara West has revealed the use of two types of chlorite green pigment (clinochlore and penninite) and copper chloride hydroxide rarely been identified in pharaonic Egyptian contexts and 'blue earth' (sodic amphibole riebeckite), not previously been reported in any Nile Valley context. This may suggest some indigenous technology being used alongside Egyptian techniques in colonial Nubia, and hopefully will prompt further investigation.[37]

With the emergence of the 25th Dynasty and the Napatan Period, a distinctive, and clearly indigenous faience appears. One can see this not only with the locally produced shabtis from the royal tombs at Kurru and Nuri,[38] but also a remarkable series of faience pectorals,[39] and other ornaments and ritual objects (Fig. 4). These ornaments tend to have a pale blue, matte glaze although polychrome faience with a slightly glossier surface is also found in this period, most spectacularly seen in a number of faience vessels recently found at Tombos (Fig. 5).[40]

36 Cf. Randall-MacIver and Woolley 1911, pls. LXVA a–b, LXVIIa; 131; Steindorff 1937, 141; Dunham and Janssen 1960, 15; Dunham 1967; Säve-Söderbergh and Troy 1991, 169.

37 Fulcher et al. 2021.

38 Cf. Dunham 1951; Haynes and Leprohon 1987.

39 Lacovara and Markowitz 2019, 128–131; Dunham 1950, pls. 49–55.

40 Rondot 2022, 390–391.

Fig. 6 *k3w* plaque, Napatan Period, c. 712–664 BC. From Sanam. Faience, H. 5.9 cm x max. W. 4.2 cm x Depth 1.6 cm. Ex Collection Lord Kitchener c. 1912. Houston Museum of Natural Science 04.2022.21.

Fig. 7 Wall applique of Apedemak, Meroitic Period, c. 1st Century AD. From Meroe. Faience, H. 24.2 cm x W. 23.4 cm x Depth 4.9 cm. World Museum, Liverpool 49.47.847 (photograph courtesy World Museum).

One in a series of votive plaques in the form of the *k3* hieroglyphs from the temple at Sanam is inscribed "making *k3w* of green faience" (Fig. 6),[41] indicating local manufacture. The Sanam faiences often have a distinctly reddish core, and a rather matte surface glaze.

An analysis project comparing samples of Napatan Nubian and Egyptian Third Intermediate and Late Period faiences was undertaken between 2014 and 2016 by the Department of Chemistry, at the University of Georgia with samples provided by Renée Stein, Director of Conservation and Chief Conservator at the Michael C. Carlos Museum at Emory University and the author. Preliminary results showed a very irregular thickness of the surface glaze layer on many of the Nubian specimens as well as a much higher copper content in them and lower sodium oxide and potassium oxide components.[42] While some of these values are similar to the Kerma faiences, there are significant differences suggesting that this was a second reinvention of the process and again as with the Classic Kerma Period, prompted by trade interruption with Egypt due to political hostility.[43]

Meroitic Nubia

The transition to the Meroitic Period sees a continuation of localized faience production, as recent analysis undertaken has shown. A project was undertaken at the Louvre to examine faiences from Sedeinga and from John Garstang's excavations in the city of Meroe by Alexander Kaczmarczyk and the Research and of Restoration of the museums of France. The analysis of the glaze layer on these faiences was carried out with X-ray fluorescence which determined that they were composed of Iron (Fe) 1.3%, Copper (Cu) 13.1%, Lead (PbO) 1.5%, Tin (Sn) 1.4%, and Silicon (Si).[44] This presents a very different composition than contemporary Egyptian faiences.[45]

The Sudanese faience glazes are usually cloudy, sometimes even opaque. This phenomenon may partly be the result of lower temperature firing. The glaze surfaces are often wavy, and small pinholes are visible on them. It has also been suggested that Egyptian Blue was added to the glaze mixtures in the Nubian faiences,[46] a feature also noted in the analysis conducted in Atlanta.[47] The bodies of many of the Meroitic faiences are often less well cemented than

41 Houston Museum of Natural Science 04.2022.21.

42 Salguero et al. 2016.

43 Contrary to Howley 2018, it is clear that there was not large-scale importation of custom-made funerary material to Napatan Nubia, cf. Lacovara 2018.

44 Sackho-Autissier 2016, 29–39.

45 Kaczmarczyk and Hedges 1983, 274–281.

46 Duma 1997.

47 Salguero et al. 2016.

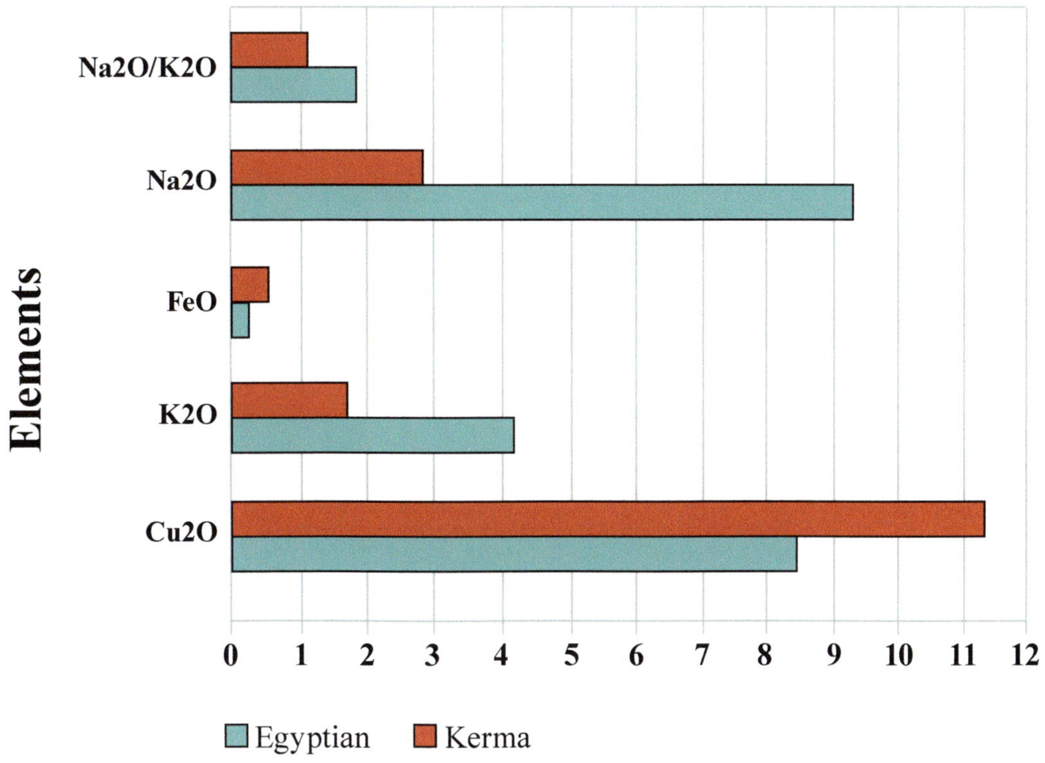

Egyptian Samples

Sample	Cu2O	K2O	FeO	Na2O	Na2O/K2O
012 glaze?	9.1	0.25	0.06	0.23	0.92
016 exterior glaze	8.46	6.27	0.13	13.85	2.21
016 interior glaze	8.48	5.84	0.85	13.81	2.36
	8.68	4.12	0.35	9.3	1.83

Nubian Samples

Sample	Cu2O	K2O	FeO	Na2O	Na2O/K2O
004 glaze	9.72	0.71	0.63	0.21	0.3
005.001 glaze	7.1	3.17	0.15	4.16	0.74
005.002 glaze + interaction	15.64	5.61	0.05	11.46	2.04
006 glaze	25.68	0.16	0.84	0.12	0.75
010 glaze?	3.41	0.13	0.78	0.35	2.02
018 glaze?	6.48	0.79	0.51	0.14	0.18
	11.33	1.76	0.49	2.74	1.01

Table 2 Comparison of the constituent elements in samples of faience from Napatan Nubia and Egypt (created by Tina Salguero and Jonathan Elias).

Fig. 8 String of Bes amulets, Late Meroitic, 100 BC–300 AD. From Karanog. Faience, Length 7.5 cm x H. 2.8 cm. Pennsylvania University Museum E7921.

Egyptian ones, but that did not prevent Nubian artisans from attempting to craft large objects such as the decorated puteals from Meroe[48] and other architectural embellishments (Fig. 7).[49]

By Post-Meroitic times, except for occasional beads and amulets which appear to be of Egyptian manufacture[50] (Fig. 8), faience is largely absent suggesting as in contemporary Egypt, the decline and eventual disappearance of the technique, due in part to the availability of glass beads.[51]

Acknowledgements

The author would like to thank Ashley Cooke, Julian Henderson, Renee Stein, Tina Salguero, Asha Bhandarkar, Darrah Johnson-McDaniel, Briel Power, Sang Lee, Hayden Evans, Chris Parsons, Hannah Walters, Chris Fleisher, Madeline Payne, Eric Formo, John Shields, Jonathan Elias, Tom Hardwick and Mike Rathke for their help in preparing this article.

48 Grzymski 2014, 165–168.

49 Cf. Maillot 2014, 783–796.

50 Woolley and Randall-MacIver 1910, 74–77.

51 Then-Obłuska and Dussubieux 2021.

Bibliography

Brovarski, E., Doll, S.K. and Freed, R.E. (eds.)
1982 *Egypt's Golden Age: The Art of Living in the New Kingdom 1558–1085 B. C.*, Boston.

Bonnet, C.
2000 *Edifices et rites funéraires á Kerma. Kerma, royaume de Nubie*, Mission archéologique de l'Université de Geneve au Soudan, Geneva.

Bonnet, C. (ed).
1990 *Kerma, royaume de Nubie*, Mission archéologique de l'Université de Geneve au Soudan, Geneva.

Davies, W.V.
2003 Kush in Egypt. A new historical inscription, *Sudan & Nubia* 7, 52–54.

D'Itria, E.
2018 Forgotten treasures: a journey (re)discovering the amulets of the Kerma Culture in the storerooms of the Museum of Fine Arts of Boston and in the Sudan National Museum of Khartoum, in: S.M. Ilaria, E. D'Itria, M. Diletta Pubblico, F.M. Rega and A. Salsano (eds.), *Current Research in Egyptology 2017 Proceedings of the Eighteenth Annual Symposium University of Naples, "L'Orientale" 3–6 May 2017*, Oxford, 54–70.

Dunham, D.
1950 *Royal Cemeteries of Kush I: El Kurru*, Cambridge, MA.
1951 Royal shawabti figures from Napata, *Bulletin of the Museum of Fine Arts, Boston* 49, no. 267, 40–48.
1967 *Second Cataract Forts II: Uronarti, Shalfak, Mirgissa*, Boston.

Dunham D. and Janssen, J.
1960 *Second Cataract Forts I: Semna and Kumma*, Boston.

Duma, G.
1997 Fayencen aus dem Sudan, *Der antike Sudan. Mitteilungen der Sudanarchäologischen Gesellschaft zu Berlin e.V.* 6, 13–23.

Friedman, F.D., Borromeo, G. and Leveque, M. (eds.)
1998 *Gifts of the Nile: Ancient Egyptian Faience* [Exhibition Catalogue], London; New York.

Firth, C.M.,
1927 *Archaeological Survey of Nubia: report for 1910-1911*, Cairo.

Fulcher, K., Siddall, R., Emmett, T.F. and Spencer, N.
2021 Multi-scale characterization of unusual green and blue pigments from the Pharaonic town of Amara West, Nubia, *Heritage* 4 (3), 2563–2579, https://doi.org/10.3390/heritage4030145.

Grzymski, K.
2014 The decorated faience puteals from Meroe, in: A. Lohwasser and P. Wolf (eds.), *Ein Forscherleben zwischen den Welten. Zum 80. Geburtstag von Steffen Wenig*, Berlin, 165–168.

Hardwick, T. and Lacovara, P.
2020/2021 A sphinx from Kerma in the Karnak Cachette, *Mitteilungen des Deutschen Archäologischen Instituts, Abteilung Kairo* 76/77, 129–140.

Hatcher, H., Henderson, J., Kaczmarczyk, A., Lacovara, P. and Vandiver, P.
2023 Kerma faience, https://www.academia.edu/98911701/Kerma_Analysis_article_March_2023_revision <last accessed 20 October 2023>.

Hayes, W.C.
1990 *The Scepter of Egypt: A Background for the Study of the Egyptian Antiquities. From the Earliest Times to the End of the Middle Kingdom*, Vol. 1, New York [first edition in 1953].

Haynes, J.L. and Leprohon, R.J.
1987 Napatan shawabtis in the Royal Ontario Museum, *Journal of the Society for the Study of Egyptian Antiquities* 17, 18–32.

Howley, K.
2018 Power relations and the adoption of foreign material culture: a different perspective from first-millennium BCE Nubia, *Journal of Ancient Egyptian Interconnections* 17, 18–36.

Kaczmarczyk, A. and Hedges, R.E.M.
1983 *Ancient Egyptian Faience: An Analytical Survey of Egyptian Faience from Predynastic to Roman Times*, Warminster.

Kingery, W.D. and Vandiver, P.
1986 *Ceramic Masterpieces: Art, Structure, Technology*, New York; London.

Knoblauch, C.
2011 Not all that glitters: a case study of regional aspects of Egyptian Middle Kingdom pottery production in Lower Nubia and the Second Cataract, *Cahiers de la céramique égyptienne* 9, 167–183.

Lacovara, P.
1991 The stone vase deposit at Kerma, in: W.V. Davies (ed.), *Egypt and Africa: Nubia from Prehistory to Islam*, London, 118–128.
1992 A new date for an old hippopotamus, *Journal of the Museum of Fine Arts, Boston* 4, 17–26.
2018 Stone Shabtis of Senkamenisken and Sudanese Society, *Nile Scribes,* https://nilescribes.org/2018/04/04/stone-shabtis-senkamenisken/.
2021 The faience industry at Kerma, *Journal of Ancient Egyptian Interconnections* 29, 32–38.

Lacovara, P. and Markowitz, Y.
2019 *Nubian Gold: Ancient Jewellery from Sudan and Egypt*, Cairo.

Maillot, M.
2014 The palace of Muweis in the Shendi Reach: A comparative approach, in: J.R. Anderson and D.A. Welsby (eds.), *The Fourth Cataract and Beyond. Proceedings of the 12th International Conference for Nubian Studies*, British Museum Publications on Egypt and Sudan 1, Leuven, 783–796.

MINIACI, G.
2019 The material entanglement in the 'Egyptian Cemetery' in Kerma (Sudan, 1750–1500 BC): Appropriation, incorporation, tinkering, and hybridisation, *Egitto e Vicino Oriente* XLII, 13–32.

MINOR, E.
2023 Faience tiles from Deir el-Ballas and Kerma: new evidence of Egyptian-Nubian relations at the foundation of the New Kingdom, in: D. KISER-GO and C.A. REDMOUNT (eds.), *Weseretkau "Mighty of Kas": Papers in Memory of Cathleen A. Keller*, Columbus, GA, 103–116.

NORDSTRÖM, H.A.
1972 *Neolithic and A-Group Sites*, Scandinavian Joint Expedition to Sudanese Nubia 3:1, Uppsala.

PIERRAT-BONNEFOIS, G.
2016/2017 Faïences de la première moitié du deuxième millénaire: la discontinuité en questions, Sésostris III et la fin du Moyen Empire, *Cahiers de Recherches de l'Institut de Papyrologie et d'Égyptologie de Lille* 31, 103–118.

VAN PELT, W.P.
2013 Revising Egypto-Nubian relations in New Kingdom Lower Nubia: From Egyptianization to cultural entanglement, *Cambridge Archaeological Journal* 23.3, 523–550.

PRISSE D'AVENNES, É.
2014 *Egyptian Art: The Complete Plates from Monuments égyptiens et Histoire de l'art égyptien*, Köln.

RANDALL-MACIVER, D. and WOOLLEY, C.L.
1911 *Buhen*, 2 vols., Eckley B. Coxe Junior Expedition to Sudanese Nubia 7–8, Philadelphia.

REISNER, G.A.
1923a *Excavations at Kerma I-III*, Harvard African Studies 5, Peabody Museum of Harvard University, Cambridge, Mass.
1923b *Excavations at Kerma V - VI*, Harvard African Studies 6, Peabody Museum of Harvard University, Cambridge, Mass.

RONDOT, V. (ed.)
2022 *Pharaon des Deux Terres. L'épopée africaine des rois de Napata: Catalogue d'exposition*, Paris.

SACKHO-AUTISSIER, A.
2016 Earthenware from the Meroitic period preserved in the Louvre Museum. Technology and production: the beginnings of research, *Dotawo* 3, 29–39.

SALAH, M. and SOUROUZIAN, H.
1987 *Official Catalogue: The Egyptian Museum Cairo*, Mainz.

SALGUERO, T., BHANDARKAR, A., JOHNSON-MCDANIEL, D., POWER, D., LEE, S., EVANS, H. and PARSONS, C. assisted by WALTERS, H., FLEISHER, C., PAYNE, M., FORMO, E. and SHIELDS, J.
2016 *Egyptian Faience: Research Update*, Department of Chemistry, University of Georgia, Unpublished Study, Atlanta.

SÄVE-SÖDERBERGH, T. and TROY, L.
1991 *New Kingdom Pharaonic Sites: The Finds and the Sites*, The Scandinavian Joint Expedition to Sudanese Nubia 5:2, Uppsala.

STEINDORFF, G.
1937 *Aniba: zweiter Band*, Mission archéologique de Nubie, 1929-1934, Glückstadt.

THEN-OBŁUSKA, J.
2022 *Beads from Excavations at Qustul, Adindan, Serra East, Dorginarti, Ballana, and Kalabsha, Part I: A-Group, post-A-Group, C-Group, N-Type, P-Type, Pan Grave, Kerma, Middle Kingdom, and New Kingdom*, The University of Chicago Oriental Institute Nubian Expedition 11, Chicago.

THEN-OBŁUSKA, J. and DUSSUBIEUX, L.
2021 Beads for the nomads of late antiquity: Chemical characterization of glass from the Blemmyan tumuli at Kalabsha, Nubia, of the mid-fourth century CE, *Archaeometry* 63.6, 1255–1271, https://doi.org/10.1111/arcm.12680.

TITE, M.S., MANTI, P. and SHORTLAND, A.J.
2007 A technological study of ancient faience from Egypt, *Journal of Archaeological Science* 34 (10), 1568–1583.

WOOLLEY, C.L. and RANDALL-MACIVER, D.
1910 *Karanog: the Romano-Nubian Cemetery*, 2 vols, Eckley B. Coxe Junior Expedition to Nubia 3–4, Philadelphia.

Part II

The gold industry of ancient Sudan

Introduction

Gold exploitation in the Middle Nile and the Eastern Desert

Julia Budka

"It is a rather general impression among Egyptologists that the sole motive for the southern advance of the Pharaohs and their steady absorption of Nubia was the desire to control the southern trade routes coming out of the Sudan and to hold the Nubian gold mines in the eastern desert, but that the land itself offered nothing which would attract conquest."[1]

Ancient Nubia is generally considered as the source of Egyptian wealth and perceived as the land of gold. As early as the Middle Kingdom, textual sources describe Egyptians making Nubians wash gold for them.[2] Tribute scenes from 18th Dynasty Egyptian contexts display submissive Nubians bringing gold and other materials to Egypt.[3] This evidence supported colonial interpretations (as exemplified in the quote by Breasted above), which have perpetuated[4] and still influence current narratives of Egyptian gold exploitation and a presumed passive role of Nubians, since they are thought to have been only acting on Egyptian orders. In Stuart Tyson Smith's words, "this classic model of core dominance and peripheral subordination downplays native agency."[5] It should, therefore, be considered a colonial stereotype built over millennia – based on ancient Egyptian textual sources dating from phases of Egyptian colonial control in Nubia – and influenced by modern colonialism in northeast Africa, to explain archaeological contexts in Nubia.

Such interpretations impact how we see the role of Nubians and their relationship with gold today. For instance, scholars took for granted that, prior to the New Kingdom colonial Period, gold mining and processing did not play a major role in Nubian society. Previous research focused mostly on Pharaonic sources,[6] despite exquisite gold objects manufactured in local styles found at Kerma, which themselves attest to local access to gold independent from Egypt.[7] Egyptocentric views of gold in the Middle Nile also consider gold jewellery found in C-Group graves in Lower Nubia to be the result of contacts with Egypt (e.g., military rewards).[8]

This part of the volume shows that recent fieldwork in Sudan is shedding new light on Nubia's gold production and processing. For example, excavations at Hosh el-Guruf (Chapter 3), in the Fourth Cataract region, yielded over 50 grindstones used to reduce gold ore, associated with a large amount of Kerma pottery.[9] Moreover, surveys in the Eastern Desert suggest that both the control of gold mines, and trade relationships with desert nomads played a major role in Nubian access to gold before Egyptian colonisation.[10] Recent excavations on Sai Island also revealed that the control of gold resources during the New Kingdom involved the participation of the local population (Chapter 4).[11] Evidence from other sites means that the continuity of gold mining/processing activities can be discussed in the longer term, from the Kerma Period, through the New Kingdom, to the Napatan Period.[12]

General research on mining

In 2010, Elizabeth Bloxam labelled ancient quarry and mining sites as "the 'forgotten' archaeological sites"[13] of Egyptian Archaeology. Although several projects have since focused on mining areas,[14] connected with the general increase in geoarchaeological research in Egypt and Sudan, this research is still relatively limited and underdeveloped. Mining expeditions have traditionally been investigated through relevant textual evidence.[15] Only in recent years have the scarce settlement remains associated with mining been considered as evidence to reconstruct the social contexts of mining activities. For example, Kate Liszka has convincingly argued that construction techniques used for dry-stone walls in the Wadi el-Hudi mining sites point to a Nubian agency within these predominately Egyptian mining settlements.[16]

1 Breasted 1906, 44.
2 E.g. the Middle Kingdom expedition inscription by Sahathor ("I forced the (Nubian) chiefs to wash gold"), see Quirke 2023, 15–16, note 11; see also Klemm, Klemm and Murr 2001, 649.
3 E.g. the famous so-called scene of tributes in the tomb of Huy, TT40, Davies and Gardiner 1926, pl. 27.
4 E.g., Adams 1970, 276; cf. Bestock 2020, 273.
5 Smith, S.T. 2003, 58.
6 Klemm and Klemm 2013, 619.
7 Minor 2012, 156; Bonnet and Honegger 2020, 220.
8 Hafsaas 2020, 171.
9 Emberling and Williams 2010, 22; Williams 2020, 188; Williams this volume.
10 Castiglioni, Castiglioni and Bonnet 2010; Castiglioni and Castiglioni 2020; Manzo 2020; Cooper 2021.
11 Budka 2021a.
12 Emberling and Williams 2010, 23. See also Lacovara and Markowitz 2019; Budka this volume (Chapter 4).
13 Bloxam 2010.
14 See, e.g., Storemyr et al. 2013; Liszka 2017; Bloxam 2015; Shaw 2021; Brand, Liszka and Kramer 2022.
15 See, e.g., Hikade 2001 and, most recently, Tallet 2023.
16 Liszka 2017.

Most of the settlement remains associated with mining and quarrying are of relatively small size and represent ephemeral camps comprising of dry-stone structures.[17] These sites, probably only seasonally or temporarily occupied, are rarely associated with abundant material culture and, as such, their exact date is likely to remain unclear.[18] Many questions remain on the realities of life in mining sites, whether this was for gold, copper or something else, and illustrate the need for a holistic approach towards mining, considering all available evidence.[19]

Bronze Age gold exploitation in the Middle Nile

Gold exploitation in the Early, Middle and Late Bronze Age is largely associated with Egyptian mining expeditions into the Eastern desert and the region of the Wadi Allaqi.[20] While scholars have stressed the presence of Nile Valley inhabitants at the sites, an, at least, limited cooperation with desert nomads has been recognised since the 1990s.[21] Within the Nile Valley, gold exploitation is mostly identified at sites dating to the New Kingdom, clustering in Upper Nubia between the Second and Third Cataracts.[22]

Little is known about the gold exploitation of the Kerma Nubians in the Middle Nile, especially in Lower Nubia and in the Batn el-Haggar – a peripheral region of the Kerma empire. Recently, Duweishat has been identified as a possible Middle Nubian gold exploitation area,[23] indicating that Kerman gold procurement in the region was overlooked by previous scholars (see Chapter 4). Evidence of gold exploitation in Duweishat going back to the time of the Old Kingdom, flourishing in later times, is nothing new,[24] but previous research has been unable to associate it definitively with Egyptians or indigenous Nubians. For the latter, the question arises as to whether these Nubian groups were Kerma Nubians, C-Group Nubians or a mixed population (see below).

Similar Middle Bronze Age activities, predating the New Kingdom have tentatively been identified in the Munich University Attab to Ferka Survey Project (MUAFS) concession between Attab and Ferka (see Chapter 4). The evidence from the northern part of the Middle Nile at Duweishat and in the MUAFS concession is supported by new findings in the area of the Fourth Cataract. At Hosh el-Guruf, there is evidence that Kerma gold procurement goes back to Middle Kerma times (see Chapter 3).[25]

To conclude, despite disparate findings, it is crucial to stress that even before the Egyptian conquest in the 18th Dynasty, Kerma people had significant knowledge of gold sources and were highly skilled in their craftsmanship. Regardless of that cultural heritage, Nubia was portrayed in Egyptian texts during the New Kingdom colonial Period as a sort of *terra nullius* to be occupied and explored.[26] At the same time, later Nubian goldwork has traditionally been seen by scholars as deriving from Egyptian models, despite the local character of Napatan and Meroitic gold objects.[27] Recent studies have acknowledged that jewellery-making techniques in use in Bronze Age Sudan are still largely unknown, making comparisons between Egyptian and Nubian productions almost impossible.[28] However, considering all available sources, including jewellery, as well as sites connected with goldworking, allows us to illustrate how crucial gold mining was on a local and indigenous level throughout Nubian history.

Bronze Age gold exploitation in the Eastern Desert

Recent surveys in the Nubian Eastern Desert, along the so-called Korosko Road, have provided evidence for water stations during the New Kingdom, but also possibly of an earlier presence at several sites.[29] Crucially, this earlier evidence does not seem to be associated with Egyptian expeditions. According to the Casteligoni brothers, Kerma Nubians were present at gold mining sites in the Eastern Desert from the Kerma Ancien phase.[30]

Apart from material culture, such as tools and ceramics, there are also some rock art and rock inscriptions along the Korosko Road which might refer to the Kerma administration of the Eastern Desert gold mines. One of the most important inscriptions is located at site KRP14 and contains finely executed hieroglyphs, including a large falcon and a lion, probably the name of a ruler of the kingdom of Kerma, Trh or Terereh.[31] Based on a close parallel to the name

17 Bloxam 2010.
18 See Klemm and Klemm 2013, passim; Klemm and Klemm 2018.
19 See, for example, the efforts by the Wadi el-Hudi Project, cf. Brand, Liszka and Kramer 2022.
20 See Auenmüller 2020 with references. Note, however, that Smith, H. S. 1994, 376 proposed an early control of the mines of Wadi Allaqi by the Nubian A-Group.
21 Klemm and Klemm 1994; Klemm and Klemm 2013; Auenmüller 2020, 42.
22 See Auenmüller 2020, 42, fig. 2.
23 Edwards 2020, 406–407.
24 Klemm and Klemm 2013, 557–564.
25 Emberling und Williams 2010; Harrell 2010; Meyer 2010.
26 Cf. Gosden 2004, 26.
27 Wenig 1978, 43; Priese 1992; Kendall 1999, 14; Török 2009, 311–312; Lacovara and Markowitz 2019, 118.
28 Guerra 2023, 476.
29 Davies and Welsby 2020.
30 Castiglioni and Castiglioni 2020; see also Budka 2021b.
31 Davies 2020, 196, fig. 15.10, pl. 15.30.

of a Kerma ruler from the execration texts of the Middle Kingdom, Vivian Davies has suggested the inscription dates to this period, corresponding to the Kerma Moyen phase.[32] Although this is certainly a possibility, I personally find Bruce Williams's suggestion of a Kerma Classique date – when the Kerma ruler was increasingly presenting himself as Egyptian to the outside world and had political influence as far away as Egypt – more likely.[33] Just before the turning point towards the end of the Kerma kingdom and the start of Egyptian colonisation, we should, therefore, picture a strong gold industry in Nubia, both along the Nile Valley and in the desert regions.

Cooperation in gold exploitation

The Kerma rulers built strong networks not only with the Hyksos kings in the north of Egypt (see Chapter 4), but also alliances towards the south and west.[34] For their goldworking business, we know that they involved former Egyptian occupants of the Lower Nubian fortresses, such as Buhen.[35] Furthermore, they must have made alliances with desert groups like the Pan Grave-people, especially for the exploitation of desert mines. I agree with Julien Cooper that desert peoples are the unknown workers behind the Egyptian gold enterprise.[36] It seems likely, that the same can be said for Kerma times and the later Napatan Period.

In conclusion, the concept of an "archaeology of interaction"[37] which appears in many respects to be crucial for understanding contact spaces in the Middle Nile should be regarded as essential to reconstruct mining activities. Communities living along the Nile were in close contact with nomads and semi-nomads and the goldworking business was clearly cooperative and involved diverse groups of people.[38]

Therefore, we can picture well-established co-optive and co-operative practices between Egyptians and Nubians in the gold mining industry over time.[39] The question arises as to whether a distinction between Egyptian and Nubian goldworking is possible at all. Research and resources might be better invested in trying to unveil the social patterns and community practices of all groups involved in the procurement of gold – focusing on aspects such as kinship, gender and lifestyle (e.g., nomadic, semi-nomadic or sedentary) – rather than on the imposing of artificial cultural groupings, so prevalent in modern archaeology.[40]

32 Davies 2020.
33 See Williams 2020, 185–186 (Tereréh being contemporaneous to Tumulus KX or KXVI).
34 See Bonnet 2021.
35 Cooper 2018.
36 Cooper 2021, 7.
37 Näser 2012; see also Knappett 2011.
38 Cf. Anfinset 2016.
39 Similar concepts are suggested for other technologies like faience production, see Minor 2023. For complex and overlapping trade routes and technological exchange between Egypt and Nubia see also the case study of copper production at Kerma: Rademakers et al. 2022.
40 For attempts to ask similar questions about stone quarry workers see Bloxam 2015; Bloxam 2020.

Bibliography

Adams, W.Y.
1970 A re-appraisal of Nubian culture history, *Orientalia* 39, 269–277.

Anfinset, N.
2016 *Metal, Nomads and Culture Contact: the Middle East and North Africa*, London; New York.

Auenmüller, J.
2020 Nubisches Gold und ägyptische Präsenz: Pharaonische Goldgewinnung in der Nubischen Wüste, in: M. Kasper, R. Rollinger, A. Rudigier and K. Ruffing (eds.), *Wirtschaften in den Bergen. Von Bergleuten, Hirten, Bauern, Künstlern, Händlern und Unternehmern*, Wien, 37–54.

Bestock, L.
2020 Egyptian fortresses and the colonization of Lower Nubia in the Middle Kingdom, in: G. Emberling and B.B. Williams (eds.), *The Oxford Handbook of Ancient Nubia*, Oxford, 271–288.

Bloxam, E.
2010 Quarrying and mining (stone), *UCLA Encyclopedia of Egyptology*, 1(1). Retrieved from https://escholarship.org/uc/item/9bb918sd.
2015 "A place full of whispers": socializing the quarry landscape of the Wadi Hammamat, *Cambridge Archaeological Journal* 25 (4), 789–814.
2020 Who were the quarry workers? Investigating the origins of stone crafting in Egypt's Eastern Desert, in: A.R. Warfe, J.C.R. Gill, C.R. Hamilton, A.J. Pettman and D.A. Stewart (eds.), *Dust, Demons and Pots: Studies in Honour of Colin A. Hope*, Leuven; Paris; Bristol, CT, 57–75.

Bonnet, C.
2021 The Kingdom of Kerma between Egypt and central Africa, in: A. Obłuski, H. Paner and M. Masojć (eds.), *Bayuda and Its Neighbours*, Nubia: Studies in the Archaeology and History of Northeast Africa 1, Turnhout, 59–70.

Bonnet, C. and Honegger, M.
2020 The eastern cemetery of Kerma, in: G. Emberling and B.B. Williams (eds.), *The Oxford Handbook of Ancient Nubia*, Oxford, 213–226.

Brand, M., Liszka, K. and Kramer, B.
2022 Living and working at the early Middle Kingdom amethyst mining settlement Site 5, Wadi el-Hudi, in: J. Sigl (ed.), *Daily Life in Ancient Egyptian Settlements: Conference Aswan 2019*, Sonderschriften des Deutschen Archäologischen Instituts, Abteilung Kairo 47, Wiesbaden, 41–55.

Breasted, J.H.
1906 *The Temples of Lower Nubia*, Chicago.

Budka, J.
2021a *Tomb 26 on Sai Island: A New Kingdom Elite Tomb and its Relevance for Sai and Beyond*, Leiden.
2021b Review: Davies, W. Vivian and Derek A. Welsby (eds) 2020. Travelling the Korosko Road: archaeological exploration in Sudan's Eastern Desert. Sudan Archaeological Research Society Publication 24. Oxford: Archaeopress, *Beiträge zur Sudanforschung* 13, 177–185.

Castiglioni, A. and Castiglioni, A.
2020 The gold mines of Kerma and exploration of the south-eastern Nubian Desert, in: W.V. Davies and D. Welsby (eds.), *Travelling the Korosko Road: Archaeological Exploration in Sudan's Eastern Desert*, Sudan Archaeological Research Society Publication 24, Oxford, 11–21.

Castiglioni, A., Castiglioni, A. and Bonnet, C.
2010 The gold mines of the Kingdom of Kerma, in: W. Godlewski and A. Łajtar (eds.), *Between the Cataracts: Proceedings of the 11th Conference for Nubian Studies, Warsaw University 27 August – 2 September 2006*, Warsaw, 263–270.

Cooper, J.
2018 Kushites expressing 'Egyptian' kingship: Nubian dynasties in hieroglyphic texts and a phantom Kushite king, *Ägypten & Levante* 28, 143–168.
2021 Between the Nile and the Red Sea: Medjay desert polities in the third to first millennium BCE, *Old World: Journal of Ancient Africa and Eurasia*, 1–22.

Davies, N. de Garis and Gardiner, A.H.
1926 *The Tomb of Huy, Viceroy of Nubia in the Reign of Tutankhamun (no. 40)*, London.

Davies, W.V.
2020 Securing the gold of Wawat: Pharaonic inscriptions in the Sudanese-Nubian Eastern Desert, in: W.V. Davies and D.A. Welsby (eds.), *Travelling the Korosko Road: Archaeological Exploration in Sudan's Eastern Desert*, Sudan Archaeological Research Society Publication 24, Oxford, 185–220.

Davies, W.V. and Welsby, D.A. (eds)
2020 *Travelling the Korosko Road: Archaeological Exploration in Sudan's Eastern Desert*, Sudan Archaeological Research Society Publication 24, Oxford.

Edwards, D.N. (ed.).
2020 *The Archaeological Survey of Sudanese Nubia, 1963–69. The Pharaonic Sites*, Oxford.

Emberling, G. and Williams, B.
2010 The Kingdom of Kush in the 4th Cataract: Archaeological salvage of the Oriental Institute Nubian Expedition 2007 season, Part 1: Preliminary report on the sites of Hosh el-Guruf and El-Widay, *Gdańsk Archaeological Museum African Reports* 7, 17–38.

Gosden, C.
2004 *Archaeology and Colonialism: Cultural Contact from 5000 BC to the Present*, Oxford.

Guerra, M.F.
2023 Towards a conclusion: Qurna in context, in: M.F. Guerra, M. Martinón-Torres and S. Quirke (eds.), *Ancient Egyptian Gold: Archaeology and Science in Jewellery (3500–1000 BC)*, Cambridge, 449–480.

HAFSAAS, H.
2020 The C-Group people in Lower Nubia: Cattle pastoralists on the frontier between Egypt and Kush, in: G. EMBERLING and B.B. WILLIAMS (eds.), *The Oxford Handbook of Ancient Nubia*, Oxford, 157–177.

HARRELL, J.A.
2010 Archaeological geology of Hosh el-Guruf, Fourth Nile Cataract, Sudan, *Gdańsk Archaeological Museum African Reports* 7, 71–83.

HIKADE, T.
2001 *Das Expeditionswesen im ägyptischen Neuen Reich: ein Beitrag zu Rohstoffversorgung und Außenhandel*, Studien zur Archäologie und Geschichte Altägyptens 21, Heidelberg.

KENDALL, T.
1999 The origin of the Napatan State: El Kurru and the evidence for the royal ancestors, in S. WENIG (ed.) *Akten der 7. Internationalen Tagung für meroitistische Forschungen vom 14. bis 19. September 1992 in Gosen/bei Berlin*, Meroitica, Schriften zur altsudanesischen Geschichte und Archäologie 15, Wiesbaden, 3–117.

KLEMM, R. and KLEMM, D.
1994 Chronologischer Abriss der antiken Goldgewinnung in der Ostwüste Ägyptens, *Mitteilungen des Deutschen Archäologischen Instituts, Abteilung Kairo* 50, 189–222.

KLEMM, D. and KLEMM, R.
2018 Ancient gold mining settlements in the Eastern Desert of Egypt and Nubia, in: J. BUDKA and J. AUENMÜLLER (eds.), *From Microcosm to Macrocosm: Individual Households and Cities in Ancient Egypt and Nubia*, Leiden, 59–66.

KLEMM, D., KLEMM, R. and MURR, A.
2001 Gold of the Pharaohs – 6000 years of gold mining in Egypt and Nubia, *Journal of African Earth Sciences* 33, 643–659.

KLEMM, R. and KLEMM, D.
2013 *Gold and Gold Mining in Ancient Egypt and Nubia*, New York.

KNAPPETT, C.
2011 *An Archaeology of Interaction: Network Perspectives on Material Culture and Society*, Oxford.

LACOVARA, P. and MARKOWITZ, Y.
2019 *Nubian Gold: Ancient Jewellery from Sudan and Egypt*, Cairo.

LISZKA, K.
2017 Egyptian or Nubian? Dry-stone architecture at Wadi el-Hudi, Wadi es-Sebua, and the Eastern Desert, *Journal of Egyptian Archaeology* 103/1, 35–51.

MANZO, A.
2020 The Nubian and Pharaonic ceramic materials, in: W.V. DAVIES and D.A. WELSBY (eds.), *Travelling the Korosko Road: Archaeological Exploration in Sudan's Eastern Desert*, Sudan Archaeological Research Society Publication 24, Oxford, 68–83.

MEYER, C.
2010 The Kingdom of Kush in the 4th Cataract: Archaeological salvage of the Oriental Institute Nubian Expedition 2007 season, Part II: Grinding stones and gold mining at Hosh el Guruf, Sudan, *Gdańsk Archaeological Museum African Reports* 7, 39–52.

MINOR, E.
2012 *The Use of Egyptian and Egyptianizing Material Culture in Nubian Burials of the Classic Kerma Period*, PhD Thesis, University of California, Berkeley.
2023 Faience tiles from Deir el-Ballas and Kerma: new evidence of Egyptian-Nubian relations at the foundation of the New Kingdom, in: D. KISER-GO and C.A. REDMOUNT (eds.), *Weseretkau "Mighty of Kas": Papers in Memory of Cathleen A. Keller*, Columbus, GA, 103–116.

NÄSER, C.
2012 Nomads at the Nile: towards an archaeology of interaction, in: H. BARNARD and K. DUISTERMAAT (eds.), *The History of the Peoples of the Eastern Desert*, Los Angeles, 80–89.

PRIESE, K.-H.
1992 *Das Gold von Meroe*, Mainz.

QUIRKE, S.
2023 Centres of goldworking in ancient Egypt: Egyptological questions and sources, in: M. F. GUERRA, M. MARTINÓN-TORRES and S. QUIRKE (eds.), *Ancient Egyptian Gold: Archaeology and Science in Jewellery (3500–1000 BC)*, Cambridge, 27–74.

RADEMAKERS, F.W., VERLY, G., DEGRYSE, P., VANHAECKE, F., MARCHI, S. and BONNET, C.
2022 Copper at ancient Kerma: a diachronic investigation of alloys and raw materials, *Advances in Archaeomaterials* 3 (1), 1–18.

SHAW, I.
2021 Procurement and liminality: Egyptian mining sites as studies in control and frontier expansion, in: N. BUCHEZ and Y. TRISTANT (eds.), *Égypte antérieure: mélanges de préhistoire et d›archéologie offerts à Béatrix Midant-Reynes par ses étudiants, collègues et amis*, Leuven; Paris; Bristol, CT, 591–605.

SMITH, H.S.
1994 The princes of Seyala in Lower Nubia in the predynastic and protodynastic periods, in: C. BERGER, G. CLERC and N. GRIMAL (eds.), *Hommages à Jean Leclant, Vol. II*, Bibliothèque d'Étude 106.2, Cairo, 361–376.

SMITH, S.T.
2003 *Wretched Kush: Ethnic Identities and Boundaries in Egypt's Nubian Empire*, London.

STOREMYR, P., BLOXAM, E., HELDAL, T. and KELANY, A.
2013 The Aswan west bank ancient quarry landscape: stone procurement, hunting, desert travel and rock-

art from the palaeolithic to the Roman period, in: D. Raue, S.J. Seidlmayer and P. Speiser (eds.), *The First Cataract of the Nile: One Region - Diverse Perspectives*, Sonderschriften des Deutschen Archäologischen Instituts, Abteilung Kairo 36, Berlin; Boston, 223–240.

Tallet, P.
2023 From stelae to rock inscriptions: a wide range of commemorative devices for mining expeditions to South Sinai in the Middle Kingdom, in: C. Ragazzoli, K. Hassan and C. Salvador (eds.), *Graffiti and Rock Inscriptions from Ancient Egypt: A Companion to Secondary Epigraphy*, Cairo, 119–135.

Török, L.
2009 *Between Two Worlds. The Frontier Region between Ancient Nubia and Egypt 3700 BC–500 AD*, Probleme der Ägyptologie 29, Leiden, Boston.

Wenig, S.
1978 *Africa in Antiquity. The Arts of Ancient Nubia and the Sudan II. The Catalogue*, New York.

Williams, B.
2020 Kush in the wider world during the Kerma period, in: G. Emberling and B.B. Williams (eds.), *The Oxford Handbook of Ancient Nubia*, Oxford, 179–200.

Chapter 3

Hosh el-Geruf, a gold-processing centre in the Fourth Cataract of the Nile

Bruce Williams[1]

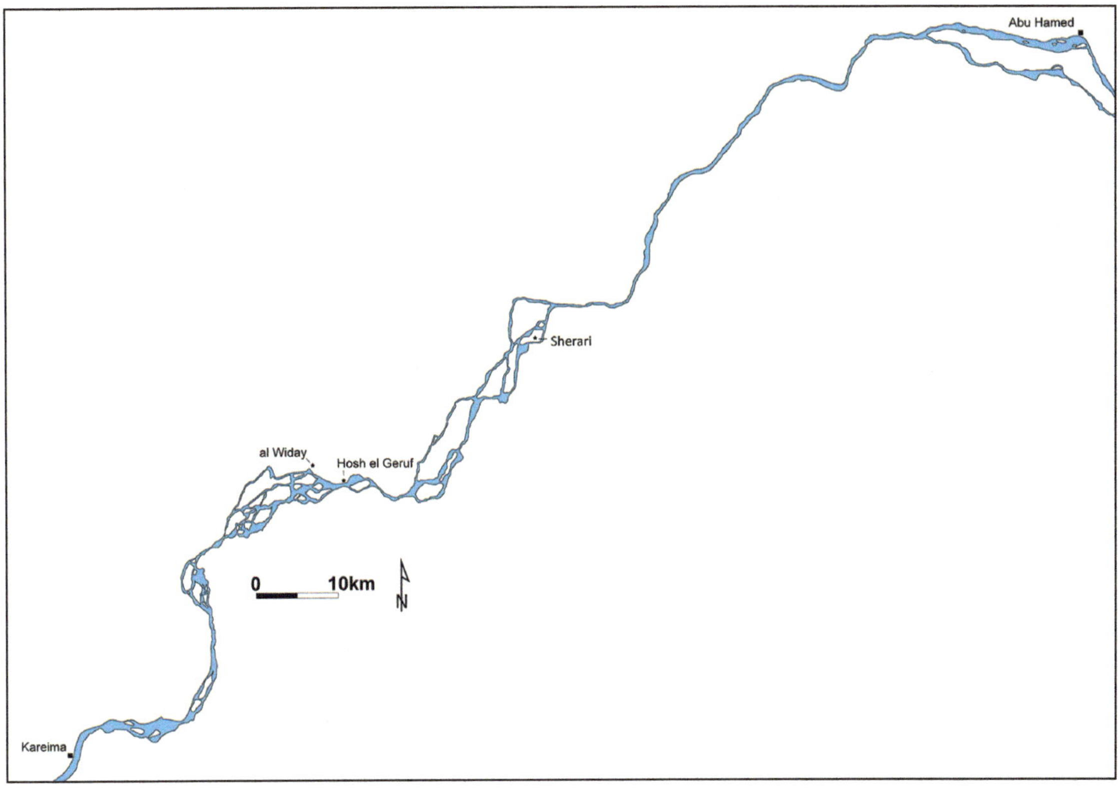

Fig. 1 Sketch map of the Fourth Cataract Region.

Abstract

Hosh el-Geruf, a site in the Fourth Cataract was used to process gold from ores recovered elsewhere in the region. While some separation of mining and reduction is well known, the distances here are unusual and they point to the existence of regional organisation in the early second millennium BC in an area that otherwise does not show signs of social complexity. This indicates that assumptions about such complexity in early Nubia need to be re-examined.

Keywords:

Fourth Cataract, gold, grindstone, industry, mining, organisation

The site of Hosh el-Geruf (alternately Hosh el-Guruf) is a relatively open area of sand, small boulders, and rock fragments nestled in a great cluster of boulder-topped outcrops of granitoid gneiss some 26 km upstream of Kareima in the Fourth Cataract.[2] The boundary between Northern and Nile States in Sudan runs through the cluster just east of the site proper, also marking the boundary between the more recent homes of the Manasir and Shaiqiyya tribes.[3]

By now the location and general topography of the Fourth Cataract of the Nile are well known (Fig. 1). The region extends from a short distance above Nuri almost to the northern tip of the Great Bend above Shemkhiya and Ginefab at Mograt Island and Abu

1 Research Associate, Polish Center of Mediterranean Archaeology, Warsaw University; Associate, the Oriental Institute of the University of Chicago; wecurbl@gmail.com.

2 For a descriptive geology, see Harrell 2010, 71–76. Many archaeological materials from the cataract remain unpublished. For a major presentation of operations on the left bank, see Welsby 2023.

3 Since archaeologists were prohibited from working in Dar al-Manasir, the Oriental Institute operations were confined to the Northern State side of the line.

Fig. 2 a: Satellite image of the Oriental Institute Nubian Expedition areas of operation 2007 (after Emberling and Williams 2010, fig. 1). b: Composite view of Hosh el-Geruf site, from the southwest. c: Composite view of Hosh el-Geruf site from the northeast (after Emberling and Williams 2010, fig. 3).

Hamed. The rocky islands that break the river into various streams – the cataract proper – extend from the Merowe/Hamdab (also known as Hamadab) Dam to above Shiri Island (northwest of Sherari on Fig. 1), for about half that distance.[4] While it is a very extended cataract region, during the high Nile season, it is entirely navigable, although the northeast-southwest direction of the river was a major impediment to navigation because the directions of the wind and the current are roughly the same. Hosh el-Geruf was located approximately halfway between the Merowe/Hamadab Dam and Shirri Island (Figs. 2–3).

The expedition researched the site in two phases (Fig. 4), first by establishing collection sites in rough

4 Note that the locality at the western end of Mograt Island is called Shellal (waterfall or cataract).

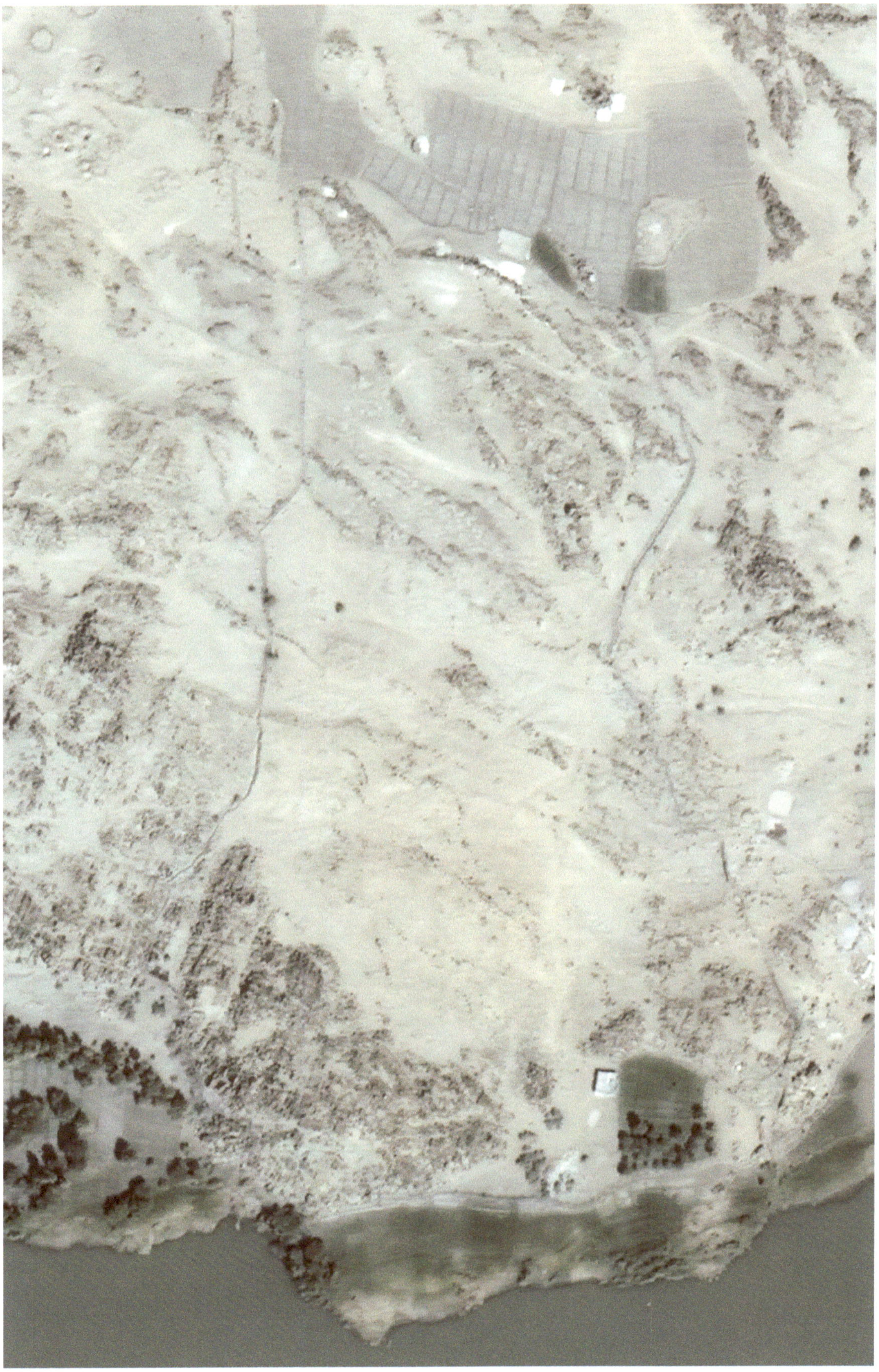

Fig. 3 Satellite view of Hosh el-Geruf site (north is up).

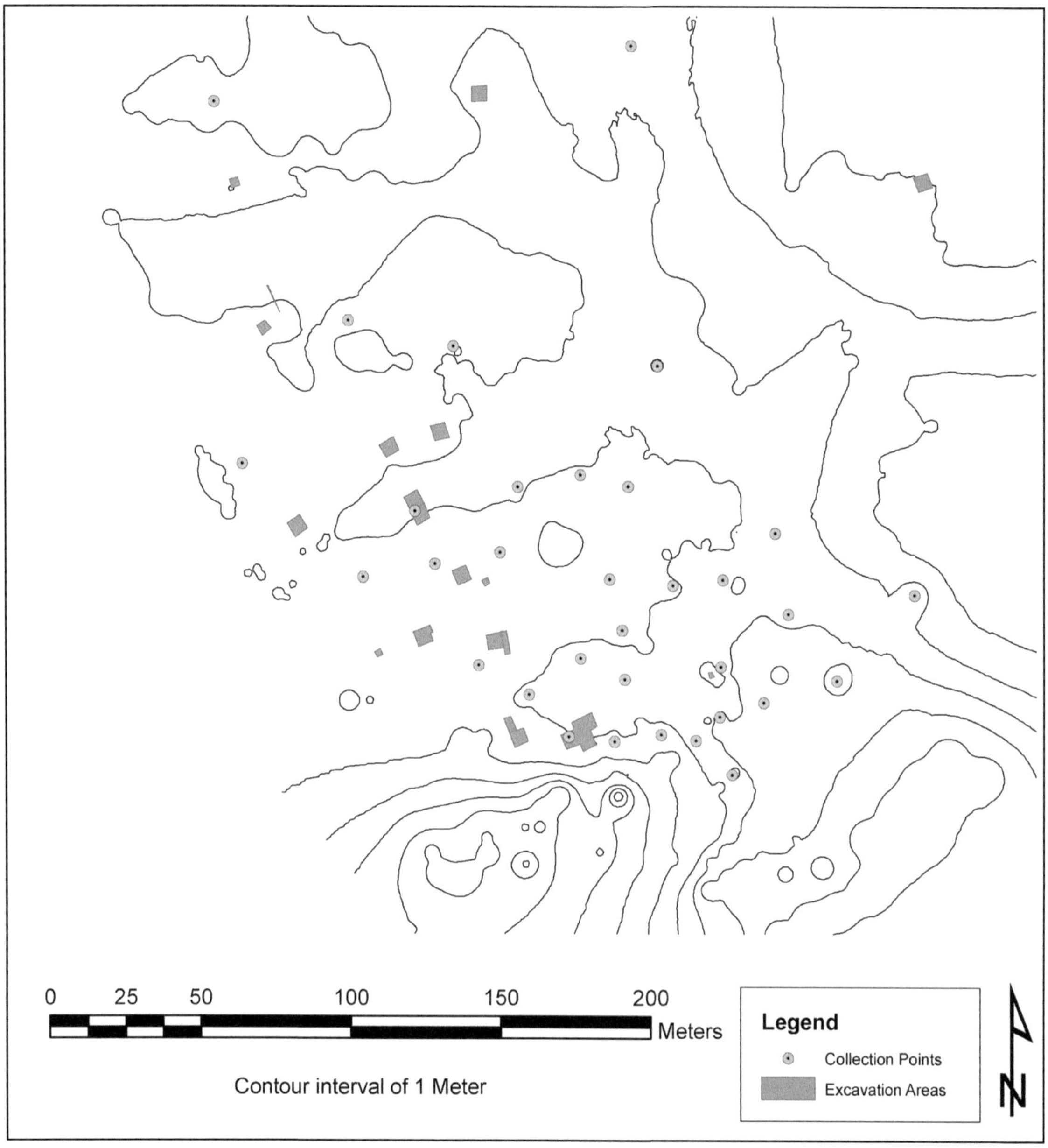

Fig. 4 Hosh el-Geruf, excavation units (rectangles) and collection units (circles).

circles about 5 meters around a stake, and second with excavation units, mostly based on 5 by 5 meter squares with some extensions.

From limited excavated areas and some surface exposure, the site appears as an outcrop of granitic gneiss that bulges upward toward the west, north, and east, forming ridges that decayed into piles of boulders with bedrock (Fig. 5a) sometimes visible at the base. These in turn decayed (Fig. 5b) and fragmented into smaller rocks, pebbles, and crumbs that spilled down the slopes. Undulations in the bedrock, sometimes visible between these higher areas also created decay products, smaller, angular fragments and crumbs, all on the surface. The entire area was subject to the deposit of windblown sand, resulting in deposits of pebbles and sand among the eminences of boulders and areas of stone cover (for general appearance see Figs. 2b–c).[5]

The site at Hosh el-Geruf appears as a collection of large grindstones (Figs. 6–7) surrounded by a dense scatter of hand grinders, globular pounding stones, angular rocks, sherds, and quartz fragments, mostly shattered. A unique combination for its scale in the Fourth Cataract region, probably the Nile Valley, the site has been severely disrupted, although the nature of disturbance does not indicate that mining was done locally.

5 Generally, Meyer and Harrell n.d.

Fig. 5 a: Hosh el-Geruf exposed granitod gneiss bedrock. b: Boulder with quartz vein, shattering (after Harrell 2010, fig. 10).

Fig. 6 a: Hosh el-Geruf site, surface with grindstones (after EMBERLING and WILLIAMS 2010, fig. 8). b: Worn grindstone. c: Deeply worn grindstone. d: Grindstone with two faces. e: Grindstone worn through (after EMBERLING and WILLIAMS 2010, fig. 11).

Fig. 7 a: Grindstone among boulders. b–d: Handstones, three views (after MEYER 2010, fig. 45).
e: Spherical quartz pounding stones (after MEYER 2010, fig. 44).

The numerous large grindstones, hammer-stones, grinders and a large concentration of shattered quartz are entirely consistent with Eastern Desert-type gold processing and almost no other kind of known ancient activity.[6]

This activity occurred most intensively in Kerma (Old Kush in this region, see General Introduction of this volume, Fig. 1) times, reviving in the Napatan Period, probably by about the time of Taharqa. A sealing of Queen Khensa, Piankhy's sister-wife, shows that the state was involved here.[7] We cannot exclude Neolithic activity, but the mining implements are consistent with the later periods.

Scattered mostly among the racks and stones were large grindstone bases (Figs. 6, 7a), globular pounding stones, often of quartz (Fig. 7c), and elongate rubbing stones (Fig. 7b). These were very numerous. Surface survey revealed that there were 62 of these grindstones on the surface of the site and mixed in with the surrounding boulders. Only one, badly decayed, but with a grindstone still on it, was in its original position and virtually all were broken (Figs. 6b–e). Some were re-used, and some had received such heavy wear on both sides that they had worn through (Fig. 6e). They were significantly larger than the domestic grindstones used to grind grain, some of which were also found here. A more systematic survey, reported on by Carol Meyer, recorded large numbers of globular stone hammers and elongate grinding stones on the surface of the site, some in concentrations that suggested that they were more or less in their original positions.[8]

The large, heavy stones were apparently used with the rounded pounding stones for crushing quartz gravel and coarse sand and grinding hand stones of hard rocks like the granitoid gneiss to pulverize it[9] prior to washing.[10] The very heavy, scooped grinding mills or stones[11] could not be moved by one person.[12] Once sunk in the ground they would make a solid surface for grinding quartz. One stone would last a very long time, though the rounded pounding stones would not. There were more shallow dished stones and elongate grindstones than heavy scooped stones.

The various excavated areas yielded no clear evidence of structures although some low-fired clay fragments showed signs of shaping that perhaps indicated some kind of oven. While it's possible that some combined mud and stone buildings were built, a style well known in the region, there was no definite evidence. Various buildings were found in places, such as Wadi Umm Rahau, agglomerations of circular foundations in mud (jalus), so there is preservation in the region. This remains an enigma for Hosh el-Geruf. Toward the north end of the site a few areas had burned debris at the surface and below. They could have been for cooking – some small grindstones for food preparation were found – but no evidence of organised fireplaces was present. Although they could have been used for heat-treating stones, again, no clear evidence was forthcoming.

6 See Klemm and Klemm 2013, 101–104 for hard rock examples, and 10–11 for wadi works, fig. 6.143 and workings near Soleb, 568 and fig. 6.223.

7 Shonkwiler 2010. For Napatan gold in the Fourth Cataract, see Welsby Sjöström 2010.

8 Meyer 2010.

9 These would be fragments that came from local veins in bedrock that disintegrated.

10 The grinding hand grinders of softer stone such as sandstone may have been used as upper flour milling stones.

11 See Edwards 2020, 227–234, workshop 16-O-12 at Attiri-Sorki, with Kerma beaker (fig. 515 R) and Old Kush-type bowls (fig. 517 MM, GG, and HH) as well as a jar (fig. 517 FF). The large grindstones are scooped (figs. 5.09–5.10) like grindstones called New Kingdom reused in Kushite times by the Klemms (Klemm and Klemm 2013, 9 and fig. 1.7, which shows a flat mill). See also Klemm and Klemm 2013, figs. 5.188, 5.246 (New Kingdom mill with multiple hollows), 5.273 (New Kingdom reused? Kushite), 5.281 (New Kingdom oval mill, deep depression as HelG), 6.32 (New Kingdom with "probably" secondary use wear from Kushite Period), 6.138 (same), 6.148 (New Kingdom flat mill), 6.149 (flat mill with globular pounders), 6.196 (New Kingdom with reuse), 6.198 (NK with reuse), 557–579 (Duweishat), 6.231 (spherical pounders, Old/MK), 6.234-235 (New Kingdom reused and Kushite), 6.247 (large New Kingdom with major later wear). Klemm and Klemm 2013, 10 consider quarrying alluvium in the wadis to be an innovation of the New Kingdom. (16-O-1 mining, modern discussed; 16-O-2 workshops at Duweishat-Jedagur, Edwards 2020, 243–250, with firmly New Kingdom pottery, figs. 551–553). The grindstones exhibit various amounts of scooping due to wear (figs. 538, 540–545, some very little, some very deep. See also Edwards 2020, 398–407. It is clear that the distinctions in the typology of grindstone bases are not discrete. See Edwards 2020, 405–407 for some chronological implications. The Hosh el-Guruf grindstone bases differ, but there is a difference not only in region, but raw material source. See Klemm and Klemm 2013, 6 and fig. 1.5 for a deeply scooped Middle Kingdom grindstone. See Edwards 2020, 101–102, 11-L-30, a hard rock mining site on the east bank about 300 meters from Askut. It is considerably downstream from Duweishat and the processing must have been in a different location. See Edwards 2020, 135–150, for a workshop 11-Q-62 at Sarras East with grindstones and a wheel base (?), but also quartz dust and fragments. The publication indicates a date possibly as early as Middle Kingdom (35), which is probably later. The handled vessel 36 could be New Kingdom or later, while V-shaped bowls 42–44 are Napatan types, as is 38, a jar with handles at the rim and neck. For discussion with illustrations of mining and processing, see Edwards 2020, 398–407.

12 Four were required to move stones for transfer to the Kareima Museum.

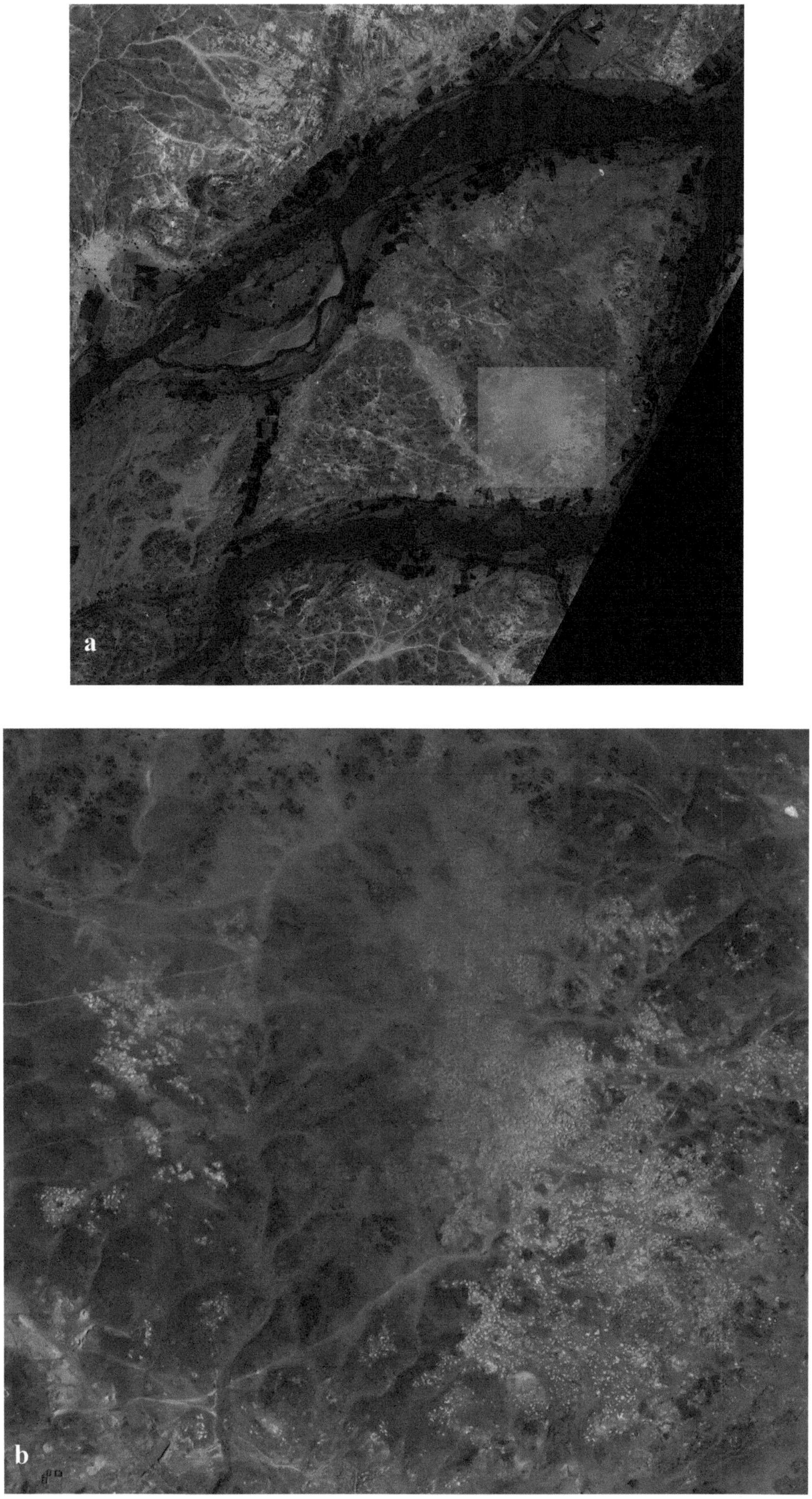

Fig. 8 a: Sherari Island, northeast area with mining area shown in light square.
b: Sherari Island mining area, wadi works (both Corona, north is up).

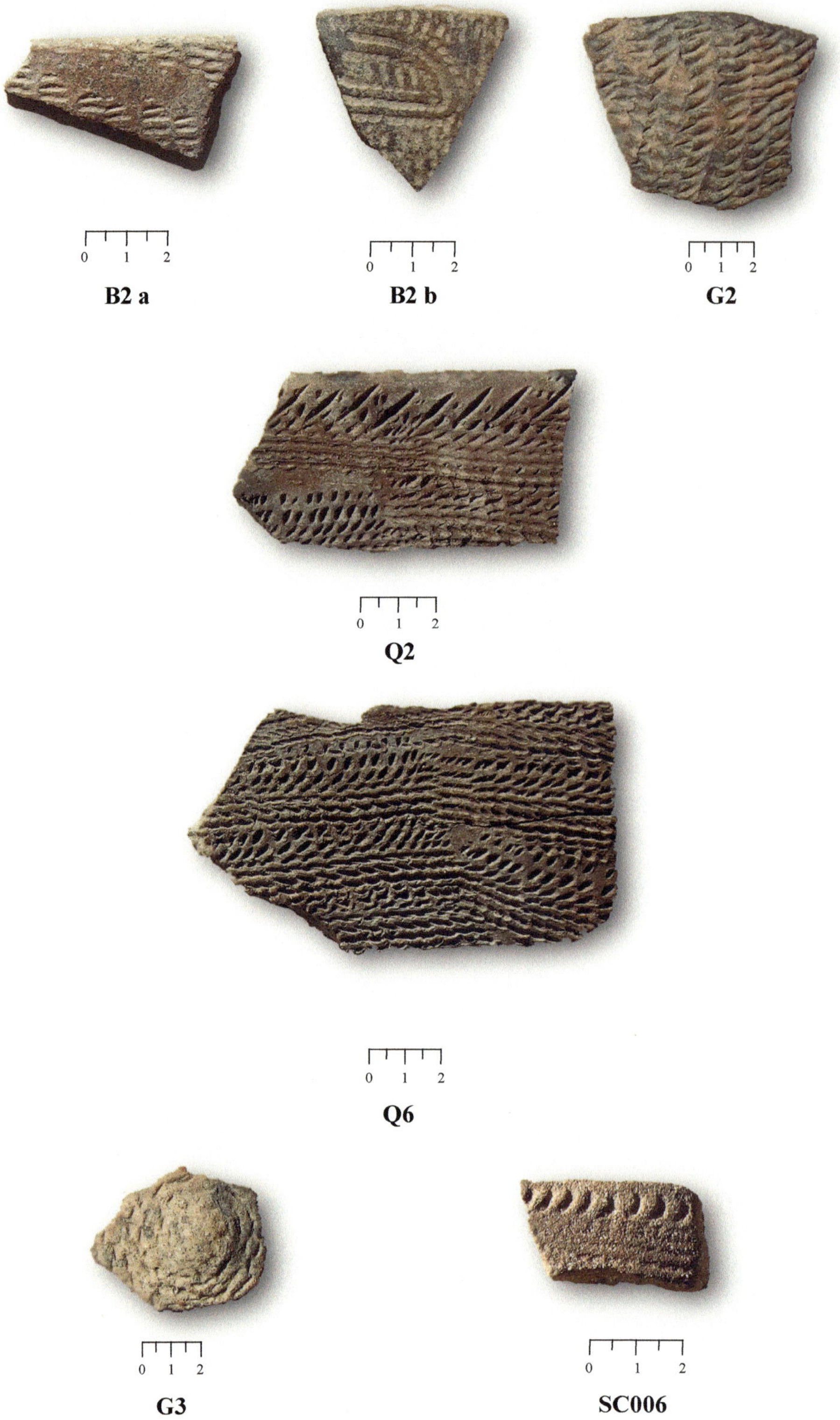

Fig. 9 Mesolithic-Neolithic pottery. Letter designates the excavation area, followed by the locus number. The lower-case letter or bag number (5/12 etc.) is the sherd lot. Surface collections are by SC plus the number.

Two kinds of mine were identified in the Eastern Desert, hard rock and wadi workings.[13] The hard rock mines followed veins, making narrow slot-like shafts in the bedrock that are quite easy to identify. No mines of this type were found at Hosh el-Geruf and none were identified in preliminary reports from the cataract region, although exploration in Dar al-Manasir was stopped after 2006. Wadi works were made to recover gold-bearing quartz and gold from veins that were exposed and disintegrated as the bedrock decayed. These consist of collections of relatively shallow pits, often of quite similar size. While there were some pits on an island near Hosh el-Geruf, they were in alluvium and probably also used to recover mud for making bricks or jalus in addition to gold-bearing material to be directly panned.[14] The one really large collection of pits that could be ancient was on Sherari Island, located between two Old Kush cemeteries (Fig. 8).[15]

I have not counted them, but there were at least several hundred in large clusters, and they were attributed to gold mining by the archaeologists.[16] While not as numerous as the pits in works near Soleb, the Sherari clusters are major.[17] The most likely reconstruction is that the gold-bearing sand and fragments were mined as at Sherari and transported by boat to Hosh el-Geruf where the ore could be reduced without obstructing the mining process. It is quite likely that there were other mining sites also that fed this processing centre. Nevertheless, it is clear that this was a regional, not local industry, and thus organised above a family level.[18] In the Fourth Cataract in modern times alluvial gold was also recovered from Nile deposits.[19]

The site of Hosh el-Geruf was quite mixed, and its pottery remains are not fully representative of the various periods and often not fully restorable. The following remarks are intended to give an impression of the various periods' diagnostic features, and not as a general presentation of the pottery from the various periods. Some types are mentioned that are not illustrated.

Hosh el-Geruf site had three major periods of use, Mesolithic-Neolithic, Old Kush (contemporary with Kerma), and early Napatan, roughly c. 750–600 BC. Currently, it is not believed that people in the Mesolithic and earlier Neolithic Periods extracted gold, so we exclude these phases from consideration of the industry.[20] Although there are a few potsherds of Christian date, there is no evidence of real activity at the site; most of the rest is Old Kush and a substantial part is Napatan.

Late Mesolithic and Neolithic pottery sherds appeared at Hosh el-Geruf in quantity. Many of these sherds were heavily worn along one or two sides, and some showed signs of deliberate shaping that would have formed them into efficient digging tools for the later gold-processing site. The strength of these sherds is much greater than those of the Kerma and Napatan Periods.

Almost all the Mesolithic-Neolithic vessels (Fig. 9) were made of a light brown to grey fabric with heavy, poorly sorted mineral temper, apparently sand.[21] It had been fired quite hard. As a rule, the vessels were decorated with impressions. Many were made by a serrated tool that was rocked against the surface to produce various decorative patterns, sometimes irregular, and they were sometimes linear. Others were made with various instruments, sometimes combined on the same vessel (Figs. 9d, g). In some cases, the gouges were deeply made (Fig. 9f), producing a strongly textured, ridged surface. Much of this decoration was also irregular, but there were also herringbone patterns (not illustrated).[22]

The Mesolithic-Neolithic pottery of this site seems to belong to a single period, and not the latest phase in the wider region.[23] It does exhibit some of the decorative diversity found in other Sudanese Mesolithic sites, notably Khartoum.

The pottery of Old Kush date (Fig. 10) parallels in part that found in the cemetery of al-Widay I some 4 kilometers to the west.[24] The pottery of this phase at Hosh el-Geruf included more simple utilitarian vessels than that at al-Widay I,[25] since the latter was a cemetery with vessels of more domestic types, mostly finer than the pottery expected at a settlement or industrial site. While the pottery has relationships with that found at Kerma itself, there are some important differences that need to be recognised. Because some

13 See above.

14 Harrell and Meyer n.d., fig. 6. Note that panning would not have been done at Hosh el-Geruf.

15 See Näser 2007, pl. 5.

16 Näser 2007.

17 Klemm and Klemm 2013, fig. 6.223. The area is huge, with what appears to be thousands of pits. Note that the ores excavated here would have also been sent elsewhere for reduction and gold recovery, very likely Soleb itself.

18 For modern family workings in wadis, see Klemm and Klemm 2013, 591–598, in the Bayuda.

19 Harrell 2010, 81–83. This was simply panned, a method not used in ancient times. Informants on Mis Island reported recovering gold from sand (wadi) deposits also and showed small gold ingots.

20 Klemm and Klemm 2013, 3–4, for example. Since gold objects are well developed by Naqada III, there must have been fairly serious prospecting and recovery by that time. See also Klemm, Klemm and Murr 2001; Klemm, Klemm and Murr 2002 and Emberling et al. 2014 generally.

21 Note that this is by grain size. The material is often angular and appears unworn, the most visible particles probably deterioration product from quartz veins.

22 Emberling and Williams 2010, fig. 24d. See also Klimaszewska-Drabot 2005.

23 Kołosowska and el-Tayeb 2003, 118; Klimaszewska-Drabot 2005, 357–58; Gatto 2006, especially pls. I–III. For an examination of the periods and their chronology, see Dittrich 2011, especially 83–100 and Usai 2020.

24 Emberling and Williams 2010, 23–28.

25 Emberling and Williams 2010, figs. 27–29, 31, 33, for example.

Fig. 10 Old Kush pottery. a–b: OK III beaker. c: Ordinary black-topped. d–f: Deeply incised bowls. g–i: Fine band-incised. j–k: Base mud applied to OK cookpots.

Fig. 11 Old Kush pottery. a–c: Pan-Grave type beakers. d–e: Red burnished jars.
f: Red burnished jar with incised decoration.

types appear in more than one culture or region, there are also ambiguities in the cultural attribution of some vessels, especially the simpler ones. The cultures of Nubia were not isolated from each other and their pottery reflects some significant associations. Several categorical types have primary associations with one or another cultural group in the region even though they occasionally occur in other cultural contexts. Some classes were actually shared.

Old Kush (Kerma) Ordinary and Old Kush (Kerma)/ Pan-Grave-type Ordinary Incised – Much of the pottery of Hosh el-Geruf and some at al-Widay consisted of open, curved bowls with simple drab or Black-topped brown exteriors and black or drab interiors, and simple smoothed, or lightly burnished surfaces. Most of the Black-topped bowls were plain (Fig. 10c), but the drab ones most often were decorated with a broad band of hatching or cross-hatching on the exterior, a pattern well known at Kerma (not illustrated, but see Figs. 10g–i for fine examples).[26] Pottery of this class is also found in post-Middle Kingdom deposits in fortresses in Nubia in Egyptian occupation debris and in Pan-Graves.[27]

Deeply Incised – An important variation of this ordinary incised pottery was deeply incised, and also not burnished (Figs. 10d–f). The incision was rather more careful than the Ordinary Incised and it generally covered the exterior, either with horizontal hatching or alternating groups of hatched lines. This kind of pottery appears rarely in the northern Kerma sites,[28] and possibly not at Kerma, but it was found in the Egyptian Second Cataract fortresses, especially the Quarry Dumps at Serra East, where it was the only Nubian pottery and even in the Southern Atbai.[29] The dumps at Serra East date to the late Middle Kingdom, indicating a Middle Kerma (Old Kush II) date for this pottery. The occurrence here and in the Second Cataract forts is telling, since it was the Medjay who are recorded as serving in the garrisons.[30] Of great interest is a contemporary deeply incised pottery with simple motifs from Eastern Sudan's Gebel Mokram Group.[31]

Old Kush (Kerma) Fine Incised – In contrast with the other incised pottery, some bowls, generally, but not always small, had a band of fine incision below the rim (Figs. 10g–i). Most often cross-hatched, the edge of the band was generally emphasised by a row of dots or even a small band of rectangles. The surfaces were red-coated, but not burnished. Incised decoration in bands on bowls appears at Kerma,[32] and red-coated incised pottery, although less carefully executed, continued to be made into the New Kingdom.[33]

Kerma Beaker and related – The fine Black-topped pottery, generally with a grey zone around the vessel, and hematite-reinforced black top (Figs. 10a–b) included beakers of two, possibly three, of the four major phases of Classic Kerma pottery as found in the great tumuli.[34] Beaker sherds were less common at Hosh el-Geruf, and without the full shape, they were not possible to date in detail.

Old Kush (Kerma) and C-Group type Simple Black-top – Ordinary, Black-topped pottery was relatively common at Hosh el-Geruf and it appeared earlier than the finest beaker pottery (Fig. 10c). Surfaces were often unburnished and the black tops generally not enriched with hematite. In the 2007 season, most of these were sherds from Hosh el-Geruf and not precisely datable, but simple open bowls were a continuing feature of Kerma pottery at al-Widay I.[35]

Kerma Jars – Simple jars with vertical necks (Fig. 11e), ordinary counterparts of beaker-type pottery are a feature of Classic Kerma,[36] as are red-polished jars with narrow necks (Not illustrated).[37]

Old Kush (Kerma) Cooking Pot – One remarkable feature of Kerma pottery is a cooking pot with an irregularly indented bottom. Most often this was made by adding a circular slab of clay to the underside and indenting it with finger or reed impressions (Figs. 10j–k). This was apparently not fired until the vessel was used, and the slab often fell away later. Several of these pieces were found at Hosh el-Geruf.

Pan-Grave type Plain and Incised Black-top – A characteristic vessel, especially in the middle and later tombs at al-Widay and at Hosh el-Geruf, was a

26 Emberling and Williams 2010, figs. 25a–i. See also, for example, Dunham 1982, 236, BLKJ CXI and CXII, various.
27 Bourriau 1991, 131 and fig. 1: 2–5; colour photographs are available also, for example UC17932 at http://www.petrie.ucl.ac.uk/, from Rifa. For excellent parallels from Hierakonpolis, see http://www.archaeology.org/interactive/hierakonpolis/nubians.html. See also Bourriau 2004.
28 Maystre 1980, pl. XLVIII, 10
29 Williams 1987, 57–58; Williams n.d.
30 See, generally, Williams 2020.
31 See Manzo 2012, figs. 85–86.
32 Dunham 1982, 230–232, BM CXIV, BKTJ CXVIII, CXIX, various. Shapes and decoration differ.
33 Personal observation by the author, Tombos and Sesebi.
34 See Emberling and Williams 2010. KX and KIV; earlier KXVI is possible. At al-Widay, there was one fine jar with a tall, concave neck (fig. 27f), and a spouted jar (fig. 27e), both consistent with a date of KX-IV.
35 Dunham 1982, 223, CXI.
36 Reisner 1923, Vol. 6, BKT XXII, figs. 248–249; Vila 1987, fig. 214. For al-Widay, see Emberling and Williams 2010, figs. 29a–b.
37 Reisner 1923, Vol. 6, RP II, fig. 266–10. For al-Widay, see Emberling and Williams 2010, fig. 29e.

Fig. 12 Napatan Period pottery. a–b: Marl jar necks. c: Pilgrim flask neck and handle. d–e: Marl jar ribbed body sherds. f: Marl jar handle. g–i: Bulged-neck jar rims. k–m: Shaped sherds, geometric. n: Possible spoon.

Black-topped beaker with a straight or inward-leaning side, broad, slightly convex base, and thickened rim, normally defined by a horizontal line incised below, sometimes with punctures (Figs. 11a–c).[38] Sometimes, the exterior of this rim was incised with hatching or cross-hatching. The black top is narrow, and generally not enhanced, but sometimes the body was red coated. In northern Nubia, this kind of pottery is characteristic of the Pan-Grave complex whose influence spread from Middle Egypt to the neighborhood of the Ethiopian Plateau.[39]

Also typical of the Old Kush Period at al-Widay are red burnished jars, some incised (Figs. 11d, e). Napatan pottery included a number of quite diagnostic sherds, such as very thin body sherds from marl amphorae, with thin, flat ribs on the exterior. There were also a number of small amphora handles of well-known Napatan amphorae, both of marl and silt-fabric vessels.

Handmade – Some of the simpler hand-made bowls found in Kerma or Pan-Grave contexts are practically indistinguishable from their earliest Napatan counterparts.[40] Some simple Black-topped sherds and possibly a few hand-made ordinary ones may belong to this phase.[41]

Only one or two sherds were likely to have come from the red burnished beakers famous from the early part of the Napatan Period (not illustrated).[42]

Ordinary Bowls – Open bowls were not characteristic of Old Kush/Kerma or later Napatan times, but there were a few rim sherds at Hosh el-Geruf, of Nile clay (not illustrated).[43]

Jars/Amphorae – The most diagnostic Napatan-type of pottery at Hosh el-Geruf was a thin-walled, well-fired clay normally called marl used for medium to large storage jars, generally amphorae with thin, flat-ribbed bodies (Figs. 12d–e) and residual handles (Fig. 12f).[44] There were also pieces of handled amphorae (not illustrated). Elongated jars or amphorae with slightly convex necks appear in Napatan times (Figs. 12a–b)[45] as do those with rib-like necks and small rims (Figs. 12g–i).[46] Bulging, thickened necks were less equivocal, on Nile clay jars with light surfaces.[47] From Hosh el-Geruf came one neck, rim and handle of a pilgrim flask (Fig. 12c).

In some cases, the surface of a jar was dark, indicating a reducing atmosphere in firing, but also possibly a mixed clay. Vessels were in the same shapes as the light pottery, notably a jar with a rim folded against a heavy roll or bulge at the neck. Sherds of Nile clay amphorae were also found at Hosh el-Geruf including side handles and one that was held to the body by a rod of clay pushed through the wall (not illustrated).

Apart from some possible, but unidentifiable, lithics, the only fairly numerous small objects were sherds that had been chipped and ground into various shapes (Figs. 12j–m). Most were geometric, but a few were apparently utilitarian. The most common were triangles, but squares, rectangles, round pieces, and one hexagon were found. Their size, ca. 2-4 cm, suggests tokens, counters, or gaming pieces. No examples were made of definitely Napatan-type pottery, a circumstance which suggests an Old Kush (Kerma) date.

A few sherds of thin, mostly hand-made pottery were ground into an oblong shape, narrow at one end and broad at the other. The shape indicates they were used as spoons or ladles (Fig. 12m).

A number of sherd tools were found, notably digging sherds, often made from Mesolithic-Neolithic pottery (Fig. 13a) and some whose function was not determined (Fig. 13b).

Conclusion

Although the Oriental Institute Nubian Expedition found significant remains of the Mesolithic-Neolithic and fewer of the Napatan Period at Hosh el-Geruf, work was overwhelmingly concentrated in the Old Kush II and III (Middle and Classic Kerma) periods. The two sites of Hosh el-Geruf and al-Widay I were related, being only 4 km distant from each other, for the main phases of activity were contemporary. However, while one was an industrial installation for the extraction of gold, the other was the formal cemetery of a small community, one that was very likely in part engaged in the labour and administration at Hosh el-Geruf itself.[48]

38 Emberling and Williams 2010, 33–35 and fig. 31.

39 For example, Bietak 1968, 117–123 for characterisation, identification, 150, see also Bietak 1982 and Bietak 1987, 123–125, and Sadr 1990. Manzo 2012, figs. 88, 92, see also de Souza 2019.

40 See Sanam, Griffith 1923, plate XVII, types IXe, Xb, the drawing is not detailed, which could conceal differences.

41 Williams 1990, fig. 26b; see also Williams 1993, figs. 85c and 87b for milled rims; for deeply grooved incised small jars, see figs. 87c–d.

42 Williams 1990, pls. 7a–c.

43 Sanam, Griffith 1923, plate XVIII, type XV, esp. a-b; see possibly Williams 1993, fig. 90b; Williams 1990, figs. 26d-e. Welsby Sjöström 2023, figs. 3.7.5–7, for example.

44 Sanam, Griffith 1923, plate XVII, types III c–e, I; Williams 1990, fig. 30e; fig. 13b, with usable handles; Vila 1980, fig. 91:4, the walls are drawn rather thick. For materials, see generally Bourriau, Nicholson and Rose 2000.

45 See Vila 1980, fig. 175, 36/4, 46/4 and 46/10.

46 Griffith 1923, plate XVII, IIIe; possibly plate XVIII, some of VIII. The publication is unclear, but for the shape, see Aston 1999, 171–172: 1588, 1591, 1592 and 1593, which are, unfortunately, Nile B2. See also Welsby Sjöström 2023, figs. 3.1.5–7, for example.

47 Williams 1990, fig. 30e.

48 Emberling and Williams 2010, 23–28 offers a general description as of 2007. For more on the relationship with Pan-Graves and the Atbai, see Manzo 2017b and 2017a, Chapter 3, especially 43–44.

0 1 2

U3

0 1 2

H3 2-2

Fig. 13 Digging sherds. a: Mesolithic-neolithic. b: Old Kush (?).

Two conclusions derived from the evidence have major consequences. First, the activity at Hosh el-Geruf was on an industrial scale; it was not some kind of family workshop. Second, the industry was regional in scope, connecting work sites of different type separated by many kilometers involving at least mining, transport of raw material, and processing. A consequential point is that this industry was not Egyptian.[49] A second consequential point is that this industry must have been maintained by a regional power which, unlike Kerma, for example, left no monumental remains or clear evidence of inequality in its cemeteries. This should not be too surprising. Wawat and other regional entities in northeast Africa had single rulers at the time of Harkhuf[50] about three centuries earlier and Kerma, possibly Sai, are the only sites with clear signs of inequality. C-Group at that time shows none, a parallel with the Fourth Cataract culture. The situation continued in the time of the Execration Texts and by the end of the Second Intermediate period, Nubia and the Atbai, under the leadership of Kush was able to act in a huge combination. Thus Egypt, while in the lead technologically and in the ability to build hierarchies, was not entirely unique in the ability to organize large-scale enterprise.

49 Gold did remain in the cataract area, even in Old Kush II. See Wolf and Nowotnick 2006, colour plate XV for a gold disk. Simple gold beads were found at al-Widay that also appear to be of local manufacture. They are not discs, but pieces of bars bent to shape. See Emberling et al. 2014, pl. 4f.

50 Hafsaas 2020, 166–168.

Bibliography

ASTON, D.A.
1999 *Elephantine XIX: Pottery from the Late New Kingdom to the Early Ptolemaic Period*, Archäologische Veröffentlichungen 95, Mainz am Rhein.

BIETAK, M.
1968 *Studien zur Chronologie der Nubischen C-Gruppe: Ein Beitrag zur Frühgeschichte Unternubiens zwischen 2200 und 1550 v.Chr.*, Berichte des Österreichischen Nationalkomitees der UNESCO -Aktion für die Rettung der nubischen Altertümer, vol. 5, Österreichische Akademie der Wissenschaften, Denkschriften der philosophisch-historischen Klasse, vol. 97, Vienna.
1982 Pfannengräber, in: W. HELCK and W. WESTENDORFF (eds.), *Lexikon der* Ägyptologie, Vol. IV, Wiesbaden, 999–1003.
1987 The C-Group and the Pan-Grave culture in Nubia, in: T. HÄGG (ed.), *Nubian Culture Past and Present*, Kungl Vitterhets Historie och Antikvitets Akademien, Konferenser 17, Stockholm, 113–128.

BOURRIAU, J.
1991 Relations between Egypt and Kerma during the Middle and New Kingdoms, in: W.V. DAVIES (ed.), *Egypt and Africa: Nubia from Prehistory to Islam*, London, 129–144.
2004 Egyptian pottery found in Kerma Ancien, Kerma Moyen and Kerma Classique graves at Kerma, in: T. KENDALL (ed.), *Nubian Studies 1998: Proceedings of the Ninth International Conference of the International Society of Nubian Studies August 21-26 1998*, Boston, 3–13.

BOURRIAU, J., NICHOLSON, P. and ROSE, P.
2000 Pottery, in: P.T. NICHOLSON and I. SHAW (eds.), *Ancient Egyptian Materials and Technology*, Cambridge, 121–147.

DITTRICH, A.
2011 *Zur Neolithisierung des Mittleren Niltals und angrenzender Regionen. Kultureller Wandel vom Mesolithikum zum Neolithikum im Nord- und Zentralsudan*, BAR International Series 228, Oxford.

EDWARDS, D.N. (ed.)
2020 *The Archaeological Survey of Sudanese Nubia 1963–69: The Pharaonic Sites*, Sudan Archaeological Research Society Publication 23, Oxford.

EMBERLING, G. and WILLIAMS, B.
2010 The Kingdom of Kush in the 4th Cataract: Archaeological salvage of the Oriental Institute Nubian Expedition 2007 season. Part 1. Preliminary report on the sites of Hosh el-Geruf and El-Widay, *Gdansk Archaeological Museum African Reports* 7, 17–38.

EMBERLING, G., WILLIAMS, B., INVOLSTAD, M. and JAMES, T.
2014 Peripheral vison: Identity at the margins of the early Kingdom of Kush, in: J.R. ANDERSON and D.A. WELSBY (eds.), *The Fourth Cataract and Beyond. Proceedings of the 12th International Conference for Nubian Studies*, British Museum Publications on Egypt and Sudan 1, Leuven, 329–336.

DUNHAM, D.
1982 *Excavations at Kerma: Part VI*, Boston.

GATTO, M.C.
2006 The most ancient pottery from the Dongola Reach (Northern Sudan), *Archéologie du Nil Moyen* 10, 73–86.

GRIFFITH, F.Ll.
1923 Oxford excavations in Nubia; XVIII. The cemetery of Sanam, *University of Liverpool Annals of Archaeology and Anthropology* 10, 73–171.

HAFSAAS, H.
2020 The C-Group people in Lower Nubia: Cattle pastoralists on the frontier between Egypt and Kush, in: G. EMBERLING and B.B. WILLIAMS (eds.), *The Oxford Handbook of Ancient Nubia*, Oxford, 157–177.

HARRELL, J.
2010 Archaeological geology of Hosh el-Guruf, Fourth Nile Cataract Sudan, *Gdansk Archaeological Museum African Reports* 7, 71–84.

KLEMM, D., KLEMM, R. and MURR, A.
2001 Gold of the Pharaohs – 6000 years of gold mining in Egypt and Nubia, *Journal of African Earth Sciences* 33, 643–659.
2002 Ancient gold mining in the Eastern Desert of Egypt and the Nubian Desert of Sudan, in: R. FRIEDMAN (ed.), *Egypt and Nubia: Gifts of the Desert*, London, 215–231.

KLEMM, R. and KLEMM, D.
2013 *Gold and Gold Mining in Egypt and Nubia, Geoarchaeology of the Ancient Gold Mining Sites in the Egyptian and Sudanese Eastern Deserts*, Berlin; Heidelberg.

KLIMASZEWSKA-DRABOT, E.
2005 Neolithic to Napatan pottery from Uli Island preliminary report, *Polish Archaeology in the Mediterranean* XVI, 357–368.

KOŁOSOWSKA, E. and EL-TAYEB, M.
2003 Pottery from the Fourth Cataract region (Sudan), *Gdansk Archaeological Museum African Reports* 2, 117–126.

MANZO, A.
2012 *Italian Archaeological Expedition to the Eastern Sudan of the University of Naples "L'Orientale": Report of the 2011 Field Season.* With contributions by Alemseged Beldados Aleho, Alfredo Crannante, Donatella Usai, and Vincenzo Zoppi, Naples.
2017a *The Eastern Sudan in its Setting. The Archaeology of a Region Far From the Nile Valley*, Cambridge Monographs in African Archaeology 94, Cambridge.
2017b The territorial expanse of the Pan-Grave culture thirty years later, *Sudan & Nubia* 21, 98–112.

MAYSTRE, C.
1980 *Akasha I*. Avec la collaboration de Erich et Margaretha Fehlmann, Frédérique van Känel, Kurt Rudin, Jürg Sedlmeier, Hans-Rudolf et Daria Zbinden-Gisler, Mission archéologique de la Fondation Henry M. Blackmer et du Centre d'*Études* Orientales de l'Université de Genève 1, Geneva.

MEYER, C.
2010 The Kingdom of Kush in the 4th Cataract: Archaeological salvage of the Oriental Institute Nubian Expedition 2007 season. Part II. Grinding stones and gold mining at Hosh el-Guruf, Sudan, *Gdansk Archaeological Museum African Reports* 7, 39–52, "Appendix A", 57–66.

MEYER, C. and HARRELL, J.
n.d. Archaeological geology. Chapter 5, in: B.B. WILLIAMS and L.A. HEIDORN (eds.), *Hosh el-Geruf, Oriental Institute Nubian Expedition, Operations in the Fourth Cataract*, Part 1.

NÄSER, C.
2007 The Humboldt University Nubian Expedition 2005: Works on Sherari and Us, in: C. NÄSER and M. LANGE (eds.), *Proceedings of the Second International Conference on the Archaeology of the Fourth Nile Cataract. Berlin, August 4th-6th, 2005*, Meroitica , Schriften zur altsudanesischen Geschichte und Archaeologie 23, Wiesbaden, 118–133.

REISNER, G.A.
1923 *Excavations at Kerma, Parts I–V*, Harvard African Studies, Vols. 5–6, Cambridge.

SADR, K.
1990 The Medjay in southern Atbai, *Archéologie du Nil Moyen* 4, 63–86.

SHONKWILER, R.
2010 The Kingdom of Kush in the 4th Cataract: Archaeological salvage of the Oriental Institute Nubian Expedition 2007 season. Part III. A Napatan seal impression from Hosh el-Guruf, *Gdansk Archaeological Museum African Reports* 7, 53–54.

DE SOUZA, A.
2019 *New Horizons: The Pan Grave Ceramic Tradition in Context*, Middle Kingdom Studies 9, London.

USAI, D.
2020 From foraging to food production. The Mesolithic and Neolithic of the Middle Nile Valley, in: G. EMBERLING and B.B. WILLIAMS (eds.), *The Oxford Handbook of Ancient Nubia*, Oxford, 101–124.

VILA, A.
1980 *La prospection archéologique de la vallée du Nil au sud de la cataracte de Dal (Nubie soudanaise). Fascicule 12: la nécropole de Missiminia I, les sepultures napatéennes*, Paris.
1987 *Le cimitière kermaïque d'Ukma Ouest: La prospection archéologique de la vallée du Nil en Nubie Soudanaise*, Paris.

WELSBY, D. (ed.)
2023 *Archaeology by the Fourth Nile Cataract. Survey and Excavations on the Left Bank of the River and on the Islands between Amri and Kirbekan. Volume I. Landscape, Toponyms and Oral History and the People, Their Settlements, Architecture and Land Use Before the Merowe Dam*, Sudan Archaeological Research Society Publication 26, Oxford.

WELSBY SJÖSTRÖM I.
2010 Golden accessories: a link to the outside world from the pyramid at site 4-F-71 (Fourth Cataract, SARS concession), *Sudan & Nubia* 14, 45–47.
2023 *Gematon: Living and Dying in a Kushite Town on the Nile. Volume III. The Pottery*, Sudan Archaeological Research Society Publication 29, Oxford.

WILLIAMS, B.
1987 The Nubian Publication Project, *Oriental Institute Annual Report* 1986-1987, 57–60.
1990 *Excavations Between Abu Simbel and the Sudan Frontier: Part 7, Twenty-fifth Dynasty and Napatan Remains at Qustul: Cemeteries W and V*, The University of Chicago Oriental Institute Nubian Expedition, vol. VII, Chicago.
1993 *Excavations at Serra East: Parts 1–5: A-Group, C-Group, Pan-Grave, New Kingdom, and X-Group Remains from Cemeteries A-G and Rock Shelters*, The University of Chicago Oriental Institute Nubian Expedition, vol. X, Chicago.
2020 Kush in the wider world during the Kerma Period, in: G. EMBERLING and B.B. WILLIAMS (eds.), *The Oxford Handbook of Ancient Nubia*, Oxford, 179–200.
n.d. A desert pottery from late Middle Kingdom fortresses, the Fourth Cataract and the Atbai (*Festschrift Ann Roth*).

WOLF, P. and NOWOTNICK, U.
2006 The third season of the Anglo-German Expedition to the Fourth Cataract of the Nile, *Sudan & Nubia* 10, 20–33.

Chapter 4

Gold exploitation in New Kingdom and Napatan Nubia

Julia Budka[1]

Abstract

The Egyptian colonial system to extract gold from the Nubian deserts and the Nile Valley is attested to in a considerable number of texts. These texts are one way to consider differences between gold production in Wawat (Lower Nubia) and Kush (Upper Nubia). This chapter moves away from the long-established interpretation of the period of Egyptian presence in Nubia being one of technological and cultural advancement, in particular in how Egypt benefited from, supposedly, previously unexplored natural resources. Instead, the focus will be on indigenous Nubian relationships with gold, from the Kerma Period to the Napatan Period. Case studies from the New Kingdom and Napatan Periods are used to provide an alternative narrative and to argue for a need to rewrite Nubia's silenced 'golden' history, especially when taking archaeological sources into account. The main aim is to highlight a seemingly long continuity of Nubian goldworking and its complex intermingling with Egyptian goldworking.

Keywords:

Nubia, gold, gold mining, wadi working, Kerma, New Kingdom, Napatan

The exploitation of gold in Nubia, well known for being rich in gold, seems to have reached a peak during the New Kingdom. Raw gold was extracted and exported from various locations across Nubia[2] and then transformed into luxury items deposited in elite and royal tombs in Egypt.[3] During the New Kingdom (c. 1550–1070 BC), Nubian gold was also sent, through Egypt, to other parts of the Egyptian empire,[4] contributing to the image of the "Golden Age" in Egypt.[5]

Ramses II's Quban stela, set up at the entrance of one of the main gold mining areas in Lower Nubia, of Wadi Allaqi, describes, in an ideological manner, the challenges of providing water for the extensive exploration of gold in the Eastern Desert.[6] Temple provisions texts also list great quantities of gold and other resources extracted from Nubia[7] and 'tribute scenes' from 18th Dynasty Egyptian contexts display submissive Nubians bringing gold and other materials to Egypt.[8] This textual and iconographic evidence supported colonial interpretations (see above, the Introduction to Part II) and the assessment of the role of Nubians and their relationship with gold. A multi-perspective approach considering all available sources for gold exploitation, and especially fresh material from recent fieldwork allows us to illustrate how crucial gold mining was on a local and indigenous level throughout Nubian history.

Prelude of the New Kingdom: Kerma goldworking

Even though gold shaped Nubian identity over millennia, only recently have scholars started challenging existing biased assumptions that consider Nubians as either passive spectators of the Egyptian exploitation of local resources, or as an oppressed population who mined gold under orders. Current research indicates a more complex picture of Nubian gold mining/processing traditions prior to New Kingdom colonisation, both in the Eastern Desert and along the Nile Valley, particularly when considering evidence from the different stages of procurement, production, and use of gold.

At the peak of the Kerma Kingdom's hegemony in the Middle Nile, evidence from Buhen demonstrates that Kerma expanded towards the gold-rich area of the Second Cataract.[9] It is very likely that the control of the Middle Kingdom fortresses by Kerma rulers was, not only, a military measure for strategic purposes, but also provided direct access to gold mines in the region and a base for the exploitation of the Wadi Allaqi area.[10] This Kerma control over Lower Nubian fortresses

1 Ludwig-Maximilians-Universität München; julia.budka@lmu.de.

2 Vercoutter 1959; Klemm and Klemm 2013.

3 E.g., Aldred 1971; Bulsinski 2015; see also Miniaci and Lacovara 2022. For a recent scientific analysis and the difficulties of differentiating Nubian and Egyptian gold alloys see Guerra, Martinón-Torres and Quirke (eds.) 2023.

4 Rainey 2015, 79.

5 Brovarski, Doll and Freed 1982.

6 Kitchen 1980, 188–193; Zibelius-Chen 1994; Klemm and Klemm 2013, 11, 294; Auenmüller 2020a.

7 Sethe 1907, 733–739; Klemm and Klemm 2013, 25.

8 E.g. the famous so-called scene of tributes in the tomb of Huy, TT40, Davies and Gardiner 1926, pl. 27.

9 Cooper 2018. For interaction processes between Kerma and Lower Nubian communities see also Walsh 2022.

10 It is noteworthy that Smith, H. S. 1994, 376 proposed the control to the mines of Wadi Allaqi as one of the key factors that the Nubian A-Group became successful traders with Egypt.

and their access to resources probably motivated the Hyksos to establish trade and direct contact with the Kerma ruler, since Nubian gold is thought to be one of the main exchange items in the Eastern Mediterranean networks of Asiatic rulers during the 15th Dynasty.[11]

Textual evidence, such as the historical inscription of Sobeknakht II at El-Kab, explains how Kerma managed to advance during the Classic Kerma into the Egyptian Eastern Desert and access previously Egyptian controlled gold mines, combining forces with "tribes of Wawat, (...), the Medjay and Punt"[12]. This illustrates, not only, the strong networks between Kerma, inner Africa, and vast regions of the Eastern Desert up to the Red Sea, but also shifting dynamics in controlling access to gold mining regions. Aaron de Souza has recently suggested the region around El-Kab and Edfu, Upper Egypt's South, should be considered as a culturally mixed area and, as such, a transitional zone between Egyptian and Nubian spheres within which gold mining was essential, not only for economic but also for political reasons.[13]

Nubia's early access to gold through trade with nomadic peoples and control of gold mining sites was recently confirmed based on evidence from the Eastern Desert, including a rock inscription at Umm Nabari referring to a Kerma ruler, which proves the reach of Kerma presence into the desert.[14] Direct exploration of gold mines by Kerma in the Eastern Desert remains to be confirmed[15] (and might remain invisible in the archaeological record[16]). However, Julien Cooper has suggested convincingly that desert peoples seem to have been the unknown workers behind the Egyptian gold enterprise.[17] It is likely that the same applies to Kerma's access to gold-rich areas of the Eastern Desert before the New Kingdom. There are noticeable differences between Middle Kingdom stone tools associated with gold mining found in the Eastern desert of Egypt and the Nile Valley, suggesting that most of the miners in the desert were community members of desert tribes rather than Nile Valley residents.[18] A closer examination of the material culture associated with mining sites in the Nubian Eastern desert and its potential reflection of various dynamics and, at certain times, different alliances between the kingdom of Kerma and nomads such as the Medjay is clearly necessary.

Although the mining areas are well known in both Egypt and Nubia, it is more difficult to trace places of further gold processing. No ancient gold workshop has been identified in the Lower Nile Valley.[19] However, there are several sites in the Middle Nile region which might have functioned as gold workshops[20] and support more nuanced interpretations of Nubian goldworking prior to Egyptian colonisation. Sites in Duweishat (Lower Nubia) associated with C-Group/Kerma people consisting of distinctive, curvilinear dry-stone structures suggest that Nubians played a role in gold processing along the Nile.[21] This contributes to challenging current narratives of Egyptians as the sole driving force of technological progress in Nubia.[22] These distinctive dry-stone structures suggest a significant role of Nubians in gold mining, not only in the Batn el-Hagar, but also in the Sesi-Delgo region further South.[23]

This idea could also be supported by Mindiq 3-P-8, a site in Kosha East in the research concession of the Munich University Attab to Ferka Survey Project (MUAFS). Described by André Vila as a Neolithic and Old Nubian habitation,[24] the general area also included Old and Middle Kerma surface material and, as such, may still have been in use at that time and/or have been used in multiple periods. Unfortunately, modern goldworking has completely destroyed the dry-stone features described by Vila and the dating can therefore not be verified. However, the similarity of the dry-stone architecture of 3-P-8 to sites such as Duweishat and its location in a rich, still exploited gold bearing area may point to a comparable original purpose of this early site connected to goldworking.[25]

Remains of ancient wadi working can be found over large areas on the East bank of the MUAFS concession, especially in the districts of Ginis and Attab. Based on the distribution of Kerma sites in the concession area, it is unlikely to be a coincidence that most sites can be found in these districts, stretching into Kosha where there is also extensive goldworking, as exemplified by site 3-P-8. Interestingly, a similar distribution pattern is apparent in the New Kingdom.[26]

Apart from site 3-P-8 and wadi working remains, there is only indirect archaeological evidence for gold exploitation on the East bank of the MUAFS concession. One particularly interesting example is

11 Ahrens and Kopetzky 2021, 295. For the trade networks of the Hyksos which included Nubia see also Gratien 2004; Mourad 2017, 382.
12 Davies 2003, 52–53.
13 Cf. de Souza 2020.
14 Davies 2020; cf. de Souza 2020, 338.
15 Cf. Castiglioni, Castiglioni and Bonnet 2010; Castiglioni and Castiglioni 2020a, 11–21; Castiglioni and Castiglioni 2020b; see also Budka 2021a.
16 Note, however, possible evidence by means of ceramics found at mining sites, see Ruffieux and Bashir 2020.
17 Cooper 2021, 7.
18 Klemm, Klemm and Murr 2001, 649.
19 See Quirke 2023 with references and sources.
20 Klemm and Klemm 2013, passim.
21 Edwards 2020, 406–407; 415. For goldworking in Duweishat see also Klemm and Klemm 2013, 557–564.
22 Cf. Liszka 2017.
23 Edwards 2020, 406–407; 415.
24 Vila 1976, 90–96.
25 See Hinterhuber 2021.
26 See Budka 2020a, 65, fig. 13 (Kerma sites) and fig. 14 (New Kingdom sites).

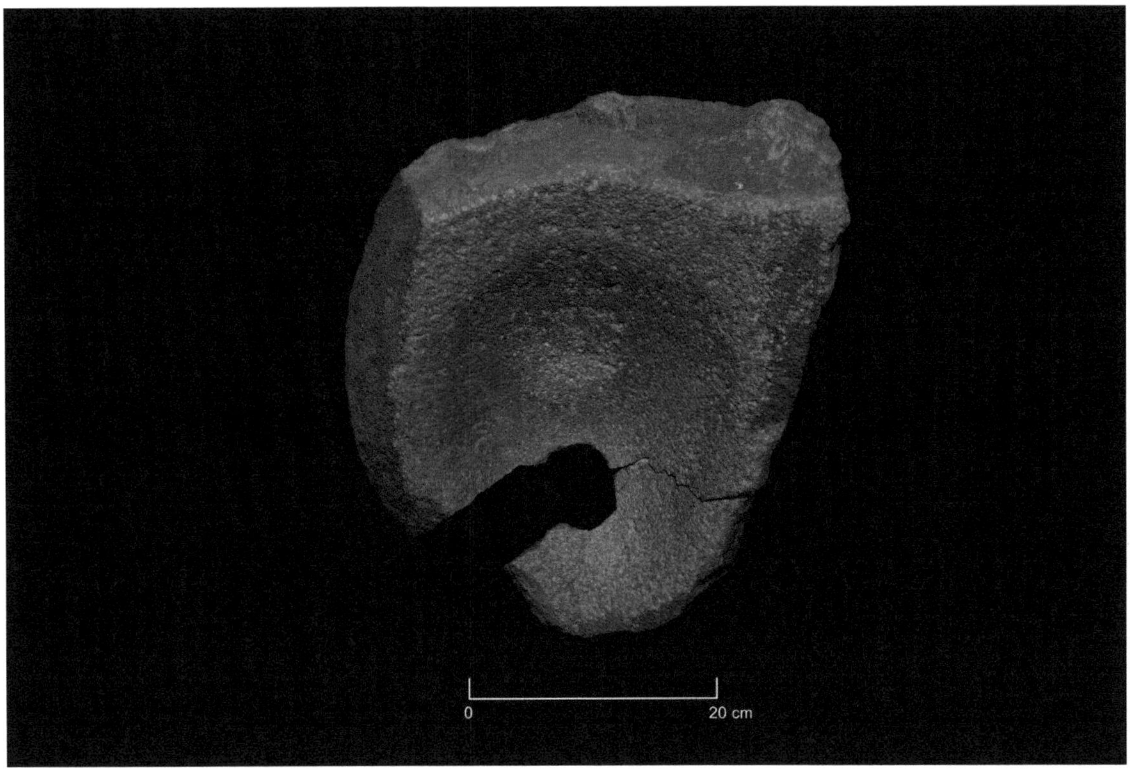

Fig. 1 Grindstone found on surface of AtW 001, northwest of Trench 1 (photo by J. Budka).

the Kerma cemetery GiE 003, located at the border between Attab and Ginis in an area covered with heaped remains of wadi working activities. This large cemetery comprises an estimated 150 tombs of which a total of 58 burial pits were excavated.[27] The oldest burials are associated with the Middle Kerma Period, but there are also Pan-Grave style burials, and most of the tombs can be dated to the Classic Kerma Period. Although little material culture was found during excavation because of looting, the finds recovered suggest a relatively wealthy community (ivory objects like fly pendants were present, as well as a bronze dagger, a royal Hyksos scarab, Kerma Black topped vessels, and imported vessels from Egypt and the Levant). In conclusion, GiE 003 is a provincial cemetery in the Kerma Kingdom's northern reaches, with evidence of continuous use from the Middle Kerma to the Classic Kerma with an intriguing presence of the Pan-Grave tradition, appearing side by side with Kerma material culture. The cemetery provides close parallels to cemeteries in the Batn el-Hagar, such as Ukma and Akasha, but also has strong similarities to the Kerma cemeteries in the closer vicinity, such as at Sai, as well as at Ferka. The association of some of the pottery from GiE 003 with the Pan-Grave horizon seems to reflect connections to nomadic people, possibly linked to desert gold mining.[28] Since these pots were found together with Kerma pottery, it is tempting to consider the persons buried with them as fully integrated members of the local community. In this respect, gold mining in the Ginis area might well have been a collaborative endeavour between several Nubian groups with different cultural backgrounds.

Other sites in the MUAFS concession which are most likely connected with gold exploitation during the Kerma Period are located on the West bank, especially in Attab West. It is remarkablable that most of these sites show a continous use from Classic Kerma to early New Kingdom times. The first case study is site AtW 002, a rectangular building built using a combination of dry-stone technique and mudbricks.[29] Documented in the 1970s by Vila and dated to the New Kingdom, this site is closely associated with so-called wadi walls and Kerma sites in the northern palaeochannel area of Attab West (extending into the Amara West district).[30] The total set of material culture excavated in

27 Budka 2022; Budka, Rose and Ward 2023, 20–24.

28 Cf. the presence of Pan-Grave style ceramics at Hosh el-Guruf at the Fourth Cataract, Emberling and Williams 2010 (see also Williams this volume).

29 See Budka, Rose and Ward 2023, 24–26.

30 For these walls and their proposed function see Dalton et al. 2023.

this structure comprised a small collection of typical settlement pottery, datable to the early 18th Dynasty, a considerable number of grindstones and several other stone tools like pounders and quartz. This finds assemblage, its location near drystone walls, and both ancient and modern goldworking sites, suggests a connection to goldworking. Maybe the site was a control post for trade and gold transport, enabling the communication between hinterland communities and the newly established Egyptian centre on Sai Island.[31] It was most likely inhabited by both Kerma Nubians and colonialists from Egypt. The former seems essential given the location of the site and the earlier network of Kerma sites in the region, in particular along the so-called northern palaeochannel, the latter are suggested by the material culture and dating of the site.

Another site in the MUAFS concession located in the Attab West district with a possible connection to goldworking is AtW 001, a settlement mound with considerable mudbrick debris and pottery-rich dump layers. Evidence suggests that the site may have already been in use in the Kerma Period – like AtW 002, and fits into a local pattern of small-scale domestic sites possibly linked to goldworking from the Kerma Period to the New Kingdom.[32] Apart from ceramics, the finds from AtW 001 included numerous stone tools such as large grindstones and pounders, testifying to grinding and crushing activities comparable to those at AtW 002. Quartz chips were found during excavation on the mound and are also traceable in the general vicinity of the site, extending into the area of site 2-T-62 (which is marked by dry-stone architecture). One large granite grindstone is of a type commonly associated with gold processing (Fig. 1). Based on the abundant 18th Dynasty material from the site, the stone tool is most likely of the same date.[33]

The functional assessment of site AtW 001 has not yet been completed. However, the site located on, what is presumably, a former island and thus close to the river, might have been linked to seasonal traffic and routes into the desert, possibly in connection with the provision of transport animals and livestock for goldworking expeditions. The parallels between AtW 001 and site 2-R-18 in the Amara West district[34] are obvious and can be used as material evidence to tentatively reconstruct gold processing in the general area as joint activities by Egyptians and Nubians.

To sum up the preliminary evidence from the MUAFS concession, there are examples of gold exploitation in the districts of Attab, Ginis and Kosha starting well before the Egyptian New Kingdom.[35] The Pan-Grave style burials in cemetery GiE 003 indicate a connection between local Kerma communities and nomadic people. An involvement of the Bronze Age groups inhabiting the region with gold mining in the Eastern desert, in addition to working in the wadi along the Nile, is therefore likely.[36] In general, the MUAFS concession with sites yielding a complex mix of material culture allows us to trace activities and social practices in a dynamic contact space shared by Kerma Nubians, Pan-Grave nomads and Egyptians. This model of shared activities also seems to hold true for the goldworking business with specific features depending on the period and the historical framework.[37]

That the MUAFS concession reflects general patterns in the Bronze Age Middle Nile rather than regional features is supported by new excavations in the Fourth Cataract area, specifically at Hosh el-Guruf. Neolithic, Kerma, and Napatan occupation phases were detected at the site, with no clear evidence of Egyptian New Kingdom activity (see Chapter 3). Numerous large grindstones were recovered, offering glimpses of early Nubian gold processing activities.[38] Harrell proposed that the grindstones were used to crush alluvial quartz ore to extract gold.[39] Such large grindstones have been interpreted as an Egyptian innovation brought to Nubia to improve gold processing.[40] However, the picture emerging from Hosh el-Guruf and other areas of Nubia suggests a local origin for this technology, indicating that a complex organisation of gold processing existed before Egyptian colonisation.[41]

New Kingdom goldworking in Nubia

It is well known that Nubian gold was among the main Egyptian economic interests for a long time span, especially during the New Kingdom.[42] Considering the above, there are strong indications that, in some parts, new questions about the long-established perception of the gold industry in New Kingdom Nubia need to be asked. So far, it has been widely assumed that from the early New Kingdom onwards gold mining expanded into the southern areas around

31 See Budka 2022.
32 Budka 2022.
33 See Budka 2022.
34 Stevens and Garnett 2017.
35 Budka 2020a, 69; Budka 2022.
36 Cf. Pan-Grave style ceramics at Hosh Guruf at the Fourth Cataract, Emberling and Williams 2010 (see also Williams this volume). See also Cooper 2021 for the role of desert nomads for Kerma's access to gold.
37 See also Quirke 2023 for the situational character of gold processing in general.
38 Emberling and Williams 2010, 20–22; Meyer 2010, 46.
39 Harrell 2010, 80–83.
40 Klemm and Klemm 2013, 609.
41 Williams 2020, 88; see also Rega 2020, 107–110 and Williams this volume.
42 Vercoutter 1959, 120–153; Müller 2013, 74–79; Morris 2018, 130.

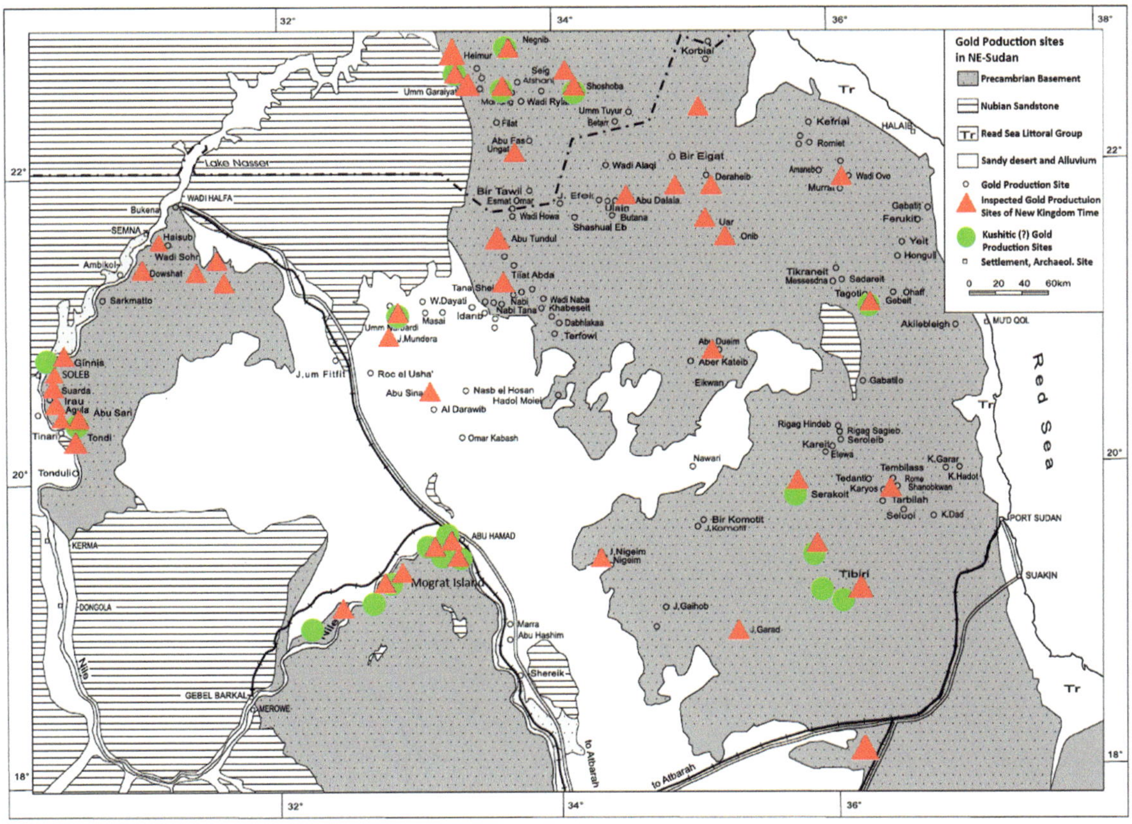

Fig. 2 Distribution map of presumed "New Kingdom" and "Kushite" gold mining sites in Nubia (map by V. Hinterhuber for the DiverseNile Project, after Klemm, Klemm and Murr 2001/Klemm and Klemm 2013).

Wadi Allaqi, as well as into Nubia's vast regions close to the Nile and the Eastern Desert, and has been seen as a technological revolution – exploiting previously unexplored resources (Fig. 2).[43] Dating these sites to the New Kingdom based on the mere existence of large grindstones, often found re-used in later Medieval buildings,[44] needs to be reconsidered. The similarity of these grindstones to Nubian examples prior to the New Kingdom suggests that an exclusively New Kingdom attribution of some of the sites is probably not as definitive as previously thought.[45] Furthermore, as will be shown in the following, it is likely that "the systematic exploration of remote desert regions during New Kingdom times"[46] was only possible through cooperation with Kerma groups and desert tribes and strongly depended on the Nubian expertise of the desert landscapes.

Textual sources from the New Kingdom tell us about the complex structure constructed by the Egyptians to extract gold from the Nubian deserts. These texts can be used to estimate differences between gold production in Wawat (Lower Nubia) and Kush (Upper Nubia). According to Egyptian texts, the amount of gold coming from Kush seems to differ from the one from Wawat.[47] This is especially the case during the reign of Thutmose III when much more gold of Wawat was registered.[48] From the time of Amenhotep III onwards, Kush seems to have gained in importance as a gold mining area as, for example, representations in the Theban tomb of viceroy Huy illustrate.[49] Textual evidence implies a decline in gold production in Ramesside times.[50]

The differences between Lower and Upper Nubia are related to geological variations and are also reflected in New Kingdom settlement patterns in Nubia.[51] Explanations for the decline in gold exploitation during the late New Kingdom still need to be sought; for this general historical and economic developments in Egypt must of course be considered.

43 Klemm and Klemm 2013, 606–614.
44 Klemm and Klemm 2013.
45 See also Mayer 2010, 48; Rega 2020.
46 Klemm, Klemm and Murr 2001, 649.
47 Vercoutter 1959, 135; Klemm and Klemm 2017, 261.
48 Morris 2018, 128–130; Budka 2020b, 404.
49 Cf. Zibelius-Chen 2013, 140. See also Klemm, Klemm and Murr 2001, 643, fig. 14.
50 Vercoutter 1959, 135.
51 Cf. Vieth 2018.

Fig. 3 Faience vessel of Khnummose from Tomb 26 on Sai Island with the title "overseer of goldworkers" (photo by C. Geiger, ©AcrossBorders Project).

Local expertise for the Egyptian colonial administration and gold exploitation

Primarily based on textual evidence, Egyptologists have acknowledged the presence of Nubians among Egyptian colonial officials,[52] and also of Nubians engaged in goldworking during the New Kingdom.[53] The latter were usually considered as prisoners of war or slaves of the Egyptian colonial state.[54] However, recent multi-facetted work and new archaeological evidence have shown that the situation in New Kingdom Nubia was much more complex.[55] Interestingly, recent evidence from Sai Island suggests that Nubians played an active role in gold exploitation and processing during the Egyptian colonial period.

Sai was one of the colonial settlements erected during the 18th Dynasty between the Second and Third Cataracts, also known as temple towns. Temples were a key feature of these towns and seem to have played an administrative role in gold exploitation in Upper Nubia.[56] It is unlikely to be a coincidence that the stretch along the eastern bank of the Nile between Ginis and Ager, comprising major New Kingdom sites like Amara West, Sai, Sedeigna and Soleb, shows the "heaped remains of ancient alluvial workings of generally scattered quartz vein detritus."[57] However, rather than be explained by a New Kingdom expansion of wadi working, much evidence points towards a continuous exploitation of gold sources in this part of the Middle Nile from at least Kerma times through to the New Kingdom (see above).

The island of Sai nicely illustrates the (almost) uninterrupted importance of the region during the Kerma Period and the New Kingdom.[58] Whereas we only have indirect evidence to suggest that the importance of the Kerman stronghold on the island must be seen in connection with gold exploitation,[59] we know more about Sai and its role for mining gold during the New Kingdom. Importantly, recent excavations at the Egyptian colonial cemetery on Sai revealed an Egyptian-style elite tomb, which yielded rich funerary equipment associated with the overseer of goldsmiths, Khnummose, and his family members.[60] The body of Khnummose was found buried with a woman's body, both placed in painted wooden coffins. An inscribed stone shabti and faience vessels (Fig. 3) record two of Khnummose's titles: '*goldworker*' and '*overseer of goldworker*'. This is the only evidence for '*overseer of goldworker*' for Upper Nubia, which illustrates the importance of Sai in the exploitation of gold during the mid-18th Dynasty.[61] The title is otherwise attested to in major Egyptian cities like Thebes, Abydos, Memphis and Per-Rameses.[62]

Fig. 4 Gold foil attached to the heart scarab of Khnummose from Tomb 26 on Sai Island (photo by M. Gundlach, ©AcrossBorders Project).

Johannes Auenmüller has traced other '*goldworkers*' active in New Kingdom Nubia,[63] in Upper Nubia, only one other individual named Bak, from Soleb, was known as a '*goldworker*'. Both Khnummose and Bak were active in the mid-18th Dynasty, the first peak of Egyptian colonisation and gold exploitation in Upper Nubia. Whether Bak was a native inhabitant of Nubia

52 See Müller 2013, passim.
53 Vercoutter 1959. Recently, Quirke 2023 has collected the titles associated with goldworking in both Egypt and Nubia.
54 Spalinger 2006, 365.
55 See Smith 2020 with references.
56 Spence et al. 2011; Klemm and Klemm 2013, 9; Vieth 2018; Stevens and Garnett 2017; Budka 2020b, 403–407.
57 Klemm, Klemm and Murr 2001, 647.
58 There is certainly a continuity in the occupation of the island; whether there was a decline in its importance during the late Classic Kerma time is still debated. This decline might be connected to trade networks with the Hyksos which ceased towards the end of the Second Intermediate Period; see Budka 2023, 55 with references.
59 See Budka 2023, 56–57.
60 Budka 2021b.
61 Lacovara and Markowitz 2019, 102–103.
62 Quirke 2023, 54, Table 2.16. For Lower Nubia, there are attestations of the title from Aniba and maybe also from Buhen.
63 Auenmüller 2020b, tables 39–41. See now also Quirke 2023, 54, Table 2.16.

Fig. 5 Gold and silver signet ring from Tomb 26 on Sai Island (photo by C. Geiger, ©AcrossBorders Project).

or one of the colonisers arriving in Soleb is impossible to answer without archaeological evidence and his skeletal remains.

Khnummose was buried at Sai with objects restricted to elite groups in New Kingdom Nubia, including a stone shabti and a stone heart scarab. Traces of gold foil were found on the heart scarab (Fig. 4), which was probably mounted in a gold bezel connected to a gold chain, a pattern typical of the mid-18th Dynasty,[64] but also already used in Classic Kerma times.[65]

A considerable amount of gold comes from Tomb 26, which is likely related to the occupation of male interments inside the tomb, including Khnummose. It is tempting to assume, despite a lack of conclusive evidence, that male individuals buried in Tomb 26 were involved in gold exploitation. Besides the remains of Khnummose, the burial goods associated with the earliest male burial in Tomb 26, presumably the father or uncle of Khnummose, are noteworthy and include a heart scarab, a set of miniature canopic jars imported from Egypt, and a gilded funerary mask. In the same burial chamber, a gold and silver finger ring was found associated with a female burial (Fig. 5).

This signet ring was possibly used as a seal in daily life and probably belonged to a male official before it was buried alongside the female individual. A similar scenario was found at Aniba Tomb S91. A woman named Taneferet was found buried with five signet rings of gold and silver[66] next to her husband, User, in the lower chamber of the monument. Interestingly, the tomb also housed the later interment of the goldsmith Khay, whose relationship with User and Taneferet remains unclear.

The burial assemblage and architecture of Tomb 26 on Sai Island allow us to assume that Khnummose and his likely family members belonged to the colonial elite culturally aligned with Egypt. However, strontium isotope analysis suggests that those people were local to the region of Sai.[67] Individuals, such as Khnummose, who were successfully assimilated into the Egyptian colonial administration functioned as 'role models'[68] for other Nubians and are to be expected at all New Kingdom sites in Nubia, as suggested by evidence from Aniba and Soleb.

This close exchange of Nubians and Egyptians in the processing of gold, as well as the active role of native Nubians in the colonial gold business probably explains why it is almost impossible to differentiate

64 Patch 2005.
65 Patrevita 2022.
66 Steindorff 1937, 111.
67 Retzmann et al. 2019. I am aware of the *caveats* raised by assessing ethnicity by means of strontium isotope only; see Schrader and Buzon this volume.
68 Morris 2018, 224.

Fig. 6 Traces of quartz working on the surface at Kajinmittar 3-P-34, Ginis East (photo by S. Patrevita, ©DiverseNile Project).

between Egyptian and Nubian goldworking, both in terms of archaeology and scientific analysis.[69] Concepts like co-option and co-operation between Egyptians and Nubians are also attested to in other technologies like faience production.[70] Within the cultural entangled milieu of New Kingdom Nubia, it is therefore probably best to discuss New Kingdom goldworking in a broad sense, avoiding artificial borders between Nubian and Egyptian gold processing which are unlikely to reflect real dynamics.

Local developments in Napatan goldworking

Although the specific Nubian character of Napatan and Meroitic gold objects was noticed quite early on[71] and recently revised,[72] there have been few attempts to contextualise the flourishing Napatan goldworking within Nubia itself. Despite clearly being influenced by Nubian New Kingdom and as far back as Kerma models, early Napatan objects have often been interpreted as re-used Egyptian imports or newly imported pieces.[73] That there was a continuity in the use of New Kingdom and Napatan goldworking sites is exemplified by the MUAFS concession and other regions (see Fig. 2). However, the Napatan gold enterprise should not only be regarded as an opportunistic reopening of New Kingdom gold mines.[74] While it is reasonable to consider a continuation of previously operational mines, this is mostly based on a presumed re-use of the large 'New Kingdom' grindstones[75], an assumption that today needs revision in the light of newly available evidence from Hosh el-Guruf (see above and Chapter 3).

In Napatan times, there are different types of evidence for goldworking in Lower and Upper Nubia. A relief of Queen Kadimalo from Semna-West indicates early Napatan awareness of the importance of controlling gold sources.[76] It mentions a victory over enemies in the "mountains of gold", implying a quick takeover of the gold mines following the Pharaonic withdrawal at the end of the New Kingdom. These mines seem to be in the Wadi Allaqi and the Eastern Desert.

A similar takeover and, as such, continuous use of Kerma and New Kingdom mines during the Napatan should be considered for Upper Nubia. Here, current fieldwork by the DiverseNile Project in the region from Attab to Ferka has the potential to shed new light on gold mining and processing in the *longue durée*. For

69 See Guerra 2023a; Quirke 2023.
70 Minor 2023.
71 Wenig 1978, 43; Priese 1999; Kendall 1999, 114; Török 2009, 311–312.
72 Lacovara and Markowitz 2019, 118.
73 Kendall 1999, 114.
74 For such a view see Klemm, Klemm and Murr 2001, 656.
75 Klemm and Klemm 2013, 611.
76 Eide et al. 1994, 35–41; Darnell 2006, 49.

instance, Vila interpreted site 3-P-34 at Ginis East as a New Kingdom gold exploitation site with clear wadi working traces and a significant amount of stone tools and pottery (Fig. 6).[77] However, recent observations suggest continuous activity at the site in Ramesside, Pre-Napatan and Napatan times, primarily based on the ceramic analysis.[78]

Gold objects like exquisite burial goods deposited in the earliest Napatan tumuli at el-Kurru are further indications that by early Napatan times gold production was already flourishing.[79] Agreeing with Peter Lacovara and Yvonne Markowitz, it has to be acknowledged that the Kushites also considered gold a strong part of their (economic) identity.[80] The mid-Napatan Period, i.e. during the 25th Dynasty, was the peak of Nubian control of gold producing areas and key trade routes.[81] Frequent royal inscriptions attest to the importance of gold and highlight Napatan rulers' numerous donations of gold to various temples[82] and the topic of abundant gold remains a common theme throughout the Napatan royal inscriptions.[83]

Nubians' intrinsic and continuous relationship with gold, long after the New Kingdom, was manifested in characteristic types of gold objects. The best examples are unique gold nuggets used as pendants in the Napatan and Meroitic Periods.[84] These have no parallels in Egypt or New Kingdom Nubia, but there is an earlier example of a gold nugget from Buhen in the Egyptian Second Intermediate Period.[85] This object probably came from Kerma, which was the ruling power in Lower Nubia during this period. These Nubian gold nuggets suggest an uninterrupted appreciation for natural materials (gold and various stones), which is a common practice in Nubian cultures.[86]

Continuity of goldworking traditions in Napatan times is also supported by Nubian crafted gold objects which are embedded in a long-lasting practice, beginning, at least, as early as the Kerma Period. Kerman goldwork in turn influenced, through New Kingdom Nubian models, later Napatan and Meroitic jewellery, examples include a granulated gold pendant from Ku. Tum. 1 at el-Kurru.[87] Granulation was a challenging technique only seldom used in Egypt during the Middle Kingdom and the New Kingdom.[88] Additionally, the pendant's rhombic design consists of a distinctive Nubian pattern, which was part of local stylistic repertoires for millennia.[89] This object's characteristic style, without contemporary parallels in Egypt, suggests a knowledge transfer within Nubia itself, where the granulation technique was in use since the Kerma Period.[90] Granulated gold objects continue to appear in the Meroitic Period.

Cylinder sheaths from Nuri, probably used as handles for fans or sistra,[91] support an independent expertise and continuous history of gold exploitation and use in Nubia.[92] These objects were made of gilded silver, a technique rarely used in Egypt, but known in Nubia since the Kerma Period (e.g., gilded-ivory fly pendants).[93] The decoration of the Napatan cylinder sheaths usually includes depictions of winged goddesses, which might suggest a connection with gender and queenship.[94] Unknown in Egypt, the extraordinary concept of Kushite queenship is reflected in the unique nature of these objects.[95]

Napatan gold objects illuminate aspects of Nubia's internal 'golden' history – unlike previously thought – it was not interrupted by the Egyptian colonial period, but continued from Kerma times through to the subsequent Meroitic Period when gold played a major role in the religious activity of Nubian rulers.[96]

77 Vila 1977, 94. See also Klemm and Klemm 2013, 568, 571, fig. 6.224.
78 Budka 2019, 21; Budka 2020a, 69.
79 Török 1997, 119.
80 Lacovara and Markowitz 2019, 118–119.
81 Eide et al. 1994, 164–176.
82 Eide et al. 1996, 438–464.
83 For example, on the Nastasen Stela, see Eide et al. 1996, 471–501.
84 Lacovara and Markowitz 2019, 27. See also Quirke 2023.
85 Bourriau 2003, 194–195.
86 For the use of natural stones in Nubian temples see Wildung 2016 with references. Note, however, that there is also evidence in Egypt for natural pebbles, see Budka 2020b, 264 with examples.
87 Dunham 1950, 13; Markowitz and Doxey 2014, 108.
88 Lacovara and Markowitz 2019, 44. See also Wilde 2013, 138; Lilyquist 1993. For a recent overview of granulation in Egypt see Guerra and Meeks 2023.
89 Kendall 1999, 14.
90 Lacovara and Markowitz 2019, 82.
91 Wenig 1978, 194; Gänsicke and Kendall 2004, 30–31; Pompei 2019, 59–74.
92 Lacovara and Markowitz 2019, 146–148.
93 Lacovara and Markowitz 2019, 85.
94 Gänsicke and Kendall 2004; Pompei 2019.
95 See Lohwasser 2001.
96 See Lacovara and Markowitz 2019.

Discussion and outlook

The archaeological evidence for indigenous goldworking in Bronze Age Nubia is patchy at best, and makes it difficult to understand the complete picture. However, new archaeological findings force us to develop an alternative narrative to the one previously established using Egyptian textual sources. In general, despite the current lack of studies on Nubian jewellery-making technologies, the goldworking business was well established in ancient Sudan during Kerma times. Gold mining in the Middle Nile Valley and the Eastern desert requires, without a doubt, specific expertise and it is likely that newly founded New Kingdom sites would have built on this local expertise. Furthermore, already before the New Kingdom there are traces of large gold mining sites in the Nile Valley, including in marginal regions of the Kerma empire, for example, in the Batn el-Hagar, the Attab-Ferka region and the Fourth Cataract (see Chapter 3). Peripheral regions like Ginis, Duweishat and Hosh el-Guruf have significant potential for a more complete and nuanced understanding of gold procurement in ancient Sudan. The Kerma Kingdom had a complex trade network, was closely connected to the Hyksos kings, and participated in globalisation processes of the Middle Bronze Age.[97] The indigenous use of Nubian gold as an important resource has previously been underestimated.

Finished objects, especially items like jewellery illustrate the expertise and skilled craftmanship of Nubian goldsmiths – irrespective of whether the gold fly pendants, the penannular earrings or other shapes and techniques are of purely Nubian origin or not.[98] As argued above, New Kingdom goldworking should be seen as a dynamic enterprise with various actors, including Egyptians, Nubians and possibly also Asiatics.[99]

To conclude, the rich evidence for Napatan and Meroitic goldworking can be used as an argument to support the long-lasting tradition of gold as an identity marker in ancient Sudan, at least from the Kerma Period onwards. Like other techniques, Nubian goldworking did not happen in an isolated sphere but in close exchange with its northern neighbours and also with desert tribes. Nubian gold processing actively influenced Egyptian goldworking and examples, such as the overseer of goldworkers Khnummose from New Kingdom Sai, illustrate the complex and entangled history of goldworking of which the complete story still waits to be written.

Acknowledgments

This chapter was written during the ERC DiverseNile Project. The project received funding from the European Research Council (ERC) under the European Union's Horizon 2020 research and innovation programme (grant agreement No. 865463). Permission to work in the field in the MUAFS concession was kindly granted by the National Corporation for Antiquities and Museums, Sudan (NCAM). Our sincere thanks go to Ghalia Garelnabi (Acting Director General in 2022), Ibrahim Musa Hamdoon (Director General in 2023) and Abdel Hai Abdel Sawy (Director of Fieldwork) as well as Huda Magzoub Elbashir (Inspector). I am grateful to all MUAFS team members involved in relevant fieldwork and especially the researchers of the ERC DiverseNile Project. Veronica Hinterhuber contributed to the assessment of the Napatan goldworking in 2021, Rennan Lemos to discussion on colonial perspectives in 2021 and 2022 and Sofia Patrevita to aspects of goldsmithing in 2022. Special thanks go to Chloë Ward for improving the written English of this text.

97 See Miniaci 2020.

98 For a recent discussion of the penannular earrings see Guerra 2023b.

99 This is also very evident in the famous so-called International Style of the Late Bronze Age – following Feldman 2006, I would argue that the identification of the origins of motifs/shapes is of less interest than to understand the hybridity and diversity of the complete process of production.

Bibliography

Ahrens, A. and Kopetzky, K.
2021 Difficult times and drastic solutions: the diffusion of looted Middle Kingdom objects found in the northern Levant, Egypt and Nubia, in: M. Bietak and S. Prell (eds.), *The Enigma of the Hyksos, volume IV: Changing Clusters and Migration in the Near Eastern Bronze Age. Collected papers of a workshop held in Vienna 4th-6th of December 2019*, Contributions to the Archaeology of Egypt, Nubia and the Levant 12, Wiesbaden, 253–313.

Aldred, C.
1971 *Jewels of the Pharaohs*, London.

Auenmüller, J.
2020a Nubisches Gold und ägyptische Präsenz: Pharaonische Goldgewinnung in der Nubischen Wüste, in: M. Kasper, R. Rollinger, A. Rudigier and K. Ruffing (eds.), *Wirtschaften in den Bergen. Von Bergleuten, Hirten, Bauern, Künstlern, Händlern und Unternehmern*, Wien, 37–54.
2020b Chapter 6: People on Sai: Prosopographical contributions to the 'social fabric' of Sai in the New Kingdom, in: J. Budka, *AcrossBorders 2: Living in New Kingdom Sai.* With contributions by Johannes Auenmüller, Annette M. Hansen, Frits Heinrich, Veronica Hinterhuber, Ptolemaios Paxinos, Nadja Pöllath, Helmut Sattmann, Sara Schnedl and Martina Ullmann, Archaeology of Egypt, Sudan and the Levant 1, Vienna, 365–394.

Bestock, L.
2020 Egyptian fortresses and the colonization of Lower Nubia in the Middle Kingdom, in: G. Emberling and B.B. Williams (eds.), *The Oxford Handbook of Ancient Nubia*, Oxford, 271–288.

Bourriau, J.
2003 The Second Intermediate Period (c. 1650–1550 BC), in: I. Shaw (ed.) *The Oxford History of Ancient Egypt*, Oxford, 184–217.

Breasted, J.H.
1906 *The Temples of Lower Nubia*, Chicago.

Brovarski, E., Doll, S.K. and Freed, R.E. (eds.)
1982 *Egypt's Golden Age. The Art of Living in the New Kingdom 1558–1085 B.C.*, Boston.

Budka, J.
2019 Towards Middle Nile biographies: The Munich University Attab to Ferka survey project 2018/2019, *Sudan & Nubia* 23, 13–26.
2020a Kerma presence at Ginis East: the 2020 season of the Munich University Attab to Ferka survey project, *Sudan & Nubia* 24, 57–71.
2020b *AcrossBorders 2: Living in New Kingdom Sai.* With contributions by Johannes Auenmüller, Annette M. Hansen, Frits Heinrich, Veronica Hinterhuber, Ptolemaios Paxinos, Nadja Pöllath, Helmut Sattmann, Sara Schnedl and Martina Ullmann, Archaeology of Egypt, Sudan and the Levant 1, Vienna
2021a Review: Davies, W. Vivian and Derek A. Welsby (eds) 2020. Travelling the Korosko Road: archaeological exploration in Sudan's Eastern Desert. Sudan Archaeological Research Society Publication 24. Oxford: Archaeopress, *Beiträge zur Sudanforschung* 13, 177–185.
2021b *Tomb 26 on Sai Island: A New Kingdom Elite Tomb and its Relevance for Sai and Beyond*, Leiden.
2022 Early New Kingdom settlement activities in the periphery of Sai Island: towards a contextualisation of fresh evidence from Attab West, *Der antike Sudan. Mitteilungen der Sudanarchäologischen Gesellschaft zu Berlin e.V.* 33, 45–61.
2023 Investigating Nubian funerary practices of marginal communities: new evidence from a Kerma cemetery at Ginis, *Egitto e Vicino Oriente* 45 (2022), 37–62.

Budka, J., Rose, K. and Ward, C.
2023 Cultural diversity in the Bronze Age in the Attab to Ferka region: new results based on excavations in 2023, *Der antike Sudan. Mitteilungen der Sudanarchäologischen Gesellschaft zu Berlin e.V.* 34, 19–35.

Bulsinski, M.
2015 *Egyptian Gold Jewellery*, Turnhout.

Castiglioni, A. and Castiglioni, A.
2020a The gold mines of Kerma and exploration of the South-Eastern Nubian Desert, in: W.V. Davies and D.A. Welsby (eds.), *Travelling the Korosko Road: Archaeological Exploration in Sudan's Eastern Desert*, Sudan Archaeological Research Society Publication 24, Oxford, 11–21.
2020b The tracks of Egyptian penetration, in: W.V. Davies and D.A. Welsby (eds.), *Travelling the Korosko Road: Archaeological Exploration in Sudan's Eastern Desert*, Sudan Archaeological Research Society Publication 24, Oxford, 22–47.

Castiglioni, A., Castiglioni, A. and Bonnet, C.
2010 The gold mines of the Kingdom of Kerma, in: W. Godlewski and A. Łajtar (eds.), *Between the Cataracts: Proceedings of the 11th Conference for Nubian Studies, Warsaw University 27 August – 2 September 2006*, Warsaw, 263–270.

Cooper, J.
2018 Kushites expressing 'Egyptian' kingship: Nubian dynasties in hieroglyphic texts and a phantom Kushite king, *Ägypten & Levante* 28, 143–168.
2021 Between the Nile and the Red Sea: Medjay desert polities in the third to first millennium BCE, *Old World: Journal of Ancient Africa and Eurasia*, 1–22.

Dalton, M., Spencer, N., Macklin, M.G., Woodward, J.C. and Ryan, P.
2023 Three thousand years of river channel engineering in the Nile Valley, *Geoarchaeology* 38, 565–587, https://doi.org/10.1002/gea.21965.

Darnell, J.C.
2006 *The Inscription of Queen Katimala at Semna: Textual Evidence for the Origins of the Napatan State,* Yale Egyptological Studies 7, New Haven.

Davies, N. de Garis and Gardiner, A.H.
1926 *The Tomb of Huy, Viceroy of Nubia in the Reign of Tutankhamun (no. 40)*, London.

Davies, W.V.
2003 Kush in Egypt: a new historical inscription, *Sudan & Nubia* 7, 52–54.
2020 Securing the gold of Wawat: Pharaonic inscriptions in the Sudanese-Nubian Eastern Desert, in: W.V. Davies and D.A. Welsby (eds.), *Travelling the Korosko Road: Archaeological Exploration in Sudan's Eastern Desert*, Sudan Archaeological Research Society Publication 24, Oxford, 185–220.

Dunham, D.
1950 *The Royal Cemeteries of Kush I. El Kurru*, Cambridge, MA.

Edwards, D.N. (ed.).
2020 *The Archaeological Survey of Sudanese Nubia, 1963–69. The Pharaonic Sites*, Sudan Archaeological Research Society Publication 23, Oxford.

Eide, T., Hägg, T., Pierce, R.H. and Török, L. (eds.)
1994 *Fontes Historiae Nubiorum. Textual Sources for the History of the Middle Nile Region Between the Eighth Century BC and the Sixth Century AD.* Vol. I: From the Eighth to the Mid-Fifth Century BC, Bergen.
1996 *Fontes Historiae Nubiorum. Textual Sources for the History of the Middle Nile Region Between the Eighth Century BC and the Sixth Century AD.* Vol. II: From the Mid-Fifth to the First Century BC, Bergen.

Emberling, G. and Williams, B.
2010 The kingdom of Kush in the 4th cataract: Archaeological salvage of the Oriental Institute Nubian Expedition 2007 season, Part 1: Preliminary report on the sites of Hosh el-Guruf and El-Widay, *Gdańsk Archaeological Museum African Reports* 7, 17–38.

Feldman, M.H.
2006 *Diplomacy by Design: Luxury Arts and an "International Style" in the Ancient Near East, 1400–1200 BCE*, Chicago; London.

Gänsicke, S. and Kendall, T.
2004 A fresh look at the cylinder sheaths from Nuri, Sudan, in: T. Kendall (ed.) *Nubian Studies 1998. Proceedings of the Ninth Conference of the International Society of Nubian Studies August 21-26, 1998, Boston, Massachusetts*, Boston, MA, 24–33.

Gratien, B.
2004 From Egypt to Kush: administrative practices and movements of goods during the Middle Kingdom and the Second Intermediate Period, in: T. Kendall (ed.), *Nubian Studies 1998: proceedings of the Ninth Conference of the International Society of Nubian Studies, August 21-26, 1998, Boston, Massachusetts*, Boston, MA, 74–82.

Guerra, M.F.
2023a Towards a conclusion: Qurna in context, in: M.F. Guerra, M. Martinón-Torres and S. Quirke (eds.), *Ancient Egyptian Gold: Archaeology and Science in Jewellery (3500–1000 BC*), Cambridge, 449–480.
2023b Making pennanular ear ornaments in Egypt, in: M.F. Guerra, M. Martinón-Torres and S. Quirke (eds.), *Ancient Egyptian Gold: Archaeology and Science in Jewellery (3500–1000 BC*), Cambridge, 369–386.

Guerra, M.F. and Meeks, N.
2023 Granulation in Egypt and the cylindrical amulet from Haraga, in: M.F. Guerra, M. Martinón-Torres and S. Quirke (eds.), *Ancient Egyptian Gold: Archaeology and Science in Jewellery (3500–1000 BC*), Cambridge, 279–286.

Guerra, M.F., Martinón-Torres, M. and Quirke, S. (eds.)
2023 *Ancient Egyptian Gold: Archaeology and Science in Jewellery (3500–1000 BC)*, Cambridge.

Harrell, J.A.
2010 Archaeological geology of Hosh el-Guruf, Fourth Nile Cataract, Sudan, *Gdańsk Archaeological Museum African Reports* 7, 71–83.

Hinterhuber, V.
2021 *Evidence for Kerma settlements and an intriguing dry-stone structure in Kosha East*, blog post, 13 May 2021. Available online at https://www.sudan-survey.gwi.uni-muenchen.de/index.php/2021/05/13/evidence-for-kerma-settlements-and-an-intriguing-dry-stone-structure-in-kosha-east/ <last accessed 13 June 2022>.

Kendall, T.
1999 The origin of the Napatan state: El Kurru and the evidence for the royal ancestors, in: S. Wenig (ed.) *Akten der 7. Internationalen Tagung für meroitistische Forschungen vom 14. bis 19. September 1992 in Gosen/bei Berlin*, Meroitica, Schriften zur altsudanesischen Geschichte und Archäologie 15, Wiesbaden, 3–117.

Kitchen, K.A.
1980 *Ramesside Inscriptions III*, Oxford.

Klemm, D. and Klemm, R.
2017 New Kingdom and early Kushite gold mining in Nubia, in N. Spencer, A. Stevens and M. Binder (eds.), *Nubia in the New Kingdom. Lived Experience, Pharaonic Control and Indigenous Traditions*, British Museum Publications on Egypt and Sudan 3, Leuven, 259–270.

Klemm, D., Klemm, R. and Murr, A.
2001 Gold of the Pharaohs – 6000 years of gold mining in Egypt and Nubia, *Journal of African Earth Sciences* 33, 643–659.

Klemm, R. and Klemm, D.
2013 *Gold and Gold Mining in Ancient Egypt and Nubia*, New York.

Lacovara, P. and Markowitz, Y.
2019 *Nubian Gold: Ancient Jewellery from Sudan and Egypt*, Cairo.

Lilyquist, C.
1993 Granulation and glass: Chronological and stylistic investigations at selected sites, ca. 2500–1400 B. C. E.,

Bulletin of the American Schools of Oriental Research 290/291, 29–94.

Liszka, K.
2017 Dry-stone architecture at Wadi el-Hudi, Wadi es-Sebua, and the Eastern Desert, *Journal of Egyptian Archaeology* 103/1, 35–51.

Lohwasser, A.
2001 Der Thronschatz der Königin Amanishakheto, in: C.-B. Arnst, I. Hafemann and A. Lohwasser (eds.), *Begegnungen. Antike Kulturen im Niltal. Festgabe für Erika Endesfelder, Karl-Heinz Priese, Walter Friedrich Reineke und Steffen Wenig*, Leipzig, 285–302.

Manzo, A.
2020 The Nubian and Pharaonic ceramic materials, in: W.V. Davies and D.A. Welsby (eds.), *Travelling the Korosko Road: Archaeological Exploration in Sudan's Eastern Desert*, Sudan Archaeological Research Society Publication 24, Oxford, 68–83.

Markowitz, Y. and Doxey, D.
2014 *Jewels of Ancient Nubia*, Boston.

Meyer, C.
2010 The Kingdom of Kush in the 4th Cataract: Archaeological salvage of the Oriental Institute Nubian Expedition 2007 season, Part II: Grinding stones and gold mining at Hosh el Guruf, Sudan, *Gdańsk Archaeological Museum African Reports* 7, 39–52.

Miniaci, G.
2020 At the dawn of the Late Bronze Age "globalization": the (re)-circulation of Egyptian artefacts in Nubia and the northern Levant in the MB II–mid MB III (c. 1710–1550 BC), *Claroscuro* 19 (2).

Miniaci, G. and Lacovara, P. (eds.)
2022 *The Treasure of the Egyptian Queen Ahhotep and International Relations at the Turn of the Middle Bronze Age (1600–1500 BCE)*, Middle Kingdom Studies 11, London.

Minor, E.
2012 *The Use of Egyptian and Egyptianizing Material Culture in Nubian Burials of the Classic Kerma Period*, PhD Thesis, University of California, Berkeley.
2023 Faience tiles from Deir el-Ballas and Kerma: new evidence of Egyptian-Nubian relations at the foundation of the New Kingdom, in: D. Kiser-Go and C.A. Redmount (eds.), *Weseretkau "Mighty of Kas": Papers in Memory of Cathleen A. Keller*, Columbus, GA, 103–116.

Morris, E.
2018 *Ancient Egyptian Imperialism*, Hoboken, NJ; Chichester.

Mourad, A.-L.
2017 Asiatics and Levantine(-influenced) products in Nubia: evidence from the Middle Kingdom to the early Second Intermediate Period, *Ägypten & Levante* 27, 381–401.

Müller, I.
2013 *Die Verwaltung Nubiens im Neuen Reich*, Meroitica, Schriften zur altsudanesischen Geschichte und Archäologie 18, Wiesbaden.

Patch, D.C.
2005 Jewelry in the early Eighteenth Dynasty, in: C.H. Roehrig, R. Dreyfus and C.A. Keller (eds.), *Hatshepsut: from Queen to Pharaoh*, New York, 191–195.

Patrevita, S.
2022 *...on the traces of Nubian goldsmithing: Gold bezels and goldsmiths and goldsmiths*, blog post, 10 Dec 2022. Available online at https://www.sudansurvey.gwi.uni-muenchen.de/index.php/2022/12/10/on-the-traces-of-nubian-goldsmithing-gold-bezels-and-goldsmiths/ <last accessed 13 October 2023>.

Pompei, A.
2019 *Napatan Cylindrical Sheaths: A Catalogue and Analysis of Precious Objects From the Royal Cemetery of Nuri*, BAR International Series 2948, Oxford.

Quirke, S.
2023 Centres of goldworking in ancient Egypt: Egyptological questions and sources, in: M.F. Guerra, M. Martinón-Torres and S. Quirke (eds.), *Ancient Egyptian Gold: Archaeology and Science in Jewellery (3500–1000 BC)*, Cambridge, 27–74.

Rainey, A.F.
2015 *The el-Amarna Correspondence*, Leiden.

Rega, F.M.
2020 Preliminary study of the macro-lithic tools collected by CeRDO in the Sudanese Eastern Desert, in: W.V. Davies and D.A. Welsby (eds.), *Travelling the Korosko Road: Archaeological Exploration in Sudan's Eastern Desert*, Sudan Archaeological Research Society Publication 24, Oxford, 99–124.

Retzmann, A., Budka, J., Sattmann, H., Irrgeher, J. and Prohaska, T.
2019 The New Kingdom population on Sai Island: application of Sr isotopes to investigate cultural entanglement in ancient Nubia, *Ägypten & Levante* 29, 355–380.

Ruffieux, P. and Bashir, M.S.
2020 The Korosko Road Project: Final report on the pottery, in: W.V. Davies and D.A. Welsby (eds.), *Travelling the Korosko Road: Archaeological Exploration in Sudan's Eastern Desert*, Sudan Archaeological Research Society Publication 24, Oxford, 164–181.

Sethe, K.
1907 *Urkunden der 18. Dynastie*. Abteilung IV, Band III, Heft 9-12, Leipzig.

Smith, H.S.
1994 The princes of Seyala in Lower Nubia in the predynastic and protodynastic periods, in: C. Berger, G. Clerc and N. Grimal (eds.), *Hommages à Jean Leclant, Vol. II*, Bibliothèque d'Étude 106.2, Cairo, 361–376.

Smith, S.T.
2020 The Nubian experience of Egyptian domination during the New Kingdom, in: G. Emberling and B.B. Williams (eds.), *The Oxford Handbook of Ancient Nubia*, Oxford, 369–394.

de Souza, A.
2020 Pots, gold, and viceroys: shifting dynamics of Egyptian-Nubian relations at the transition to the New Kingdom, from the viewpoint of Middle Nubian pottery at Tell Edfu, *Ägypten & Levante* 30, 313–343.

Spalinger, A.J.
2006 Covetous eyes south: the background to Egypt, in: E.H. Cline and D. O'Connor (eds.), *Thutmose III: A New Biography*, Ann Arbor, 344–369.

Spence, K., Rose, P.J., Bradshaw, R., Collet, P., Hassan, A., MacGinnis, J., Masson, A. and van Pelt, P.
2011 Sesebi 2011, *Sudan & Nubia* 15, 34–38.

Steindorff, G.
1937 *Aniba. Zweiter Band*, Service des Antiquités de l'Egypte. Mission archéologique de Nubie 1929–1934, Glückstadt.

Stevens, A. and Garnett, A.
2017 Surveying the Pharaonic Desert Hinterland of Amara West, in: N. Spencer, A. Stevens and M. Binder (eds.), *Nubia in the New Kingdom: Lived Experience, Pharaonic Control and Indigenous Traditions*, British Museum Publications on Egypt and Sudan 3, Leuven, 227–306.

Török, L.
2009 *Between Two Worlds. The Frontier Region between Ancient Nubia and Egypt 3700 BC–500 AD*, Probleme der Ägyptologie 29, Leiden; Boston.

Vercoutter, J.
1959 The gold of Kush, *Kush* 7, 120–153.

Vila, A.
1976 *La prospection archéologique de la vallée du Nil au sud de la Cataracte de Dal. Fascicule 4: District de Mograkka (Est et Ouest). District de Kosha (Est et Ouest)*, Paris.
1977 *La prospection archéologique de la vallée du Nil au Sud de la Cataracte de Dal (Nubie Soudanaise). Fascicule 5: District de Ginis (Est et Ouest)*, Paris.

Vieth, J.
2018 *Die ägyptischen Tempelstädte des Neuen Reiches in Nubien: Eine siedlungs- und landschaftsarchäologische Studie*, PhD dissertation, Ludwig-Maximilians-Universität München. Available at: https://edoc.ub.uni-muenchen.de/24988/ <last accessed 08. September 2023>.

Walsh, C.
2022 Marginal communities and cooperative strategies in the Kerma pastoral state, *Journal of Ancient Near Eastern History* 9 (2), 195–220.

Wenig, S.
1978 *Africa in Antiquity. The Arts of Ancient Nubia and the Sudan II. The Catalogue*, New York.

Wilde, H.
2013 Technologie und Kommunikation. Innovationsschübe vor dem Hintergrund der Außenbeziehungen Altägyptens, in: E. Kaiser and W. Schier (eds.) *Mobilität und Wissenstransfer in diachroner und interdisziplinärer Perspektive*, Berlin; Boston, 115–150.

Wildung, D.
2014–2015 Prähistorische Votive in einem meroitischen Heiligtum, *Mitteilungen des Deutschen Archäologischen Instituts, Abteilung Kairo* 70–71, 463–469.

Williams, B.
2020 Kush in the wider world during the Kerma period, in: G. Emberling and B.B. Williams (eds.), *The Oxford Handbook of Ancient Nubia*, Oxford, 179–200.

Zibelius-Chen, K.
1994 Die Kubanstele Ramses II. und die nubischen Goldregionen, in: C. Berger, G. Clerc and N. Grimal (eds.), *Hommages à Jean Leclant, Vol. II*, Bibliothèque d'Étude 106.2, Cairo, 411–417.
2013 Nubien wird ägyptische Kolonie, in: S. Wenig and K. Zibelius-Chen (eds.), *Die Kulturen Nubiens – ein afrikanisches Vermächtnis*, Dettelbach, 135–155.

Part III

Animal and vegetal resources and foodways in ancient Sudan

Introduction

Foodways in ancient Sudan

Julia Budka

Cooking practices and foodways in general provide information on a range of aspects, including social ones such as subsistence strategies, nutrition, and health.[1] In the Nile Valley they are often considered in relation cultural diversity. Randi Haaland has labelled Nubia as "a culinary cross-road between Africa and the Near East."[2] The obvious contrast between Sahelian Africa with its 'Porridge-and-Pot' culinary tradition and the 'Bread-and-Oven' world in Egypt has been discussed based on ethnographic, archaeological, iconographic and textual evidence.[3] To contextualise this contrast, Elena Garcea highlights the importance of sorghum in prehistoric Sudan, used as both temper in pottery and of course for consumption in the form of porridge (Chapter 5). The topic of early food production in Sudan is therefore essential to understand developments in later periods. For example, we can trace bread consumption in elite contexts with ritual functions at Kerma and Meroe.[4]

After the New Kingdom, Jeremy Pope suggested, using textual evidence, that the porridge-tradition in Sudan could be a possible Napatan social marker.[5] The question arises whether similar social reflections can also be found in the multicultural and dynamic setting of Bronze Age Sudan. In any case, the appearance of Egyptian-style bread moulds at Kerma city dated to before the heyday of the site during Classic Kerma times, is remarkable and indicative of the above mentioned "culinary cross-road", suggesting an integration of at least some aspects of the 'Bread-and-Oven' world in Nubia as early the Bronze Age, at least in elite ritual contexts.[6]

More recently, multidisciplinary approaches have focused on food traditions in Sudan, in particular during the Napatan and Meroitic Periods (i.e., the Iron Age).[7] These preliminary studies suggest heterogeneous Napatan food cultures. This heterogeneity can be explained through the existence of complex encounters between the local Nubian population and foreigners, specifically Egyptians in these Iron Age Periods. Recent advances in understanding the domestication of summer crops such as sorghum[8] also highlight regional patterns, stressing that we must consider several "Nubias" when it comes to foodways (see Chapters 7 and 9 in this volume).[9]

A review of ethnographic, archaeological, iconographic and epigraphic evidence regarding culinary traditions in the Middle Nile from a diachronic perspective still needs to be undertaken.[10] Textual sources, representations, and archaeological data are available for several periods and traditions which means that transformations of social practices in various communities, on both a regional and supra-regional level, can be addressed from a historical perspective. As is shown by Stuart Tyson Smith in Chapter 9, foodways in New Kingdom Nubia are especially well traceable and appear as highly complex.

Most of the contributions in this part of the volume illustrate the large variety of evidentiary sources and approaches for the study of food in ancient Sudan, including animal and vegetal resources and various aspects of foodways. Prehistorian Elena Garcea presents a chapter on early food production and food producers in prehistoric Sudan (Chapter 5) including a discussion on the importance of cattle and cattle cultures in Sudan. This ties in nicely with the assessment of the C-Group cattle management in the Second Cataract area by Shayla Monroe (Chapter 6). She focuses on regional variations in the morphology of cattle in Kerma, Lower Nubia and Pharaonic Egypt and discusses the potential for different land use between these territories due to both variations in local ecology, and divergent political strategies and their consequences for pastoralist production.

1 See, e.g., Gosden and Hather 1999; Twiss 2019 for the general importance of food studies in archaeology; Graff 2020 for an archaeology of cuisine and cooking.

2 Haaland 2009.

3 E.g. Haaland 2007; Haaland 2009; Haaland 2012.

4 Haaland 2012.

5 Pope 2013 and, after substantial criticism also as a slightly revised version, Pope 2018.

6 For bread moulds at Kerma see Chaix and Grant 1993, 402–403 with references. A diachronic study of bread moulds in ancient Sudan is still pending and a clear desideratum; well-known are the Napatan and Meroitic bread moulds, see, e.g., Anderson et al. 2007, 89–90 with references and a discussion whether bread was actually made in these moulds or something else (there is evidence of the use of sorghum at Dangeil, whereas wheat and barley are attested in Lower Nubian sites like Qasr Ibrim).

7 Baldi 2018; Matthews and Nowotnick 2019; Nowotnick and Matthews 2020; Nowotnick and Matthews 2022.

8 See Fuller 2004; Fuller 2013; Fuller and Lucas 2020.

9 See Lemos 2020.

10 See Baldi 2018.

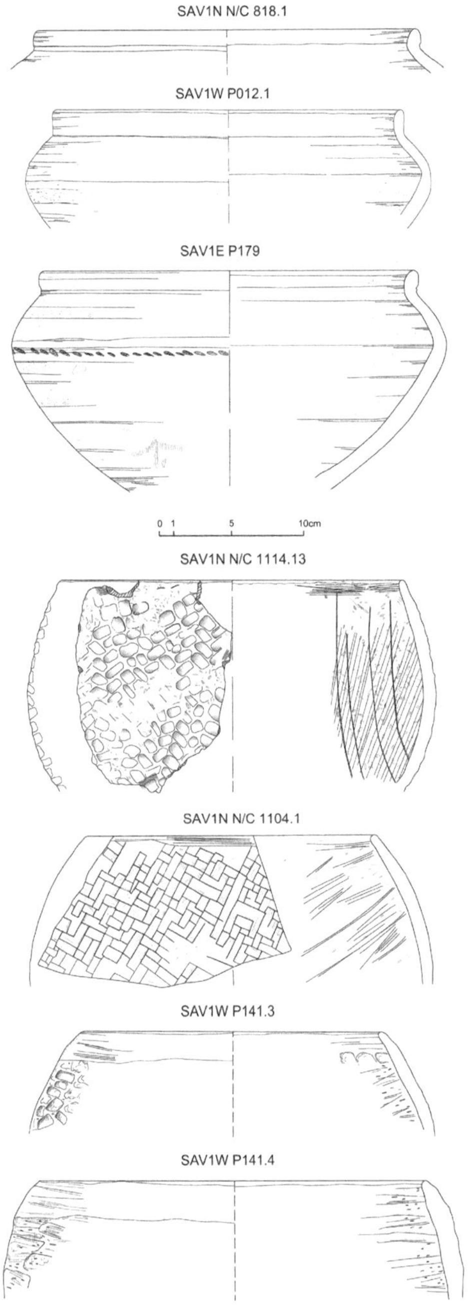

Fig. 1 Examples of Egyptian-style and Nubian-style cooking vessels from the New Kingdom town of Sai (illustration by J. Budka, ©AcrossBorders Project).

Frits Heinrich, Annette Hansen and Philippa Ryan discuss the management of vegetal resources in Bronze Age Nubia, using Sai Island (18th Dynasty town) and Amara West (Ramesside town) as their main case studies, providing a perspective from colonial towns during the New Kingdom (Chapter 7). They show the complex interplay of water availability, seasonality, geology, and technology and how this co-determines the vegetation and the nature of agriculture. The results reflect resilience strategies and a sophisticated circular economic system in Bronze Age Sudan built on a diverse crop curriculum, a wide range of managed wild plant resources, and the use of crop processing waste for non-food products.[11]

An interdisciplinary method relevant for food studies is offered by Sarah Schrader and Michele Buzon in their contribution on isotopic and skeletal approaches to diet and mobility in Nubia (Chapter 8). This chapter illustrates the important role the study of isotopes has for migration studies in the Middle Nile, in particular for New Kingdom Nubia, as well as the rich potential for future isotope analysis in the region.

This part of the book is concluded by Stuart Tyson Smith (Chapter 9) on foodways and cultural entanglements in New Kingdom Nubia, demonstrating the embeddedness of food in social and political history. He focuses on domestic foodways and presents data from Askut in Lower Nubia and Tombos in Upper Nubia; intercultural interactions between colonists and local populations and their impact on diet and food are also discussed.

Foodways in Bronze Age Sudan: an overview

There are many rich sources of information for the study of food cultures in Bronze Age Sudan, especially from the Nile Valley. Primary sources include cooking wares, particular through the use organic residue analysis, faunal remains and botanical remains from domestic sites, and also material from cemeteries.

Cooking wares in Bronze Age Sudan

Ceramics are well attested throughout the ages and vessels connected with eating, cooking and storage are commonly found in Bronze Age settlements. There are clear differences regarding the Egyptian-style and the Nubian-style corpora, not only in terms of shape but also regarding the technology with Egyptian vessels typically being wheel-made, as opposed to their hand-made Nubian counterparts (Fig. 1).[12] Egyptian style cooking pots of the 18th Dynasty found both in Egypt proper and in Sudan tell an intriguing story of cultural entanglement and intercultural intermingling. This includes not just the importation of vessels from Egypt and the mechanisms involved, but also the existence of hybrid vessels, as well as the two-directional technological and manufactural exchanges evident in the production of ceramic cooking vessels.[13]

11 This is nicely comparable to a recent study (Le Moyne et al. 2023) on ecological flexibility between the Neolithic and Kerma Periods at the site of Kadruka.

12 See Smith 2003; Budka 2019 with references.

13 See Budka 2016; Budka 2020, 221–226 with references; see also Chapters 9 and 12, this volume. Hybrid vessels are also attested at various sites in Egypt, especially at Elephantine and Edfu, see Raue 2017; de Souza 2020.

Most excavated New Kingdom sites in Nubia (e.g., urban sites like Sai Island, Amara West, Sesebi, but also rural sites like AtW 001 and AtW 002 in the hinterland of Sai) show a side-by-side use of Egyptian wheel-made cooking pots and Nubian-style hand-made pots with basketry impression or incised decoration, sometimes with notched rim decoration or black-topped rims (see above, Introduction to Part I and below, Chapter 9).[14]

Within the framework of cultural encounters in the Middle Nile Valley during the Bronze Age, the amount, size and shape of different cooking vessels have been used as indicators for common or diverse culinary practices.[15] Seemingly distinctive cuisines have been postulated for the important case study of Askut. Smith notes a high frequency of Nubian cooking pots during the New Kingdom[16] and from this infers the presence Nubian servants and/or wives at Egyptian colonial sites (see also Chapter 9).[17] Despite an association of Nubian cooking pots primarily with Nubian women, there is no direct evidence that cooking was a predominantly female activity.[18] Although I agree with Smith that a gendered structure of household responsibilities is indeed likely (see Chapter 9), we should also consider a situational component for cooking activities.[19] There might have been seasonal differences, as well as regional variations and it is also likely that cooking was not always the task of the same person.

The New Kingdom town of Sai yielded a remarkable composite mixture of Nubian and Egyptian cooking pots – imported and locally made Egyptian wheel-made cooking pots, as well as Nubian-style products were used in the same contexts (see Fig. 1). Interestingly, during Sai's heyday in the later reign of Thutmose III and Amenhotep II, Nubian cooking pot variants outnumber the Egyptian ones and dominate the cooking assemblage, very similar to the findings in Askut (see Chapter 9). By this time, Egyptian style cooking pots are often made in local fabrics and not any longer imported from Egypt. This is particularly significant, as the ceramics corpus from the New Kingdom town of Sai becomes generally more sophisticated in the mid-18th Dynasty and decorated imports from Egypt increase compared to earlier levels. Thus, the cooking pots are more likely to reflect social realities and community practises than trade networks, such as, for example, wine and oil amphoras.

That there might be "close links between ceramic technological production and cultural identity"[20] is shown by several archaeological case studies from various regions in the ancient world. However, findings from New Kingdom Nubia suggest that individual choices and group dynamics were sometimes more significant than cultural identities.[21] We must consider multiple lifestyles within the New Kingdom temple towns which first reflect social practices rather than ethnicity or identity. I believe that hybrid vessels in urban sites like Sai and rural sites like AtW 001 (see above, introduction to Part I) attest to what emerges as a complex mixture of lifestyles which transformed both the indigenous and colonial society, resulting in the new diversity which shaped New Kingdom Nubia and leading to several 'Nubias'.[22]

Faunal and botanical evidence for Nubian foodways

To understand foodways at specific sites and in larger regions, faunal and botanical evidence is of course crucial (see Chapters 5, 6, 7 and 9). For the Kerma Period, preliminary research comparing faunal remains from Kerma city and a rural site (Gism el-Arba) suggests parallels as well as certain differences between the two sites.[23] Research on New Kingdom colonial towns in Nubia emphasise that here, typical "Egyptian" versus typical "Nubian" strategies and corresponding faunal and botanical sets are not found. Rather, intercultural mixing is obvious, supporting the picture provided by ceramic evidence, especially cooking ware.[24]

For faunal remains in colonial Nubia, the evidence for the consumption of fish offers intriguing information about cultural entanglement, as Smith discusses in Chapter 9. Furthermore, the presence of pigs in the temple towns is noteworthy and appears to be linked to the establishment of colonial centres, contrasting with Nubian cultural sites (and maybe of rural sites, but this needs to be confirmed by future research). In New Kingdom Egypt, pork is one of the main sources of meat[25] and a preference for the slaughtering of young animals is evident across different settlements.[26] Similarly, evidence from the northern sector of the Egyptian town of Sai also suggests that during the early New Kingdom pigs were the third most important domesticated species (Fig. 2). They were slaughtered at the optimum age for meat consumption suggesting a similar preference for tasteful and tender meat in 18th Dynasty Sai. It is not surprising that pigs were slaughtered young, since they are sexually active at a very early age and they produce a high number

14 See also Budka 2022 with references.
15 See, e.g., Smith 2003.
16 Smith 2003, 119.
17 Smith 2003, 43–53, 190–193, 204. See also his contribution in this volume, Chapter 9.
18 Smith 1995; Smith 2003; see also Smith this volume for an updated discussion.
19 Budka 2020, 414–415.
20 Pierce 2013, 529.
21 Spencer 2014, 47.
22 See Lemos 2020.
23 See Chaix 2006.
24 See Budka 2020, 420 and Chapter 9 in this volume.
25 See, e.g., Ikram 1995, 29–33; Bertini 2014, 306–308.
26 See, e.g., at Amarna, Kemp 2012, 219–220.

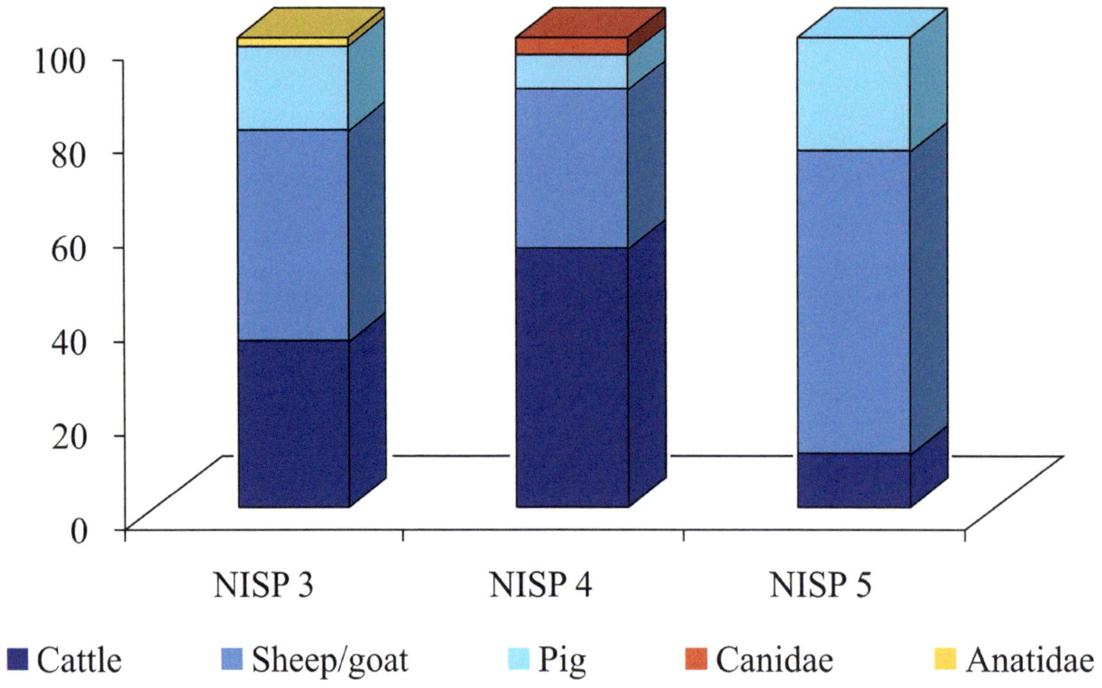

Fig. 2 Distribution of mammal and avian fauna from SAV1 North, Sai Island (NISP%) (illustration and data: Konstantina Saliari, ©AcrossBorders Project).

of piglets. Perhaps the few older pigs at SAV1 North were for breeding purposes.[27] Unfortunately, the faunal remains of pigs from the New Kingdom for this sector at Sai are too ephemeral or poorly preserved to estimate their size.[28]

Pigs have been reported from other Egyptian sites in Nubia, for example at Askut (see Chapter 9), but for now Sai represents one of, if not the, earliest attestations. In Ramesside times, for example, a neonate piglet was found in the western chamber of the pyramid tomb G301 at Cemetery D of Amara West.[29] However, there is only limited evidence for pigs at indigenous Nubian sites prior to Medieval times. They are markedly rare at the site of Kerma, both in the town and in the cemeteries.[30] It can be very tentatively suggested that the presence of pigs in the earliest levels of New Kingdom Sai supports the assessment of the town as founded for colonial purposes with a primarily Egyptian lifestyle.[31] It should be stressed that the percentage of pigs in the earliest level at Sai is higher than in the following phases of occupation (see Fig. 2), which would support an import of these animals from Egypt to Sai for meat consumption during at the time of the town's foundation – when the town was strongly dependent on external supplies.[32]

In regards to crops, the preference for barley or emmer could be a possible indicator of a more "Egyptian" or "Nubian" character of a site.[33] Of the two cereals encountered at New Kingdom Sai, barley is more abundant than emmer wheat. This is like the situation at nearby and partly contemporary Amara West[34] but contrasts with what has been observed in New Kingdom Egypt. It is often suggested that barley primarily served as an ingredient for beer and as animal fodder. The dominance of barley in Egyptian archaeobotanical assemblages until the New Kingdom has led this view to be challenged by botanists who emphasise barley's role as primarily a human food.[35] The apparent dominance of barley over emmer wheat at New Kingdom Sai needs to be investigated further

27 There is evidence for pig pens in the southern part of the town (still unpublished), so breeding very likely took place at Sai.

28 This information is based on an unpublished report by the archaeozoologist working on the faunal remains from SAV1 North, Konstantina Saliari.

29 BINDER, SPENCER and MILLET 2011, 53. Evidence for pigs from the town of Amara West is still unpublished (Neal Spencer, personal communication, September 2023).

30 See, e.g., CHAIX 1988.

31 Also SMITH this volume, interprets the pigs at Askut as evidence for Egyptian influence.

32 See BUDKA 2020, 424–426.

33 See HEINRICH and HANSEN 2020.

34 RYAN 2017.

35 See CAPPERS et al. 2014.

Fig. 3 Hybrid cooking pot MUAFS 082/2023
(photo by J. Budka, photo edits by C. Ward, © DiverseNile Project).

but seems to support a site-specific and colonial Nubia-specific occurrence of crops.[36]

All in all, recent archaeological and bioarchaeological research at Nubian sites in the Nile Valley has led to the understanding that local foodways were established in colonial temple towns, which are neither completely Egyptian nor completely Nubian but rather evidence of a complex cultural entanglement process.

Organic residue analysis

Organic residue analysis (ORA) is useful to understand complex foodways in New Kingdom Nubia in more detail. So far, there has only been one case study published of ORA for nine samples from Askut and the new set of samples discussed by Smith in this volume (see Chapter 9). The lipid analysis indicates strongly divergent traditions of food production that differ according to the manufacture of the vessel (Egyptian or Nubian tradition)[37] and may suggest a stronger specialisation in the use of Egyptian cooking vessels.[38] While recent analyses determined the study of organic remains in cooking pots from Amara West as very limited,[39] a proof of concept ORA of six cooking pots from Sai was successful.[40] Interestingly, this, as yet, unpublished analysis from New Kingdom contexts did not show any differences between the contents of Egyptian and Nubian cooking pots – this is based on the analysis of three imported Egyptian cooking pots and three locally produced hand-made pots. Of much interest is another small proof of concept study ORA of cooking pots from site AtW 001 at Attab West.[41] Twelve selected samples yielded a recovery rate of 50%, with six cooking vessels yielding interpretable lipid profiles. GC-C-IRMS analyses were carried out on the sherds (n=6; Table 1) to determine the $\delta^{13}C$ values of the major fatty acids, $C_{16:0}$ and $C_{18:0}$, and ascertain the source of the lipids extracted, through the use of the $\Delta^{13}C$ proxy.[42]

36 Heinrich and Hansen 2020.

37 See Smith 2003, 113–124.

38 Smith this volume.

39 Spencer 2014, 55.

40 This proof of concept was undertaken by my LMU colleagues Philipp Stockhammer and Maxime Rageot to whom I am very grateful. Philipp Stockhammer provided in general on several occasions useful information concerning ORA analysis.

41 Analysis was undertaken by Julie Dunne and her team, University of Bristol (Dunne, Haberfield and Evershed 2023). For the site see most recently Budka, Rose and Ward 2023, 26–30.

42 Dunne, Haberfield and Evershed 2023. The text summarising the results of the analysis is based on this unpublished report.

Sample name	Object number	Original find number	Context/ find spot	Part of the pot	Lipid concentration (µg g-1)	$\delta^{13}C_{16:0}$	$\delta^{13}C_{18:0}$	$\Delta^{13}C$	Attribution
ATW01	DN 001	MUAFS 011-1/ 2022	WP 653 = AtW 001, surface	Nubian cooking pot, rim sherd	5.4	-22.8	-24,4	-1.6	Ruminant adipose
ATW02	DN 002	MUAFS 011-2/ 2022	WP 653 = AtW 001, surface	Egyptian cooking pot, rim sherd	4.1	-18.8	-18.7	0.1	Ruminant/ non-ruminant/ plant
ATW03	DN 003	MUAFS 035/ 2023	AtW 001, T2, SU 1257	Nubian cooking pot, bodysherd	32	-23.8	-23.4	0.4	Non-ruminant adipose
ATW04	DN 004	MUAFS 082/ 2023	AtW 001, T2, SU 1263	Hybrid cooking pot, bodysherd	4.2	-19.2	-23.5	-4.2	Ruminant dairy
ATW08	DN 008	MUAFS 208/ 2023	AtW 001, T2, SU 1289	Nubian cooking pot, bodysherd	13.4	-22.7	-24.6	-1.9	Ruminant adipose
ATW10	DN 010	MUAFS 258/ 2023	AtW 001, T2, SU 1309	Nubian cooking pot, bodysherd	4.2	-16.3	-16.7	-0.4	Plant

Table 1 Sample name, object number, context, part of the pot, lipid concentrations (µg g^{-1}), $\delta^{13}C$ and $\Delta^{13}C$ values and attributions of Attab West Bronze Age vessels (after Dunne, Haberfield and Evershed 2023).

One of the most interesting results is the lipid profile of ATW04, the hybrid cooking pot MUAFS 082/2023 (Fig. 3, see also above, Introduction to Part I). The residue from this vessel is within the ruminant dairy region, with a $\Delta^{13}C$ value of -4.2 ‰, suggesting it was used to process dairy products (e.g., milk, butter or cheese), from ruminants such as cattle, sheep or goat. The results from two vessels (ATW01 and ATW08, both Nubian-style cooking pots) plot within the ruminant adipose region with Δ13C values of -1.6 and -1.9 ‰, confirming they were used to process carcass products from domesticates such as cattle, sheep or goat or, possibly, hunted wild ruminants. The residue from vessel ATW03 (Nubian-style cooking pot; Δ13C value of 0.4 ‰) is within the non-ruminant adipose range. The residues from vessels ATW02 and ATW10, an Egyptian-style and Nubian-style cooking pot, are between the ruminant and non-ruminant regions with Δ13C values of 0.1 and -0.4 ‰, respectively. Vessel ATW10 contains lipid distributions indicative of plant processing. Vessel ATW02 was likely used to process mixtures of ruminant and non-ruminant products, either contemporaneously or at different times. Non-ruminant products may originate either from pig/warthog or other fauna such as reptiles. Since the faunal results from site AtW 001 are not yet available, this remains unclear for now. Although, given their presence in neighbouring urban sites such as Sai and Amara West, pig seems most likely. Since ATW02 is an Egyptian-style cooking vessel, this might support the originally "foreign" character of pig meat being consumed in New Kingdom Nubia (see above).

The small set of ORA samples from Bronze Age Nubia might not be enough to interpret the extent of actual diversity but is nevertheless of relevance. Forthcoming chemical analyses of larger sets of samples promise to provide critical information and help to understand social practices attached to vessels, including questions of cultural identity and diversity. A future correlation with the archaeozoological and archaeobotanical analyses[43] will allow the different methodological approaches to supplement each other (e.g., bee products can only be identified through residue analyses, while meat cuts can only be identified via archaeozoology). This integrative step will produce the best possible understanding of site-specific cooking practices, which are relevant for reconstructing cultural and/or group identities (see already the case study of Askut, Chapter 9).

43 See, e.g., Ryan 2017; Heinrich and Hansen 2020.

Towards an understanding of food systems in Bronze Age Sudan

As highlighted above and in the chapters of this part of the volume, questions on foodways are complex and are best approached with multidisciplinary methods, taking advantage of recent advances in archaeological science.[44] Combining chemical residue analyses with the results of animal bone studies and botanical evidence has considerable potential, as has the general isotopic approach (see Chapter 8). Following Kelly Reed, the application of the 'food system' concept considering "all the processes and infrastructure involved in feeding a population"[45] seems especially promising. For Bronze Age Sudan, the different styles of cooking vessels, the actual cooking spaces, the fuel used for cooking, as well as specific devices such as so-called fire dogs can be considered (see also Chapter 9).[46]

For the Bronze Age Middle Nile, organic residue analyses (ORA) are an urgent desideratum since there are only limited published data from Askut.[47] The lipid analyses of hybrid vessels might offer important information about food traditions which might overlap and change in times of complex cultural encounters.

Future results of faunal analysis from different regions of Bronze Age Sudan will help in interpreting the relationship between sedentary groups inhabiting the Nile Valley and contemporaneous mobile groups migrating between the Nile Valley and the (semi-)desert regions to the west.[48] Comparisons of preferences regarding animal protein sources (e.g., fish vs. domestic mammals) and husbandry strategies might also help to identify groups with different cultural and/or social backgrounds.

Altogether, this volume presents the first tentative steps towards a better understanding of foodways in Bronze Age Sudan, considering not only supra-regional developments and correlations to Egypt, but also site-specific patterns which might be regional or reflect the specific eating and drinking preferences of individual communities.

44 See also Reed and Ryan 2019.

45 Reed 2021, 57.

46 For the importance to include pots and tools into the study see Dietler 2010, 207–226. For fuel for cooking in Egypt and Nubia see Budka et al. 2019.

47 Smith 2003; Smith this volume.

48 E.g. Wadi Hariq: Jesse et al. 2004; Pöllath 2006; cf. also Gatto 2014; Weschenfelder 2014.

Bibliography

Anderson, J.R., D'Andrea, C.A., Logan, A. and Ahmed, S.M.
2007 Bread moulds from the Amun temple at Dangeil, Nile state: an addendum, *Sudan & Nubia* 11, 89–93.

Baldi, M.
2018 Livelihood activities and food tradition in Kushite Nubia, in: I. Incordino, S. Mainieri, E. D'Itria, M.D. Pubblico, F.M. Rega and A. Salsano (eds.), *Current Research in Egyptology 2017: Proceedings of the Eighteenth Annual Symposium, University of Naples "L'Orientale" 3-6 May 2017*, Oxford, 19–32.

Bertini, L.
2014 13: Faunal remains at Kom Firin, in: N. Spencer (ed.), *Kom Firin II: The Urban Fabric and Landscape*, British Museum Research Publication 192, London, 306–311.

Binder, M., Spencer, N. and Millet, M.
2011 Cemetery D at Amara West: the Ramesside period and its aftermath, *British Museum Studies in Ancient Egypt and Sudan* 16, 47–99.

Budka, J.
2016 Egyptian cooking pots from the Pharaonic town of Sai Island, Nubia, *Bulletin de liaison de la céramique égyptienne* 26, 285–295.
2019 Pottery of the Middle and the New Kingdom from Lower and Upper Nubia, in: D. Raue (ed.), *Handbook of Ancient Nubia, Vol. 1*, Berlin; Boston, 465–489.
2020 *AcrossBorders 2: Living in New Kingdom Sai.* With contributions by Johannes Auenmüller, Annette M. Hansen, Frits Heinrich, Veronica Hinterhuber, Ptolemaios Paxinos, Nadja Pöllath, Helmut Sattmann, Sara Schnedl and Martina Ullmann, Archaeology of Egypt, Sudan and the Levant 1, Vienna.
2022 Early New Kingdom settlement activities in the periphery of Sai Island: towards a contextualisation of fresh evidence from Attab West, *Der antike Sudan. Mitteilungen der Sudanarchäologischen Gesellschaft zu Berlin e.V.* 33, 45–61.

Budka, J., Geiger, C., Heindl, P., Hinterhuber, V. and Reschreiter, H.
2019 The question of fuel for cooking in ancient Egypt and Sudan, *EXARC Journal* 1/2019, https://exarc.net/issue-2019-1/ea/question-fuel-cooking-ancient-egypt-and-sudan.

Budka, J., Rose, K. and Ward, C.
2023 Cultural diversity in the Bronze Age in the Attab to Ferka region: new results based on excavations in 2023, *Der antike Sudan. Mitteilungen der Sudanarchäologischen Gesellschaft zu Berlin e.V.* 34, 19–35.

Cappers, R.T.J., Heinrich, F., Kaaijk, S., Fantone, F., Darnell, J. and Manassa, C.
2014 Barley revisited: Production of barley bread in Umm Mawagir (Kharga Oasis, Egypt), in: K. Accetta, R. Fellinger, P.L. Gonçalves, S. Musselwhite and W.P. van Pelt (eds.), *Current Research in Egyptology 2013. Proceedings of the Fourteenth Annual Symposium*, Oxford, Havertown, 49–63.

Chaix, L.
1988 Cinquième note sur la faune de Kerma (Soudan). Campagnes 1987 et 1988, in: C. Bonnet, B. Privati, C. Simon, L. Chaix, P. De Paepe (eds.), *Les fouilles archéologiques de Kerma (Soudan), Genava, n.s.* 36, 27–29.
2006 New data about rural economy in the Kerma culture: the site of Gism el-Arba (Sudan), in: K. Kroeper, M. Chłodnicki and M. Kobusiewicz (eds.), *Archaeology of Early Northeastern Africa. In Memory of Lech Krzyżaniak*, Studies in African Archaeology 9, Poznań, 25–38.

Chaix, L. and Grant, A.
1993 Palaeoenvironmental and economy at Kerma, northern Sudan during the third millennium B.C.: Archaeozoological and botanical evidence, in: L. Kryzaniak, M. Kobusiewicz and J. Alexander (eds.), *Environmental Change and Human Culture in the Nile Basin and Northern Africa Until the Second Millennium B.C.*, Poznań, 399–404.

Dalton, M., Spencer, N., Macklin, M.G., Woodward, J.C. and Ryan, P.
2023 Three thousand years of river channel engineering in the Nile Valley, *Geoarchaeology* 38/5, 565–587, https://doi.org/10.1002/gea.21965.

Dietler, M.
2010 *Archaeologies of Colonialism: Consumption, Entanglement, and Violence in Ancient Mediterranean France*, Berkeley, CA.

Dunne, J., Haberfield, G. and Evershed, R.P.
2023 *Organic residue analysis of Bronze Age pottery from Attab West, Sudan: Report*, University of Bristol, unpublished report for the ERC DiverseNile Project, LMU Munich.

Fuller, D.Q.
2004 Early Kushite agriculture: archaeobotanical evidence from Kawa, *Sudan & Nubia* 8, 70–74.
2013 14. Agricultural innovation and state collapse in Meroitic Nubia: The impact of the Savannah package, in: C.J. Stevens, S. Nixon, M.A. Murray and D.Q. Fuller (eds.), *Archaeology of African Plant Use*, London, 165–177.

Fuller, D.Q. and Lucas, L.
2020 Savanna on the Nile: long-term agricultural diversification and intensification in Nubia, in: G. Emberling and B.B. Williams (eds.), *The Oxford Handbook of Ancient Nubia*, Oxford, 927–953.

Gatto, M.
2014 Peripatetic nomads along the Nile: Unfolding the Nubian Pan-Grave culture of the Second Intermediate Period, *Journal of Ancient Egyptian Interconnections* 6 (1), 11–28.

Gosden, C. and Hather, J.G.
1999 *The Prehistory of Food. Appetites for Change*, London; New York.

Graff, S.R.
2020 Archaeology of cuisine and cooking, *Annual Review of Anthropology* 49, 337–354.

HAALAND, R.
2007 Porridge and pot, bread and oven: food ways and symbolism in Africa and the Near East from the Neolithic to the present, *Cambridge Archaeological Journal* 17 (2), 165–182.
2009 Ancient Nubia: a culinary cross-road between Africa and the Near East, in: H. HAFSAAS-TSAKOS and A. TSAKOS (eds.), *Connecting South and North: Sudan Studies from Bergen in Honour of Mahmoud Saleh*, Bergen, 41–58.
2012 Changing food ways as indicators of emerging complexity in Sudanese Nubia: from Neolithic agropastoralists to the Meroitic civilisation, *Azania: Archaeological Research in Africa* 47, 327–342.

HEINRICH, F.B.J. and HANSEN, A.M.
2020 Mud bricks, cereals and the agricultural economy. Archaeobotanical investigations at the New Kingdom town, in: J. BUDKA, *AcrossBorders 2, Living in New Kingdom Sai*, Archaeology of Egypt, Sudan and the Levant 1, Vienna, 275–349, 480–488 (plates).

IKRAM, S.
1995 *Choice Cuts: Meat Production in Ancient Egypt*, Orientalia Lovaniensia Analecta 69, Leuven.

JESSE, F., KRÖPELIN, S., LANGE, M., PÖLLATH, N. and BERKE, H.
2004 On the periphery of Kerma – The Handessi Horizon in Wadi Hariq, Northwestern Sudan, *Journal of African Archaeology* 2, 123–164.

KEMP, B.J.
2012 *The City of Akhenaten and Nefertiti: Amarna and its People*, London.

LEMOS, R.
2020 Material culture and colonization in ancient Nubia: Evidence from the New Kingdom cemeteries, in: C. SMITH (ed.), *Encyclopedia of Global Archaeology*, Cham, https://doi.org/10.1007/978-3-319-51726-1_3307-1.

LE MOYNE, C., ROBERTS, P., HUA, Q., BLEASDALE, M., DESIDERI, J., BOIVIN, N. and CROWTHER, A.
2023 Ecological flexibility and adaptation to past climate change in the Middle Nile Valley: A multiproxy investigation of dietary shifts between the Neolithic and Kerma periods at Kadruka 1 and Kadruka 21, *PLoS One*, 2023 Feb 2;18(2):e0280347, doi: 10.1371/journal.pone.0280347.

MATTHEWS, S. and NOWOTNICK, U.
2019 Culinary interactions: connecting foodways in Early Iron Age Africa, *Azania: Archaeological Research in Africa* 54(4), 468–486.

NOWOTNICK, U. and MATTHEWS, S.
2020 Meroe, Sudan: Connecting Foodways. Ein neues Projekt zu Esstraditionen in Nordost-Afrika und ihren kulturellen Verflechtungen, *e-Forschungsberichte des Deutschen Archäologischen Instituts* 2020 (1), 78–84.
2022 Small enclosure, big meals: Meroitic cooking in regional perspective, *Der antike Sudan. Mitteilungen der Sudanarchäologischen Gesellschaft zu Berlin e.V.* 33, 19–32.

PÖLLATH, N.
2006 Mid-Holocene pastoralism in North-Western Sudan: cattle bone finds from Wadi Hariq and their cultural implications, in: K. KROEPER, M. CHŁODNICKI and M. KOBUSIEWICZ (eds.), *Archaeology of Early Northeastern Africa. In Memory of Lech Krzyżaniak*, Studies in African Archaeology 9, Poznań, 321–324.

POPE, J.
2013 Epigraphic evidence for a 'Porridge-and-Pot' tradition on the ancient Middle Nile, *Azania: Archaeological Research in Africa* 48(4), 473–497.
2018 The "gum-eaters" of Nubia revisited, in: T.A. BÁCS, Á. BOLLÓK and T. VIDA (eds.), *Across the Mediterranean – Along the Nile: Studies in Egyptology, Nubiology and Late Antiquity Dedicated to László Török on the Occasion of His 75th Birthday* 1, Budapest, 503–514.

PIERCE, K.V.L.
2013 *Living and Dying Abroad: Aspects of Egyptian Cultural Identity in Late Bronze Age and Early Iron Age Canaan*, UCLA Electronic Theses and Dissertations, Los Angeles.

RAUE, D.
2017 Nubian pottery on Elephantine Island in the New Kingdom, in: N. SPENCER, A. STEVENS and M. BINDER (eds.), *Nubia in the New Kingdom: Lived Experience, Pharaonic Control and Indigenous Traditions*, British Museum Publications on Egypt and Sudan 3, Leuven, 525–536.

REED, K.
2021 Food systems in archaeology: Examining production and consumption in the past, *Archaeological Dialogues* 28(1), 51–75, https://doi.org/10.1017/S1380203821000088.

REED, K. and RYAN, P.
2019 Lessons from the past and the future of food, *World Archaeology* 51:1, 1–16, DOI: 10.1080/00438243.2019.1610492.

RYAN, P.
2017 From raw resources to food processing: Archaeobotanical and ethnographic insights from New Kingdom Amara West and present-day Ernetta Island in Northern Sudan, in: L. STEEL and K. ZINN (eds.), *Exploring the materiality of food 'stuffs': Transformations, symbolic consumption and embodiments*, London, 15–38.

SMITH, S.T.
1995 *Askut in Nubia. The Economics and Ideology of Egyptian Imperialism in the Second Millennium B.C.*, Studies in Egyptology, London; New York.
2003 *Wretched Kush. Ethnic Identities and Boundaries in Egypt's Nubian Empire*, London; New York.

DE SOUZA, A.
2020 Melting pots: Entanglement, appropriation, hybridity, and assertive objects between the Pan-Grave and Egyptian ceramic traditions, *Journal of Ancient Egyptian Interactions* 27, 1–23.

Spencer, N.
2014 Creating and re-shaping Egypt in Kush: Responses at Amara West, *Journal of Ancient Egyptian Interconnections* 6(1), 42–61.

Twiss, K.C.
2019 *The Archaeology of Food: Identity, Politics, and Ideology in the Prehistoric and Historic Past*, Cambridge.

Weschenfelder, P.
2014 Linking the Eastern Desert and the Nile Valley: Pan-Grave people from the late Middle Kingdom to the early New Kingdom, in: J.R. Anderson and D.A. Welsby (eds.), *The Fourth Cataract and Beyond. Proceedings of the 12th International Conference for Nubian Studies*, British Museum Publications on Egypt and Sudan 1, Leuven, 357–366.

Chapter 5

Early food production and food producers in prehistoric Sudan

Elena A.A. Garcea[1]

Abstract

Early food production in Sudan dates between the sixth and the fourth millennium BC. With the onset of the Neolithic period, it replaced hunting-gathering and engaged food producers in the extraction, management and use of domestic resources introduced from Southwest Asia (cattle, caprines, wheats and barley) and locally domesticated (sorghum). The Neolithic marked the decline of egalitarian societies and the emergence of social inequality based on the value of wealth and capital as symbols of power and ostentation in life and after death. It also implied the adoption of a series of social patterns and cultural behaviours in all sectors of human life and funerary traditions, spanning from settlement systems to social roles and individual engagements and affecting relationships, prestige values, ideology and symbols.

Keywords:

Early food production, Neolithic, pastoralism, agro-pastoralism, Sudan

Introduction

Multiple conditions of previous hunting-gathering communities laid the foundations for the emergence of food production with the adoption of animal and plant domestic species. Hunter-gatherers had developed a delayed-return economy consisting of intensification of resource exploitation, control over wild animal and plant life cycles, food processing and storing and considerable levels of technical knowledge accumulation with the development of a variety of artefactual assemblages.[2]

The so-called Neolithisation process involved economic, organisational, biological, and health transformations and changes. Not only it changed the ways for obtaining food, but it also changed the ways of preparing and cooking it as well as using it for symbolic purposes. Human communities internalised this process in their social, material and mental systems. They developed and shared repetitive cultural customs, including socially symbolic rites of passage, such as birth, initiation, adulthood, marriage, death as well as territorial movements.[3] Sudan's archaeology of the sixth/fifth and fourth millennia BC is particularly informative in this respect. While the sixth/fifth millennia BC featured a gradual process of cultural and social changes that received certain visual manifestations, the fourth millennium BC witnessed an explosion of cultural and symbolic values, which had, however, matured over the previous centuries.

Domestic cattle, caprines, wheats and barley have no local wild ancestors in Africa and were imported from Southwest Asia, appearing in Egypt from the end of the seventh millennium BC and in Sudan from the first half of the sixth millennium BC.[4] Initially, they were only gradually and intermittently introduced in the social and economic organisation of local African communities. Attempts to domesticate some African endemic wild species, such as aurochs, sorghum, pearl millet and other plants, also occurred.[5]

A variety of cultural units developed in Sudan's Neolithic and include a number of technological and cultural continuities and changes in all artefactual productions. Even though Neolithic habitations are less documented than cemeteries in the Middle Nile Valley, they existed and were occupied for long periods, paving the way for the formation of hierarchical settlement systems and anticipating complex political organisations.[6]

Environmental conditions in the early and middle Holocene

The early Holocene (10,000–6300 BC) is characterised by a humid period with African summer monsoon, which ended the hyper-arid (<10 mm annual rainfall) spell of the final Pleistocene Last Glacial Maximum. At the onset of the Holocene in North Africa, the tropical rain front of the Inter-Tropical Convergence Zone (ITCZ) moved 700–1000 km northward. The ITCZ is where humid and dry air masses converge and affect rainfall, producing alternating humid and dry periods. Thanks to the northward ITCZ shift and local groundwater, the Sahelian savanna extended northward and several perennial lakes developed in western Sudan, supporting generalised wetter conditions that terminated later in Sudan than in Egypt.[7] Also the

1 Department of Letters and Philosophy, University of Cassino and Southern Latium, Italy; e.garcea@unicas.it.

2 Garcea 2020; Sadig 2010; Sadig 2013.

3 Dittrich 2013.

4 Garcea 2020.

5 Fuller, Willcox and Allaby 2011; Fuller and Hildebrand 2013; Garcea, Karul and D'Ercole 2016; Gifford-Gonzalez and Hanotte 2013.

6 Garcea 2020; Langlois et al. 2019.

7 Williams, M. 2019.

flow of the Middle Nile River did not decline in step with climate deterioration in the Sahara, but later and only temporarily thanks to the monsoonal effects on the Nile headwaters.[8] Local ecosystems responded differently and moister environments persisted in certain ecological niches even during the dry and cold spell that occurred around 6300 BC (8.2 ka BP).[9]

During the middle Holocene, beginning from the end of the seventh millennium BC, environmental conditions changed and savanna environments gave way to drier habitats.[10] In western Sudan, aridity increased in an easterly direction with the driest areas being those closer to the Nile, outside the floodplain.[11] At the end of the African Humid Period, around 5000 BC, the Nile's floods became irregular and the western tributaries of the main river, Wadi Howar and Wadi el-Melik, receded and eventually dried out c. 4000–2800 BC.[12] Nevertheless, climate deterioration has not always been negative for human occupation. Drier conditions in certain areas favoured it, while it was prevented in the early Holocene wet periods, such as the Kerma plain[13] and the Middle Wadi Howar, which was too swampy for long-term stays during the early Holocene.[14]

While environmental changes influenced human behaviour to some extent, no cause-effect scenarios of environmental and cultural changes should be envisaged to understanding human adoption of domesticated animals and plants. Numerous lines of evidence demonstrate that climate change was not the most important factor of cultural and economic transition leading to food production in north-eastern Africa,[15] even though human response to monsoonal withdrawal might have led to a gradual increase of mobile settlement organisation, which resulted to suit animal herding.[16]

The relationship between environmental conditions and human behaviour was reciprocal as human communities also had an impact on the environment. In fact, the practises of tending domesticating and domestic animals and plants and producing and preparing food affected the formation of ecological niches.[17] Analyses of the micromorphology, mineralogy and isotopic composition of degraded dung deposits from East African Pastoral Neolithic sites demonstrated that herders contributed to create persistent anthropogenic hotspots that enriched and restructured savanna ecosystems.[18] Niche dynamic metrics also showed that the climatic niche of animal production in Africa significantly expanded with respect to wild terrestrial ungulates due to husbandry practises and adaptation strategies to climate change with increasing aridification.[19]

Deferred beginnings of food production in prehistoric Sudan

Southwest Asian domesticates reached Africa through multiple routes. Corridors between the Levant and Egypt could be both overland and maritime across the Nile Delta or the Red Sea.[20] Besides the Nile Valley, an eastern potential route, particularly for caprines, may have gone through the northern flank of the Sinai and/or the southern tip of the peninsula, crossing the Gulf of Suez.[21] Livestock also spread across North Africa and the Sahara following longitudinal directions, initially being restricted within winter-rain regions.[22] The delay in the adoption of domestic livestock in Sudan, with respect to the Sahara, and crops, with respect to Egypt, may be because Sudan has mostly received summer rains throughout the Holocene. The boundary between summer and winter rainfall currently lies along the Khartoum longitude but passed further north during the early/middle Holocene.[23]

Domesticates reached Nubia through several waves of migrations and not as a package. Some livestock may have been introduced into the Middle Nile Valley from the Sahara through longitudinal cultural contact rather than large migrations of Saharan groups.[24] Others could have followed the routes of domestic cereals through the Nile Valley, the Sinai desert, and the southern Red Sea Hills.[25]

Animal herding was a discontinuous, leapfrog process before it led to full-fledged nomadic pastoralism according to a multi-stage dispersal with different economic solutions.[26] It took up to 2000 years before it covered the entire Sudanese country, from the beginning of the sixth millennium in northern Sudan (Kerma), early fifth millennium BC in central Sudan, end of fifth millennium BC in western Sudan (Wadi Howar) and southern Gezira, and middle fourth millennium BC in eastern Sudan (Fig. 1). Domestic barley and wheat sporadically appeared in Sudan towards the end of the sixth millennium BC and sorghum was locally

8 Hildebrand et al. 2018.
9 Zerboni and Nicoll 2018.
10 Macklin et al. 2013; Williams, M. 2019.
11 Hildebrand et al. 2018.
12 Hildebrand et al. 2018.
13 Macklin et al. 2013.
14 Keding 2000.
15 Adelsberger et al. 2020; Zerboni 2013.
16 Dunne et al. 2018.
17 Fuller et al. 2018.
18 Marshall et al. 2018.
19 Phelps et al. 2019.
20 Bar-Yosef 2013; Linseele, Holdaway and Wendrich 2016.
21 Kindermann and Riemer 2021.
22 di Lernia 2022.
23 Williams, M. 2019.
24 Dunne et al. 2018.
25 Out et al. 2016; Salvatori, Usai and Lecointe 2016.
26 Garcea 2016; Garcea 2020; see also di Lernia 2022.

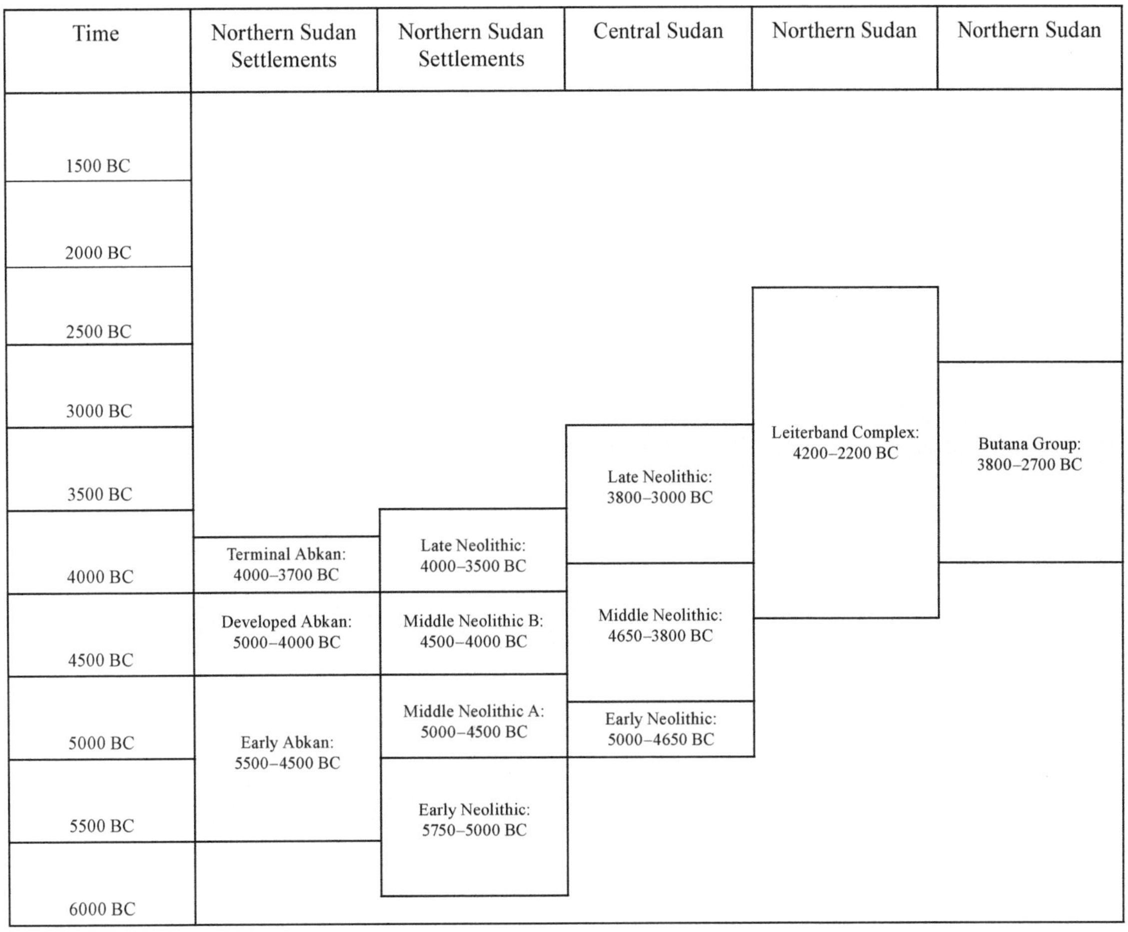

Fig. 1 Chronological timespans of main Neolithic cultural units.

domesticated c. 3500 BC.[27] The exploitation of Sudanese sorghum clearly fits in the conceptual perspective that rejects a dichotomy between wild and domestic forms based on arbitrary thresholds, and emphasises intermediate hybrid communities.[28] Its domestication was an intentional and unintentional continuum in time and space and its use and consumption at different cultivation/domestication stages corroborates to the leapfrog domestication process that selected animal and plant species underwent.

Demic or cultural diffusion?

How did Southwest Asian domestic species arrive to Northeast Africa and how were they incorporated in the local subsistence economy? The first question regards whether Southwest Asian food producers expanded in Northeast Africa bringing along their economic means of subsistence (demic diffusion), or Northeast African hunter-gatherers adopted herding/farming practises in their local economic systems (cultural diffusion). In the former case, changes may be detected in the genetic pool of local human populations, in the latter, long-term genetic continuity may be recognisable across shifting cultural transitions. Up-to-date genetic studies illustrate a complex mosaic of interactions between food producers and autochthonous foragers.[29]

Groups with gracile morphological features possibly migrated from the southern Levant and mixed with local robust hunter-gatherers, resulting in a progressive decrease in cranio-facial robusticity and relative increase in cranial height.[30] On the other hand, morphometric tooth analysis supports continuity between Mesolithic and Early Neolithic populations from El-Barga with slight dietary changes at the beginning of the Neolithic,[31] and from El-Khiday with possibly *in situ* selection for a reduction in cranial robusticity and dental size.[32] Therefore, population

27 Brass et al. 2022.
28 Bogaard et al. 2021.
29 Sirak, Sawchuk and Prendergast 2022.
30 Crevecoeur 2012.
31 Benoiston, Bayle and Crevecoeur 2018.
32 Irish and Usai 2021.

replacement or admixture seemingly occurred, but was a slow and gradual process that became biologically evident at least one millennium after the acquisition of food production.[33] A phase of genetic admixture is genetically documented 4000–3000 BC in Northeast Africa, involving local groups with ancestry similar to present-day Dinka people and allochthonous groups with ancestry similar to ancient Levantine people. The amount of Dinka-related ancestry decreased very slowly and only partially, suggesting repeated admixtures between herders and foragers and in some cases predating the introduction of domestication practises.[34] Finally, archaeological data from the Levant and North Africa with similar raw materials and stone tools suggest that small groups of mobile people were likely to have continually moved in both directions between the two regions, practicing regular exchanges of goods.[35]

Regarding the second question on how domestic animals were incorporated in the local subsistence economy, non-consecutive and pluridirectional scenarios from herding as an incipient supplement to full-fledged nomadic pastoralism have been considered.[36] They take into account at least four multi-stage solutions: 1) contemporary, independent settlements of hunter-gatherers and herders in the same areas; 2) hunter-gatherers adopting a few domestic animals with no visible cultural changes; 3) early herders with some, but not all, visible cultural changes; and 4) full nomadic pastoralists. As these scenarios also concern mobility patterns and settlement systems, they are described below (see Settlement organisation).

Continuities and discontinuities in material cultures

Neolithic material cultures exhibit technological and behavioural continuities and changes with discontinuities, which appear in artefactual productions, settlement systems and funerary customs. One of the most characteristic continuities appears in several ceramic decorative techniques, using rocker, alternately pivoting stamp and simple impressions.[37] On the other hand, substantial changes occurred at various stages of ceramic manufacturing processes, such as raw material selection, decorative motifs (e.g., use of unevenly serrated combs), surface treatment (burnishing) and use.[38] Ceramics acquired a central role not only in domestic practises but also in funerary customs, including their use as grave goods and/or ceremonial items. Caliciform beakers represent a Neolithic hallmark. They originated in the Upper Egypt's Tasian culture and spread to Nubia from the beginning of the fifth millennium BC and in central Sudan from the end of the fifth millennium BC, persisting until the Late Neolithic. While in Egypt they occur in both settlement and funerary contexts,[39] in Sudan they mostly appear as grave goods and only exceptionally in habitations. Exceptions were observed at El-Multaga in central Sudan, dating to the fifth millennium BC, and in the Lower Wadi Howar (Abu Tabari) and Jebel Abyad, dating to the beginning of the fourth millennium BC.[40] It has been suggested that the large assortment of ceramic shapes, decorations and surface treatments would hint at the emergence of specialised potters.[41]

Concerning lithic industries, both débitage and retouched tools are also common in cemeteries. They could be made of a variety of raw materials. In general, the procurement and exchange of certain items, including raw materials (e.g., porphyry and rhyolite) and finished products (e.g., gouges and polished stone tools), intensified as a response to the new forms of social power that developed through the control or ownership of domestic livestock.[42] Ground stone axes, gouges, mace-heads, palettes, grinders, rubbers and querns were more common than retouched tools in central Sudanese cemeteries.

Finally, the production of a large set of non-utilitarian items complements utilitarian productions and marks another turning point of early food producers. They include bracelets, necklaces, pendants, earrings, lip-plugs, beads, combs, cosmetic containers, cosmetic palettes and figurines made in a multiplicity of raw materials (e.g., wild and domestic animal bones, elephant and hippopotamus ivory, ostrich eggshell, Red Sea shells, agate, malachite, zeolite, amazonite, carnelian, obsidian).[43]

Cultural units

The earliest domesticated species is the skull of a cattle that was dated 5750 BC and came from a tomb in the El-Barga cemetery (Fig. 2).[44] Slightly later Neolithic habitation remains are located nearby, at Wadi El-Arab and exhibit Early Neolithic burnished ceramics decorated with the rocker technique. Conversely, Middle Neolithic productions are undecorated or decorated with simple impressions under the rim and can be black-topped or rippled, resembling Abkan productions (see below).[45]

33 Benoiston, Bayle and Crevecoeur 2018.
34 Sirak, Sawchuk and Prendergast 2022.
35 Caneva 2016.
36 Garcea 2016; Garcea 2020.
37 D'Ercole et al. 2017.
38 Garcea and D'Ercole 2018.
39 Jesse 2006–2007.
40 Jesse 2006–2007.
41 Salvatori, Usai and Lecointe 2016.
42 Garcea 2020.
43 Garcea 2020.
44 Honegger 2005; Honegger 2019.
45 Honegger 2014; Honegger 2019; Honegger and Williams 2015.

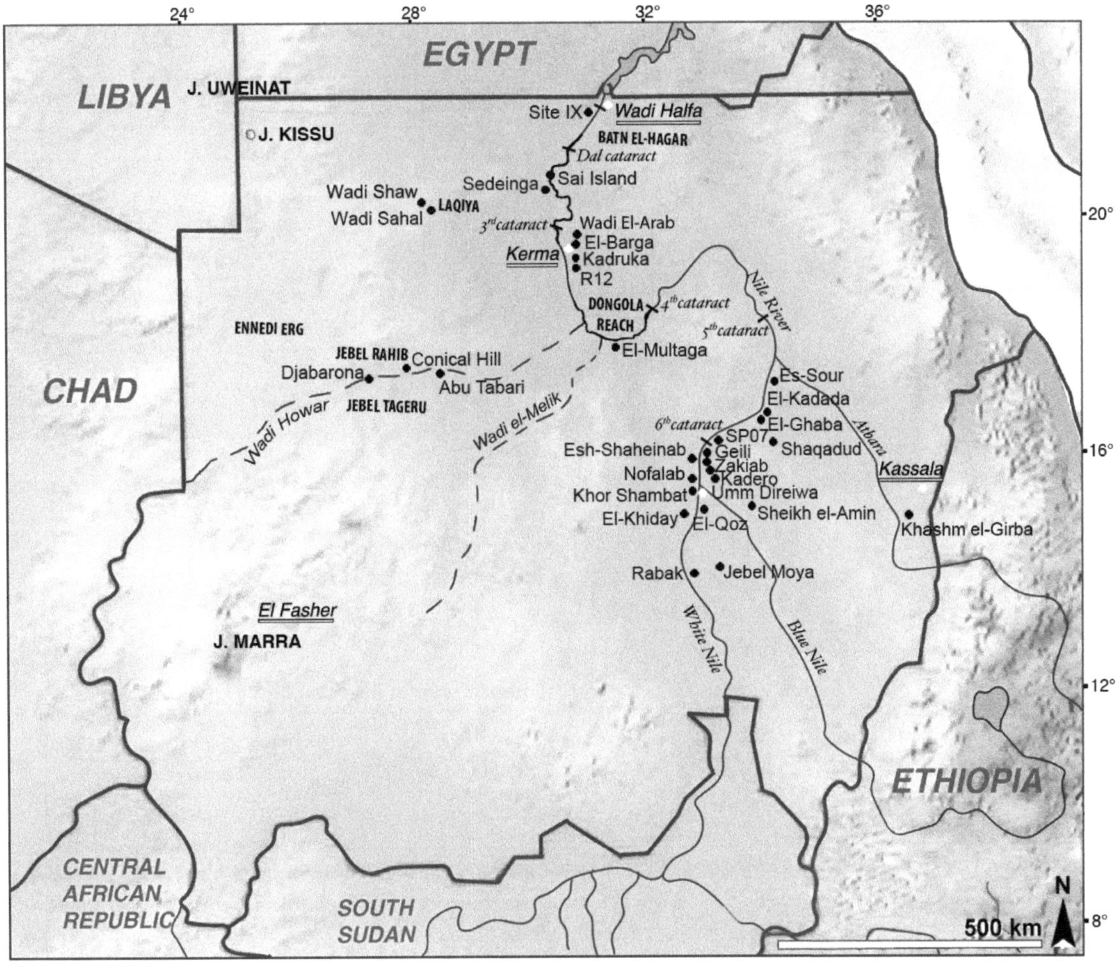

Fig. 2 Map of the Neolithic sites mentioned in the text.

The *Abkan* culture (Figs. 1, 3) was first identified around the village of Abka (Site IX) near the Wadi Halfa-Second Cataract[46] and extended to the Western Egyptian Desert at Nabta-Kiseiba, the Laqiya region and the Dongola Reach (Karat group).[47] It covers the period between 5500 and 3700 BC. Nordström divided it into three chronologically distinct phases: Early Abkan (5500–4500 BC), Developed Abkan (4500–4000 BC) and Terminal Abkan (4000–3700 BC).[48] Ceramic pastes consisted of Holocene silty Nile alluvial clay, rich in quartz and plagioclase, instead of previously used Pleistocene primary clay, and mineral and organic tempers (charcoal particles and herbivore dung).[49] New vessel shapes and different surface treatments appeared. Surfaces are burnished, mostly undecorated (Figs. 4.3–4) and often black-topped (Figs. 4.1–2). The few decorations (plain zigzags made with the rocker technique, paired dots made with the alternately pivoting stamp technique and simple impressions) are usually limited to the rim (Fig. 4.5). Developed Abkan ceramics display an increase of black-topped, red-polished, plain or rippled vessels.[50] Early Abkan lithic tool-kits consist of groovers, denticulates, notched pieces, sidescrapers, simple and carinated endscrapers and broad lunates. The increase of scrapers has been related to hide preparation.[51] Quartz is still the most abundant raw material, but is complemented with other rocks, such as agate, carnelian and chalcedony. Developed Abkan tool-kits show an increase of microlithic elements. Abkan rock art exhibits numerous engravings with human figures tending livestock.[52] Unlike most other Neolithic units in Sudan, the Abkan only represents habitations without cemeteries.

46 Myers 1960.
47 Lange and Nordström 2006; Nordström 1972; Shiner 1968.
48 Nordström 2006.
49 D'Ercole 2017; Garcea 2020.

50 Nordström 2006.
51 Shiner 1968.
52 Nordström 2006.

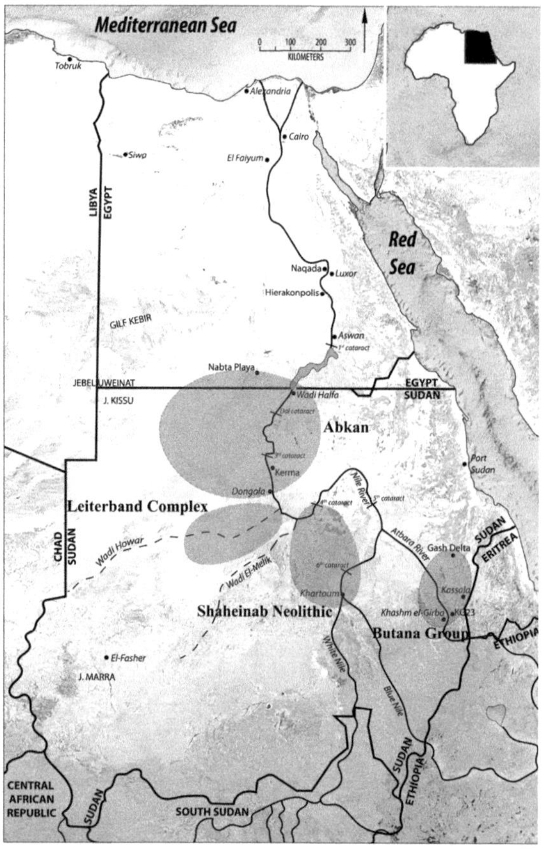

Fig. 3 Geographic distribution of main Neolithic cultural units.

Fig. 4 Abkan pottery: 1–2. Black-topped; 3–4. Undecorated; 5. Ripple ware with impressed decoration on the rim (after Garcea 2020, fig. 6.1, with permission by Springer).

In central Sudan, the Neolithic period is locally known as *Shaheinab Neolithic* (5000–3800 BC) after the eponymous site of Esh-Shaheinab, located on an ancient left bank of the Nile, 50 km north of Omdurman.[53] This site includes an Early Neolithic settlement with numerous hearths and a burial ground that was established in the Late Neolithic (fourth millennium BC) and continued to be used in later periods. Pottery displays a large variety of decorations made with the rocker, alternatively pivoting stamp and simple impressions.[54] Motifs are extremely variable with zigzags applied in all directions, horizontal, vertical, oblique or even forming concentric, curvilinear lines. Rocker decorations form dotted zigzags (Figs. 5.1–8), plain zigzags (Figs. 5.9–10) and zigzags with "vees and dots" (Figs. 5.11–14), the latter made with unevenly serrated edged combs. Alternately pivoting stamped decorations make parallel lines (Figs. 5.15–17) and occasionally dotted wavy lines (Fig. 5.18), the latter being only made with two-pronged tools in the Neolithic. Plain black-, brown- and red-burnished pottery (Figs. 5.19–21), which is usually thinner (3 mm thick), is also characteristic. Stone industries show scarcely diversified tool-kits with a decrease in the number and quality of microliths in favour of large flake tools, such as denticulates and scrapers. Perforators are also frequent and could be used for a variety of purposes, namely making pottery repair holes, drilling eggshell and stone beads or piercing hide.[55] Quartz is the most frequent raw material also in central Sudan, but came from riverbeds instead of outcrops as in northern Sudan. Other materials, such as Nile pebbles, fossil wood and volcanic rocks, that is, basalt, porphyry and rhyolite, were preferably employed to make larger tools. Porphyry and rhyolite were typically used to make gouges (Figs. 6.1–3) and broken pieces were reused for the production of other tools.[56] Almost in front of Esh-Shaheinab, on the right bank of the Nile, an Early Neolithic habitation was also reoccupied with a Late Neolithic cemetery at Geili.[57]

The Neolithic period in western Sudan is mainly known from its habitations. Early herders' economy was based on the exploitation of rare cattle and caprines, wild fauna and aquatic resources. Differences exist between the traditions in north-western Sudan and the Wadi Howar and between those in the Lower and Middle Wadi Howar, east and west of Jebel Rahib. While north-western Sudan was under the influence of Abkan groups who reached the Wadi

53 Arkell 1953.
54 Garcea 2020.
55 Caneva 1988; Haaland 1987.
56 Kapustka et al. 2019.
57 Caneva 1988.

Fig. 5 Esh-Shaheinab pottery: 1–8. Rocker dotted zigzags; 9–10. Rocker plain zigzags; 11–14. Rocker zigzags with vees and dots; 15–17. Alternately pivoting stamped parallel lines; 18. Alternately pivoting stamped dotted wavy lines; 19–21. Plain burnished pottery (photos by R. Ceccacci 2006).

Fig. 6 1–3. Gouges; 4–5. Darfur axes (1–3. ©Charles University, Faculty of Arts, photo by L. Varadzin 2011; 4–5. African Archaeology Archive Cologne, ID: 6059710, photo by E. Cziesla).

Shaw and Wadi Sahal in the Laqiya area,[58] the Wadi Howar region was characterised by the *Leiterband* complex (4200–2200 BC).[59] Being closer to the Nile Valley, the Lower Wadi Howar permitted contacts with Shaheinab Neolithic groups, as similar ceramics indicate. Conversely, the Middle Wadi Howar, which was too swampy for previous foragers' settlements, became the main centre for cattle herding.[60] Leiterband pottery combines characteristic Nilotic decorative techniques, such as rocker impressions made with tools with plain, evenly serrated and unevenly serrated edges, and local interpretations. One of the latter are decorative patterns made with the return technique producing ladder-like impressions (Fig. 7).[61] In general, vessel surfaces are mostly red or red-brown, usually entirely decorated. Stone tools follow a trend similar to pottery, displaying general components, including microliths, borers and lunates, as well as

58 Lange and Nordström 2006.

59 Jesse and Keding 2007.

60 Jesse et al. 2013.

61 Keding 2006.

local characteristic, such as Darfur axes (Figs. 6.4–5).[62] Finally, thumbnail, convex/circular endscrapers suggest connections with Tenerian and other Pastoral sites in the southern Sahara.[63] Burials are present but no isolated cemetery was recorded in the Wadi Howar. Grave goods occasionally occur in Leiterband burials, but are limited to personal ornaments and do not reflect a comparable social hierarchy as in the Nile Valley.[64]

Food production did not reach eastern Sudan until the middle fourth millennium BC. It is associated with the *Butana Group* (3800–2700 BC), featuring an agropastoral economy with large quantities of domesticated animals and domesticated cereals.[65] Very large (8–10 ha) and thickly stratified (2 m) sites, surrounded by smaller specialised locations, arose between the Atbara and Gash Rivers by the fourth millennium BC, suggesting the formation of nucleated resident communities. Imported grave goods (Red Sea shells) in some tombs and possible symbols of authority or rank, including administrative devices and imported porphyry mace-heads, indicate the development of complex social hierarchies.[66] Alongside local traditions, Butana Group ceramics (Fig. 8) display similarities with the Nile Valley, particularly with Pre-Kerma and occasionally Late Neolithic and A-Group productions. These cultural relations seemingly developed along an overland route from the confluence of the Atbara and Nile Rivers to the Fourth Cataract area, which connected eastern Sudan to Upper Nubia.

Fig. 7 *Leiterband* pottery (African Archaeology Archive Cologne, ID: 6064271, photo by B. Keding).

Settlement organisation

Nearly everywhere in Sudan, there are instances of herders who settled at the same sites previously occupied by foragers (e.g., 8-B-76 on Sai Island, Kadruka, El-Kadada, Kadero, El-Qoz, SP07 on Jebel Sabaloka East, Esh-Shaheinab, Geili, Khor Shambat, El-Khiday, Shaqadud midden, Conical Hill, Abu Tabari).[67] Different hypotheses may be advanced regarding herders' initial low-mobility organisational system. Early stock raising probably consisted of a few animals that could be managed without nomadic transhumance. Moreover, even at a more advanced stage of pastoralism, some communities stay in one settlement all year-round, as the Masaai in Kenya and Tanzania do. Other pastoralists split their group and keep some people at residential camps, while a few of them move with the herds to areas of good forage.[68]

The Neolithic site of Kadero is a good example of a permanent base-camp used all year round.[69] Lipid residues confirmed low mobility of livestock at this site even with a developed pastoral economy, which involved specific animal management practises with the selection of C_4 plants, including wild sorghum and wild millet growing in the savannas close to the site.[70]

At the same time, new territories (e.g., Kerma plain and Middle Wadi Howar) were occupied in the fifth millennium BC and, after 4000 BC, herders mostly expanded their geographic areas of influence and acquired access to a wide range of exotic materials and goods. Only at this stage, large-scale pastoralists shifted to nomadism, which was an efficient system for both animals and humans in increasingly arid environments. As these nomadic herders moved, they needed stable alliances with the dwellers they came in contact with, stimulating a system of long-distance trade and alliances and developing a symbiotic relationship with other

62 Jesse 2021.

63 Garcea 2013; Gifford-Gonzalez 2008.

64 Jesse and Keding 2002.

65 Barron et al. 2020; Manzo 2011; 2017; Vella Gregory and Brass 2021; Winchell 2013.

66 Manzo 2017; Manzo 2019.

67 Garcea 2020.

68 Gifford-Gonzalez 2005.

69 Chłodnicki, Kobusiewicz and Kroeper 2011.

70 Dunne et al. 2018.

Fig. 8 Butana Group pottery (after Garcea 2020, fig. 7.6, with permission by Springer).

populations.[71] As social complexity increased, social networks became stronger and social units contracted in smaller areas.[72]

Among the scenarios mentioned above (see paragraph on Demic or cultural diffusion?), Scenario 1 was recorded in both northern and central Sudan. Here, contemporary, independent settlements of hunter-gatherers and herders existed during the second half of the sixth millennium and beginning of the fifth millennium BC, for example, on Sai Island at Sites 8-B-10C and 8-B-76, and on the Blue Nile at Sheikh Mustafa and Sheikh el-Amin. Scenario 2 regards hunter-gatherers who adopted a few domestic animals but did not display visible cultural changes. This scenario was particularly common in north-western Sudan and the Egyptian Western Desert, where hunter-gatherers adopted a negligible number of domesticates (less than 1%) during the sixth millennium BC and underwent minimal changes in their subsistence and material culture, according to a 'pastro-foraging' form of economy, which preceded full-fledged pastoralism in the fifth millennium BC.[73] These incipient herders living in desert areas may have slowed down the process of domesticate adoption in order to minimise the risks of becoming dependent on livestock. Scenario 3 of early herders with some, but not all, visible cultural changes is particularly evident in numerous Neolithic settlements located in northern, central and western Sudan. It can be observed, for example, at Abkan sites, most sites in the Dongola Reach, Es-Sour, Nofalab, Zakiab, Umm Direiwa, Shaqadud midden, El-Khiday (16-D-5,

71 Caneva 2016.

72 Garcea and Hildebrand 2009.

73 Kuper and Riemer 2013, see also Kindermann and Riemer 2021.

16-D-6), Rabak, Sheikh el-Amin, and most sites in the Wadi Howar. These sites developed a low-mobility settlement strategy often organised around base-camps near increasingly contracting water pools and task-specific localities for raw material acquisition and/or wild game hunting. As the Nile offered permanent resources, the shift to mobility was a consequence, rather than a requisite of pastoralism. Finally, Scenario 4 of specialised pastoralism concerns groups with large herds who shifted to a nomadic settlement organisation, developing large cemeteries and ephemeral settlements.

Cemeteries as social units

Cemeteries became significant social units, as they were the most tangible evidence for established social hierarchies and the places that could represent permanent cultural symbols, unlike ephemeral nomadic camps.[74] Human communities had no standardised funerary practises but performed differentiated customs in burials and commemoration of the ancestors. Adults and children of both sexes were buried with no evident age or sex correlation with grave goods richness, and females could have equally important roles as males. A large variety of utilitarian and non-utilitarian grave goods often, but not always, accompanied them. Two major types of cemeteries were established in northern and central Sudan. Some were used over long time periods and include hundreds of burials according to a carefully planned spatial organisation. Others, possibly belonging to small communities (i.e., Sedeinga and cemetery A at El-Kadada), comprise less than a hundred graves and were used for relatively short periods, but still including several generations.[75]

In northern Sudan, site R12, dating from the end of the sixth millennium BC and mostly covering the fifth millennium BC, already reveals social codes based on the richness of the grave goods and funerary rituals involving sacrifice and consumption of cattle.[76] Kadruka consists of around 20 cemeteries that were in use throughout the fifth millennium BC and exhibit different burial customs, suggesting that several communities used it.[77] One of the earliest cemeteries at Kadruka, KDK23 (dated to the first half of the fifth millennium BC) was considered as a sort of "island of the dead".[78] It includes individuals of both sexes and all ages and was organised in rows separated by narrow corridors with the youngest individuals (new-born babies and infants) at the top of the mound and the richest concentrated nearby. Four individuals show traumas due to interpersonal violence.[79] Toward the second half of the fifth millennium BC, rich tombs at other Kadruka cemeteries were assigned to local chieftains, testifying to increasingly marked social inequality and ranking.[80]

In central Sudan, Ghaba is a large cemetery that was used for about 1300 years, from the very beginning of the fifth to the beginning of the fourth millennium BC, being contemporary to Kadruka in Upper Nubia in its first phase, and to Esh-Shaheinab in the later phase.[81] It yielded 265 burials and its size and wealth suggested that Ghaba refers to a substantial population of a comparable scale to Upper Egypt.[82] Kadero (first half of the fifth millennium BC) is another large cemetery with 218 burials organised into ten clusters with the richest graves located in the central part of the burial ground.[83] Funerary goods vary from none, to a few vessels and personal adornments, up to numerous and diversified offerings.

Funerary customs further flourished during the fourth millennium BC. At El-Kadada (first half of the fourth millennium BC), which included three cemeteries (A, B, and C), some graves in cemetery A were cut into each other, suggesting that several generations used this cemetery without knowing the location of older burials.[84] A narrow empty strip separates five or six groups of burials containing 10–12 individuals. Each of them includes one or two tombs with rich offerings and others with less varied goods or even no objects. Children burials (<6 years old) are laid inside reused ceramic storage vessels and are placed within or near the habitation. The burials in cemetery C were arranged according to a south-north axis. In a few tombs, secondary burials were interred contemporaneously and placed against the edge of the funerary pits or around the main deceased, attesting to the practise of human sacrifices for certain high rank people. The richest tomb (KDD86/128–129–130-131) contains a central individual, a male with a large bucranium behind him, covered with red ochre, three other human bodies and two dogs placed around the edge of the pit.[85] Chieftaincies with the emergence of a person of authority and power arose particularly during the fourth millennium BC, but it is not possible to determine whether the power of the chiefs buried in these cemeteries was political, economic or religious (or all three of them).

74 Garcea 2020.
75 Reinold 2006.
76 Salvatori and Usai 2008.
77 Reinold 2001; Reinold 2006.
78 Alarashi et al. 2021; Sellier et al. 2019.
79 Maines et al. 2017; Sellier et al. 2019.
80 Reinold 2001; Reinold 2006.
81 Salvatori and Usai 2019b; Salvatori, Usai and Lecointe 2016.
82 Williams, B. 2006.
83 Chłodnicki, Kobusiewicz and Kroeper 2011.
84 Reinold 2000; Reinold 2001; Reinold 2007.
85 Reinold 2000; Reinold 2001; Reinold 2007.

Domestic food management and cultural implications

The management of domestic food had at least three essential cultural implications. Even before domestic species represented a new food resource, they were part of the funerary sphere as symbols of power, wealth or ostentation. Animal burials and sacrifices as funerary ceremonies suggest that communities may have genealogically integrated animals, particularly horned and hoofed ruminants, in their social sphere.[86]

Secondly, the exploitation and management of domestic species implied a change in the way people consumed foods, cooked them and transformed them into products that were not readymade in nature. Besides being more nutritious and more storable, these new products also affected the appearance, taste and potential for cultural meanings of food.[87]

Finally, the new economic Neolithic system may have influenced the type of exchanged items, affecting the selection of domestic animal and plant species together with artefactual items that represented valued goods. Dittrich also pointed out that the efforts for obtaining and maintaining these animals and plants must have prevailed over the attempts to exploit them as subsistence basis.[88]

Animals

With respect to sedentary agriculture, animal husbandry is a preferred form of adaptation to semi-arid/arid environments as it can resort to resilient adaptation strategies to cope with environmental uncertainties and economic pressures. Currently, 20% of the Sudanese population still engages in herding activities.[89] Pastoralists are able to exploit regions with a low resource base by raising livestock, which are energy converters of non-edible resources into edible foodstuff for humans.[90] In contrast to meat feeding, the consumption of milk and dairy products allows exploiting living animals as well as cattle blood, as is currently the case in East Africa.[91] Lipid analysis of organic residues in ceramic vessels from Neolithic sites in North Africa, including Kadero in central Sudan, demonstrated that a considerable part of them contained dairy products (47%), confirming that secondary products were already appreciated and consumed from at least the mid-fifth millennium BC, if not earlier.[92]

Wild aurochs lived in Sudan and are archaeologically documented from c. 50,000 years ago.[93] Nevertheless, genetic data rule out successful indigenous domestication.[94] The closest place of origin of Northeast African domestic cattle, goat and sheep is the southern Levant, where they date from 8400–8200 BC.[95] Domesticated animals arrived earlier in the desert areas than in the Nile Valley. Cattle is securely dated from 6000 BC in the Eastern Sahara at site E-75-8 at Nabta Playa;[96] the earliest caprines were found in the Sinai Peninsula, dating from about 6250 BC[97] and at Farafra Oasis from 6000 BC.[98] Domestic caprines may have arrived even earlier in the Red Sea Hills of Egypt, where an undated feature at Sodmein cave containing caprine remains is stratigraphically earlier than another feature dated 6200 BC.[99]

Even when domestic livestock were available, Early Neolithic herders continued to rely mainly on wild resources, supplementing them with domestic animals. The percentage of domestic livestock can very also between contemporary and near-by sites, such as for example Kadero, where they made up 81% of the total (domestic and wild) faunal remains, and Esh-Shaheinab or Geili, where they represented less than 25%.[100] Cattle often prevailed over small livestock, such as for example at Kadero, Khor Shambat 1, Kadruka, R12, Nofalab, Umm Direiwa, El-Kadada, Zakiab and the Wadi Howar (e.g., Djabarona 84/13 and Abu Tabari S02/1).[101]

The custom of burying animal remains predates the acquisition of domestic animals. A burial from site 6-B-36, dating to the Qadan period (c. 14,000–10,000 BC), included two vertebrae of a large ungulate, probably wild aurochs, that were related to a possible funerary feast.[102] Other burials displayed bucrania at Jebel Sahaba, another Qadan site.[103] Possibly following up on this ancient tradition, domestic animals were not introduced in Sudan as a food resource, but as funerary elements. The earliest remains of domestic cattle in Nubia, dated 5750 BC, consist of a cattle skull placed in the burial of a child facing an adult male.[104] Several other sites (e.g., R12, Kadruka, Ghaba, Kadero and El-Kadada) revealed one or more bucrania as grave goods[105] and cattle skins as burial coverings (e.g., at Kadruka).[106] These

86 Russell 2007.
87 Fuller et al. 2018; Roffet-Salque et al. 2018.
88 Dittrich 2013.
89 Casciarri and Ahmed 2009.
90 Dyson-Hudson and Dyson-Hudson 1982.
91 Gifford-Gonzalez 2005.
92 Dunne et al. 2018.
93 Osypińska et al. 2021.
94 Stock and Gifford-Gonzalez 2013.
95 Roffet-Salque et al. 2018.
96 Wendorf and Schild 2001.
97 Linseele et al. 2014.
98 Gautier 2014.
99 Vermeersch et al. 2015.
100 Garcea 2020.
101 Dunne et al. 2018; Dunne et al. 2021; Garcea 2020.
102 Yeshurun 2018.
103 Wendorf 1968.
104 Honegger 2014.
105 Chłodnicki, Kobusiewicz and Kroeper 2011; Reinold 2000; Salvatori and Usai 2008; Salvatori, Usai and Lecointe 2016.
106 Reinold 2001.

offerings were interpreted as expressions of prestige, authority and/or wealth.[107]

Animal offerings do not only consist of cattle remains but also include small livestock and appear in a variety of funerary customs. A few sacrificial lambs and rare goat skulls were found at R12.[108] Caprines were also unearthed in seven burials at El-Kadada.[109] Sheep could be represented by either their full bodies, such as at Kadruka,[110] or only by their teeth, such as at El-Multaga.[111] One of the sheep from Kadruka was adorned with a necklace of amazonite beads around its neck.[112] These animal remains occur together with other funerary offerings such as personal ornaments, ceramic vessels, figurines or stone and bone tools, suggesting they were equally regarded as symbolically meaningful items.

Plants

Besides proving that ceramic vessels were used as containers of dairy products mentioned above, organic residues demonstrated that also vegetal products were processed in pots. At Kadero, 40% of the vessels were used as containers of substances of plant origin.[113] Lipids derived from plant processing were also found at Khor Shambat 1 and corroborate the phytolith evidence observed on grinding stones. No domestic plants were recovered at these sites, indicating instead an intensive exploitation of wild grasses of Panicoideae and wild fruits of *Ziziphus spina-christi* and *Celtis integrifolia*.[114]

Also the most common domestic cereals, wheats and barley, had no wild ancestors in Africa and were imported from Southwest Asia. Their regular cultivation became established in northern Egypt (Fayum and Merimde) in the mid-fifth millennium BC. In Sudan, they are known from botanical macro remains, pollen, phytoliths and starch remains on dental calculus in burials from R12 (c. 5300–5100 BC), Ghaba (5620–5480 and 4730–4540 BC) and Kadruka 1 (mid-fourth millennium BC).[115] While it is irrefutable that these Near Eastern cereals were valued in northern and central Sudan as early as the second half of the sixth millennium BC, they are not as widely spread as domestic livestock and only come from funerary contexts. Furthermore, it is not possible to determine whether they derived from local farming, as some authors claim[116] or were imported from elsewhere. In fact, other authors do not associate the presence of the earliest wheat and barley in burials with the beginning of agriculture in Sudan.[117] It seems more reasonable to associate the presence of these cereals in burials and their ritual consumption with the first appearance of wild aurochs and domestic cattle as funerary offerings. It should also be noted that there must have been technical challenges in cultivating wheat and barley as they are winter-rain cereals and can hardly grow in summer-rain regions without irrigation.

Conversely, summer rain-fed wild cereals, such as sorghum and millet, grew in North Africa and were locally domesticated. Evidence of wild sorghum gathering dates from c. 8000–7000 BC in the Egyptian Western Desert and from 5700–3750 BC in Sudan.[118] In the central Sahara, cultivation of wild cereals, including sorghum, is attested from c. 8200 BC.[119] Sorghum was domesticated in Sudan and represents the earliest evidence of its domestication in the world, c. 3500 BC.[120] Early cultivation occurred in the eastern Sudanic grasslands.[121] Site KG23 at Khashm el-Girba, belonging to the Butana Group,[122] provided the earliest evidence for its incipient domestication from c. 3500 BC, and Jebel Moya, in the southern Gezira, 350 km south-west of KG23, from 2500–2100 BC.[123] At Jebel Moya, sorghum occurs in a 70 cm thick Neolithic deposit also containing domestic cattle and sheep/goat.[124] MicroCT scanning of ceramic sherds from KG23 confirmed domestic sorghum at 3700–2900 BC.[125] The archaeobotanial assemblage from KG23 analysed by MicroCT scanning contained both wild (26%) and domesticated (69%) sorghum. Considering that domesticated morphology prevailed, Barron et al. advocate that the domestication process was nearing or at fixation by 3700–2900 BC and that cultivation had begun earlier, contradicting the hypothesis of a slow evolutionary process of sorghum domestication.[126] These authors also claim that domesticated sorghum was brought to the area rather than being locally domesticated. Finally, they observe that some communities may have preferred domesticated types, while others continued to exploit wild forms.

Sorghum could be used for consumption as well as for pottery tempering. Its seeds could be prepared in household ceramic pots and consumed as porridge, unlike domestic wheat and barley that were consumed

107 Salvatori and Usai 2008.
108 Pöllath 2008.
109 Bonnet et al. 1989.
110 Reinold 2000.
111 Peressinotto et al. 2004.
112 Reinold 2000.
113 Dunne et al. 2018.
114 Dunne et al. 2021.
115 Madella et al. 2014; Out et al. 2016; Reinold 2000; Ryan et al. 2016.
116 Salvatori and Usai 2019a; Salvatori and Usai 2019b.
117 Fuller and Hildebrand 2013; Garcea 2020; Hildebrand et al. 2018.
118 Barron et al. 2020.
119 Mercuri et al. 2018.
120 Vella Gregory and Brass 2021.
121 Fuller and Hildebrand 2013.
122 Manzo 2017.
123 Brass et al. 2022; Vella Gregory and Brass 2021.
124 Brass et al. 2022.
125 Barron et al. 2020.
126 Barron et al. 2020.

as bread and cooked in communal baking ovens in Egypt, northern Sudan and the Near East.[127] The cultural and adaptive boundary of these traditions lies precisely in Nubia, which represented a crossroads between bread-eating populations to the north and porridge-eating people to the south. In later times, bread consumption in Nubia was part of elitist ritual functions, as attested in Kerma and Meroe.[128] The role of ritual consumption of cereals originating from the Mediterranean world even in historical times reinforces the hypothesis that they were introduced into Nubia for these purposes as early as the Neolithic period.

Final remarks

Increasing social complexity is rooted in the Neolithic. This period marked the decline of egalitarian societies and the emergence of social inequality based on the value of wealth and capital as symbols of power and ostentation. It implied the adoption of a series of social patterns and cultural behaviours in all sectors, spanning from settlement systems to social roles and individual engagements, and affecting relationships, prestige values, ideology and symbols.[129]

The general picture of early food production and food producers in prehistoric Sudan depicts the spread of emerging interconnected communities. Increased trade, exchange and long-distance relationships favoured the acquisition and accumulation of valuable goods. Domestic animals and plants seemingly arrived in Nubia as part of traded goods together with other precious raw materials and finished products that first appeared in the tombs of emerging elites as early as the fifth millennium BC and increased in the fourth millennium BC. Items of Red Sea shells, ivory, malachite and amazonite were imported from East Africa possibly through intermediation of Butana Group peoples, who reached the Nile Valley and Upper Nubia across the Atbara Valley and the Fourth Cataract and interacted with Pre-Kerma, Late Neolithic and A-Group communities.[130] To the west, the Libyan Desert acted as Nubia's hinterland and, at the same time, contacts with Saharan groups developed. In the rainy seasons, the Laqiya region could offer extensive pastures for the herds of A-Group populations. Finally, from their base-camps in the Middle Wadi Howar the transhumant herders producing Leiterband pottery moved toward the west (Ennedi Erg and Sahara) and the south (Jebel Tageru).[131]

The prevalence of livestock, especially cattle, as funerary offerings in Nubia and the surrounding deserts over domestic plants testifies to a lifestyle mainly based on pastoralism that started in the Neolithic and continued in later periods.[132] While domestic animals gradually spread all over the country, domestic cereals remained restricted to Nubia and eastern Sudan due to unfavourable environmental conditions elsewhere.

Acknowledgements

I would like to cordially thank Julia Budka for inviting me to participate in the *DiverseNile Seminar Series 2021* on "Cultural Diversity in Northeast Africa" and to present a lecture and for proposing me to contribute an article to this volume. I am also grateful for her comments on an earlier version of this paper.

127 Dittrich 2017; Haaland 2007.
128 Haaland 2012.
129 Caneva 2016.
130 Manzo 2017.
131 Jesse 2021; Jesse et al. 2013; Keding 2006.
132 See Dubosson 2020.

Bibliography

Adelsberger, K., Lewis, J., Dodd, J.P., Hill, D., Smith, J.R. and Garcea, E.A.A.
2020 Mid-Holocene environmental change and human occupation at Sai Island, northern Sudan, *Geoarchaeology* 35, 803–818.

Alarashi, H., Gourichon, L., Khalidi, L., Chambon, P., Sellier, P., Maines, E., Aoudia, L., Anderson, P., Baumann, M. and Langlois, O.
2021 Survival kit for the afterlife or instruction manual for prehistorians? Staging artefact production in Middle Neolithic cemetery Kadruka 23, Upper Nubia, Sudan, *Antiquity* 2021, 1–8, https://doi.org/10.15184/aqy.2021.151.

Arkell, A.J.
1953 *Shaheinab*, London.

Barron, A., Fuller, D.Q., Stevens, C., Champion, L., Winchell, F. and Denham, T.
2020 Snapshots in time: MicroCT scanning of pottery sherds determines early domestication of sorghum (*Sorghum bicolor*) in East Africa, *Journal of Archaeological Science* 123, 105–259.

Bar-Yosef, O.
2013 Nile valley-Levant interactions: an eclectic review, in: N. Shirai (ed.), *Neolithisation of Northeastern Africa*, Berlin, 237–247.

Benoiston, A.-S., Bayle, P. and Crevecoeur, I.
2018 Biological affinity of the Mesolithic and Neolithic populations from El-Barga, Sudan: the dental remains, in: M. Honegger (ed.), *Nubian Archaeology in the XXIst Century: Proceedings of the Thirteenth International Conference for Nubian Studies*, Leuven, 805–815.

Bogaard, A., Allaby, R., Arbuckle, B.S., Bendrey, R., Crowley, S., Cucchi, T., Denham, T., Frantz, L., Fuller, D., Gilbert, T., Karlsson, E., Manin, A., Marshall, F., Mueller, N., Peters, J., Stépanoff, C., Weide A. and Larson, G.
2021 Reconsidering domestication from a process archaeology perspective, *World Archaeology* 56, 56–77.

Bonnet, C., Chaix, L., Lenoble, P., Reinold, J. and Valbelle, D.
1989 Sépultures à chiens sacrifiés dans la vallée du Nil, *Cahiers de Recherches de l'Institut de Papyrologie et d'Egyptologie de Lille* 11, 25–39.

Brass, M., Vella Gregory, I., Awad, A., Adam, A., Abdallah, R. and Alawad, O.
2022 An archaeology of pastoralism and agropastoralism in the Sudan, in: *Oxford Research Encyclopedia of Anthropology*, New York, 1–22.

Caneva, I. (ed.)
1988 *El Geili. The History of a Middle Nile Environment. 7000 B.C.–A.D. 1500*, BAR International Series 424, Oxford.

Caneva, I.
2016 Domestic livestock, pastoral nomadism and complex societies in the Nile valley: reflections on old questions, *Origini* 39, 101–118.

Casciarri, B. and Ahmed, A.G.M.
2009 Pastoralists under pressure in present-day Sudan: an introduction, *Nomadic Peoples* 13, 10–22.

Chłodnicki, M., Kobusiewicz, M. and Kroeper, K. (eds.)
2011 *Kadero: The Lech Krzyzaniak Excavations in the Sudan*, Poznań.

Crevecoeur, I.
2012 First anthropological insights on the early Holocene funerary assemblages from El-Barga, in: M. Honegger (ed.), *Kerma 2011-2012 Soudan*, Neuchâtel, 19–28.

D'Ercole, G.
2017 *Ceramic Manufacturing Techniques and Cultural Traditions in Nubia from the 8th to the 3rd Millennium BC: Examples from Sai Island*, Cambridge Monographs in African Archaeology 96, Oxford.

D'Ercole, G., Garcea, E.A.A., Eramo, G. and Muntoni, I.M.
2017 Variability and continuity of ceramic manufacturing of prehistoric pottery from Upper Nubia, Sudan: An ethnographic comparison, *Journal of Archaeological Science: Reports* 16, 553–563.

di Lernia, S.
2022 Earliest herders of the central Sahara (Tadrart Acacus Mountains, Libya): A punctuated model for the emergence of pastoralism in Africa, *Journal of World Prehistory* 36, 531–594.

Dittrich, A.
2013 Continuity, change and material memory: Taking a temporal perspective on the Neolithisation in Northeastern Africa, in: N. Shirai (ed.), *Neolithisation of Northeastern Africa*, Berlin, 43–64.
2017 Neolithization in progress – The advent of domesticates in Northeastern Africa, in: S. Burmeister and R. Bernbeck (eds.), *The Interplay of People and Technology: Archaeological Case Studies on Innovations*, Berlin Studies of the Ancient World 43, Berlin, 61–103.

Dubosson, J.
2020 Cattle cultures in ancient Nubia, in: G. Emberling and B.B. Williams (eds.), *The Oxford Handbook of Ancient Nubia*, Oxford, 908–926.

Dunne, J., di Lernia, S., Chłodnicki, M., Kherbouche, F. and Evershed, R.P.
2018 Timing and pace of dairying inception and animal husbandry practices across Holocene North Africa, *Quaternary International* 471, Part A, 147–159.

Dunne, J., Jórdeczka, M., Chłodnicki, M., Hardy, K., Kubiak-Martens, L., Moskal-del Hoyo, M., Osypińska, M., Portillo, M., Sobkowiak-Tabaka, I., Delgado-Raack, S., Bobrowski, P., Breeze, P.S., Drake, N., Manning, K. and Evershed, R.P.
2021 Holocene resource exploitation along the Nile: diet and subsistence strategies of Mesolithic and Neolithic societies at Khor Shambat 1, Sudan, *Antiquity* 95, 1426–1445.

Dyson-Hudson, N. and Dyson-Hudson, R.
1982 The structure of East African herds and the future of East African herders, *Development and Change* 13, 213–238.

FULLER, D.Q. and HILDEBRAND, E.
2013 Domesticating plants in Africa, in: P. MITCHELL and P. LANE (eds.), *The Oxford Handbook of African Archaeology*, Oxford, 507–527.

FULLER, D.Q., WILLCOX, G. and ALLABY, R.G.
2011 Cultivation and domestication had multiple origins: arguments against the core area hypothesis for the origins of agriculture in the Near East, *World Archaeology* 43, 628–652.

FULLER, D.Q. and GONZALEZ CARRETERO, L.
2018 The archaeology of Neolithic cooking traditions: archaeobotanical approaches to baking, boiling and fermenting, *Archaeology International*, 21, 1, 109–121.

GARCEA, E.A.A. (ed.)
2013 *Gobero: The No-Return Frontier. Archaeology and Landscape at the Saharo-Sahelian Borderland*, Frankfurt am Main.

GARCEA, E.A.A.
2016 Multi-stage dispersal of Southwest Asian domestic livestock and the path of pastoralism in the Middle Nile Valley, *Quaternary International* 412, Part B, 54–64.
2020 *The Prehistory of the Sudan*, Cham.

GARCEA, E.A.A. and D'ERCOLE, G.
2018 What do we see when we see a decoration? An overview on the pottery from Sai Island and Esh Shaheinab, in: J. KABACINSKI, M. CHŁODNICKI, M. KOBUSIEWICZ and M. WINIARSKA-KABACINSKA (eds.), *Desert and the Nile. Prehistory of the Nile Basin and the Sahara. Papers in Honour of Fred Wendorf*, Poznań, 153–181.

GARCEA, E.A.A. and HILDEBRAND, E.A.
2009 Shifting social networks along the Nile: Middle Holocene ceramic assemblages from Sai Island, Sudan, *Journal of Anthropological Archaeology* 28, 304–322.

GARCEA, E.A.A., KARUL, N. and D'ERCOLE, G.
2016 Southwest Asian domestic animals and plants in Africa: routes, timing and cultural implications, *Quaternary International* 412, Part B, 1–10.

GAUTIER, A.
2014 Animal remains from the Hidden Valley Neolithic Site, Farafra Oasis, in: B.E. BARICH, G. LUCARINI, M.A. HAMDAN and F.A. HASSAN (eds.), *From Lake to Sand: The Archaeology of Farafra Oasis, Western Desert, Egypt*, Florence, 369–374.

GIFFORD-GONZALEZ, D.
2005 Pastoralism and its consequences, in: A.B. STAHL (ed.), *African Archaeology: A Critical Introduction*, Oxford, 187–224.

GIFFORD-GONZALEZ, D. (ed.)
2008 *Adrar Bous: Archaeology of a Central Saharan Granitic Ring Complex in Niger*, Tervuren.

GIFFORD-GONZALEZ, D. and HANOTTE, O.
2013 Domesticating animals in Africa, in: P. MITCHELL and P. LANE (eds.), *The Oxford Handbook of African Archaeology*, Oxford, 491–505.

HAALAND, R.
1987 *Socio-Economic Differentiation in the Neolithic Sudan*, BAR International Series 350, Oxford.
2007 Porridge and pot, bread and oven: Food ways and symbolism in Africa and the Near East from the Neolithic to the present, *Cambridge Archaeological Journal* 17, 165–182.

HILDEBRAND, E.A., GARCEA, E.A.A., FLORENZANO, A. and MERCURI, A.M.
2018 Multiscalar perspectives on Holocene climatic and environmental changes in the Sahara and Nile Corridor, with special consideration of archaeological sites on Sai Island, Sudan, in: A.M. MERCURI, C. D'ANDREA, R. FORNACIARI and A. HÖHN (eds.), *Plants and People in Africa's Past: Progress in African Archaeobotany*, New York, 215–245.

HONEGGER, M.
2005 El-Barga: un site clé pour la compréhension du Mésolithique et du début du Néolithique en Nubie, *Revue de Paléobiologie* 10, 95–104.
2014 Recent advances in our understanding of prehistory in Northern Sudan, in: J.R. ANDERSON and D.A. WELSBY (eds.), *The Fourth Cataract and Beyond. Proceedings of the 12th International Conference for Nubian Studies*, British Museum Publications on Egypt and Sudan 1, Leuven, 19–30.
2019 The Holocene prehistory of Upper Nubia until the rise of the Kerma kingdom, in: D. RAUE (ed.), *Handbook of Ancient Nubia, vol. 1*, Berlin; Boston, 217–238.

HONEGGER, M. and WILLIAMS, M.
2015 Human occupations and environmental changes in the Nile valley during the Holocene: The case of Kerma in Upper Nubia (northern Sudan), *Quaternary Science Reviews* 130, 141–154.

IRISH, J.D. and USAI, D.
2021 The transition from hunting-gathering to agriculture in Nubia: dental evidence for and against selection, population continuity and discontinuity, *Proceedings of the Royal Society, B, Biological Sciences* 288, 20210969, https://doi.org/10.1371/journal.pone.0108517.

JESSE, F.
2006–2007 Un nouvel aspect du Néolithique au Wadi Howar (nord du Soudan) – des vases caliciformes, *Cahiers de Recherches de l'Institut de Papyrologie et d'Egyptologie de Lille* 26, 187–196.
2021 From hunters to herders: The Libyan desert in prehistoric times, in: G. EMBERLING and B.B. WILLIAMS (eds.), *The Oxford Handbook of Ancient Nubia*, Oxford, 250–269.

JESSE, F. and KEDING, B.
2002 Death in the desert – burials in the Wadi Howar Region (Eastern Sahara), in: JENNERSTRASSE 8 (ed.),

Tides of the Desert: Contributions to the Archaeology and Environmental History of Africa in Honour of Rudolph Kuper, Africa Praehistorica 14, Köln, 277–293.

2007 Holocene settlement dynamics in the Wadi Howar Region (Northern Sudan) and the Ennedi Mountains (Chad), in: O. Bubenzer, A. Bolten and F. Darius (eds.), *Atlas of Cultural and Environmental Change in Arid Africa*, Africa Praehistorica 21, Köln, 42–43.

Jesse, F., Keding, B., Lenssen-Erz, T. and Pöllath, N.

2013 'I hope your cattle are well': archaeological evidence for early cattle-centred behaviour in the Eastern Sahara of Sudan and Chad, in: M. Bollig, M. Schnegg and H.-P. Wotzka (eds.), *Pastoralism in Africa: Past, Present and Future*, New York, 66–103.

Kapustka, K., Lisá, L., Bajer, A., Buriánek, D., Varadzin, L. and Varadzinová, L.

2019 Gouges: iconic artifacts of the early Neolithic period in Central Sudan, *African Archaeological Review* 36, 505–534.

Keding, B.

2000 New data on the Holocene occupation of the Wadi Howar region (Eastern Sahara/Sudan), in: L. Krzyzaniak, K. Kroeper and M. Kobusiewicz (eds.), *Recent Research Into the Stone Age of Northeastern Africa*, Poznań, 89–104.

2006 Pottery of the Wadi Howar – traditions, transformations and their implications, in: K. Kroeper, M. Chlodnicki and M. Kobusiewicz (eds.), *Archaeology of Early Northeastern Africa. In Memory of Lech Krzyżaniak*, Studies in African Archaeology 9, Poznań, 235–259.

Kindermann, R. and Riemer, H.

2021 From complex hunter-gatherers in the Eastern Sahara to the Early Nile Neolithic, in: J. M. Rowland, G. Lucarini and G. J. Tassie (eds.), *Revolutions. The Neolithisation of the Mediterranean Basin: The Transition to Food Producing Economies in North Africa, Southern Europe and the Levant*, Berlin, 203–229.

Kuper, R. and Riemer, H.

2013 Herders before pastoralism: prehistoric prelude in the Eastern Sahara, in: M. Bollig, M. Schnegg and H.-P. Wotzka (eds.), *Pastoralism in Africa: Past, Present and Future*, New York, 31–65.

Lange, M. and Nordström, H.-A.

2006 Abkan connections – The relationship between the Abkan culture in the Nile Valley and early Nubian sites from the Laqiya region (Eastern Sahara, Northwest Sudan), in: K. Kroeper, M. Chłodnicki and M. Kobusiewicz (eds.), *Archaeology of Early Northeastern Africa. In Memory of Lech Krzyżaniak*, Studies in African Archaeology 9, Poznań, 297–312.

Langlois, O., Durrenmath, G., Khalidi, L., Karrar, H.K.A., Cez, L., Gourichon, L., Sambo, H. and Pruvost, C.

2019 Chronicle of a destruction foretold: a belated 61 reassessment of the preservation status of Neolithic habitation sites in the Kadruka concession (Northern Dongola Reach, Sudan), *Sudan & Nubia* 23, 61–67.

Linseele, V., Holdaway, S.J. and Wendrich, W.

2016 The earliest phase of introduction of Southwest Asian domesticated animals into Africa. New evidence from the Fayum Oasis in Egypt and its implications, *Quaternary International* 412, Part B, 11–21.

Linseele, V., Van Neer, W., Thys, S., Phillipps, R., Cappers, R., Wendrich, W. and Holdaway, S.

2014 New archaeozoological data from the Fayum "Neolithic" with a critical assessment of the evidence for early stock keeping in Egypt, *PLoS ONE* 9, e108517, https://doi.org/10.1371/journal.pone.0108517.

Macklin, M.G., Woodward, J.C., Welsby, D.A., Duller, G.A.T., Williams, F.M. and Williams, M.A.J.

2013 Reach-scale river dynamics moderate the impact of rapid Holocene climate change on floodwater farming in the desert Nile, *Geology* 41, 695–698.

Madella, M., García-Granero, J.J., Out, W.A., Ryan, P. and Usai, D.

2014 Microbotanical evidence of domestic cereals in Africa 7000 years ago, *PLoS One* 9, e110177, https://doi.org/10.1371/journal.pone.0110177.

Maines, E., Sellier, P., Chambron, P. and Langlois, O.

2017 Burying children and infants at Kadruka 23: New insights into juvenile identity and disposal of the dead in the Nubian Neolithic, in: E. Murphy and M. Le Roy (eds.), *Children, Death and Burial: Archaeological Discourses*, Oxford, 43–56.

Manzo, A.

2011 *Italian Archaeological Expedition to the Eastern Sudan of the University of Naples "L'Orientale": 2010 Field Season*, Naples.

2017 *Eastern Sudan in its Setting: The Archaeology of a Region far from the Nile Valley*, Oxford.

2019 Eastern Sudan in the 3rd and 2nd millennia BC, in: D. Raue (ed.), *Handbook of Ancient Nubia, vol. 1*, Berlin; Boston, 335–365.

Marshall, F., Reid, R.E.B., Goldstein, S., Storozum, M., Wreschnig, A., Hu, L., Kiura, P., Shahack-Gross, R. and Ambrose, S.H.

2018 Ancient herders enriched and restructured African grasslands, *Nature* 561, 387–390.

Mercuri, A.M., Fornaciari, R., Gallinaro, M., Vanin, S. and di Lernia, S.

2018 Plant behaviour from human imprints and the cultivation of wild cereals in Holocene Sahara, *Nature Plants* 4, 71–81.

Myers, O.H.

1960 Abka again, *Kush* 8, 174–181.

Nordström, H.-A.

1972 *Neolithic and A-group sites*, Uppsala.

2006 The discovery of the Neolithic in Nubia, *ArchéoNil* 16, 31–39.

Osypińska, M., Osypiński, P., Belka, Z., Chłodnicki, M., Wiktorowicz, P., Ryndziewicz, R. and Kubiak, M.
2021 Wild and domestic cattle in the ancient Nile Valley: marks of ecological change, *Journal of Field Archaeology* 46, 7, 429–447.

Out, W.A., Ryan, P., García-Granero, J.J., Barastegui, J., Maritan, L., Madella, M. and Usai, D.
2016 Plant exploitation in Neolithic Sudan: a review in the light of new data from the cemeteries R12 and Ghaba, *Quaternary International* 412, Part B, 36–53.

Peressinotto, D., Schmitt, A., Lecointe, Y., Pouriel, R. and Geus, F.
2004 Neolithic nomads at El Multaga, Upper Nubia, Sudan, *Antiquity* 78, 54–60.

Phelps, L.N., Broennimann, O., Manning, K., Timpson, A., Jousse, H., Mariethoz, G., Fordham, D.A., Shanahan, T.M., Davis, B.A.S. and Guisan, A.
2019 Reconstructing the climatic niche breadth of land use for animal production during the African Holocene, *Global Ecology and Biogeography* 2019, 1–21.

Pöllath, N.
2008 Tools, ornaments and bucrania: the animal remains, in: S. Salvatori and D. Usai (eds.), *A Neolithic Cemetery in the Northern Dongola Reach: Excavations at Site R12*, London, 59–77.

Reinold, J.
2000 *Archéologie au Soudan: Les civilisations de Nubie*, Paris.
2001 Kadruka and the Neolithic in the northern Dongola Reach, *Sudan & Nubia* 5, 2–10.
2006 Les cimetières préhistoriques au Soudan – coutumes funéraires et systèmes sociaux, in: I. Caneva and A. Roccati (eds.), *Acta Nubica: Proceedings of the X International Conference of Nubian Studies*, Rome, 139–162.
2007 *La nécropole néolithique d'el-Kadada au Soudan central*, Paris.

Roffet-Salque, M., Gillis, R., Evershed, R.P. and Vigne, J.-D.
2018 Milk as a pivotal medium in the domestication of cattle, sheep and goats, in: C. Stépanoff and J.-D. Vigne (eds.), *Hybrid Communities: Biosocial Approaches to Domestication and Other Trans-Species Relationships*, London, 127–143.

Russell, N.
2007 The domestication of anthropology, in: R. Cassidy and M. Mullin (eds.), *Where the Wild Things are Now*, London, 27–48.

Ryan, P., Out, W.A., García-Granero, J.J., Madella, M. and Usai, D.
2016 Plant macroremains from the white deposits and skeletons of Ghaba and R12 cemeteries. Identification and implications, in: S. Salvatori, D. Usai and Y. Lecointe (eds.), *Ghaba: An Early Neolithic Cemetery in Central Sudan*, Frankfurt, 109–120.

Sadig, A.M.
2010 *The Neolithic of the Middle Nile region: An Archaeology of Central Sudan & Nubia*, Kampala.
2013 Reconsidering the 'Mesolithic' and 'Neolithic' in Sudan, in: N. Shirai (ed.), *Neolithisation of Northeastern Africa*, Berlin, 23–42.

Salvatori, S. and Usai, D. (eds.)
2008 *A Neolithic cemetery in the Northern Dongola Reach: Excavations at Site R12*, Sudan Archaeological Research Society 16, London.

Salvatori, S. and Usai, D.
2019a The Mesolithic and Neolithic in Sudan, in: D. Raue (ed.), *Handbook of Ancient Nubia, vol. 1*, Berlin; Boston, 171–194.
2019b The Neolithic and 'Pastoralism' along the Nile: A dissenting view, *Journal of World Prehistory* 32, 251–285.

Salvatori, S., Usai, D. and Lecointe, Y. (eds.)
2016 *Ghaba: An Early Neolithic Cemetery in Central Sudan*, Frankfurt.

Sellier, P., Aoudia, L., Maines, E. and Chambon, P.
2019 A Neolithic burial ground from Upper Nubia as seen from recent work at Kadruka 23, *Sudan & Nubia* 23, 68–76.

Shiner, J.
1968 The cataract tradition, in: F. Wendorf (ed.), *The Prehistory of Nubia, Vol. 2*, Dallas, 535–629.

Sirak, K.A., Sawchuk, E.A. and Prendergast, M.E.
2022 Ancient human DNA and African population history, in: *Oxford Research Encyclopedia of Anthropology*, New York, 1–43.

Stock, F. and Gifford-Gonzalez, D.
2013 Genetics and african cattle domestication, *African Archaeological Review* 30, 51–72.

Vella Gregory, I. and Brass, M.
2021 Sudan, Prehistory of, in: C. Smith (ed.), *Encyclopedia of Global Archaeology*, Cham, 1–17.

Vermeersch, P.M., Linseele, V., Marinova, E., Van Neer, W., Moeyersons, J. and Rethemeyer, J.
2015 Early and Middle Holocene human occupation of the Egyptian Eastern Desert: Sodmein Cave, *African Archaeological Review* 32, 465–503.

Wendorf, F.
1968 Site 117: A Nubian final Paleolithic graveyard near Jebel Sahaba, Sudan, in: F. Wendorf (ed.), *The Prehistory of Nubia, Vol. 2*, Dallas, 954–995.

Wendorf, F. and Schild, R. (eds.)
2001 *Holocene Settlement of the Egyptian Sahara: The Archaeology of Nabta Playa*, vol. 1, New York.

Williams, B.
2006 A-Group society in the context of North eastern Africa, in: K. Kroeper, M. Chłodnicki and M. Kobusiewicz (eds.), *Archaeology of Early Northeastern Africa. In Memory of Lech Krzyżaniak*, Studies in African Archaeology 9, Poznań, 177–194.

WILLIAMS, M.
2019 *The Nile Basin: Quaternary Geology, Geomorphology and Prehistoric Environments*, Cambridge.

WINCHELL, F.
2013 *The Butana Group Ceramics and Their Place in the Neolithic and Post-Neolithic of Northeast Africa*, BAR International Series 2459, Oxford.

YESHURUN, R.
2018 Taphonomy of old archaeofaunal collections: New site-formation and subsistence data for the Late Paleolithic Nile Valley, *Quaternary International* 471, Part A, 35–54.

ZERBONI, A.
2013 Early Holocene palaeoclimate in North Africa: an overview, in: N. SHIRAI (ed.), *Neolithisation of Northeastern Africa*, Berlin, 65–82.

ZERBONI, A. and NICOLL, K.
2018 Enhanced zoogeomorphological processes in North Africa in the human-impacted landscapes of the Anthropocene, *Geomorphology* 331, 22–35.

Chapter 6

C-Group cattle management in the Second Cataract area

Shayla Monroe[1]

Abstract

Here, I present a brief osteometric comparison of cattle from two archaeological assemblages in ancient Sudan. These measurements are reviewed in the context of regional variation in the size and shape of cattle in Kerma, Lower Nubia, and pharaonic Egypt. The evolutionary and ecological principles of variation and breed formation are described. Archaeological studies comparing cattle stature across ancient Europe and ancient Rome are considered, and then factors likely to have contributed to stature variations in Nile Valley cattle populations are discussed, including differential land use between the territories of Egypt, Lower Nubia, and Kerma, variations in local ecology, and divergent political trajectories and their associated implications for pastoralist production.

Keywords:

Cattle, Sudan, Nubian C-Group, Kerma, ecology, zooarchaeology

The Egyptian fortress of Askut was erected near the Second Cataract of the Nile River ca. 1850 BC. Askut was one of a series of fortresses erected in the Middle Kingdom to buffer the boundaries of the pharaonic state from the growing political threat of Kerma to the south (Fig. 1).[2] The fort was excavated in the 1950s by Alexander Badawy and the archaeological assemblage offers a unique perspective on a sphere of prolonged ethnic interaction in the political and cultural borderlands between ancient Egypt and ancient Nubia. The ceramic assemblages and associated material were analysed by Stuart Tyson Smith.[3] My dissertation research focused on Askut's faunal remains.[4] In its own right, Askut's full faunal assemblage tells a story of herding, and some hunting, in an ancient colonial context. It is the cattle remains, however, that are particularly interesting because the individual specimens are so very curiously *small.*

My osteometric study of cattle reared by the C-Group at the Second Cataract found that they were much smaller than the Kerma cattle studied by Louis Chaix[5] by nearly every measure. Furthermore, when compared to the mean measurements of cattle bones from multiple sites through time, the Askut cattle are smaller by almost every available measure, with the only two similarly sized populations being found at Wadi Howar[6] and Gebelein (see Fig. 1).[7] Excluding Wadi Howar for the moment, what the Askut and Gebelein cattle have is that members of the Nubian C-Group apparently reared them both.

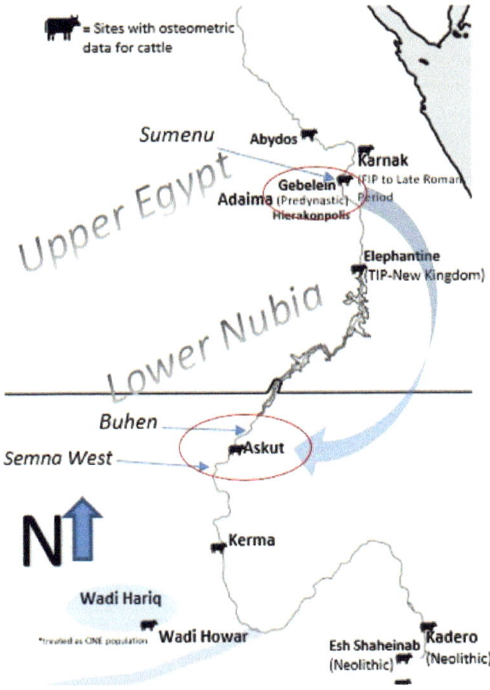

Fig. 1 Map of selected osteometric data set for cattle in the Nile Valley region (S. Monroe).

Chaix[8] used the length and breadth of Third Lower Molars as a proxy for animal size. Table 1 below compares the measurements for Askut specimens against those of Kerma. Here, the range of Third Lower Molar measurements for Askut is shown to be lower that than of Kerma, a first line of evidence that Askut cattle were smaller than Kerma cattle overall.

1 Department of Anthropology, Harvard University; shaylamonroe@fas.harvard.edu.

2 Smith 1991; Wegner 1995.

3 Smith 1995; see also Chapter 9 in this volume.

4 Monroe 2021.

5 Chaix 2007.

6 Pöllath and Peters 2006.

7 Chaix 2007.

8 Chaix 2007.

Element	Kerma (N)	Askut (N)	Kerma Min	Askut Min	Kerma Max	Askut Max	Kerma Mean	Askut Mean	Kerma S.D	Askut S.D.
Length M3	37	5	38.2	34.29	41.5	38.17	38.2	36.82	1.8	1.66
Breadth M3	29	9	14.8	13.5	17	14.74	14.8	13.85	1	0.56

Table 1 Comparison of Lower Molar 3 measurements: Kerma vs. Askut. S.D.= Standard Deviation.

Dimension	Kerma (N)	Askut (N)	Kerma Min	Askut Min	Kerma Max	Askut Max	Kerma Mean	Askut Mean	Kerma S.D	Askut S.D.
Glpe	177	14	54.6	40.31	72	67.43	64.3	58.4	3.5	5.9
Bp	183	14	27.2	26.17	38	33.56	32.9	29.2	2.6	2.2
SD	171	13	21.7	21.18	32.6	28.42	24.1	23.8	2.3	1.9
Bd	164	13	25.9	23.67	39.4	33.24	30.6	28.2	2.5	2.6

Table 2 Osteometric comparison of Phalanx 1: Kerma vs. Askut. S.D.= Standard Deviation.

Most of Chaix's comparative stature data comes from measurements of the various dimensions of first, second, and third phalanges.[9] By comparing all of the measured dimensions of the anterior first phalanx, Chaix found statistical differences between Neolithic Nile Valley cattle, Predynastic Egyptian cattle, and Kerma cattle.[10] Table 2 shows that the maximum dimensions of the Kerma proximal phalanges are larger than the Askut phalanges for all of Askut's time periods. The aggregate proximal phalanx measurements suggest that the cattle acquired at Askut came from a population that was decidedly smaller than Kerma cattle.

The next set of graphs take the mean of Askut's phalanx measurements, accounting for several dimensions, and compare Askut's mean measurements with those of other archaeological cattle populations. Figures 2, 3, and 4 show measurements taken according to the standards in von den Driesch[11] and show that the proximal phalanges found at Askut were shorter in length than at least four other Nile Valley cattle populations described below, and narrower in proximal width than those of the other groups, with the exception of Egyptian Predynastic cattle.

Studies of C-Group cattle are rare. Bangsgaard found so little evidence of cattle in her study of C-Group settlements that she, logically, cast doubt as to whether the C-Group even *had* cattle.[12] However, we have evidence from two populations of cattle associated with C-Group settlements, and they are both characterised by noticeably small-statured individuals. I am not sure if this is due to (a) the geopolitical position of the C-Group causing them to raise their cattle in harsher environments, whereas Kerma people had access to more abundant grasslands to the south, (b) a simple difference in cattle phenotype/breed/genetics, or (c) Kerma cattle were larger due to the Kerma polity facilitating and supporting long-term breeding and improvement, similarly to the ancient Egypt state farther north.

It is likely that the size differences between Kerma and C-Group cattle are associated with multiple interrelated factors. The foremost question addressed in this chapter is: do the skeletal differences between C-Group, Kerma, and Egyptian cattle reflect different environments, different choices, or possibly a complex combination of political, ecological/environmental, and economic circumstances and decisions. To illustrate how these factors have played out elsewhere, I will repeatedly refer to two better documented cases: that of ancient Dynastic Egypt, where written records augment what can be gleaned from archaeofaunal remains, and Rome in the eras of its Republic and its Imperium, where written records are supported by the study of osteometric data spanning centuries. Human communities, including cattle pastoralists, vary a great deal in how they manage plant, animal, and land resources. Even communities living in close

9 Chaix 2007.
10 Chaix 2007.
11 von den Driesch 1976.
12 Bangsgaard 2014.

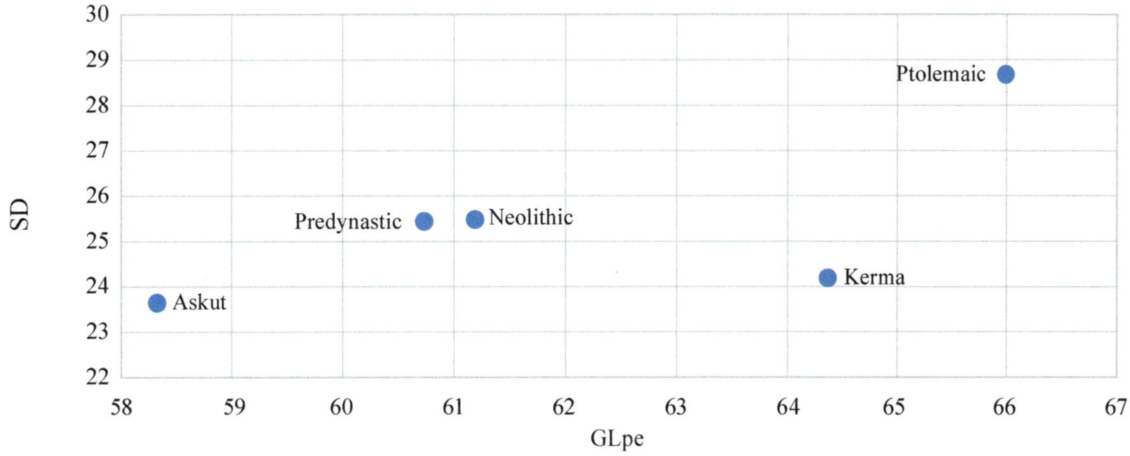

Fig. 2 Plot of proximal phalanx mean narrowest diameter (SD) x mean length (GLpe) for 5 cattle populations.

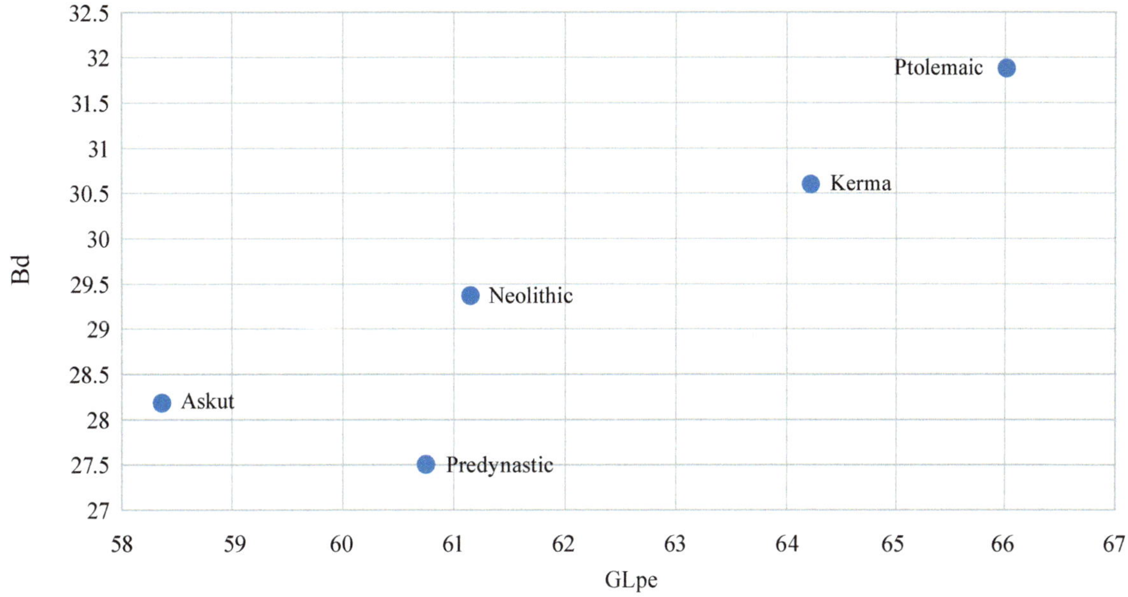

Fig. 3 Plot of proximal phalanx mean distal breadth (Bp) x mean length (GLpe) for 5 cattle populations.

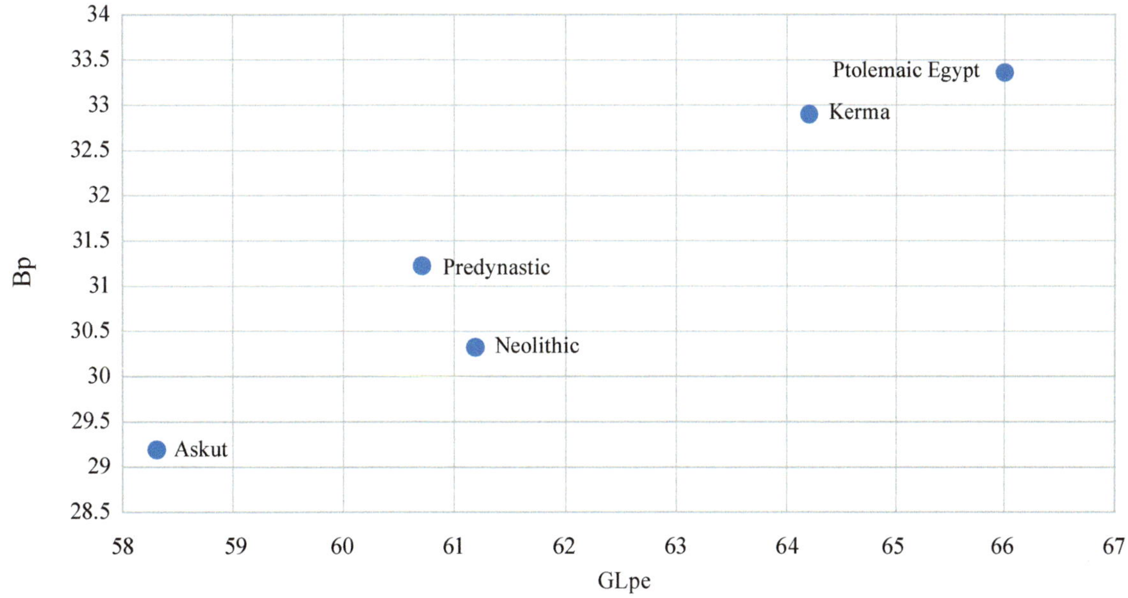

Fig. 4 Plot of proximal phalanx mean proximal breadth (Bp) x mean length (GLpe) for 5 cattle populations.

geographic proximity can differ in their strategies for using the landscape they share. Agrodiversity is a concept used to detect spatial and temporal variations in the way that humans manage biophysical resources and species exploiting for food production. Agrobiodiversity, a lens within agrodiversity, in essence, seeks to understand how people manage their "land, water, and biota as a whole."[13]

Historically, cattle keeping in Africa has been adaptable to a variety of cultures, economies, and ecosystems. For domesticated animals, humans are very much a part of their ecology. Herders make decisions, including sexually selective processes, and create conditions that act upon the bodies of cattle during their lifetime development and over the course of generations. Perhaps turning the lens of agrobiodiversity toward the ancient Nile Valley can help us examine the interplay between decisions and conditions that have long term, visible effects on ancient cattle populations. Cattle size cannot be used as a straightforward proxy for environmental conditions, but it may prove a productive starting point for understanding the diversity of ecological strategies employed by state and non-state pastoralists in the ancient Middle Nile Valley.

Cattle stature and archaeology

Herders face economic, geographic, topographical, and environmental circumstances that have both intentional and unintentional effects on the size of cattle.[14] A variety of archaeological studies have documented changes in stature over time in more extensively studied European cattle populations, and these offer some perspectives on the cattle in Nubia.[15] In pre-imperial Rome, skeletal elements of improved cattle populations grew in three dimensions simultaneously: body length, body width, and body depth. It appears that, in some areas around Rome, width and depth were selected for before height, while in other regions, what MacKinnon refers to as "stockiness" (being skeletally robust and heavily muscled) did not increase, even when body width did.[16] MacKinnon connects regional increases in cattle stature over time with agricultural and demographic changes related to the changing nature of the Roman state.[17] Reasons for these changes in cattle morphology included the pressing demand for meat for aggregated urban human populations and those of the standing, pre-Imperium Roman army, leading to selection for larger-bodied cattle. As well, he cites the import of larger cattle phenotypes into Rome from foreign locales, with the Epirote breed from Greece being one possible example.

Breed formation is multicausal, and cattle are subject to some of the same evolutionary principles affecting the relationship between the body size of wild species and their environment. Ecological principles seek to explain aspects of that relationship, such as Allen's Rule, which correlates animal size, mass, and shape with climate and environmental conditions.[18] As such, evolutionary principles must be taken into consideration even when looking at changes in domesticated animals over time.

Acquiring and providing an optimal diet for cattle depends on many things, including climate, altitude, species competition in the landscape, as well as the herder mobility, the human ability to move cattle towards richer food sources. Felius and colleagues argue that the overall gradual decrease in size among European cattle after the Bronze Age was an adaptation to seasonal food scarcity associated with severe winters.[19] Breeding larger cattle requires an optimal diet for the herds year-round.

Defining improvement

MacKinnon describes the process of *improvement* as the selective manipulation of variable traits such as meat weight, traction power, and other qualities that might be more dependent on localised environments.[20] For examples, smaller cattle tend to need less water, so they could very well have the advantage over larger breeds in arid environments. Individual phenotypic and behavioural traits can offer different practical advantages, and desirability of these traits can largely depend on what the herd keeper's day-to-day and long-term priorities. It is logical to raise or acquire cattle with traits that are relevant to and harmonious with one's economic circumstances. Animals known for being obedient or strong can save household managers among pastoralists time and energy.[21] Cattle breeding communities might select for these traits when they are "worth" more than size, coat colour, or projected milk and meat yield. Choices in trait selection have consequences, and if repeated, can eventually result changed genetic makeup of a cattle population.

Without aDNA, it may not be possible to attribute morphological differences in ancient Nile Valley Bos populations as breeds, regional variations, or phenotypic clusters. It is difficult to know whether we are cataloguing separate "breeds" or simply aggregations of local variation from adaptation to microregions. MacKinnon theorises as to whether distinct cattle "breeds" are zooarchaeologically recognizable through biometric data. While breeds in

13 Brookfield and Stocking 1999.
14 Bopp-Ito et al. 2018.
15 Rizzetto, Crabtree and Albarella 2017; Trentacoste et al. 2021; Jeanjean et al. 2023.
16 MacKinnon 2010.
17 MacKinnon 2010.
18 Ayala and Avise 2014.
19 Felius et al. 2014.
20 MacKinnon 2010.
21 Gifford-Gonzalez 2013.

the modern sense are defined by genetic information, MacKinnon describes ancient breeds in the Roman Empire as loosely conforming to regional types.[22] For Kerma, Chaix's study categorises distinct facial morphology of cattle across the various regions subject to the Kerma state, recognising that there are physically distinct types.[23] However, stature appears fairly consistent across these Kerma types because their minimum measurements are consistently larger than those at Askut.

Ancient knowledge of phenotypic manipulation

Stature is not the only physical trait manipulated by ancient cattle keepers. It appears that ancient herders also selected for other traits, such as coat colour and horn morphology. As this chapter focuses on evidence from archaeology, there can be less emphasis here on perishable traits like coat colour. However, coat colour's importance in selecting breeding pairs, has been demonstrated on the part of ancient Egyptian cattle breeders.[24] It makes sense that breeders who knew how to select for coat colour also knew how to select for other phenotypic traits and expressions.

We know coat colour was important for some cattle-centred rituals in Egypt[25] It could be that separate sets of breeders within Egypt and Kerma may have had separate aims: some could breed for meat weight, some could breed for traction and transport, some could breed animals for their beauty and phenotypic appropriateness for ritual requirements.

Ancient Egyptian illustrations of horn shape show an early example of humans exploiting natural variation to modify cattle phenotypes. Wild cattle have long horns to protect themselves against predators, and also, among males, to compete with one another for access to mates. Long horns, however, can make cattle more dangerous and difficult for human handling.[26] Short-horned taurine cattle first appear in early Bronze Age Mesopotamia. By the Egyptian Second Intermediate Period (1782 to 1550 BC), short-horned cattle became gradually more prevalent in Egyptian wall paintings, until they become the dominant form.[27]

The circumstances under which a population becomes a "breed" are complex: there are cultural, economic, and ecological factors at play.[28] Citing examples of African cattle breeds with localised advantages in immunity and milk production, Gifford-Gonzalez goes on to state that: "The evolutionary histories of these breeds are necessarily entangled with those of their herders, whose lives depended, to one degree or another, upon their prudent management, and whose fortunes rose or fell upon the animals' resilience and productivity."[29]

In order to become distinct from other populations in a species, a "breed" must reproduce in isolation, meaning that there would be minimal mating between cattle from different geographic regions.[30] The separation might not be simply geographic. Theoretically, cultural/linguistic or political borders might exist across which people would not trade cattle. However, historically, that may not stop people who have good reasons to engage in trade. This leads to the question of whether or not Egyptian breeders would have kept native Egyptian stock separate from cattle acquired in war, trade, and tax tribute. With so many cattle to choose from within their territory, Egyptian breeders might have had an abundance of specimens from which to choose desirable phenotypic traits, selecting for body size, shape, horn shape, and coat colour.

State-driven breed improvement

By exploring the patterns of ancient state-driven breed improvement, I argue that in addition to the internal motivation of herding peoples, external motivations and coercion from above may affect cattle, if the herding group is subordinated within a political hierarchy. In some cases, , the aims of complex polities and the aims of herders might be one and the same, such as herd growth optimization. In other contexts, herders might be guided more by risk-reduction strategies, such as East African herders selecting for smaller, "tougher" cattle that withstand the practices of bleeding and give milk under drought conditions. In any case, the state may use power, economic rewards, and influence, to sway herders towards certain management and breeding practices that conflict with their own, local interests.

In addition to ideological or aesthetic motivations, early states had two very practical incentives for rewarding the breeding of larger cattle: the provisioning of aggregated/urban population provisioning and military provisioning. Population increases associated with intensified grain production would have resulted in a growing population of humans that also needed, or wanted, some form of animal protein. Human population aggregation, such as we see in the ancient urban centres of the Kerma polity and Egypt, can create pressure on cattle-herders to breed livestock that are taller, stronger, "meatier", or more productive if they are primarily dairy cattle.[31] Not all Egyptian and Kerma communities were heavy meat-eaters, and beef was apparently reserved for special occasions,

22 MacKinnon 2010.
23 Chaix and Grant 1992.
24 Gardiner 1942; Schwabe 1984.
25 Ibid.
26 Felius et al. 2014.
27 Epstein 1971; Brewer 2001; Felius et al. 2014.
28 Gifford-Gonzalez 2013.
29 Gifford-Gonzalez 2013, 7.
30 MacKinnon 2010.
31 MacKinnon 2010.

ritual settings, or otherwise elite contexts. However, with the decrease in nearby wild animals that could be hunted, livestock and small stock served a practical purpose of supplementing the cereal-based diets of Bronze Age Nile Valley peoples.[32]

While the matter of "feeding cities", or aggregated human populations, with livestock has been addressed methodologically by Zeder, and specifically in ancient Egypt by Redding, the provisioning ancient states' military forces, is more challenging and, outside of the Roman Empire, has been less studied.[33] Hesse and Wapnish examined archaeofaunal assemblages from ancient military settlements in Southwestern Asia,[34] and my dissertation examined the food refuse at the Egyptian military fortress of Askut, in an effort to answer some questions about provisioning the troops stationed there.[35] Askut's assemblage differed from those Hesse and Wapnish examined transport animals (i.e., equids) were much less common than predicted by their model.[36] Only a few scattered equid elements at Askut, and, even with horses found at nearby fortresses such as Buhen, it appears that provisioning of troops in pharaonic Egypt was relied on river transport.[37]

That Kerma was logistically capable of feeding a substantial army, there is no doubt. Military provisioning may have mirrored that of neighbouring Egypt, with the Nile River was used as a thoroughfare to transport food and supplies. In Egypt, documents attest that state-owned cattle herds were managed at the city of Kom el-Hisn, and local leaders were obligated to deliver animals for temple offerings and for provisioning troops.[38] Given the enormousness of Kerma's cattle wealth attested up to around 1750 BC, a similar strategy seems well within the capabilities of the Kerma state.[39]

To imagine how extensively ancient militarism might affect cattle size, once again, we look to the Republic Era of Rome, during which military units and legionnaires had to be fed en masse. According to MacKinnon, the size of Roman cattle increased during this time, likely due at least in part to the need to feed the armies.[40] Once the Roman state moved into its Imperial Age, in which war was largely waged abroad, filling the bellies of legionnaires was outsourced to occupied territories from which food resources could be requisitioned.[41]

Cattle size continued to increase during the Roman Imperial Era, with the new impetus being the increased need to supplement imported grain with protein to feed urban Roman populations. Felius and colleagues note that during the Pax Romana, an age of sustained Roman Imperialism, political and economic stability made it easier for larger cattle from Rome's centre to be exported out into distant provinces.[42] Likewise, local cattle in the Roman provinces grew in size after Roman hegemony was established.[43]

It is interesting that large cattle essentially disappeared from Rome after the fall of the Empire.[44] Not only does this support the association of state influence with increased cattle size, but it also suggests that – at least for Rome – breeding cattle for size was a top-down process, serving the interests of the state apparatus. But not necessarily the long-term requirements of the herds. Without the state, politically driven incentives for breeding larger cattle, such as provisioning military or urban populations in exchange for remuneration, may have been subordinated to local interests and motives. While Felius and colleagues suggest a breeding "system had that *regressed* to *primitive* practices"[45] [emphasis mine], I propose that local herders acting in their own interests and that of their herds with a combination of ecological knowledge and intention that was neither "regressive" nor "primitive".

Cattle stature and land use

It is challenging to uncover the relationship between cattle stature and land use in ancient times using archaeological methods alone. In pharaonic Egypt, we do know something of the relationship between cattle rearing and land use and allocation from written records. Cattle were herded in those areas of pharaonic Egypt's territory not suited for crop production: the marshes, the drylands borders, the bush between settlements, and the wadis. Such marginal areas were occupied by hunters and herders, as well as people producing and harvesting commodities like honey, wood, and salt.[46] A substantial cattle pasturing took place in the Nile Delta region, taking advantage of a salt marsh ecosystem between marine water and fresh tides. The plants that grow in this area are tolerant of salt water, and some saline vegetation species can actually respond favourably to the stimulation provided by grazing animals.[47] Movement of the animals disturbs the soil and encourages herbs, grasses, and shrubs in this category to proliferate

32 Saffirio 1972; Ikram 2012, 199, 229.
33 Zeder 1991; Redding 1992.
34 Hesse and Wapnish 1985.
35 Monroe 2021.
36 Hesse and Wapnish 1985.
37 Clutton-Brock 1974; Raulwing and Clutton-Brock 2009.
38 Redding 1992; Moreno Garcia 1999.
39 Chaix and Grant 1992; Chaix 2007.
40 MacKinnon 2010.
41 Sidebottom 2004.
42 Felius et al. 2014.
43 Groot 2017; Trixl, Steidl and Peters 2017.
44 Felius et al. 2014.
45 Felius et al. 2014.
46 Moreno Garcia 2017.
47 Dítětová et al. 2016.

after the herds move on. Herds benefit from lightly salty vegetation in place of salt licks. Lobban argues that ancient Egypt's intense plant cultivation in the Nile Delta in part developed to produce fodder for its expanding cattle population.[48] In ancient Egypt, the optimal locations for pasturing would have likely changed seasonally in response to the yearly inundation of the Nile. Administrators could pasture cattle in one part of Egypt and then transfer them, by walking or by boat, to another area where beef was required. Livestock were sent live throughout Egypt according to the requirements of the state, and slaughtered only when they reached the recipient site.[49] The process of cattle distribution illustrates the capability of the Egyptian state to manage animal resources from production to consumption, across several political and ecological zones, to provision thousands of workers and staff for state projects.[50] Longer-distance movements of livestock were mainly accomplished via cattle boats, rather than overland.

While we do not have a corresponding written record from Kerma, we can assume that state societies had to factor in regional ecological knowledge into managing agricultural and pastoralist production. For Kerma and its outliers, I fear that we are some years away from the amassing the magnitude of remote sensing data and associated landscape information that might lend insights of the detail built up for the ancient Egyptian state.[51]

MacKinnon notes that in ancient Rome, some fields that served for animal pasturage were used for cultivation in alternate years.[52] This pattern of alternate use is widespread in traditional Africa and Eurasian agronomy; soils depleted by the planting of cereal grains can be enriched by the urine and dung of cattle and small stock. Practices such as this one can exacerbate differences in natural land quality over time, and it can take several years to several decades for environmental, demographic, economic, or political changes to influence decisions concerning land-use allocation.[53]

Theoretically, shifts in cattle size and shape might also be associated with a reduction in transhumant mobility. Hafsaas notes a gradual reduction in the mobility of the Nubian C-Group, which is supported by human dental evidence of a gradually increasing dietary reliance on grain.[54] However, the two C-Group samples with published measurements do not show appreciable difference in cattle stature over time.

Using other species in conjunction with *Bos*

An analysis of agrobiodiversity must consider contexts in which domesticated species are raised in combination with one another. The goals and priorities of cattle keepers often change in areas where cattle coexist with equids, and change in other ways when cattle are kept with caprines. Equids can provide draft power, and this means that bulls and oxen can be used for other purposes or consumed as food. MacKinnon notes that Pliny documents the use of donkeys rather than oxen to plough areas of the Roman empire in which the soils were drier and less dense.[55] Considerations of cattle size and agrobiodiversity in the ancient Nile Valley should therefore aim to take into account the contexts and frequency in which cattle and donkeys are found at the same site.

Unlike in European contexts, where, after the introduction of the horse collar, diminished cattle populations are associated with increased use of horses for ploughing and increased human consumption of grain,[56] horses in the Nile Valley arrive fairly late, and then they are largely associated with warfare rather than farming.[57] In terms of smaller equids, in the case of the ancient Nile Valley and southeastern Sahara, donkeys aided in mobility and transport rather than intensified farming.

Ethnoarchaeological studies of East African pastoralist groups, such as the Maasai, shows how donkeys can aid in the mobility of cattle herding groups by transporting supplies and group members, such as babies and elders, who might not otherwise travel as well.[58] Donkeys are valuable in for mobility in arid lands because they can go without water for two to three days.[59] Among the archaeological sites west of the Third Cataract that contain evidence of donkeys (i.e. Laqiya, Wadi Hariq, and Wadi Howar, see Fig. 1),[60] Wadi Howar also contains cattle that are small in stature, similar to those found in the C-Group enclaves mentioned above.[61] By 4000 BC, Wadi Howar's contribution to the flow of the Nile river had diminished substantially, compared to previous times.[62] It is conceivable that people facing an ongoing scarcity of water, like the last human populations of Wadi Howar, would simultaneously select smaller cattle that do better in arid environments, while also employing donkeys, with their complementary ability to weather aridity, for transport.

48 Lobban 1989.
49 Papazian 2013.
50 Papazian 2013.
51 Cf. Grzymkski 2004; Budka 2020.
52 MacKinnon 2010.
53 Brookfield and Stocking 1999.
54 Hafsaas 2006; Beckett and Lovell 1994.
55 MacKinnon 2010.
56 Felius et al. 2014.
57 Spalinger 2007; Spalinger 2008; Schrader et al. 2018; Turner 2021.
58 Marshall and Wiessbrod 2011.
59 Förster 2007.
60 Förster 2007.
61 Pöllath and Peters 2006; Monroe 2021.
62 Nicoll 2004; Pachur and Kröpelin 1987.

Conclusions

Many factors influence the phenotypic traits of domesticated cattle, some of which are more easily isolated than others. Zooarchaeological analyses show that the average size and shape of largely contemporaneous cattle in the ancient Nile Valley varied according to region and political territory. While future research must aim to acquire finer chronological resolution, this chapter was a first step in summarising the related political and ecological factors that would influence divergent cattle morphology among animals cared for by pharaonic Egyptians, Kerma people, and C-Group Nubians.

Bibliography

Ayala, F.J. and Avise, J.C.
2014 *Essential Readings in Evolutionary Biology*, Baltimore.

Bangsgaard, P.
2014 Nubian faunal practices: Exploring the C-Group "Pastoral Ideal" at nine cemeteries, in: J.R. Anderson and D.A. Welsby (eds.), *The Fourth Cataract and Beyond. Proceedings of the 12th International Conference for Nubian Studies*, British Museum Publications on Egypt and Sudan 1, Leuven, 437–355.

Beckett, S. and Lovell, N.C.
1994 Dental disease evidence for agricultural intensification in the Nubian C-Group, *International Journal of Osteoarchaeology* 4 (3), 223–239.

Bopp-Ito, M., Deschler-Erb, S., Vach, W. and Schibler, J.
2018 Size diversity in Swiss Bronze Age cattle, *International Journal of Osteoarchaeology* 28 (3), 294–304.

Brewer, D.J.
2001 Cattle, in: D.B. Redford (ed.), *The Oxford Encyclopedia of Ancient Egypt*, Oxford, 242–244.

Brookfield, H. and Stocking, M.
1999 Agrodiversity: definition, description and design, *Global Environmental Change* 9 (2), 77–80.

Budka, J.
2020 Kerma presence at Ginis East: the 2020 season of the Munich University Attab to Ferka survey project, *Sudan & Nubia* 24, 57–71.

Chaix, L.
2007 Contribution to the knowledge of domestic cattle in Africa: the osteometry of fossil Bos taurus from Kerma, Sudan (2050–1750 BC), in: G. Grupe and J. Peters (eds.), *Skeletal Series and Their Socio-Economic Context*, Rahden, 120–249.

Chaix, L. and Grant, A.
1992 Cattle in ancient Nubia, *Anthropozoologica* 16, 61–66.

Clutton-Brock, J.
1974 The Buhen horse, *Journal of Archaeological Science* 1 (1), 89–100.

Dítětová, Z., Dítě, D., Eliáš, P. and Galvánek, D.
2016 The impact of grazing absence in inland saline vegetation–a case study from Slovakia, *Biologia* 71 (9), 980–988.

Epstein, H.
1971 *The Origin of Domestic Animals of Africa*, Revised Edition, New York; London; Munich.

Felius, M., Beerling, M.L., Buchanan, D.S., Theunissen, B., Koolmees, P.A. and Lenstra, J.A.
2014 On the history of cattle genetic resources, *Diversity* 6 (4), 705–750.

Förster, F.
2007 With donkeys, jars and water bags into the Libyan Desert: the Abu Ballas Trail in the late Old Kingdom/First Intermediate Period, *British Museum Studies in Ancient Egypt and Sudan* 7, 1–36.

Gardiner, A.H.
1942 Writing and literature, in: J.R. Harris (ed.), *The Legacy of Egypt*, Oxford, 53–79.

Gifford-Gonzalez, D.
2013 Animal genetics and African archaeology: why it matters, *African Archaeological Review* 30, 1–20.

Groot, M.
2017 Developments in animal husbandry and food supply in Roman Germania Inferior, *European Journal of Archaeology* 20 (3), 451–471, doi:10.1017/eaa.2016.31.

Grzymski, K.
2004 Landscape archaeology of Nubia and central Sudan, *African Archaeological Review* 21, 7–30.

Hafsaas, H.
2006 *Cattle Pastoralists in a Multicultural Setting: the C-Group People in Lower Nubia 2500–1500 BCE*, The Lower Jordan River Basin Programme Publications 10, Bergen.

Hesse, B. and Wapnish, P.
1985 *Animal Bone Archaeology: From Objectives to Analysis*, Washington, DC.

Ikram, S.
2012 From food to furniture: animals in ancient Nubia, in: M.M. Fisher, P. Lacovara, S. Ikram and S. D'Auria (eds.), *Ancient Nubia: African Kingdoms on the Nile*, Cairo, 210–228.

Jeanjean, M. Mureau, C., Forest, V. and Evin, A.
2023 Morphometric evolution of the domestic triad, in western *Gallia Narbonensis* (southern France, Languedoc), between the 2nd c. BC and the 4th c. AD: Preliminary and critical use of log size index for diachronic analysis, *Quaternary International* 662–663, 13–25, https://doi.org/10.1016/j.quaint.2022.07.001.

Lobban, Jr., R.A.
1989 Cattle and the rise of the Egyptian state, *Anthrozoös* 2 (3), 194–201.

MacKinnon, M.
2010 Cattle 'breed' variation and improvement in Roman Italy: connecting the zooarchaeological and ancient textual evidence, *World Archaeology* 42 (1), 55–73.

Marshall, F. and Weissbrod, L.
2011 Domestication processes and morphological change: Through the lens of the donkey and African pastoralism, *Current Anthropology* 52 (S4), S397–S413.

Monroe, S.L.
2021 *Colonizing Cattle: The Zooarchaeology of a Military Frontier in the Egyptian-Nubian Borderlands*, PhD dissertation, University of California, Santa Barbara.

Moreno García, J.C.
1999 *Ḥwt et le milieu rural égyptien du IIIe millénaire. Economie, administration et organisation territoriale,* Bibliothèque de l'Ecole des Hautes Etudes Sciences Historiques et Philologiques 337, Paris.
2017 Trade and power in ancient Egypt: Middle Egypt in the late third/early second millennium BC, *Journal of Archaeological Research* 25, 87–132.

Nicoll, K.
2004 Recent environmental change and prehistoric human activity in Egypt and Northern Sudan, *Quaternary Science Reviews*, 23 (5-6), 561–580.

Pachur, H.J. and Kröpelin, S.
1987 Wadi Howar: Paleoclimatic evidence from an extinct river system in the southeastern Sahara, *Science* 237 (4812), 298–300.

Papazian, H.
2013 The central administration of the resources in the Old Kingdom: Departments, treasuries, granaries and work centers, in: J.C. Moreno García (ed.), *Ancient Egyptian Administration*, Handbook of Oriental Studies, Section 1: The Near and Middle East 104, Leiden, 41–83.

Pöllath, N. and Peters, J.
2006 On the possible use of the LSI scaling technique for stature analysis in cattle, *Revue de Paléobiologie* 24 (Vol. spec. 10), 225–235.

Raulwing, P. and Clutton-Brock, J.
2009 The Buhen horse: Fifty years after its discovery (1958–2008), *Journal of Egyptian History* 2 (1), 1–106.

Redding, R.W.
1992 Egyptian Old Kingdom patterns of animal use and the value of faunal data in modelling socioeconomic systems, *Paléorient* 18 (2), 99–107.

Rizzetto, M., Crabtree, P.J. and Albarella, U.
2017 Livestock changes at the beginning and end of the Roman period in Britain: issues of acculturation, adaptation, and 'improvement', *European Journal of Archaeology* 20 (3), 535–556, doi:10.1017/eaa.2017.13.

Saffirio, L.
1972 Food and dietary habits in ancient Egypt, *Journal of Human Evolution* 1 (3), 297–305.

Schrader, S.A., Smith, S.T., Olsen, S. and Buzon, M.
2018 Symbolic equids and Kushite state formation: A horse burial at Tombos, *Antiquity* 92 (362), 383–397.

Schwabe, C.W.
1984 A unique surgical operation on the horns of African bulls in ancient and modern times, *Agricultural History* 58 (2), 138–156.

Sidebottom, H.
2004 *Ancient Warfare: A Very Short Introduction*, Oxford.

Smith, S.T.
1991 Askut and the role of the Second Cataract forts, *Journal of the American Research Center in Egypt* 28, 107–132.
1995 *Askut in Nubia: The Economics and Ideology of Egyptian Imperialism in the Second Millennium BC*, London; New York.

Spalinger, A.J.
2007 The Army, in: T. Wilkinson (ed.), *The Egyptian World*, London, 118–128.
2008 *War in Ancient Egypt: The New Kingdom*, Malden, MA; Oxford.

Trentacoste, A., Nieto-Espinet, A., Guimarães, S., Wilkens, B., Petrucci, G. and Valenzuela-Lamas, S.
2021 New trajectories or accelerating change? Zooarchaeological evidence for Roman transformation of animal husbandry in Northern Italy, *Archaeological and Anthropological Sciences* 13, 1–22.

Trixl, S., Steidl, B. and Peters, J.
2017 Archaeology and zooarchaeology of the Late Iron Age-Roman transition in the province of Raetia (100 bc–100 ad), *European Journal of Archaeology* 20 (3), 431–450, doi:10.1017/eaa.2016.25.

Turner, S.
2021 *The Horse in New Kingdom Egypt: Its Introduction, Nature, Role and Impact*, Wallasey.

von den Driesch, A.
1976 *A Guide to the Measurement of Animal Bones from Archaeological Sites*, Cambridge, MA.

Wegner, J.W.
1995 Regional control in Middle Kingdom Lower Nubia: the function and history of the site of Areika, *Journal of the American Research Center in Egypt* 32, 127–160.

Zeder, M.A.
1991 *Feeding Cities: Specialized Animal Economy in the Ancient Near East*, Washington, DC.

Chapter 7

The management of vegetal resources in Bronze Age Nubia

Frits Heinrich[1], Annette M. Hansen[2] and Philippa Ryan[3]

Abstract

This chapter provides an overview of the vegetal resources of Bronze Age Nubia. After providing a brief introduction to, and historiography of, archaeobotanical research in Nubia, we first describe the ecological context in which plants in Nubia grow and show how the complex interplay water availability, seasonality, geology, and technology co-determine the vegetation and the potential and nature of agriculture. We then reflect on the management of the vegetal resources and distinguish between taxa that naturally occur in the environment and those that are cultivated as crops on the fields, which were mostly introduced to Nubia from other regions. We then continue to discuss different practical categories of plants and their uses (e.g., cereals, pulses, fruit trees) and reflect on their attestation and potential use in Nubia. While there are currently few archaeobotanical studies for the study area and period, the results thus far attest a diverse crop curriculum, a wide range of managed wild plant resources, and the use of crop processing waste as by-products that were upcycled into products for other non-food sectors. These practices both reflect resilience strategies and a sophisticated circular economic system in Bronze Age Nubia.

Keywords:

Plant life, crops, wild plants, vegetal resource management, archaeobotany, Nubia

1 Research Group Interdisciplinary Historical Food Studies (FOST), Department of History, Archaeology, Arts, Philosophy and Ethics, Vrije Universiteit Brussel (VUB), Brussels, Belgium; Research Group Industrial Microbiology and Food Biotechnology (IMDO), Department of Bioengineering Sciences, Vrije Universiteit Brussel (VUB), Brussels, Belgium; Frits.Heinrich@vub.be.

2 Research Group Interdisciplinary Historical Food Studies (FOST), Department of History, Archaeology, Arts, Philosophy and Ethics, Vrije Universiteit Brussel (VUB), Brussels, Belgium; Annette.Hansen@vub.be.

3 Royal Botanic Gardens, Kew, UK; p.ryan@kew.org.

Introduction

Plant life is one of the most important resources available to any society past or present, and Bronze Age Nubia was no exception.[4] Not only are plants at the basis of the terrestrial food chain from which almost all animal and human foodstuffs are derived, but in the premodern world plants were also at the basis of, or at least played a pivotal role in, almost all production chains in non-food sectors. In this chapter we aim to provide a comprehensive overview and assessment of the diverse vegetal resources available in Bronze Age Nubia and reflect on their uses, management, and visibility by looking primarily at the archaeobotanical evidence. We will begin with a brief survey of the different types of evidence we have for the vegetal resources and the historiography of their study for Bronze Age Nubia. Subsequently, we will reflect on the ecological context and the constraints it imposed on plants; here we will also treat human strategies and technologies employed to mitigate these constraints. We will then proceed to discuss the different taxa, both cultivated and wild plants, available in Nubia during the Bronze Age and their uses and importance.

Studying human plant use in Nubia

Due to their omnipresence in the physical environment and socioeconomic importance in daily life, plants and plant use leave behind a diverse array of types of evidence. These do not only include references in the written sources, iconographic depictions, and archaeological objects related to their production, storage, processing, or consumption (e.g., tools, granaries, cooking installations, ceramics), but also physical remains of the plants themselves. While in most places the conservation of organic materials is contingent on them being charred following purposeful or accidental exposure to fire, being mineralised under moist conditions, or ending up in waterlogged anaerobic conditions, in hyper-arid regions such as Nubia materials may be preserved in a desiccated state, provided they are out of reach of groundwater and Nile floods. This can allow for exceptional preservation and a wealth of materials, including plant-based artefacts (e.g., textiles and wooden implements). Archaeological plant remains

4 We here use the definition of Nubia as the region extending from the First Cataract at Aswan through modern Khartoum and from the Red Sea in the east to the Libyan Desert in the west, following Kipfer 2021.

are studied through the discipline of archaeobotany (also known as ethnoarchaeobotany, or instead as palaeoethnobotany in North America), which can be defined as the study of past human-plant relationships in the broadest sense, addressing all aspects of such interactions from gathering or cultivating to the processing, storage, preparation, consumption, trade, and discard of plant materials as well as all techniques and implements used in such processes. While the use of plants for food is often a focus, other plant uses such as for fuel, fodder, textiles, dyes, and construction materials are also studied, as is the use of plants as medicinal, ritual, or pharmaceutical ingredients. Within archaeobotany there are further subdisciplines that look at different types of plant remains.

Most archaeobotanists study what are called macro-remains: the seeds and fruits of plants and associated plant parts. These are identified using morphological identification criteria (and with the help of a stereomicroscope, botanical reference collection, and plant atlases) and are subsequently quantified. While seeds and fruits may be found in any archaeological context (e.g., floors and surface levels), those related to cooking (e.g., ovens and hearths) and waste disposal (e.g., middens) are often the richest in archaeobotanical remains. Contexts in which plant remains were used as temper such as mudbricks, clay ovens and pottery also tend to be rich in archaeobotanical material, while seeds and fruits may also leave behind identifiable impressions in mudbrick constructions and pottery.[5] Taxonomically, macro-archaeobotanical remains can often be identified at the species or sub-species level depending on the surviving plant parts. Interdisciplinary approaches in which macro-archaeobotanical insights and evidence from written sources are combined can be useful in improving interpretations of ancient plant names,[6] help in the quantification of documentary sources,[7] and aid in the interpretation of price data of in-kind prices expressed in plant material.[8] Macro-remains are also suitable for various types of scientific analyses. These include ancient DNA studies (for which desiccated material has much potential), C14 dating (in which seeds and fruits may provide better results than wood or charcoal as they represent a single year), and stable isotope analyses that may provide insights into manuring (nitrogen), watering practices (carbon), and provenance (oxygen, strontium), though many of these new techniques have not yet, or not yet widely, been applied to Nubian case studies to date.

Phytolith studies is another subdiscipline of archaeobotany. It focuses on phytoliths: microscopic silica bodies that form in plant tissues of certain groups of plants, including grasses, sedges, and palms. While the taxonomic zoom of phytoliths is usually limited to the family or genus level (rarely at species level), they can provide useful insights, especially when macro-remains are not present, either because they were destroyed or derive from plant parts that typically do not survive as charred macro-remains (such as leaves). Anthracology and dendroarchaeology are archaeobotanical disciplines that study archaeological charcoal and wood respectively, with many specialists working on both materials. The use of wood in construction and tools, fuel, and the make-up and management of woodland resources are foci here, while wood may also be used for dendrochronology. The discipline of palynology studies archaeological pollen. While the other disciplines discussed above obtain their materials from anthropogenic contexts, palynologists take soil cores from within the landscape, preferably from layers that were wet while pollen from the environment were being deposited (e.g., lake sediments). The results, which are typically at the family level, are also less directly linked to human activity, but rather to diachronic developments of the vegetation in the wider landscape and can for instance be used in assessing historical environmental and climate change. Lastly, ethnoarchaeobotany is the ethnographic and ethnobotanical study of traditional plant use, agriculture, food preparation, and associated practices to learn more about their historical counterparts and to be able to better interpret their archaeological remains. This can be very valuable in assessing and reconstructing rather practical and mundane aspects of the plant economy on which the written sources tend to remain silent; ethnoarchaeobotanical insights can sometimes also be applied in experimental archaeology. While under threat by modernization worldwide, various traditional practices have been maintained in some form in modern Nubia or were until quite recently (especially in comparison to Egypt).

Though archaeobotanical studies are a more recent branch of scholarship than in Egypt, they have a substantial and ongoing tradition in Nubia.[9] It has been noted that the overall number of modern and

5 See Hansen, Walker and Heinrich 2017 for clay ovens; Heinrich and Hansen 2020 for a historiography of mudbrick evidence in Egypt and Sudan; Fuller, Macdonald and Vernet 2007 and Fuller et al. 2014 for a discussion of impressions on pottery.

6 Heinrich and Wilkins 2013/2014.

7 Heinrich and van Pelt 2017a; 2017b.

8 van Pelt and Heinrich 2019.

9 Examples of earlier studies include Erroux 1980; van Zeist 1983; 1987; Chaix 1984; Rowley-Conwy 1989; Chaix and Grant 1993. For an overview of recent archaeobotanical scholarship in Nubia, we refer the reader to the literature review by Fuller 2015 and the overviews provided in Fuller and Lucas 2021 and Heinrich and Hansen 2020. Examples of Nubian Bronze Age phytolith studies may be found in Ryan, Cartwright and Spencer 2012; 2016, Ryan 2018 and Le Moyne et al. 2023; those for charcoal and wood in Cartwright 2001; 2018; those for plant archaeogenetics in Palmer et al. 2009 and Pérez-Escobar et al. 2022, and those for ethnoarchaeobotany in Ryan 2017 and Ryan et al. 2021; 2022.

Fig. 1 Typical small agricultural plot with faba bean (*Vicia faba*) and date palm trees (*Phoenix dactylifera*) on low lying land. Note the strip of woody vegetation at the top of the river embankment (left), and the scattered Acacia spp. trees towards the desert's edge (right). Sai Island, Eastern shore, close to the Pharaonic town, January 2015 (photo by F. Heinrich).

systematic studies of settlements and habitation sites remains very limited in Nubia, also for the Bronze Age. Furthermore, much scholarship, often due to the nature of archaeological priorities, is focused on archaeobotanically-speaking less representative cemetery and temple sites and contexts.[10] The most extensively studied habitation sites for Bronze Age Nubia are the New Kingdom islands towns of Sai[11], inhabited in the Early and Middle Bronze Age by the Kerma people and in the Late Bronze Age by both Egyptians and Nubians, and Amara West[12], the administrative centre of Upper Nubia during the Ramesside Period in the Late Bronze Age and inhabited by Egyptians and Nubians.

Ecological context

Nubia is situated in the Sahara Desert and has a warm desert climate (BWh in the Köppen classification) with very limited and unreliable rainfall, especially in the north of between 3–75 mm per year; there vegetation is largely absent and limited to the Nile Valley, though grasses and herbs occur along some paleochannels and wadi areas depending on ground water and incidental rains may occur elsewhere. South of the Fifth Cataract and in the Red Sea lowlands, annual rainfall is higher (75–400 mm – yet also unreliable), and the vegetation graduates into becoming more Sahelian consisting of semi-desert scrub and grasses and a greater density of woody plants along the wadis.[13] With limited and unreliable rainfall, and in the absence of aquifers such as those that occur in the Egyptian Western Desert, agriculture is almost exclusively reliant on water from the river Nile and its annual flooding after the monsoons in the Ethiopian highlands.

It will come as no surprise that one of the primary limiting factors on human exploitation of vegetal resources in Nubia is water: its limited availability poses constraints both for plant growth and the amount of available arable land. This limited availability has deeply intertwined temporal and spatial aspects that furthermore have an intricate relationship with technology. In spatial terms, in much of Nubia, unlike in Egypt, local geography with steep and high riverbanks

10 See Fuller 2015; Fuller and Lucas 2021, for a discussion.

11 Heinrich and Hansen 2020.

12 Ryan, Cartwright and Spencer 2012; 2016; Ryan and Spencer 2013; Cartwright and Ryan 2017.

13 Darbyshire et al. 2015.

Fig. 2 Opportunistic agriculture on a makeshift plot using the residual soil moisture to cultivate different pulses at the bottom of a small creek and sandbank islet after river water receded. Sai Island, Eastern shore, close to the Pharaonic town, January 2015 (photo by F. Heinrich).

along the Nile reduces the size of the floodplain and flood basins, hence reducing the amount of naturally inundated land as well as the potential for storing water.[14] This would have led to a more fragmented agricultural landscape with smaller plots along a much narrower strip of cultivation along the river than one would have seen in the Egyptian Nile Valley and Delta (see Fig 1).

The situation may have been somewhat different in areas with more favourable geographic conditions such as the Seleim Basin in the Dongola Reach, where groundwater may be reached further inland with the help of wells.[15] Furthermore, through the use of water-lifting devices such as the shaduf, higher lying land could be irrigated perennially, and a combination of small channels and a succession of shadufs could be used to bridge greater height differences. While this constitutes an investment of additional labour, the method was efficacious and in parts of Nubia was in use, alongside the sāqiyah waterwheel, until the rise of the diesel generator a few decades ago. Another form of perennial irrigation would have been the manual watering of kitchen and vegetable gardens, for which archaeologically plots associated with houses have been encountered at the Pharaonic settlement at Amara West.[16] The relative scarcity of arable land would moreover have made the many islands that characterise the middle and upper Nile landscape valuable assets. The larger islands (such as Amara, Ernetta, and Sai) have the attractive feature that they offer four rather two shorelines, while the many smaller and sometimes temporary islands were open to more opportunistic exploitation.[17] Similarly, the gradual receding of the water levels from the flood into the next summer would have opened up temporary land in the riverbed of any seasonally flowing channels (depending on depth), allowing for impromptu cultivation on makeshift 'fields' of interannually variable dimensions (see Fig. 2 and Fig. 3).

The temporal aspect of water availability in Nubia is mostly defined by the seasonality of the Nile flood and the inundation of arable land that could afterwards be cultivated. The timing of the floods made Nubia very suitable for the cultivation of winter crops. These could be sown after the waters had receded and complete their lifecycles before the hot and dry late spring and

14 Welsby 1996.
15 Ryan 2017.
16 Ryan 2017.
17 Ryan 2017.

Fig. 3 Opportunistic agriculture on a makeshift plot using the residual soil moisture to cultivate different pulses at the bottom of river shore embankment after river water receded. Sai Island, Eastern shore, close to the Pharaonic town, January 2015 (photo by F. Heinrich).

early summer and the next flood season. This did not fully exclude the option of cultivating summer crops, including watermelons and melons, for instance by planting them close to the summer bed of the river,[18] on seasonal islands, or by using the shaduf.[19] Only after the spread of more efficient Hellenistic water lifting technology from Egypt, such as the sāqiyah, during the Late Meroitic and Post-Meroitic Periods, summer crops would become more important.[20] This has been argued to have eventually led to a transformation of the farming system towards a regime in which double-cropping and agricultural intensification with summer cash crops would play a central role.[21]

Cultivating crops versus managing wild plant resources

Plants can be legitimately categorised in different manners, and, as archaeobotanists are wont to do, in this survey of plants available during the Nubian Bronze Age, we will take a combined approach. On the one hand, we will follow genetic relationships (e.g., for the cereals and the pulses), while on the other we will group them along the lines of functional uses by humans (e.g., vegetables and oil crops). A further distinction that we will make, and one that is especially important because the theme of this book is on resources and their management, is whether the plant in question was cultivated as a crop or exploited as it naturally occurred in the environment as a wild plant.

Insights from ethnographic studies about the role of wild plants today within agricultural communities across Africa and in Sudan teach us they were likely important in most preindustrial societies.[22] However, as wild resources are often a more informal sector of the economy, they tend to be underrepresented in written sources. This can make it difficult to quantitatively assess use and to qualify them conceptually: for instance, how were distinctions between 'wild' and 'cultivated' plants made?[23] Notable exceptions to scarcer references are medical or magical texts, that often include a wide range of wild taxa among ingredients, though this is not always representative of

18 Fuller 2015.
19 Ryan 2017.
20 Clapham and Rowley-Conwy 2007.
21 Fuller 2015.
22 Barucha and Pretty 2010; Al-Battal 1991.
23 Cf. Frayn 1975; Frayn 1979; Zocchi et al. 2022.

regular plant use in society at large.[24] In addition, when wild plants bring forth products that are commercially important products (e.g., incense, spices, other exotics), we find more references.[25] For attestations of everyday use, archaeobotanical evidence is one of the most important sources with which to recognize the historical use of wild taxa. A complicating factor however can be that while a wild plant may have certain known uses, us encountering it at an archaeological site does not always mean it was used for that purpose. Especially plants with obscure medical or magical uses mentioned in written sources, depending on the archaeological context they were found in, may often just represent weeds or material that ended up in the settlement accidentally from the wider environment.[26] In rare cases new methodologies, such as the chemical analysis of dental calculus in human remains, make it possible to obtain direct evidence for wild plant consumption. Using this technique, the consumption of the tubers of purple nutsedge (*Cyperus rotundus*) could for instance be shown at Al Khiday.[27] The assessment of modern ecology and vegetation, as well as ethnoarchaeobotanical investigations into modern ethnographic wild plant use can also be informative in modelling wild plant use in the past. While humans can both purposefully and unwittingly affect the natural vegetation of their environment, the qualitative presence of certain wild taxa in an area is typically a constant on human timescales, especially in the ancient world. In fact, most of the wild plants that were available in Nubia during the Bronze Age were also available during the Neolithic and would throughout the Meroitic, Medieval, and Ottoman Periods remain available until this day. As with most natural resources – the obvious other example in the Nubian and Egyptian contexts being water and irrigation – some form of active management to regulate access and use likely was necessary to avoid overexploitation (with the exception perhaps of any exploited edible leafy weeds that grow within and around farmers' fields). While our evidence for Nubia is limited, from both historical and ethnographic evidence we know that throughout history wild vegetal resources were not always a true 'free for all', with some control being exerted over them through (*de facto*) private ownership, community governance,[28] or state-imposed legislation.

For cultivated plants, or crops, the situation is a bit more complex. Most cultivated plants are domesticates: plants of which the characteristics have been altered through artificial selection by humans, and that for completing their life cycles to a greater or lesser extent rely on humans. Cultivation therefore requires a much more intense form of management: farming. Most of our crops come from only a limited number of centres of domestication. This logically means that outside of these areas, they were introduced at some point before which they were not available. Similarly, crops could disappear again from the curriculum of available taxa if their cultivation was discontinued. Archaeobotanists are therefore very interested in crop histories, both in terms of the timing of new regional introductions as well as diachronic shifts in crop selection.[29] The crops that are attested for Bronze Age Nubia, which we will discuss below, mainly belong to the so-called *Neolithic Package*, a curriculum of founder crops originating from the Fertile Crescent that were introduced in Nubia during the Neolithic after having been brought upstream along the Nile through Egypt.[30]

Cereals

Cereals are plants from the Poaceae (or grasses) family that are used as food by humans.[31] The collection of grains from wild stands of grasses by hunter-gatherers was instrumental in their ultimate domestication that heralded the advent of farming. Throughout the ancient world cereals became the most important category of staple, and their primary use was, as it is today, that of a grain crop from which bread and porridge can be made. In Nubia the transition to agriculture during the Neolithic was likely a gradual process and the collection of local panicoid grasses (such as *Brachiaria* sp. and *Echinochloa* sp.) is evident from grave finds.[32] Though the evidence for cultivated cereals is scant during the Neolithic and primarily relates to cemetery contexts, both six-row hulled barley (*Hordeum vulgare* ssp. *vulgare*) and emmer wheat (*Triticum turgidum* ssp. *dicoccon*) are attested.[33] The first evidence for domestic cereal storage infrastructure appears during the pre-Kerma Period at Sai.[34] Based on grave finds, analogous to those from the Neolithic, it has been suggested that the practice of collecting wild grasses, either for subsistence or because of cultural significance, continued into the Kerma Period.[35] In lieu of larger and systematic archaeobotanical studies of domestic contexts from the earlier periods much with respect to the use of wild grasses and the nature of transition to full-fledged agriculture, for now remains obscured. While the evidence for the Kerma Period remains limited, it is however clear that emmer wheat

24 Cf. Bauer Petrovska 2012.
25 Cf. Diego Espinel 2017; Manzo 2017.
26 Fahmy 1997; Malleson 2015; Antolín et al. 2016; Dunne et al. 2022.
27 Buckley et al. 2014.
28 Cf. Ostrom 1991.
29 Cf. Heinrich 2017.
30 See also Garcea this volume.
31 For an introduction into cereal taxonomy and morphology for historians and archaeologists see Heinrich 2019.
32 Out et al. 2016.
33 Ibidem.
34 Geus 2004; Hildebrand 2007.
35 Ryan 2018.

and barley had become major crops. Besides regular six-row hulled barley, an unusual local variety of six-row barley – that morphologically behaves as if it is a two-row form – has been noted at New Kingdom Amara West. Usually, six-row barley has two groups of three grains 'per row', but in this variety, each side has one central grain with two sterile lateral bracts.[36] This form of barley may have been present during the Kerma Period already. It has also been argued that a different type of barley, two-row hulled barley (*Hordeum vulgare* ssp. *distichon*), was present during the Kerma Period,[37] though in light of the above, such finds should be re-examined so as to determine whether these specimens are truly of the two-row form, or instead represent the Nubian six-row form.[38]

As the evidence from the Pharaonic towns at both Amara West and Sai illustrates, six-row hulled barley and emmer wheat remained the dominant cereals during the New Kingdom.[39] Interestingly, this is where we see an apparent divergence from the pattern observed in Egypt. Whereas in Egypt emmer wheat, which had been of secondary importance since the Old Kingdom, gradually becomes more important at the expense of six-row hulled barley,[40] barley remains dominant in Nubia.[41] Evidence from domestic contexts at Amara West suggests that as in Egypt proper, emmer wheat held a higher social status than barley: in smaller houses without formal storage areas proportionally more barley was found than emmer wheat, whereas in large villas with dedicated storage facilities, the situation was reversed.[42] While culturally often underappreciated, agriculturally barley has many advantages, including comparatively high yields, low nutrient requirements, and greater resistance to drought and salinity.[43] In the ecological context of Nubia (with a *de facto* smaller arable, as outlined above), these could have been important reasons for continuing the cultivation of barley. In fact, while emmer wheat was later replaced by other cereals, six-row hulled barley remained to be an important crop until the mid-20th century.[44] Thus far there has been no evidence to suggest that any summer cereals, such as different millets or sorghum, the latter of which may have been domesticated in the east of Sudan,[45] were cultivated in Nubia until at least a few hundred years after the New Kingdom.[46]

Both six-row hulled barley and emmer wheat are so-called 'hulled' cereals. As opposed to 'free threshing' or 'naked' cereals, in hulled cereals the chaff (i.e., the palea and lemma) is tightly fitted around the kernel. It therefore does not come easily during threshing, requiring a second processing step, dehusking or dehulling, to get rid of the chaff. This process moreover needs to be carried out piecemeal as grain is needed for consumption, since dehusking may damage the kernel risking spoilage. Archaeological experiments, following the excavation of a Second Intermediate Period bakery in the Kharga Oasis, have shown that while dehusking is required for hulled wheats such as emmer wheat due to their very tough and substantial chaff, the process is optional for barley. Barley chaff is more brittle rather than tough and is less voluminous, and it can therefore more easily be ground and sieved out of the fraction post grinding if desired, though leaving some in need not adversely affect product quality, as is the case with traditional Greek *paximadi* bread.[47] Interestingly, similar practices have been documented ethnobotanically in a contemporary Nubian village near Amara West.[48] While both six-row hulled barley and emmer wheat would have been used for breads and porridges, barley would have been important for beer as well. Non-alcoholic beverages, often referred to as barley waters, for which there is both evidence from the wider ancient world,[49] as well as ethnobotanical evidence from Nubia,[50] would have also been made from barley.

In addition to food, cereals would have also provided important resources for non-food applications: their straw and chaff. Besides uses as animal bedding or fodder, this material could be chopped up very finely to serve as temper in pottery.[51] If chopped up more coarsely, it could serve as temper providing structural integrity for mudbricks used in construction and in dung cakes used as fuel.[52] The economic importance of this resource, which is sometimes categorised as 'crop processing waste' should not be underestimated, and terms such as 'by-product' or 'secondary product' would be more apt. With the shift to naked wheat in Egypt and Sudan from the Greco-Roman Period onwards, the importance of chaff especially would grow, leading to its commoditization, as from naked cereals it can be collected much more economically: all

36 The identification of the Nubian six-row barley that behaves like the two-row form was first clarified at Qasr Ibrim through ancient DNA analysis by Palmer et al. 2009.
37 Erroux 1980
38 Some of the older literature, such as Erroux 1980 and Chaix 1984, also identifies "four-row hulled barley" – which is no longer recognised and should be interpreted as six-row hulled barley.
39 Ryan, Cartwright and Spencer 2012; Heinrich and Hansen 2020.
40 Murray 2000a.
41 Cartwright and Ryan 2017; Heinrich and Hansen 2020.
42 Cartwright and Ryan 2017.
43 For discussions see Cappers et al. 2014; Heinrich 2017; Heinrich, Hansen and Erdkamp 2021.
44 Ryan et al. 2022.
45 See Beldados and Costantini 2011.
46 Fuller 2004. For a discussion, see Heinrich and Hansen 2020.
47 Cappers et al. 2014.
48 Ryan et al. 2022.
49 Heinrich 2019.
50 Ryan et al. 2022.
51 See D'Ercole this volume.
52 Heinrich and Hansen 2020; El Dorry 2023a.

at once and centrally at the threshing floor, rather than over time after piecemeal dehusking at the consumer's home. This development for instance can be seen in the difference between the amounts of chaff encountered in the mudbricks from the New Kingdom town on Sai Island and those from the Ottoman fortress built on top of it.[53]

Pulses

Pulses are a group of grain crops from the Fabaceae (or legume) family of which the dried seeds are used.[54] Our evidence for pulses in Bronze Age Nubia is very limited, with only lentil (*Vicia lens*) and pea (*Lathyrus oleraceus*) being encountered in small numbers at Amara West,[55] and only a single specimen of grass pea (*Lathyrus sativus*) at Sai,[56] while the first evidence for faba bean (*Vicia faba*) – which today is omnipresent in Nubian agriculture and cuisine (e.g., in the modern Egyptian and Sudani staple *ful medammes*) – is later and dates from Napatan Kawa.[57] The first attestations in Nubia of cowpea (*Vigna unguiculata*) and lablab bean (*Lablab purpureus*) are situated in the Post-Meroitic and Christian Periods,[58] while for white lupine (*Lupinus albus*) and chickpea (*Cicer arietinum*) the date of their introduction in Nubia is unclear as far as the archaeobotanical evidence is concerned. Due to the very small sample size (with for the period only two habitation sites at which systematic archaeobotanical research has been conducted to date), and the potential role of recovery issues, it would of course be dangerous to generalize the absence or rareness of certain pulses too starkly. The evidence from Egypt, where much more work has been conducted for the Bronze Age, however, would also suggest that only limited selection of pulses was available, with some taxa, such as faba bean, only becoming more ubiquitous from the Greco-Roman Period onwards.[59] Why crops such as faba bean and chickpea, which had been part of the original Neolithic crop curriculum from the Fertile Crescent, only later became popular along the Nile is unclear. Agriculturally pulses are attractive crops, as they require very little to no fertilization due to having a symbiotic relationship with nitrogen fixing bacteria on their root nodules, which also makes them suitable for green manuring, though it is possible that these advantages were less relevant in the Nilotic context.[60] Nutritionally pulses are complementary with cereals such as barley and wheat with respect to their essential amino acid composition. Culinarily they are versatile: while they can be prepared by themselves in mashes, stews, and soups, they can also be ground like cereals, with which they were often mixed in bread and porridge preparations, as both historical and ethnographic evidence shows. On the other hand, another constant through time and space was that pulses had a lower status than cereals.[61] Lastly, it should be noted that though pulses were primarily used as grain crops, the same species may have other uses as well: ethnobotanically it was for instance found that the leaves of pea were commonly consumed as a leafy vegetable on Ernetta Island, and that this use was considered to be more important than using the pea as a pulse crop.[62]

Fruit trees

For Bronze Age Nubia different wild and cultivated fruits have been attested in the archaeobotanical record. The fruit of the doum palm (*Hyphaene thebaica*), which occurs naturally in Nubia, is among the more common of these. The mesocarp of the fruit, the fruit flesh, has a sweet-tart flavour and today is a beloved children's snack, while the rind can be used to produce molasses-like liquids and the unripe kernel can be ground into a flour.[63] The tree is traditionally more common in Sudan than in Egypt, though it would appear that its importance declined from the 1950s onwards with it being cleared in different places.[64] For another palm tree encountered in Nubia, the date palm (*Phoenix dactilyfera*), the opposite development may have taken place. While the date palm is ubiquitous today, Bronze Age finds are rarer for Nubia and its cultivation must have been limited.[65] The written evidence seems to support this, as even by the Meroitic Period the Roman geographer Strabo claims that in Kush date trees are rare and only found in royal gardens.[66] Besides their fruits, both taxa of palm tree provide materials with other uses, such as wood for construction and fuel, while the leaves and petioles (leafstalks) can be used for making different types of basketry,[67] roofing, (cosmetic) fencing, and

53 Heinrich and Hansen 2020, cf. the discussion in van der Veen 1999.

54 For an introduction into pulses for historians and archaeologists, see Heinrich and Hansen 2019.

55 Ryan 2017. Recently, new genetic insights have placed lentil in the genus Vicia with *Vicia lens* as its new name; formerly it was known as *Lens culinaris*. Similarly, pea, formerly *Pisum sativum* was moved to the genus Lathyrus and is now called *Lathyrus oleraceus*.

56 Heinrich and Hansen 2020.

57 Fuller 2004.

58 Fuller 2015.

59 See El Dorry 2023b for a discussion.

60 Cf. Heinrich, Hansen and Erdkamp 2021.

61 Heinrich and Hansen 2019.

62 Ryan 2017.

63 Mubarak et al. 1982; Ryan, Cartwright and Spencer 2012.

64 Ryan 2017.

65 Ryan et al. 2022.

66 Strab. 17.2.2, cf. Heinrich and Hansen 2020.

67 Wendrich 2000.

agricultural windbreaks,[68] while the fibres of the (pseudo)bark can be used for coarse textiles.[69] While in the historical context such uses have mainly been discussed for the date palm, due to a focus on Egypt where that taxon was most important, ethnographic evidence shows they also apply to the doum palm.[70] Unique to the doum palm is the use of its seed for small objects such as beads, buttons, and small containers (Fig. 4).

Another fruit tree for which we have evidence is the sycamore fig (*Ficus sycamorus*), and it appears to have been quite abundant at Amara West, yet it was more rare at Sai.[71] Christ's thorn (*Ziziphus spina-chirsti*), sometimes referred to as 'jujube', is yet another wild fruit tree that was exploited. The small, and rather tart, fruits of the tree resemble miniature apples, about the size of a marble, and have relatively large endocarps at their core. While the amount of flesh per fruit is limited, larger trees can carry thousands of fruits and they are both used as an opportunistic snack and for more elaborate preparations; the written sources suggest that Christ's thorn may have also been used in certain bread preparations.[72] Archaeological finds of grape (*Vitis vinifera*) are very rare for the Bronze Age in Nubia, being only attested at New Kingdom Semna West,[73] with a contemporary find at Sai likely being later period contamination;[74] from the Napatan and Meroitic Periods onwards, grape would start to occur more frequently.[75]

Fig. 4 Container for the storage of kohl for cosmetic uses made from the seed of a doum palm (*Hyphaene thebaica*) fruit; the stick is functions as the applicator to apply kohl to the eyes. This modern specimen was bought from Bedouin in the Dongola Reach by Frits Heinrich in January 2014 (photo by A.M. Hansen; photo edits by A.J. Bronkhorst).

Melons, watermelons, and other cucurbits

Different cucurbits, including watermelons and colocynths, are commonly encountered at Bronze Age sites in Nubia, among others at Kerma,[76] and New Kingdom Amara West,[77] Gala Abu Ahmed,[78] and Sai,[79] though their identification to species level can be challenging. Besides being used for their fruit flesh, their seeds are edible and are often toasted, though oil can also be extracted from them. The domestication of watermelon (*Citrullus lanatus*) is still under investigation, though Northeast Africa and modern Sudan in particular, have been suggested as the centre of domestication.[80] Recent archaeogenomic analyses of desiccated material from a New Kingdom Period desert site close to Amara West (2-R-65) for instance indicated that many 'watermelon' seeds were in fact a hybrid mix of *Citrullus mucosospermus* and *Citrullus lanatus* ssp. *vulgaris*, and they showed most similarity to types used for their edible seeds.[81] Another plant in this group of which the seeds are common in the archaeological record is the colocynth (*Citrullus colocynthis*).[82] This plant is widely used for medicinal purposes and as fodder for donkeys, but also for its edible seeds that can be roasted, ground into a flour, or pressed for an oil that used to be important as lamp oil in some regions.[83] While normally a wild plant, in the Ernetta and Abri areas in Nubia, it was observed being cultivated as if a crop, with elderly farmers claiming that this practice was far more common in the past;[84] the possibility can therefore not be excluded that this practice had a historical parallel.

68 Heinrich and Hansen 2020, cf. Heinrich and Hansen 2021.
69 Vogelsang-Eastwood 2000.
70 Orwa et al. 2009.
71 Ryan, Cartwright and Spencer 2012; Heinrich and Hansen 2020.
72 Tallet 2015.
73 van Zeist 1983.
74 Heinrich and Hansen 2020.
75 Fuller 2015.
76 Chaix 1984.
77 Ryan, Cartwright and Spencer 2012.
78 Kahlheber 2013.
79 Heinrich and Hansen 2020.
80 Paris 2015.
81 Pérez-Escobar et al. 2022.
82 Kahlheber 2013.
83 Yaniv, Shabelsky and Schafferman 1999.
84 Ryan et al. 2022.

Vegetables, and oil and fibre crops

The evidence for vegetable crops as well as oil and fibre crops is extremely scant for Bronze Age Nubia, with almost none of the 'regular' crops from these categories for which we have evidence in Egypt being attested.[85] In terms of fibre crops, the earliest archaeobotanical evidence for flax (*Linum usitatissimum*) – of which linen is made, which was the most common type of textile in Ancient Egypt[86] – is from Amara West,[87]while the earliest find of (Old World) cotton (*Gossypium* sp.) dates to Meroitic Qasr Ibrim.[88] Flax can be used as both a fibre crop and oil crop, in which case it is referred to linseed (though specially bred cultivars tend to be used for the different purposes). Other dedicated oil crops such as sesame (*Sesamum indicum*) and safflower (*Carthamus tinctorius*) first appear at Qasr Ibrim, and later elsewhere, from the Post-Meroitic and Christian Period onwards.[89] For radish (*Raphanus sativus*), of which the root is commonly eaten while its seeds can be pressed for oil,[90] and poppy (*Papaver somniferum*), there is no extant Nubian evidence. A striking dissimilarity can be observed when comparing the list of fruits, vegetables, and condiments that we have from Ancient Egyptian evidence compiled by Mary Anne Murray with that of any of the Nubian Bronze Age sites: with the exception of some of the fruits, most are missing in the latter case.[91]

The issues with respect to the small number of extant studies and potential issues of recovery, explored above for pulses, may to some extent also apply to our dearth in evidence for vegetables and oil and fibre crops. There however may also be other, not necessarily mutually exclusive, complementary explanations. It would not be an unreasonable hypothesis that animal sourced materials could have been more prevalent in Nubia than their vegetal counterparts: butter and lard could have been used instead of oils,[92] while skins, hides, leather, wool, and goat hair could be used instead of plant fibres.[93] Taxa that are primarily known for other uses could moreover in some cases have had secondary roles as oil or fibre crops or vegetables. Grape and watermelon seeds (see above), for instance, are rich in oils and could be pressed to obtain these; additionally, doum and date palms were used as sources of fibres,[94] while we have ethnobotanical evidence for the use of pea leaves as a leafy vegetable (see above).

It is also possible that instead of on cultivated crops, Nubian communities during this period relied more strongly on wild plant alternatives. In some of the written sources it has for instance been suggested that white lotus (*Nymphaea lotus*) hearts may have played a role in certain preparations of bread.[95] From modern practices we know that the unripe berries and buds of karira (*Capparis deciduas*) are furthermore widely used as pickled vegetables, while ethnobotanical fieldwork in the Sikoot showed that wild plants such as amaranth (*Amaranthus* spp.), arugula (*Eruca vesicaria*), African jute (*Corchorus fascicularis*), cheeseweed (*Malva parviflora*), damascisa (*Glinus lotoides*), and purslane (*Portulaca oleracea*) were commonly collected as leafy vegetables.[96] Though they are widely attested in the archaeobotanical record, their interpretation is difficult, as they may have ended up in archaeological contexts through a variety of pathways besides exploitation for food, such as having been weeds or having been present in animal dung that was used as fuel.[97] Wild sources of vegetable oils would include both the seeds of colocynth (see above) and those of the castor bean plant (*Ricinus communis*). The seeds of the desert date or balanos (*Balanites aegypitiaca*) and the tubers of the tiger nut (*Cyperus esculentus*) have also been suggested as potential sources of oil.[98] The rhizomes of tiger nut were furthermore eaten as a vegetable, and had various other uses, such as being an addition to beers and breads.[99] Possible wild sources of plant fibres used for producing widely diverse products including textiles, matting, basketry, brushes, and objects, include various wild grasses, common reed (*Phragmites communis*), giant reed (*Arundo donax*), and various sedges, most famously papyrus (*Cyperus papyrus*).[100]

Wood and other tree products

Woody plants have may have diverse potential uses: they may provide timber and other products for construction and tools, firewood for use of fuel (or fuel making where charcoal making is practiced), fodder for animals, though they may also provide resins and gums. The most important native trees and woody plants in Nubia are sycamore fig (*Ficus sycomorus* – though it has become rarer), doum palm (*Hyphaene thebaica*), Christ's thorn (*Ziziphus spina-christi*) and different species of tamarisk (*Tamarix* sp.)

85 Fuller 2015; Ryan, Cartwright and Spencer 2016; Heinrich and Hansen 2020.

86 Vogelsang-Eastwood 2000.

87 Ryan, Cartwright and Spencer 2012.

88 Fuller 2015.

89 Ibidem.

90 The use of which has been suggested for Roman Egypt but is contested – see Serpico and White 2000a for a discussion.

91 Murray 2000b, 610.

92 Cf. Serpico and White 2000a.

93 Cf. van Driel-Murray 2000; Vogelsang-Eastwood 2000.

94 Wendrich 2000.

95 Tallet 2015.

96 Ryan et al. 2022.

97 Heinrich and Hansen 2020, for a discussion.

98 Serpico and White 2000a. Cf. Murray 2000b.

99 Murray 2000b; Tallet 2015.

100 Wendrich 2000; Leach and Tait 2000; Vogelsang-Eastwood 2000.

Fig. 5 Left: thorny bushes of *Acacia sp.* being used to close-off a dilapidated building that serves as a night shelter for sheep, as indicated by the thick layer of sheep dung pellet at the entrance and inside the structure. Sai Island, Eastern shore, close to the Pharaonic town, January 2015 (photo by F. Heinrich).

and acacia (*Acacia* sp.), including *Acacia nilotica* and *Acacia senegal*. The densest concentrations of woody plants may be found as thickets close to the embankment of the river (cf. Fig. 1). The exception is the doum palm, of which the managed specimens are found somewhat more inland, though their numbers have declined in favour of dates cultivated on plantations (see above). Due to its deep roots, acacia may also be found further inland, for instance around wadis and where the groundwater levels permit; acacia is also at the core of the Sahelian savanna forests to the south. A woody plant that is currently exploited for fuel, but for which archaeological evidence is lacking, is the Apple of Sodom (*Calotropis procera*), and it too may be found further away from the river. Today acacia wood, also because of the charcoal industry, is the most important type of wood for fuel use.

At New Kingdom Amara West, the sycamore fig (*Ficus sycomorus*), was the most important woody taxon used for fuel in domestic contexts, while to a lesser extent doum palm (*Hyphaene thebaica*), Christ's thorn (*Ziziphus spina-christi*) and different species of tamarisk (*Tamarix* spp.) and acacia (*Acacia* spp.) played a role.[101] Sycamore fig was also dominant in terms of the desiccated wood encountered at the site, including as wood of choice for coffins and funerary articles.[102] Evidence from the broader Kerma Period primarily yields desiccated wood and charcoal from mainly acacias, though tamarisk, Christ's thorn, and karira (*Capparis decidua)* also occurred; as this evidence exclusively comes from cemetery contexts it is difficult to interpret or compare to material from domestic contexts. Evidence for (imported) Mediterranean and Near Eastern woody taxa, as are sometimes encountered in Egypt is absent for Nubia.[103] Though archaeological evidence is limited, ethnographic observations show that acacia is commonly used in construction, for instance in lintels above doorways and windows in mudbrick constructions. The thorny branches of acacia can also be observed to be used for animal pens or to close off animal shelters at night (Fig. 5). Live acacia trees are also a source of fodder for animals, in particular goats, who are not deterred by the thorns and may climb into larger trees.

Some trees produce resins or gums that both today and in the past were applied for diverse uses. While gums are formed during internal decomposition

101 Cartwright and Ryan 2017.

102 Ryan, Cartwright and Spencer 2012.

103 See Gale et al. 2000.

processes of cellulose, contain large amounts of sugar, and are water soluble, resins are formed through the oxidation of essential oils in plants and are not water soluble; gum-resins, naturally occurring combinations of the two, are common in some families. Today, Sudan is one of the world's most important producers of Gum Arabic, which is obtained from Acacia sp. trees. While *Acacia senegal* is the primary commercial species in use and is believed to produce the best quality gum, other species, such as the ubiquitous Nile acacia (*Acacia nilotica*) may be used as well. Due to their water solubility, gums may be used as binders and adhesives, such as in glue and paint – as was attested for paint remains from New Kingdom Sai[104] – though they may also be used as incense.[105] In Nubia, and the areas immediately to its east and south, the main taxa providing gum-resins come from the Burseraceae family: frankincense (*Boswellia* spp.) and myrrh (*Commiphora* spp.). While the main commercial species from these genera are *Boswellia sacra* and *Commiphora myrrha* respectively, for both there are various other species that, as is apparent from ethnographic evidence, were or may have been used for the same purpose in the past. Gum-resins have diverse applications ranging from use in religious ceremonies, to varnish, and of course, incense.[106] In the Egyptian context, gums and gum-resins are often associated with Nubia, either as the place of origin or transit,[107] and they would have therefore likely been among the most important local vegetal resources for exchange or export.

Conclusion

In this chapter we provided an overview of the vegetal resources of Bronze Age Nubia from the perspective of the archaeobotanical evidence, which we placed in its ecological and technological context. While the relative scarcity of systematically archaeobotanically sampled and studied habitation sites forms an impediment for understanding the full extent of potential vegetal resources used, there are some important observations that can be made so far. It is apparent from the evidence available that the Bronze Age Nubian vegetal economy was a diverse and balanced system between the crops that were cultivated and the wild plant resources that were managed and collected. While this deserves more investigation in future studies, especially considering the importance of wild resources, this seems to relate to the inhabitants' keen awareness of their ecological context and limitations particularly in respect to water and the necessity to develop technologies and resilience strategies to sustain their societies. In the same vein, key resilient staple crops such as hulled six-row barley remain important throughout the Bronze Age and beyond. Moreover, the use of crop processing waste for multiple activities from tempering mudbricks and plasters to use as fodder and fuel attests a circular economic system, and even upcycling, through using waste from one sector as by-products to feed into other non-food sectors. The data so far is encouraging and there is much potential for the future study of Bronze Age Nubian sites in investigating the extent of plant use on sites and furthermore placing the current results into a more complete regional reconstruction of agricultural practices and resource management in the longue durée.

104 Fulcher et al. 2022.

105 For an overview, see Newman and Serpico 2000.

106 See Serpico and White 2000b, for an overview.

107 Cf. Diego Espinel 2017; Manzo 2017.

Bibliography

AL-BATAL, S.
1991 *Traditional Agricultural Technology in Nubia: Continuity and Change*, University of Khartoum, Khartoum.

ANTOLÍN, F., BERIHUETE AZORÍN, M. and LÓPEZ-BULTÓ, O.
2016 Archaeobotany of wild plant use: Approaches to the exploitation of wild plant resources in the past and its social implications *Quaternary International*, 404A, 1–3, DOI: 10.1016/j.quaint.2016.01.029.

BHARUCHA, Z. and PRETTY, J.
2010 The roles and values of wild foods in agricultural systems, *Philosophical Transactions of the Royal Society B: Biological Sciences* 365.1554, 2913–2926.

BAUER PETROVSKA, B.
2012 Historical review of medicinal plants' usage, *Pharmacognosy Reviews* 6(11), 1–5.

BELDADOS, A. and COSTANTINI, L.
2011 Sorghum exploitation at Kassala and its environs, North Eastern Sudan in the second and first millennia BC, *Nyame Akuma* 75, 33–39.

BUCKLEY, S., USAI, D., JAKOB, T., RADINI, A. and HARDY, K.
2014 Dental calculus reveals unique insights into food items, cooking and plant processing in prehistoric central Sudan, *PLOS One* 9(7), e100808, 1–10.

CAPPERS, R.T.J., HEINRICH, F.B.J., KAAIJK, S., FANTONE, F., DARNELL, J. and MANASSA, C.
2014 Barley revisited: production of barley bread in Umm Mawagir (Kharga Oasis, Egypt), in: K. ACCETTA, R. FELLINGER, P. LAURENÇO GONÇALVES, S. MUSSELWHITE and W.P. VAN PELT (eds.), *Current Research in Egyptology 2013. Proceedings of the Fourteenth Annual Symposium*, Oxford; Havertown, 49–63.

CARTWRIGHT, C.
2001 The plant remains, in: D.A. WELSBY (ed.), *Life on the Desert Edge: Seven Thousand Years of Settlement in the Northern Dongola Reach, Sudan, Volume II*, Sudan Archaeological Research Society Publication 7, London, 556–567.
2018 Charcoal and wood, in: D.A. WELSBY (ed.), *A Kerma Ancien Cemetery in the Northern Dongola Reach, Excavations at site H29*, Sudan Archaeological Research Society, Oxford, 207–210.

CARTWRIGHT, C.R. and RYAN, P.
2017 Archaeobotanical research at Amara West in New Kingdom Nubia, in: N. SPENCER, A. STEVENS and M. BINDER (eds.), *Nubia in the New Kingdom: Lived Experience, Pharaonic Control and Indigenous Traditions,* British Museum Publications on Egypt and Sudan 3, Leuven, 271–286.

CHAIX, L.
1984 Troisième note sur la faune de Kerma (Soudan). Campagnes 1983 et 1984, in: C. BONNET, N. FERRERO, C. SIMON, L. CHAIX, and S.M. AHMED, *Les fouilles archéologiques de Kerma (Soudan), Genava, n.s.* 32, 31–34.

CHAIX, L. and GRANT, A.
1993 Palaeoenvironment and economy at Kerma, Northern Sudan, during the third millennium B.C.: archaeozoological and botanical evidence, in: L. KRZYŻANIAK, M. KOBUSIEWICZ and J.A. ALEXANDER (eds.), *Environmental Change and Human Culture in the Nile Basin and Northern Africa until the Second Millennium B.C.*, Studies in African Archaeology 4, Poznań, 399–404.

CLAPHAM, A.J. and ROWLEY-CONWY, P.A.
2007 New discoveries at Qasr Ibrim, Lower Nubia, in: R.T.J. CAPPERS (ed.), *Fields of Change: Progress in African Archaeobotany*, Groningen Archaeological Studies 5, Groningen, 157–164.

DARBYSHIRE, I., KORDOFANI, M., FARAG, I., CANDIGA, R. and PICKERING, H. (eds.)
2015 *The Plants of Sudan and South Sudan. An Annotated Checklist*, Royal Botanic Gardens, Kew, Richmond.

DIEGO ESPINEL, A.
2017 The scents of Punt (and elsewhere): trade and functions of sntr and ʿ ntw during the Old Kingdom, in: I. INCORDINO and P.P. CREASMAN (eds.), *Flora Trade Between Egypt and Africa in Antiquity*, Oxford; Philadelphia, 21–48.

DUNNE, J., SALVATORI, S., MARITAN, L., LINSEELE V., GILLARD, T., BREEZE P., DRAKE, N., EVERSHED, R.P. and USAI, D.
2022 Wild food: Plants, fish and small animals on the menu for early Holocene populations at al-Khiday, Central Sudan, *African Archaeological Review* 39, 255–281, DOI: 10.1007/s10437-022-09490-w.

EL DORRY, M.
2023a It's a dung job. Exploring fuel disc production in Egyptian monasteries, in: L. BLANKE and J. CROMWELL (eds.), *Monastic Economies in Late Antique Egypt and Palestine*, Cambridge, 212–232.
2023b Forbidden, sprouted, stewed: an archaeobotanical and historical overview of fava beans in ancient Egypt, in: M. EL DORRY (ed.) *Food and Drink in Egypt and Sudan: Selected Studies in Archaeology, Culture, and History*, Bibliothèque d'Étude 184, Cairo, 87–103.

ERROUX, J.
1980 Examen de quelques grains d'orge provenant d'une tombe de l'île de Saï, in: L. JOURDAN (ed.), *Sacrifices de moutons dans des tombes Kerma de l'Ile de Saï (vallée du Nil, début du deuxième millénaire avant J.-C.) et leur signification rituelle*, Mémoires archéologiques 1, Valbonne, 86–90.

FAHMY, A.F.E.-D.
1997 Evaluation of the weed flora of Egypt from Predynastic to Graeco-Roman times, *Vegetation History and Archaeobotany* 6, 241–247, DOI: 10.1007/BF01370445.

FRAYN, J.M.
1975 Wild and cultivated plants: A note on the peasant economy of Roman Italy, *Journal of Roman Studies* 65, 32–39.
1979 *Subsistence Farming in Roman Italy*, London.

Fulcher, K., Spencer, N., Budka, J. and Stacey, R.J.
2022 Polysaccharide paint binding media at two Pharaonic settlements in Nubia, *Heritage* 5 (3), 2028–2040.

Fuller, D.Q.
2004 Early Kushite agriculture: archaeobotanical evidence from Kawa, *Sudan & Nubia* 8, 70–74.
2015 The economic basis of the Qustul Splinter State: cash crops, subsistence shifts, and labour demands in the Post-Meroitic transition, in: M.H. Zach (ed.), *The Kushite World: Proceedings of the 11th International Conference for Meroitic Studies, Vienna, 1.–4. September 2008*, Beiträge zur Sudanforschung. Beiheft 9, Vienna, 33–60.

Fuller, D.Q., Macdonald, K. and Vernet, R.
2007 Early domesticated pearl millet in Dhar Nema (Mauritania): evidence of crop processing waste as ceramic temper, in: R.T.J. Cappers (ed.), *Fields of Change: Progress in African Archaeobotany*, Groningen Archaeological Studies 5, Groningen, 71–76.

Fuller, D.Q., Denham, T., Arroyo-Kalin, M., Lucas, L., Stevens, C.J., Qin, R., Allaby, R. and Purugganan, M.D.
2014 Convergent evolution and parallelism in plant domestication revealed by an expanding archaeological record, *Proceedings of the National Academy of Sciences* 111(17), 6147–6152.

Fuller, D.Q. and Lucas, L.
2021 Savanna on the Nile: Long term agricultural diversifications and intensification in Nubia, in: G. Emberling and B.B. Williams (eds.), *The Oxford Handbook of Ancient Nubia*, Oxford, 927–953.

Geus, F.
2004 Pre-Kerma storage pits on Sai Island, in: T. Kendall (ed.), *Nubian Studies 1998, Proceedings of the Ninth Conference of the International Society of Nubian Studies, August 21–26, 1998, Boston, Massachusetts*, Boston, 46–51.

Gale, R., Gasson, P., Hepper, N. and Killen, G.
2000 Wood, in: P.T. Nicholson and I. Shaw (eds.), *Ancient Egyptian Materials and Technology*, Cambridge, 334–371.

Hansen, A.M., Walker, B.J. and Heinrich, F.B.J.
2017 'Impressions' of the Mamluk agricultural economy. Archaeobotanical evidence from clay ovens (*ṭābūn*) at Tall Ḥisbān (Jordan), *Tijdschrift voor Mediterrane Archeologie* 56, 58_69.

Heinrich, F.B.J.
2017 Modelling crop-selection in Roman Italy. The economics of agricultural decision making in a globalizing economy, in: T.C.A. de Haas and G.W. Tol (eds.), *The Economic Integration of Roman Italy. Rural Communities in a Globalizing World*, Mnemosyne Supplements History and Archaeology of Classical Antiquity 404, Leiden; Boston, 141–169.
2019 Cereals and bread, in: P. Erdkamp and C. Holleran (eds.), *The Routledge Handbook of Diet and Nutrition in the Roman World*, London; New York, 101–115.

Heinrich, F.B.J. and Hansen, A.M.
2019 Pulses, in: P. Erdkamp and C. Holleran (eds.), *The Routledge Handbook of Diet and Nutrition in the Roman World*, London; New York, 116–128.
2020 Mud bricks, cereals and the agricultural economy. Archaeobotanical investigations at the New Kingdom town, in: J. Budka, *AcrossBorders 2. Living in New Kingdom Sai,* Archaeology of Egypt, Sudan and the Levant 1, Vienna, 275–349, 480–488 (plates).
2021 A hard row to hoe. Ancient climate change from the crop perspective, in: P. Erdkamp, J.G. Manning and K. Verboven (eds.), *Climate Change and Ancient Societies in Europe and the Near East. Diversity in Collapse and Resilience*, Palgrave Studies in Ancient Economies, London, 25–80.

Heinrich, F.B.J. and Wilkins, D.A.
2013/2014 Beans, boats and archaeobotany: a new translation of *phasolus* or why the Romans ate neither kidney beans nor cowpeas, *Palaeohistoria* 55/56, 149–176.

Heinrich, F.B.J. and van Pelt, W.P.
2017a Graantransport en graanprijzen in Ramessidisch Egypte. Het recto van P. Amiens en P. Baldwin gekwantificeerd, *Tijdschrift voor Mediteranne Archeologie* 28(56), 1–12.
2017b Ramessidische graantransporten, landerijen en landbelastingen botanisch gekwantificeerd: Het verso van Papyrus Amiens + Baldwin, in: G. Aalbersberg, S. Boersma and M. Schepers (eds.), *Paleo-Palfenier: met Rita van Egypte tot Ezinge*, Groningen, 23–34.

Heinrich, F.B.J., Hansen, A.M. and Erdkamp, P.
2021 Roman isotopes and economic meaning: millets, manure, mobility, marine signals, and Malthus, *Archaeological and Anthropological Sciences* 13, article number 44, 1–13.

Hildebrand, E.
2007 The significance of Sai Island for early plant food production in Sudan, *Cahiers de Recherches de l'Institut de Papyrologie et d'Égyptologie de Lille* 26, 173–181.

Kahlheber, S.
2013 The fruit and seed remains, in: F. Jesse, B. Eichhorn and S. Kahlheber, Archaeobotanical Investigations at the Gala Abu Ahmed Fortress in Lower Wadi Howar, Northern Sudan, *Sudan & Nubia* 17, 33–41.

Kipfer, B.A.
2021 Nubia, in: *Encyclopedic Dictionary of Archaeology*, Cham, https://doi.org/10.1007/978-3-030-58292-0.

Leach, B. and Tait, J.
2000 Papyrus, in: P.T. Nicholson and I. Shaw (eds.), *Ancient Egyptian Materials and Technology*, Cambridge, 227–253.

Le Moyne, C., Roberts, P., Hua, Q., Bleasdale, M., Desideri, J., Boivin, N. and Crowther, A.
2023 Ecological flexibility and adaptation to past climate change in the Middle Nile Valley: A multiproxy investigation of dietary shifts between the Neolithic

and Kerma periods at Kadruka 1 and Kadruka 21, *PLoS One* 18 (2), e0280347. DOI: 10.1371/journal.pone.0280347

MALLESON, C.
2015 Flora of Ancient Egypt, in: I. SHAW and E. BLOXHAM (eds.), *The Oxford Handbook of Egyptology*, Oxford, 125–150.

MANZO, A.
2017 "They shall come to trade at Iken." Ports and river in second millennium BCE Nubia, in: I. INCORDINO and P.P. CREASMAN (eds.), *Flora Trade Between Egypt and Africa in Antiquity*, Oxford; Philadelphia, 75–100.

MUBARAK, M.O., BARI, E.A., WICKENS, G.E. and WILLIAMS, M.A.J.
1982 The vegetation of the Central Sudan, in: M.A.J. WILLIAMS and D.A. ADAMSON (eds.), *A Land Between Two Niles: Quaternary Geology and Biology of the Central Sudan,* Rotterdam, 143–164.

MURRAY, M.
2000a Cereal production and processing, in: P.T. NICHOLSON and I. SHAW (eds.), *Ancient Egyptian Materials and Technology*, Cambridge, 505–536.
2000b Fruits, vegetables, pulses and condiments, in: P.T. NICHOLSON and I. SHAW (eds.), *Ancient Egyptian Materials and Technology*, Cambridge, 609–655.

NEWMAN, R. and SERPICO, M.
2000 Adhesives and binders, in: P.T. NICHOLSON and I. SHAW (eds.), *Ancient Egyptian Materials and Technology*, Cambridge, 475–494.

OSTROM, E.
1991 *Governing the Commons. The Evolution of Institutions for Collective Action*, Cambridge.

ORWA, C., MUTUA, A., KINDT, R., JAMNADASS, R. and SIMONS, A.
2009 *Agroforestree Database: a Tree Reference and Selection Guide Version 4.0*, World Agroforestry Centre, Kenya. https://www.worldagroforestry.org/output/agroforestree-database <last access 1. October 2023>.

OUT, W., RYAN, P., GARCÍA-GRANERO, J., BARASTEGUI, J., MARITAN, L., MADELLA, M. and USAI, D.
2016 Plant exploitation in Neolithic Sudan: A review in the light of new data from the cemeteries R12 and Ghaba, *Quaternary International* 412, 36–53.

PALMER, S.A., MOORE, J.D., CLAPHAM, A.J., ROSE, P. and ALLABY, R.G.
2009 Archaeogenetic evidence of ancient Nubian barley evolution from six to two-row indicates local adaptation, *PlosOne* 4(7), e6301, 1–7.

PARIS, H.S.
2015 Origin and emergence of the sweet dessert watermelon, *Citrullus lanatus*, *Annals of Botany* 116(2), 133–148.

PÉREZ-ESCOBAR, O.A., TUSSO, S., PRZELOMSKA, N.A.S., WU, S., RYAN, P., NESBITT, M., SILBER, M.V., PREICK, M., FEI, Z., HOFREITER, M., CHOMICKI, G. and RENNER, S.S.
2022 Genome sequencing of up to 6,000-year-old Citrullus seeds reveals use of a bitter-fleshed species prior to watermelon domestication, *Molecular Biology and Evolution* 39(8), msac168.

ROWLEY-CONWY, P.
1989 Nubia AD 0–550 and the "Islamic" agricultural revolution: preliminary botanical evidence from Qasr Ibrim, Egyptian Nubia, *Archéologie du Nil Moyen* 3, 131–138.

RYAN, P.
2017 From raw resources to food processing: Archaeobotanical and ethnographic insights from New Kingdom Amara West and present-day Ernetta Island in Northern Sudan, in: L. STEEL and K. ZINN (eds.), *Exploring the Materiality of Food 'Stuffs': Transformations, Symbolic Consumption and Embodiments*, Abingdon; New York, 15–38.
2018 Plants as grave goods: Microbotanical remains (phytoliths) from the white deposits in the graves, in: D.A. WELSBY (ed.), *A Kerma Ancien cemetery in the Northern Dongola Reach, excavations at site H29*, Sudan Archaeological Research Society, Oxford, 203–206.

RYAN, P., CARTWRIGHT, C. and SPENCER, N.
2012 Archaeobotanical research in a pharaonic town in ancient Nubia, *The British Museum Technical Research Bulletin* 6, 97–107.
2016 Charred macroremains (seed, fruits) and phytoliths from Villa E.12.10 at Amara West, a Pharaonic town in Northern Sudan, in: U. THANHEISER (ed.), *News from the Past: Progress in African Archaeobotany,* Groningen, 95–114.

RYAN, P. and SPENCER, N.
2013 Diet and plant-use at Amara West, *Egyptian Archaeology* 42, 18–20.

RYAN, P., HASSAN, M., SAAD, M., JAEGER, M. and CARTWRIGHT, C.
2021 The biocultural heritage and historical ecology of date palm cultivation in Nubian villages, northern Sudan, *Sudan & Nubia* 25, 24–39.

RYAN, P., KORDOFANI, M., SAAD, M., HASSAN, M., DALTON, M., CARTWRIGHT, C. and SPENCER, N.
2022 Nubian agricultural practices, crops and foods: Changes in living memory on Ernetta Island, northern Sudan, *Economic Botany* 76(3), 250–272.

SERPICO, M. and WHITE, R.
2000a Oil, fat and wax, in: P.T. NICHOLSON and I. SHAW (eds.), *Ancient Egyptian Materials and Technology*, Cambridge, 390–429.
2000b Resins, amber and bitumen, in: P.T. NICHOLSON and I. SHAW (eds.), *Ancient Egyptian Materials and Technology*, Cambridge, 430–474.

TALLET, P.
2015 Food in ancient Egypt, in: J. WILKINS and R. NADEAU (eds.), *A Companion to Food in the Ancient World*, Chichester, 319–325.

VAN DER VEEN, M.
1999 The economic value of chaff and straw in arid and temperate zones, *Vegetation History and Archaeobotany* 8, 221–224.

van Driel-Murray, C.
2000 Leatherwork and skin products, in: P.T. Nicholson and I. Shaw (eds.), *Ancient Egyptian Materials and Technology*, Cambridge, 299–319.

van Pelt, P.W. and Heinrich, F.B.J.
2019 Emmer wheat and barley prices in the late New Kingdom: A Ramesside price paradox resolved, *Journal of Egyptian Archaeology* 104(1), 103–107.

van Zeist, W. A.
1983 Fruits in foundation deposits of two temples, *Journal of Archaeological Science* 10, 351–354.
1987 The plant remains, in: A. Vila, *La cimetière Kermaïque d'Ukma Ouest: La prospection archéologique de la vallée du Nil en Nubie Soudanaise*, Paris, 247–255.

Vogelsang-Eastwood, G.
2000 Textiles, in: P.T. Nicholson and I. Shaw (eds.), *Ancient Egyptian Materials and Technology*, Cambridge, 268–298.

Welsby, D.A.
1996 *The Kingdom of Kush. The Napatan and Meroitic Empires*, London.

Wendrich, W.Z.
2000 Basketry, in: P.T. Nicholson and I. Shaw (eds.), *Ancient Egyptian Materials and Technology*, Cambridge, 254–267.

Yaniv, Z., Shabelsky, E. and Schafferman, D.
1999 Colocynth: Potential arid land oilseed from an ancient cucurbit, in: J. Janick (ed.), *Perspectives on New Crops and New Uses*, Alexandria, 257–261.

Zocchi, D.M., Bondioli, C., Hosseini, S.H., Miara, D.J., Musarella, C.M., Mohammadi, D., Manduzai, A.K., Issa, K.D., Sulaiman, N., Khatib, C., Ahmed, H.M., Faraj, T.A., Amin, H.I.M., Hussain, F.H.S, Faiz, A., Pasqualone, A., Heinrich, F., Fontefrancesco, M.F. and Pieroni, A.
2022 Food security beyond cereals: A cross-geographical comparative study on acorn bread heritage in the Mediterranean and the Middle East, *Foods* 11, 3898, 1–39, DOI: 10.3390/foods11233898.

Chapter 8

Isotopic and skeletal approaches to diet and mobility in ancient Nubia

Sarah Schrader[1] and Michele Buzon[2]

Abstract

In this chapter, we discuss previous isotopic research that has focused on diet and mobility in the ancient Nile Valley, with particular focus on Nubia. While dietary interpretations from carbon and nitrogen from bone collagen have been discussed elsewhere, carbonate in the Nile Valley has not been fully appreciated. We present new carbon and nitrogen data from carbonate tissues coupled with strontium to examine if and how childhood diet and migration status are related. We assess isotopic data from Tombos, Qurneh, Saqqara, Amara West, as well as the Scandinavian Joint Expedition's Pharaonic and C-Group samples. Our analysis suggests dietary practices were different between these samples. Tombos, Pharaonic, and C-Group all have markedly varied carbon values, which may suggest a more Nubian C_4-based diet. The other samples, Qurneh, Saqqara, and Amara West, are all much more similar, which may reflect a stricter Egyptian C_3-diet, or may be the effect of a small sample size. At Tombos, there does appear to be a difference between individuals who have a local strontium isotope signature and those that do not. However, this needs to be explored further as strontium should be coupled with other isotopes to confirm migration. This chapter illustrates the important contribution isotopes have made to dietary and migration studies in the Nile Valley while simultaneously highlighting the potential for future isotope analysis in the region.

Keywords:

Carbonate, strontium, carbon, nitrogen, foodways, migration, Nubia

Introduction

The human history of the Nile Valley spans millennia; during this time, there was a plethora of complex human interactions, as populations moved, boundaries changed, and people intermingled. Archaeologically, this is very fruitful ground as countless questions can be asked regarding but not limited to, sociopolitical change, everyday life, and the exploitation of resources. Using isotope science to address these questions is not only popular, but highly informative. Within the Nile Valley, there is a long history of isotope studies that have addressed topics such as human and animal diet, migration, climate change, and weaning.[3] The field is continuously developing as new archaeological sites are discovered and state-of-the-art isotopic methods are established.

However, isotopic studies are not always the ideal methodological approach and these techniques do come with limitations. For example, while the hot and arid environment of the Nile Valley macroscopically preserves bones, on a microscopic level there is often significant destruction to biomolecules. Several studies report limited to no success with such analyses, which is likely due to diagenetic, or post-depositional, processes associated with the extreme environment.[4]

In this contribution, we discuss previous isotopic research in the Nile Valley, with a particular focus on dietary and mobility isotopes. We discuss the various human tissues (e.g., bone collagen, dental enamel carbonate) that have been isotopically examined and pay particular attention to those tissues that are more resilient to diagenetic alteration. We review previous publications that have used these approaches and document methodological and topical trends in the field. Additionally, new carbon and strontium data from dental enamel are presented from Tombos, Qurneh, Saqqara, Amara West, and the Pharaonic as well as C-Group populations (Scandinavian Joint Expedition to Lower Nubia, discussed further below). We use carbon to infer dietary practices and strontium to elucidate possible scenarios of migration, both at the individual and population levels. Through this multi-isotope approach, we aim to elucidate the intersection of locality and diet in diverse Nubian populations, spanning the C-Group through Napatan Periods (c. 2300–664 BC). While many isotopic studies have been conducted in the Nile Valley, this chapter makes a unique contribution by comparing dental enamel carbon and strontium isotope data from these Nile Valley samples.

1 Faculty of Archaeology, Leiden University, The Netherlands; s.a.schrader@arch.leidenuniv.nl.

2 Department of Anthropology, Purdue University, USA; mbuzon@purdue.edu.

3 Buzon and Richman 2007; Buzon and Simonetti 2013; Buzon, Smith and Simonetti 2016; Buzon and Bowen 2010; Eerkens et al. 2018; Iacumin et al. 1996; Schrader 2019; Stantis et al. 2019; Stantis et al. 2020; Stantis et al. 2021.

4 For examples see Schrader 2019; Stantis et al. 2021; Thompson, Chaix and Richards 2008.

Dietary and mobility isotopic studies in the Nile Valley

Before discussing our new dataset and interpretations, we present a brief explanation of isotopes and previous applications to archaeological contexts. We focus specifically on carbon and strontium, as these are the isotopes examined in this chapter. There are other resources that discuss other isotopes applied to the Nile Valley, including nitrogen, oxygen, lead, and others.[5]

The foundations of isotope archaeology

Isotopes have been studied archaeologically for decades, providing an excellent basis for paleodietary studies and continued research.[6] Originally stemming from an interest in carbon-14 dating methods, research in this area gradually developed into broader applications including dietary reconstruction as well as mobility, life history, demography, disease, and paleoenvironmental studies.[7] With the development of mass-spectrometry technology, refined measurements of specific isotopes and their relative abundances became possible. Protocol to identify postmortem degradation have also been developed, increasing the reliability of the method.

In addition to the examination of various isotopes, multiple human tissues began to be assessed. Bone is composed of both organic and inorganic materials; the former, bone collagen, makes up approximately 30% of dry bone and the latter, bone carbonate, composes the other 70% of dry bone.[8] Controlled feeding studies have indicated that collagen isotope ratios reflect dietary proteins, whereas carbonate isotope ratios are derived from the total diet.[9] One integral component of bone is that it remodels throughout the life course. The speed with which a bone remodels depends on the bone; ribs are said to remodel approximately every two to five years, whereas the femur can take ten years or more to completely turnover.[10] Teeth also contain both organic as well as inorganic material. Dentine, the inner portion of the tooth extending from the crown to root, is approximately 30% organic.[11] Dental enamel, located on the crown surface, is largely composed of inorganic carbonate hydroxyapatite, making it particularly resistant to degradation.[12] Primary dentine, deposited during tooth formation, does not remodel during life; however, secondary and sometimes tertiary dentine do remodel.[13] Conversely, dental enamel does not change during life, but rather is essentially locked in at the time of production (*in utero*-15 years, depending on the tooth).[14]

Carbon

By analysing the ratio of the isotopes ^{13}C to ^{12}C, expressed as $\delta^{13}C$, archaeologists are able to infer broad patterns of plant consumption. More specifically, scientists can differentiate a predominately C_3-based plant diet (e.g., wheat, rice, many vegetables and fruits) from a C_4-based plant diet (e.g., sorghum, millet).[15] There is an approximate 5‰ enrichment between plant $\delta^{13}C$ values of plants and those of human bone collagen, and a further 5-6‰ enrichment between collagen and carbonate tissues.[16] Thus, we can expect bone collagen $\delta^{13}C$ values for C_3 diets to range from -33‰ to -23‰ (mean collagen approximately -19‰; mean carbonate approximately -12‰) and bone collagen $\delta^{13}C$ values for C_4 diets to range from -14‰ to -9‰ (mean collagen approximately -8‰; mean carbonate approximately -1‰).[17] There is a third photosynthetic pathway, CAM plants, that have $\delta^{13}C$ values intermediary to C_3 and C_4; however, they are not common in the Nile Valley and likely were not consumed as foods. Going beyond C_3/C_4 foods, it is also possible to use carbon isotopes to distinguish between marine and terrestrial diets. Because the main source of carbon for marine animals is dissolved carbonate ($\delta^{13}C$=0‰), which differs from atmospheric CO_2, ($\delta^{13}C$= -7‰), we can expect a 7‰ difference between terrestrial and marine environments.[18] Carbon values, primarily from dental enamel carbonate, can also be used to assess when weaning from breastmilk to solid foods occurred. Studies comparing dental enamel from multiple teeth have shown a dietary shift at the time of weaning, namely a general enrichment in $\delta^{13}C$ increasing with age.[19] For example, at the Dakhleh Oasis (Roman Egypt), there is a significant difference between preweaning and postweaning teeth, and it is estimated that complete weaning occurred by the age of 3 years old.[20]

Nitrogen values provide information on trophic level, wherein nitrogen is accumulated through steps in the food chain. Each step results in an approximately

5 See Buzon and Bowen 2010; Dupras and Schwarcz 2001; Iacumin et al. 1996; Iacumin et al. 1998; Schrader 2019; Simonetti et al. 2021; Thompson et al. 2005; Thompson, Chaix and Richards 2008; Touzeau et al. 2013; White 1993; White, Longstaffe and Law 2004.

6 See Britton 2018.

7 Katzenberg and Waters-Rist 2019.

8 Note that a small percentage of non-collagenous proteins, proteoglycans, lipids, and trace element substitutions are also present in bone; Katzenberg and Waters-Rist 2019.

9 Ambrose and Norr 1993; Kellner and Schoeninger 2007; Tieszen and Fagre 1993.

10 Hedges et al. 2007; Parfitt 2002; Xia et al. 2018.

11 Pilloud and Heim 2018.

12 Plomp et al. 2020

13 Cox and Sealy 1997; Hillson 1996.

14 Dupras and Tocheri 2007; Hillson 1996.

15 Smith and Epstein 1971.

16 Ambrose and Norr 1993; Passey et al. 2005.

17 DeNiro and Epstein 1978; Dupras and Tocheri 2007; Lee-Thorp, Sealy and van der Merwe 1989; Schoeninger and DeNiro 1984.

18 Katzenberg and Waters-Rist 2019.

19 Wright and Schwarcz 1998.

20 Dupras and Tocheri 2007.

3-5‰ increase, or enrichment, of $\delta^{15}N$ values.[21] For example, legumes have a $\delta^{15}N$ of 0‰; $\delta^{15}N$ values for herbivores are variable, but usually fall within 3-6‰; carnivores living in the same environment would then have $\delta^{15}N$ values greater than 6‰. In addition to trophic levels, nitrogen isotopes can also speak to freshwater fish consumption. As we might expect, the consumption of freshwater fish results in a more enriched $\delta^{15}N$ value, but also, will be accompanied by an increase in $\delta^{13}C$ values. The increase of $\delta^{13}C$ is markedly variable, given that, even within the same body of water, freshwater plants have various resources of carbon (e.g., atmospheric CO_2, water CO_2, soil bicarbonate and carbonate, organic carbon from plants and animals).[22] For example, Katzenberg and colleagues found that $\delta^{13}C$ values of fish bones ranged from -8.1 to -27.0‰ within the same body of water (little Sea of Lake Baikal).[23]

Previous studies of carbon and nitrogen from bone collagen in the Nile Valley have illustrated variation in diet across time and space. Differences between Egyptian and Nubian populations, with the former having a predominately C_3 diet and the latter having a mixed C_3/C_4 diet, have been put forward.[24] For example, Saqqara, Abydos, and Asyut samples all have strong C_3 isotopic values, suggesting a diet including wheat, barley, vegetables, and fruits.[25] Whereas, Kerma individuals have a mixed C_3/C_4 diet, suggesting they consumed sorghum or millet, or ate animals who were foddered on C_4 plants.[26] However, it should be noted that results from bone collagen have been limited due to poor preservation, as collagen is vulnerable to diagenesis.

While previous publications have summarised carbon and nitrogen collagen values from the Nile Valley, carbonate values have largely been overlooked.[27] However, several isotopic studies using carbonate tissues, abbreviated here as $\delta^{13}C_{CARB}$, have been conducted using Nile Valley samples. Iacumin and colleagues examined both bone collagen and bone carbonate from Gebelein (Predynastic 4950–2950 BC and First Intermediate Period 2120–1990 BC) and Asyut (First Intermediate Period) as well as unknown samples (probably from the Dynastic Period) and unknown mummy samples (bone carbonate *n* = 24).[28] The values between sites and time periods were markedly similar and reflect a largely C_3 diet ($\delta^{13}C_{CARB}$ -15.3‰ to -13.2‰; = -14.38 ± 0.48). Later, Buzon and Bowen examine the feasibility of using oxygen isotopes in the Nile Valley and in doing so, also present dental enamel carbonate data from the Nubian site of Tombos (*n* = 30).[29] Carbonate values from this sample were much more varied ($\delta^{13}C_{CARB}$ -13.4‰ to -7.4‰; = -11.81 ± 1.0), indicating a stronger C_4 component to the Nubian diet, which is congruent with other regional isotopic studies.[30]

Touzeau and colleagues examined carbon in bone and dental enamel carbonate, in addition to other tissues and isotopes (sulfur, hair, and soft tissue), in Egyptian mummies dating from 2500 BC–500 AD (*n* = 36).[31] Carbonate in bone and dental enamel both suggested a predominately C_3 diet (bone $\delta^{13}C_{CARB}$ -15.68‰ to -11.50‰; = -14.3 ± 0.9; enamel $\delta^{13}C_{CARB}$ -13.20‰ to -10.74‰; = -11.6 ± 0.7); these values are markedly similar to those reported above[32] and the authors also note a notable continuity in carbonate values over thousands of years of Egyptian history. Dental enamel carbonate was also less negative than bone carbonate (both within and between individuals, on average 2.7‰ less negative), which the authors suggest may be due to weaning practices. It is possible that milk, originating from C_4 fed animals, or millet gruel was introduced to infants and toddlers as part of the weaning process.[33]

Stantis and colleagues examined both mobility and dietary practices via strontium, oxygen, and carbon from dental carbonate at the site of Tell el-Daba in the Nile Delta (*n*=75).[34] Tell el-Daba is important as it is the capital city of the Hyksos, who are thought to have originated in the Near East and ruled Lower Egypt from the Delta during the Second Intermediate Period (c. 1638-1530 BC). Carbon values reported here are largely C_3, like other Nile Valley studies (enamel $\delta^{13}C_{CARB}$ -13.5‰ to -9.6‰; = -11.4 ± 0.7). Interestingly, there was no significant difference in carbon values between locals and non-locals, suggesting similar dietary patterns during childhood. Stantis and co-authors note a wider variety of foods consumed in non-locals, as illustrated by a broader $\delta^{13}C$ range (non-locals $\delta^{13}C_{CARB}$ -13.5‰ to -9.6‰, locals $\delta^{13}C_{CARB}$: -12.1‰ to -10.3‰).[35] These findings may also speak to the abundance of C_3 vegetation in both Egypt and the Near East during the Bronze Age.

Strontium

The movement of people across the landscape can provide important information to understand how resources were accessed and utilised through time.

21 Bocherens and Drucker 2003; O'Connell et al. 2012; Schwarcz and Schoeninger 1991.
22 Katzenberg and Waters-Rist 2019.
23 Katzenberg et al. 2012.
24 Schrader 2019.
25 Iacumin et al. 1996; Thompson et al. 2005.
26 Iacumin et al. 1998; Thompson, Chaix and Richards 2008.
27 See Schrader 2019.
28 Iacumin et al. 1996.
29 Buzon and Bowen 2010.
30 Ciesielska et al. 2021; Iacumin et al. 1998; Schrader 2019; Thompson, Chaix and Richards 2008.
31 Touzeau et al. 2014.
32 See Iacumin et al. 1996.
33 Touzeau et al. 2014.
34 Stantis et al. 2021.
35 Stantis et al. 2021.

For instance, in Bronze Age Nubia, the control of land by Kerma or Egyptians may have resulted in the relocation of individuals. Markers of geographic origin, such as isotopic signatures, are often used to investigate if migration, defined as one-way, long-term, permanent relocation, has occurred. However, mobility, understood as movement across shorter distances within more limited cultural or political boundaries, may also have occurred.[36] The ability to trace these transfers depends on particulars of the isotope system being used and the documented variability between regions of interest.

Isotope analyses can be used to identify first-generation immigrants who spent time in another location while their dental tissues were developing during childhood, or more recently though skeletal tissues if tissues are intact. Strontium isotope analysis ($^{87}Sr/^{86}Sr$) has been used in many global locations to trace movements across the landscape. Geological variability in the age and composition of bedrock is needed between a particular site and a likely place of origin for immigrants. Younger rocks and rocks with low Rb content generally have lower $^{87}Sr/^{86}Sr$ values with older, Rb-rich rocks, such as granite, that are characterised by higher values.[37] It is also important that local foods are being consumed, which would reflect the local geology; the importation of nonlocal foods as well as the consumption of sea salt can override local signatures.[38]

The Nile Valley provides some geological differences along the river, which are the basis for this method. Below the First Cataract, formations are characterised by Dakhla chalk, Esna shale and Theban limestone; Nubia generally consists of pre-Cambrian Basement Complex covered with Nubian Sandstone complex, with outcrops of granite at the cataracts.[39] The determination of a local $^{87}Sr/^{86}Sr$ signature is usually accomplished by analysing local small animals with local home ranges in order to characterize the biologically available strontium.[40]

Strontium isotope research in the region over the last two decades beginning with Buzon and colleagues[41] has established some consistency ($^{87}Sr/^{86}Sr$ with other archaeological indications of identity) in the documentation of individuals who may have originated in Egypt and moved to Nubia during the colonial activities of the Egyptian empire, particularly at the Third Cataract site of Tombos. Very little research has been done on samples in Northeast Africa outside of the Nile River Valley. However, as more samples are analysed by various researchers at numerous sites in the region,[42] it has become clear that there is much overlap in $^{87}Sr/^{86}Sr$ values.[43] The addition of other isotope systems may provide a sharper picture of movements. For example, variability in Pb ($^{206}Pb/^{204}Pb$, $^{207}Pb/^{204}Pb$, $^{208}Pb/^{204}Pb$, $^{208}Pb/^{206}Pb$ $^{207}Pb/^{206}Pb$) and Nd ($^{143}Nd/^{144}Nd$) isotope can be used to corroborate the interpretations based on Sr isotope ratios.[44]

Oxygen isotope analysis ($\delta^{18}O$) has also been used in this region. Oxygen isotopes vary in relation to hydrological, geographical, and climatological factors such as temperature, humidity, rainfall, latitude, elevation and distance from the coast.[45] These values are complicated by isotopically variable groundwater (wells) and river water as well as water use strategies such as irrigation, storage, and boiling.[46] However, this method has proven valuable in distinguishing individuals from desert oases from the river valley[47] and may provide a useful method to explore the movement of people in Nubia into and from the Eastern and Western Deserts.

Materials and methods

Here we present new carbonate data, paired with previously published strontium data, from various ancient sites, including: Tombos, Qurneh, Saqqara, Amara West, Pharaonic, and C-Group (the last two of which are composed of various sites, excavated as part of the Scandinavian Joint Expedition to Sudanese Nubia; *N*=104; Fig. 1).

Materials

Tombos

Tombos is located at the Third Cataract of the Nile in Sudan. Remains in the nearby town reveal structure foundations and a wall/dry moat system that outlined a large, fortified area, which may have been the ancient fortress of Taroy.[48] Excavations and analyses since 2000 have revealed three main burial areas: North (middle-class chamber tombs and pits primarily dating to the New Kingdom Period), East (tumulus graves that begin in the late New Kingdom and continue into the early Napatan Period), and West (pyramid, chapel, and chamber tombs along with pit tombs primarily dating to

36 Gregoricka 2021.
37 Faure 1977.
38 Fenner and Wright 2014.
39 Burke et al. 1982; Whiteman 1971.
40 Price, Burton and Bentley 2002.
41 Buzon, Simonetti and Creaser 2007.
42 Buzon, Simonetti and Creaser 2007; Buzon, Smith and Simonetti 2016; Buzon and Simonetti 2013; Kozieradzka-Ogunmakin 2021; Osypinska et al. 2021; Retzmann et al. 2019; Schrader et al. 2019; Simonetti et al. 2021; Stantis et al. 2020; Touzeau et al. 2013.
43 Buzon, Guilbault and Simonetti 2023.
44 Simonetti et al. 2023.
45 Longinelli 1984
46 Buzon and Bowen 2010; Buzon, Schrader and Bowen 2018.
47 Dupras and Schwarcz 2001.
48 Smith and Buzon 2018.

the New Kingdom with some reuse in the early Napatan). The skeletal remains are curated at Purdue University. Previous research has indicated a possible local strontium range, based off small mammals, to be 0.70710-0.70783.[49] However, as discussed above, using strontium alone only provides preliminary evidence of mobility; additional testing, including further isotopic studies are necessary, to substantiate these data.

Qurneh
The site of Qurneh is located in the necropolis at Thebes and the individuals included are associated with a New Kingdom date. The remains are curated in the Duckworth Collection at the University of Cambridge. Note that no local strontium range has been determined.

Saqqara
The remains from the Saqqara necropolis, near Cairo, are associated with a New Kingdom date. They are curated in the Duckworth Collection at the University of Cambridge (labelled as Memphis in the collection). A local strontium range has yet to be established.

Amara West
Amara West is a site located between the Second and Third Cataracts in Sudan that contains burials dating to the New Kingdom and early Napatan Periods (~1300 BC–800 BC). The remains are curated at The British Museum. A tentative local strontium range is 0.70633-0.70802, which was also developed using small mammals.[50]

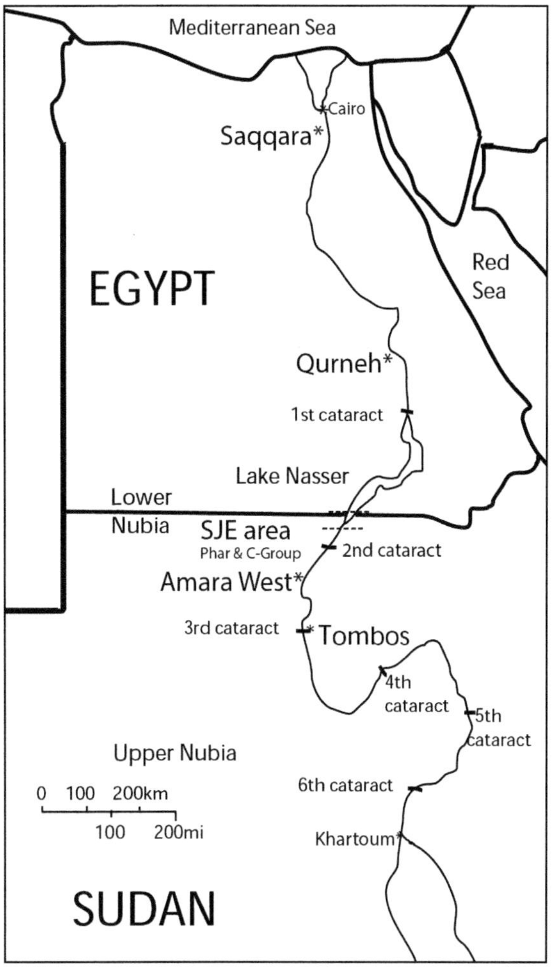

Fig. 1 Locations of samples examined.

Pharaonic
The collection marked 'Pharaonic' comes from the Scandinavian Joint Expedition to Nubia sites located from the modern Egyptian border to ~60km south. These individuals were buried in Egyptian style, date to 1650–1350 BC, and are curated in the Biological Anthropology Laboratory at the University of Copenhagen. At this time the local strontium range for the First to Second Cataract region is unclear; although faunal data have been published, the complicated geology makes the utility of migration studies – using strontium alone – limited.[51] The application of additional isotopes to the study of migration may clarify this issue.

C-Group
The C-Group remains come from cemeteries associated with this culture excavated by the Scandinavian Joint Expedition to Nubia (2000–1600 BC) in the region from the modern Egyptian border to ~60km south. They are curated in the Biological Anthropology Laboratory at the University of Copenhagen. For notes on local strontium range, please see information above regarding Pharaonic sample, as both the C-Group and Pharaonic populations inhabited the same region.

Methods

Sex and age-at-death in adults were estimated according to accepted bioarchaeological techniques, namely pelvic and cranial morphology.[52] Age-at-death for non-adults was estimated according to bone fusion and dental eruption, both of which are widely used in bioarchaeology.[53] Age at tooth formation was estimated using well-documented dental development data and later categorised in four

49 Buzon and Simonetti 2013.
50 Spencer et al. in review.
51 Buzon and Simonetti 2013.
52 Brickley and McKinley 2004; Buikstra and Ubelaker 1994.
53 AlQahtani, Hector and Liversidge 2010; Brickley and McKinley 2004; Buikstra and Ubelaker 1994.

	FEI	IEC	MC	AD	Total
Tombos	1	12	30	5	48
Qurneh	0	0	12	0	12
Saqqara	0	0	14	0	14
Amara West	2	3	1	0	6
Pharaonic	0	0	9	0	9
C-Group	0	0	13	0	13
Total	3	15	79	5	102

Table 1 Demographic distribution.

groups: Foetal/Early Infancy (FEI), Infancy and Early Childhood (IEC), Middle Childhood (MC), and Early Adolescence (AD).[54]

Best practices for destructive isotope sampling were followed at all stages of research and publication.[55]

Carbonate

The enamel surface was burred to remove any adhering contaminants. Approximately 10mg of dental enamel was taken from the crown of the tooth, using a Dremel fitted with a diamond blade. These samples were then treated with 5% NaOCl (Sodium hypochlorite), then rinsed. A 0.1 mol acetic acid solution was added. This process was repeated for three days. Samples were rinsed and dried prior to analysis.[56] Dental carbonate was analysed using a TermoFinnigan Delta V Isotope Ratio Mass Spectrometer (Purdue Stable Isotope Facility, Department of Earth and Atmospheric Sciences, Purdue University).

Strontium

The strontium data presented in this study comes from published sources.[57] The analyses were completed at the Radiogenic Isotope Facility in the Department of Earth and Atmospheric Sciences, University of Alberta and the University of Notre Dame Midwest Isotope and Trace Element Research Analytical Center (MITERAC). Samples were prepared in a class 1000 cleanroom facility and prepared using previously published methods.[58]

Statistical analysis

Shapiro-Wilk tests and Q-Q plots were used to test for normality. Due to the fact that dental enamel is formed at various times in the life course (*in utero* to young adolescence) depending on the tooth, we also statistically examined age distribution based on tooth formation between sites; this was done via a Kruskal-Wallis test. Pearson's *t*-tests were used to compare strontium and carbonate values. ANOVA was employed to examine dental enamel carbonate values between all samples. LSD post-hoc tests were conducted, following the ANOVA, to better understand the relationship between strontium and carbon at specific sites. Statistical analyses were conducted in SPSS (version 29.0) and plots were made in R version 4.2.0[59] with the ggplot2 package.[60]

Results

Initial statistical testing confirmed that data were normally distributed. A Kruskal-Wallis test confirmed that there are no differences in the distribution of age at dental enamel formation between sites ($H[5] = 4.224, p=0.518$).

Results of the dental carbonate isotope analysis were markedly variable. Across the six sample populations included here, carbon values ranged from -13.85‰ to -6.22‰ and strontium values ranged from 0.70658 to 0.70912 (Table 2; Fig. 2). An ANOVA, comparing carbonate values from each of the samples, indicates that these populations had significantly different carbon values ($F(5), 98) = [3.007], p = 0.014$).

Carbon values from Tombos have a wide range and likely include both C_3 and C_4 consumers. As reported elsewhere, there is also a relatively wide range of

54 AlQahtani, Hector and Liversidge 2010; Hillson 1996; Turner et al. 2009; Table 1.
55 Vaiglova et al. 2023
56 Koch, Tuross and Fogel 1997.
57 For full description of methods see Buzon, Simonetti and Creaser 2007; Buzon and Simonetti 2013; Buzon, Smith and Simonetti 2016; Schrader et al. 2019.
58 Buzon, Simonetti and Creaser 2007; Buzon and Simonetti 2013.
59 R Core Team 2020.
60 Wickham 2016.

Site	n	$\delta^{13}C_{CARB}$			$^{87}Sr/^{86}Sr$		
		Min/Max		SD	Min/Max		SD
Tombos	49	-13.85 to -7.42‰	-12.22‰	1.15	0.70661-0.70912	0.70767	0.00045
Saqqara	12	-12.93 to -11.38‰	-12.27‰	0.55	0.70745-0.70807	0.70774	0.00022
Qurneh	14	-13.29 to -10.89‰	-12.37‰	0.72	0.70731-0.70798	0.70777	0.00018
Pharaonic	9	-13.23 to -6.22‰	-11.27‰	2.61	0.70658-0.70764	0.70740	0.00033
C-Group	13	-13.12 to -7.05‰	-11.01‰	1.75	0.70735-0.70807	0.70764	0.00020
Amara West	7	-13.30 to -11.94‰	-12.66‰	0.43	0.70741-0.70763	0.70753	0.00007

Table 2 Dental enamel carbon and strontium results.

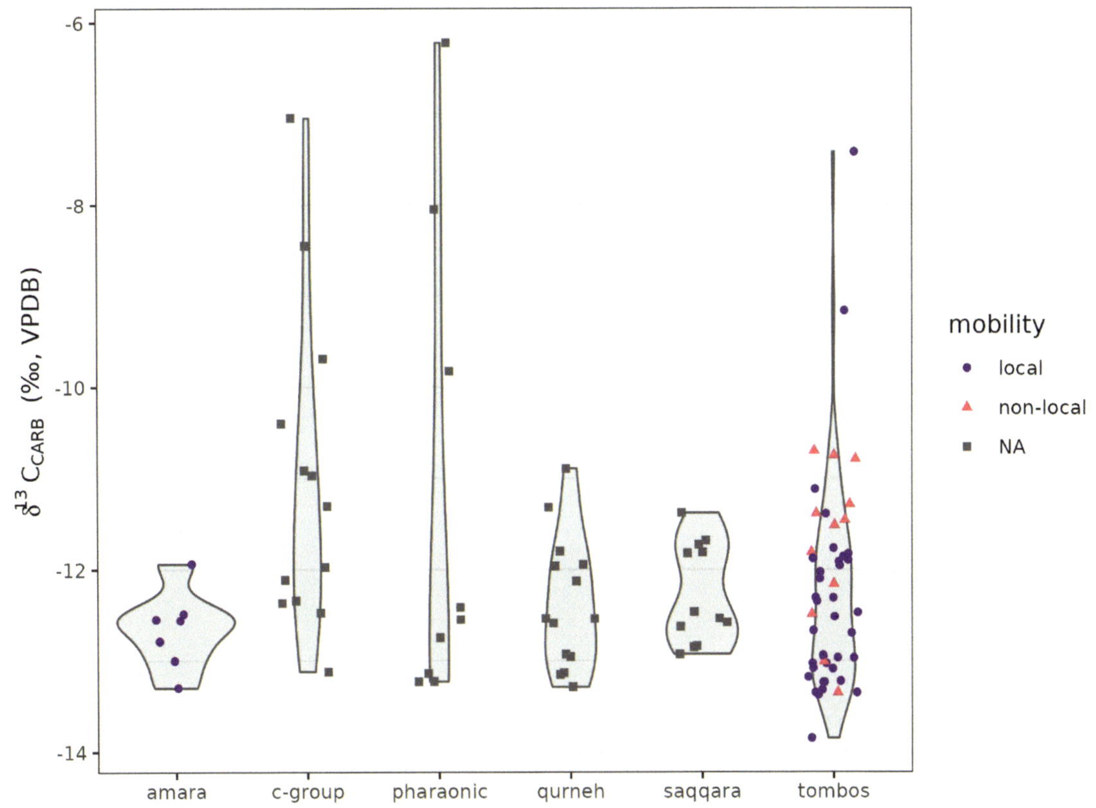

Fig. 2 Carbonate values for all samples.

strontium values.[61] There are two carbon outliers: TOM-24 and TOM-111 (discussed further below). When carbon and strontium are contrasted (outliers removed), there is a significant positive relationship ($r[47] = 0.345$, $p = 0.018$). If we compare carbon results between those individuals whose strontium values fall within the local range, versus those individuals whose strontium values are outside the local range (i.e., possible first-generation migrants), there is also a significant difference between these groups (t [47] = -1.764, $p = 0.042$; Table 3; Fig. 3). As noted above, further research needs to be done to confirm that these individuals are in fact migrants; however, the strontium data do suggest this. The two

61 Buzon, Simonetti and Creaser 2007; Buzon and Simonetti 2013.

Site	n	$\delta^{13}C_{CARB}$			$^{87}Sr/^{86}Sr$		
		Range		SD	Range		SD
Non-Local	11	-13.35 to -10.70‰	-11.69‰	0.90	0.70705-0.70912	0.70823	0.00054
Local	38	-13.85 to -7.42‰	-12.37‰	1.18	0.70661-0.70781	0.70751	0.00024

Table 3 Tombos local versus non-local carbon and strontium results

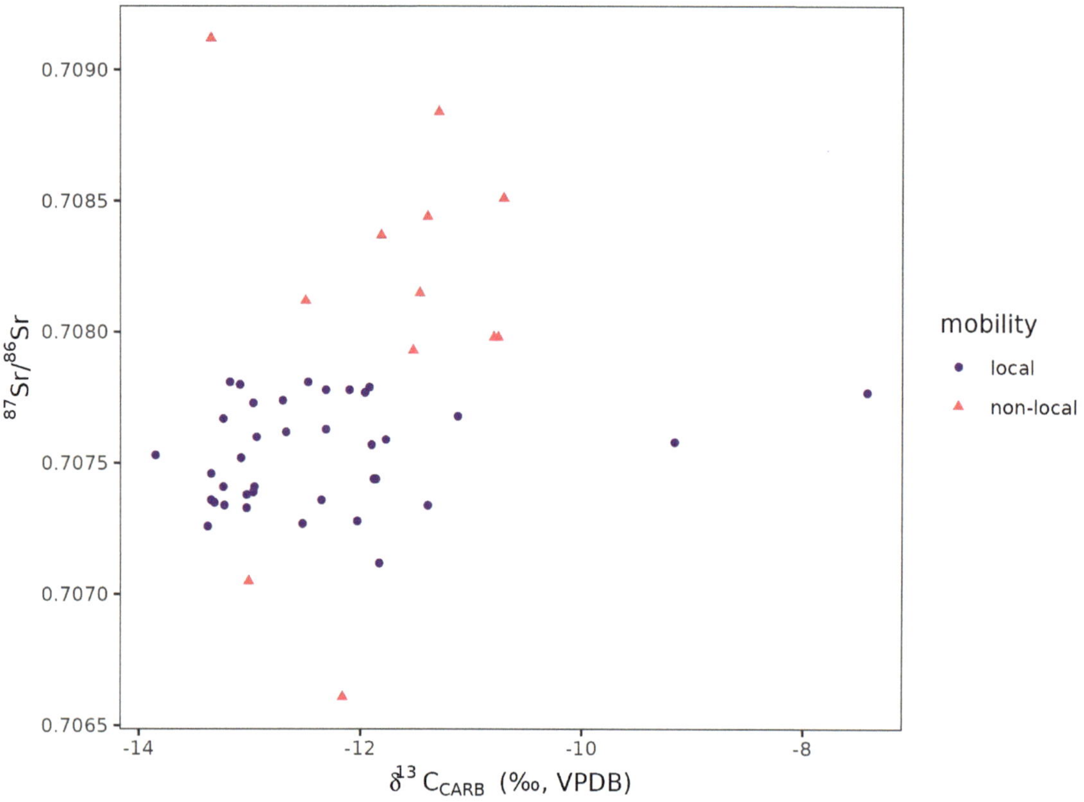

Fig. 3 Tombos locals versus non-locals carbon values compared.

carbon outliers, TOM-24 and TOM-111, have enriched carbon values ($\delta^{13}C_{CARB}$ -7.42 and -9.16, respectively), suggesting a stronger C_4 component to their diet to the rest of the Tombos sample. Both individuals have what can tentatively be interpreted as local strontium values (0.70777 and 0.70758, respectively). LSD post-hoc tests revealed that carbon values from the Tombos sample significantly differed from both Pharaonic and C-Group samples (p = 0.047, 95% C.I. = [-1.89, -0.01]; p = 0.004, 95% C.I. = [-2.01, -0.40], respectively). Interestingly, if Tombos 'locals' are differentiated from 'non-locals,' the same LSD post-hoc tests indicates that only the Tombos locals actually differ from Pharaonic and C-Group (p = 0.024, 95% C.I. = [-2.05, -0.15]; p =0.002, 95% C.I.= [-2.18, -0.53]), while the Tombos non-locals are not statistically significantly different (p = 0.472 , 95% C.I. = [-1.57, 0.73]; p = 0.206, 95% C.I. = [-1.73, 0.38]).

The Pharaonic and C-Group samples also have wide carbon ranges (7.01‰, 6.07‰), similar to that of Tombos (6.43‰). There is no significant correlation between carbon and strontium in either the Pharaonic or C-Group samples (r[9]= -0.615, p=0.078; r[13]= 0.190, p=0.535). LSD post-hoc tests indicate that the Pharaonic sample is significantly different than the Tombos locals, Qurneh, and Amara West samples (p=0.024, 95% C.I. = [-2.05, -0.15]; p=0.049, 95% C.I. = [-2.20, -0.01]; p=0.035, 95% C.I. = [0.10, 2.69]). Similarly, the C-Group is significantly different from Tombos local, Saqqara, Qurneh, and Amara West samples when a LSD post-hoc was conducted (p=0.002, 95% C.I. = [-2.18, -0.53]; p=0.017, 95% C.I.

= [-2.29, -0.23]; p=0.008, 95% C.I. = [-2.35, -0.37]; p=0.008, 95% C.I. = [0.45, 2.85]).

Dental enamel carbon from Saqqara, Qurneh, and Amara West are all relatively similar with less than 2.5‰ range within each sample (1.55‰, 2.4‰, 1.36‰, respectively). Carbon and strontium values for Saqqara and Amara West are not correlated (r[12]= -0.157, p=0.627; r[7]= -0.528, p=0.224); however, for Qurneh, carbon and strontium have a statistically significant negative relationship (r[14]= -0.624, p=0.017). While a local strontium range has been estimated for Amara West, all individuals with carbon data were deemed to be local—thus, more refined comparison of local versus non-local, as was done with the Tombos sample, is not possible here.

Discussion

The data presented here suggest a complex relationship between locality, chronology, and dietary practices during the second to first millennia BC in the Nile Valley. Statistical testing does suggest that there was a difference between carbon consumption between the six samples examined here. It is important to remember that, for the most part, this reflects childhood dietary practices as the enamel that was isotopically tested was formed in utero to young adolescence. Strontium values are also complicated because recent research has shown that strontium alone cannot establish first generation migrant status in the Nile Valley, but rather must be coupled with additional isotopes.[62] Nonetheless, these new carbonate data do suggest that diets varied across the Nile Valley.

The carbon values per site suggest that all six samples likely regularly consumed C_3 foods, including wheat, and barley, as well as common Nile Valley fruits and vegetables (e.g., onions, leaks, lentils, peas, dates). The Tombos, Pharaonic, and C-Group samples have a wide range of carbon values, indicating that at least some individuals were consuming C_4 foods (e.g., sorghum, millet) or were consuming the products of animals (e.g., milk, blood, meat) that were foddered on C_4 foods. One could make the argument that this is a geographic or environmental byproduct (i.e., C_4 foods grow in hotter climates). While this is certainly true, exceptions include Amara West, which has a distinctly C_3 dental enamel carbonate range and is south of the C-Group/Pharaonic area of occupation. We therefore argue, as others have done before us, that foods consumed are socially meaningful decisions that are made by agents, rather than passive selection of foods that are available.[63]

At Tombos, we found a positive relationship between carbon values and strontium values. Stantis et al. found similar results in their study of Tell el-Daba.[64] However, given that strontium geology is so complex, particularly in the Nile Valley, it is difficult at this time draw to conclusions about how these two values might be influencing one another.[65] If we use small mammal strontium values to estimate locality, we found that dental enamel carbon values between 'locals' and 'non-locals' did significant differ, with the former eating a higher proportion of C_3 foods and the latter consuming more C_4 foods. Within the complex colonial sphere of Tombos, this dietary juxtaposition is particularly interesting. Schrader has made the argument that C_4 foods were culturally selected by Nubians whereas C_3 foods were a more Egyptian food.[66] This doesn't preclude that Nubians consumed C_3 foods, as they were readily available and composed vegetables and fruits, which were certainly a sizeable portion of the Egyptian and Nubian diet. But, millet and sorghum possibly played an important cultural role in distinguishing Nubians from Egyptians, which may have been particularly relevant in a colonial sphere. Non-locals potentially moving to Tombos from other areas in Nubia may have consumed C_4 foods in childhood, while people who lived at Tombos in an Egyptian colonial environment, much like Amara West, may have consumed predominately C_3 foods in their childhood. It is equally possible that the non-locals were consuming a C_4-based gruel or animal by-products from C_4-fed animals.[67] Bone collagen data suggests this may have been the case throughout the life course.[68]

The wide carbon ranges found in both the C-Group and Pharaonic samples may also be explained by this Nubian cultural selection of C_4 foods argument. The C-Group were an indigenous Nubian group, occupying Lower Nubia from c. 2300–1800 BC. Given this Nubian heritage, they may also have consumed more C_4 and fed their children a higher proportion of C_4 foods than Egyptian counterparts. The Pharaonic sample is a bit more difficult to assess; these are individuals who were buried in the First-Second Cataract region in an Egyptian burial style—however, there is still debate as to whether they were Egyptians who migrated into this colonial space during the New Kingdom, or whether they were locals (e.g., C-Group, Nubian) who took on an Egyptian identity to survive and possibly advance within a colonial environment.[69] It is possible that the data presented here support the latter; that the Pharaonic samples were biologically Nubian and were thus raised

62 Buzon, Guilbault and Simonetti 2023.

63 Bourdieu 1977; Bourdieu 1984; Löfgren 2015.

64 Stantis et al. 2021.

65 Buzon, Guilbault and Simonetti 2023.

66 Schrader 2019.

67 Dupras 2001; Dupras and Tocheri 2007; Touzeau et al. 2014.

68 Schrader 2019.

69 Smith 1998; Smith and Buzon 2014.

on Nubian C_4 foods during childhood and then as they grew older decided to take on Egyptian identity, thereby explaining their burial status. However, additional research is needed to confirm this hypothesis.

Saqqara, Qurneh, and Amara West carbonate values are all markedly similar. There is limited variation within the samples, although this may be due to a limited sample size. It is also quite possible that these samples simply reflect carbon values of an Egyptian-based diet. If we compare the $\delta^{13}C$ ranges of Saqqara, Qurneh, and Amara West, they are all very similar to previous research conducted on dental enamel carbonate tissues discussed above.[70] Based on these results, we can tentatively conclude that, for these samples, nearly all of the foods consumed by these individuals were C_3. This is perhaps not surprising given the strong C_3 dietary practices of Egyptians. As mentioned above, the case of Amara West is particularly interesting, given the colonial nature of the site. There are meaningful differences between Amara West and Tombos, both of which are Egyptian colonial outposts in colonised Nubia, that might explain these findings. First, Amara West was founded and occupied much later than Tombos (Ramesside Period, ~1300–1100 BC, versus initial colonization, ~1450 BC). It is possible that the dietary distinctions between Nubian and Egyptian no longer existed by the Ramesside Period. Secondly, the strontium data suggest that all individuals that we have carbonate data for are local. Perhaps a similar pattern that we see at Tombos, where the non-local individuals have a more C_4 signal and the local individuals have a more C_3 signal, would also be visible at Amara West, but is currently obscured by the small sample size. Lastly, it is also possible that the community of Tombos nurtured a transcultural space where eating Egyptian and Nubian foods was accepted. Previous research by Buzon and Smith has suggested that life at Tombos was relatively peaceful, that Nubians and Egyptians living in this space were healthy, and that a certain coexistence was encouraged as a way to promote the success of the empire.[71]

Lastly, it is important to again highlight that because we are examining dental enamel tissues here, we are discussing childhood dietary practices, which may include breastfeeding and/or weaning. While more research needs to be done on this topic in the region, we do acknowledge that this variable could be impacting our results and subsequent interpretations. The fact that age-at-enamel formation did not differ significantly between sites, lends credence to the argument that these patterns might in fact reflect dietary differences. It is quite possible that, because Egyptians and Nubians identified with the foods they consumed in a meaningful way, in feeding these foods to their children they were instilling this very identity into future generations.

Conclusion

The new carbon data presented here suggests a dynamic social landscape where individuals and communities used food as a way to define and maintain identities. These data can be used as a springboard for additional research into dietary and migration practices in ancient Nubia and the Nile Valley. For example, additional carbonate data from other sites would help to support or refute our interpretations of Egyptian/Nubian dietary practices. We have mentioned the poor preservation of collagen in the region, likely due to the harsh environment. However, hair keratin has been shown to be a viable alternative to bone collagen.[72] Additional carbon and nitrogen studies from hair would provide more substantive interpretations of ancient dietary practices through the life course.

As discussed above, strontium should be coupled with other isotopes to confirm or refute migration.[73] If these multi-isotope studies were conducted on all samples discussed here, we would be able to more thoroughly examine the intersection of migration and diet as was preliminarily done here with the Tombos sample. Local ranges are also needed for several samples as well as the Nile Valley more broadly.

These isotopic contributions, in addition to the excavation and analysis of new archaeological sites, will certainly advance our understanding of Nubian and Nile Valley diet and migration. As has been argued elsewhere, isotope analysis has made a profound impact on the field and will continue to do so.

Acknowledgements

The authors wish to acknowledge our collaboration with co-Director Stuart Tyson Smith on the Tombos archaeological project and the support and assistance provided by the Sudanese National Corporation for Antiquities and Museums and the town of Tombos in our many seasons of excavations. The University of Copenhagen, University of Cambridge Duckworth Collection, and The British Museum generously allowed the sampling of materials from their collections for this study. The isotopic research was supported National Science Foundation grant BCS-0917815, Dutch Research Council (NWO VI.Vidi.201.153), National Geographic Society, American Philosophical Society, American Association of Physical Anthropologists, Purdue Alumni Association and Purdue University College of Liberal Arts Research Incentive grant. Sample preparation and analysis was completed in collaboration with Gabriel Bowen and Antonio Simonetti.

70 See Touzeau et al. 2014.

71 Smith 2003; Buzon and Richman 2007.

72 Schrader and Smith 2022.

73 Buzon, Guilbault and Simonetti 2023.

Bibliography

ALQAHTANI, S.J., HECTOR, M.P. and LIVERSIDGE, H.M.
2010 Brief communication: The London atlas of human tooth development and eruption, *American Journal of Physical Anthropology* 142, 481–490.

AMBROSE, S.H. and NORR, L.
1993 Experimental evidence for the relationship of the carbon isotope ratios of whole diet and dietary protein to those of bone collagen and carbonate, in: B. LAMBERT and G. GRUPE (eds.), *Prehistoric Human Bone: Archaeology at the Molecular Level*, Berlin, 1–37.

BOCHERENS, H. and DRUCKER, D.
2003 Trophic level isotopic enrichment of carbon and nitrogen in bone collagen: case studies from recent and ancient terrestrial ecosystems, *International Journal of Osteoarchaeology* 13, 46–53.

BOURDIEU, P.
1977 *Outline of the Theory of Practice*, Cambridge.
1984 *Distinction: A Social Critique of the Judgement of Taste*, Cambridge.

BRICKLEY, M.B. and MCKINLEY, J.I.
2004 *Guidelines to the Standards for Recording Human Remains*, IFA Paper No. 7, Reading.

BRITTON, K.
2017 A stable relationship: Isotopes and bioarchaeology are in it for the long haul, *Antiquity* 91 (358), 853–864.

BUIKSTRA, J. and UBELAKER, D.
1994 *Standards for Data Collection from Human Skeletal Remains*, Fayetteville.

BURKE, W.H., DENISON, R.E., HETHERINGTON, E.A., KOEPNICK, R.B., NELSON, H.F. and OTTO, J.B.
1982 Variation of seawater $^{87}Sr/^{86}Sr$ throughout Phanerozoic time, *Geology* 10 (10), 516–519.

BUZON, M.R. and BOWEN, G.J.
2010 Oxygen and carbon isotope analysis of human tooth enamel from the New Kingdom site of Tombos in Nubia, *Archaeometry* 52, no. 5, 855–868.

BUZON, M.R. and RICHMAN, R.
2007 Traumatic injuries and imperialism: The effects of Egyptian colonial strategies at Tombos in Upper Nubia, *American Journal of Physical Anthropology* 133 (2), 783–791.

BUZON, M.R., SCHRADER, S. and BOWEN, G. J.
2018 Isotopic approaches to mobility in northern Africa: A bioarchaeological examination of Egyptian/Nubian interaction in the Nile Valley, in: M.C. GATTO, D. MATTINGLY, N. RAY and M. STERRY (eds.), *Burials, Migration and Identity in the Ancient Sahara and Beyond*, Cambridge, 223–246.

BUZON, M.R., SIMONETTI, A. and CREASER, R.A.
2007 Migration in the Nile Valley during the New Kingdom Period: A preliminary strontium isotope study, *Journal of Archaeological Science* 34 (9), 1391–1401.

BUZON, M.R. and SIMONETTI, A.
2013 Strontium isotope ($^{87}Sr/^{86}Sr$) variability in the Nile Valley: Identifying residential mobility during ancient Egyptian and Nubian sociopolitical changes in the New Kingdom and Napatan Periods, *American Journal of Physical Anthropology* 151 (1), 1–9.

BUZON, M.R., SMITH, S.T. and SIMONETTI, A.
2016 Entanglement and the formation of the ancient Nubian Napatan state, *American Anthropologist* 118 (2), 284–300.

BUZON, M.R., GUILBAULT, K.A. and SIMONETTI, A.
2023 Exploring intersectional identities and geographic origins in ancient Nubia at Tombos, Sudan, *Bioarchaeology International*, https://doi.org/10.5744/bi.2022.0029.

CIESIELSKA, J.A., STARK, R.J., OBŁUSKI, A., BOIVIN, N. and ROBERTS, P.
2021 Multi-isotope analysis of dietary variation among the Early Christian communities of northern Sudan, *Journal of Archaeological Science: Reports* 37, 103016.

COX, G. and SEALY, J.
1997 Investigating identity and life histories: Isotopic analysis and historical documentation of slave skeletons found on the Cape Town Foreshore, South Africa, *International Journal of Historical Archaeology* 1 (3), 207–224.

DENIRO, M.J. and EPSTEIN, S.
1978 Influence of diet on the distribution of carbon isotopes in animals, *Geochimica et Cosmochimica Acta* 42 (5), 495–506.

DUPRAS, T.L. and SCHWARCZ, H.P.
2001 Strangers in a strange land: Stable isotope evidence for human migration in the Dakhleh Oasis, Egypt, *Journal of Archaeological Science* 28 (11), 1199–1208.

DUPRAS, T.L. and TOCHERI, M.W.
2007 Reconstructing infant weaning histories at Roman period Kellis, Egypt using stable isotope analysis of dentition, *American Journal of Physical Anthropology* 134 (1), 63–74.

EERKENS, J.W., DE VOOGT, A., DUPRAS, T.L., FRANCIGNY, V. and GREENWALD, A.M.
2018 Early childhood diets on the Nile: $\Delta^{13}C$ and $\Delta^{15}N$ in serial samples of permanent first molars in an elite Meroitic population from Sai Island, Sudan, *International Journal of Osteoarchaeology* 28 (5), 552–562.

FAURE, G.
1977 *Principles of Isotope Geology*, New York.

FENNER, J.N. and WRIGHT, L.E.
2014 Revisiting the strontium contribution of sea salt in the human diet, *Journal of Archaeological Science* 44, 99–103.

GREGORICKA, L.A.
2021 Moving forward: A bioarchaeology of mobility and migration, *Journal of Archaeological Research* 29, 581–635.

HEDGES, R.E.M., CLEMENT, J.G., THOMAS, D.L. and O'CONNELL, T.C.
2007 Collagen turnover in the adult femoral mid-shaft: Modelled from anthropogenic radiocarbon tracer measurements, *American Journal of Physical Anthropology* 133, 808–816.

HILLSON, S.
1996 *Dental Anthropology*, Cambridge.

IACUMIN, P., BOCHERENS, H., MARIOTTI, A. and LONGINELLI, A.
1996 An isotopic palaeoenvironmental study of human skeletal remains from the Nile Valley, *Palaeogeography, Palaeoclimatology, Palaeoecology* 126 (1–2), 15–30.

IACUMIN, P., BOCHERENS, H., CHAIX, L. and MARIOTH, A.
1998 Stable carbon and nitrogen isotopes as dietary indicators of Ancient Nubian populations (northern Sudan), *Journal of Archaeological Science* 25 (4), 293–301.

KATZENBERG, M.A., MCKENZIE, H.G., LOSEY, R.J., GORIUNOVA, O.I. and WEBER, A.
2012 Prehistoric dietary adaptations among hunter-fisher-gatherers from the Little Sea of Lake Baikal, Siberia, Russian Federation, *Journal of Archaeological Science* 39 (8), 2612–2626.

KATZENBERG, M.A. and WATERS-RIST, A.
2019 Stable isotope analysis: A tool for studying past diet, demography, and life history, in: M.A. KATZENBERG and A.L. GRAUER (eds.), *Biological Anthropology of the Human Skeleton*, Oxford, 469–504.

KELLNER, C.M. and SCHOENINGER, M.J.
2007 A simple carbon isotope model for reconstructing prehistoric human diet, *American Journal of Physical Anthropology* 133 (4), 1112–1127.

KOCH, P.L., TUROSS, N. and FOGEL, M.L.
1997 The effects of sample treatment and diagenesis on the isotopic integrity of carbonate in biogenic hydroxylapatite, *Journal of Archaeological Science* 24 (5), 417–429.

KOZIERADZKA-OGUNMAKIN, I.
2020 Isotope analysis and radiocarbon dating of human remains from El-Zuma, in: M. EL-TAYEB and E. CZYŻEWSKA-ZALEWSKA (eds.), *Early Makuria Research Project. El-Zuma Cemetery*, Leiden, 220–227.

LEE-THORP, J.A., SEALY, J.C. and VAN DER MERWE, N.J.
1989 Stable carbon isotope ratio differences between bone collagen and bone apatite, and their relationship to diet, *Journal of Archaeological Science* 16, no. 6, 585–599.

LÖFGREN, O.
2015 Anthropology of everyday life, in: J.D. WRIGHT (ed.), *International Encyclopedia of Social & Behavioral Sciences*, Amsterdam, 323–326.

LONGINELLI, A.
1984 Oxygen isotopes in mammal bone phosphate: A new tool for paleohydrological and paleoclimatological research?, *Geochimica et Cosmochimica Acta* 48, 385–390.

O'CONNELL, T.C., KNEALE, C.J. TASEVSKA, N. and KUHNLE, G.G.C.
2012 The diet-body offset in human nitrogen isotopic values: A controlled dietary study, *American Journal of Physical Anthropology* 149 (3), 426–434.

OSYPINSKA, M., OSYPINSKI, P., BELKA, Z., CHLODNICKI, M., WIKTOROWICZ, P., RYNDZIEWICZ, R. and KUBIAK, M.
2021 Wild and domestic cattle in the ancient Nile Valley: Marks of ecological change, *Journal of Field Archaeology* 46, 429–447.

PARFITT, A.M.
2002 Misconceptions (2): Turnover is always higher in cancellous than in cortical bone, *Bone* 30 (6), 807–809.

PASSEY, B.H., ROBINSON, T.F., AYLIFFE, L.K., CERLING, T.E., SPONHEIMER, M., DEARING, M.D., ROEDER, B.L. and EHLERINGER, J.R.
2005 Carbon isotope fractionation between diet, breath CO_2, and bioapatite in different mammals, *Journal of Archaeological Science* 32 (10), 1459–1470.

PILLOUD, M.A. and HEIM, K.
2018 Dental development, in: S.L. LÓPEZ VARELA (ed.), *The Encyclopedia of Archaeological Sciences*, Chichester, 1–4.

PLOMP, E., VON HOLSTEIN, I.C.C., KOOTKER, L.M., VERDEGAAL-WARMERDAM, S.J.A., FOROUZANFAR, T. and DAVIES, G.R.
2020 Strontium, oxygen, and carbon isotope variation in modern human dental enamel, *American Journal of Physical Anthropology* 172 (4), 586–604.

PRICE, T.D., BURTON, J.H. and BENTLEY, R.A.
2002 The characterization of biologically available strontium isotope ratios for the study of prehistoric migration, *Archaeometry* 44, 117–135.

R CORE TEAM
2020 *R: A Language and Environment for Statistical Computing*, Vienna.

RETZMANN, A., BUDKA, J., SATTMANN, H., IRRGEHER, J. and PROHASKA, T.
2019 The New Kingdom population on Sai Island: Application of Sr isotopes to investigate cultural entanglement in Ancient Nubia, *Ägypten & Levante* 29, 355–380.

SCHOENINGER, M.J. and DENIRO, M.J.
1984 Nitrogen and carbon isotopic composition of bone collagen from marine and terrestrial animals, *Geochimica et Cosmochimica Acta* 48 (4), 625–639.

SCHWARCZ, H.P. and SCHOENINGER, M.J.
1991 Stable isotope analyses in human nutritional ecology, *American Journal of Physical Anthropology* 34 (S13), 283–321.

SCHRADER, S.
2019 *Activity, Diet and Social Practice: Addressing Everyday Life in Human Skeletal Remains*, Cham.

SCHRADER, S.A., BUZON, M.R., CORCORAN, L. and SIMONETTI, A.
2019 Intraregional $^{87}Sr/^{86}Sr$ variation in Nubia: New insights from the Third Cataract, *Journal of Archaeological Science: Reports* 24, 373–379.

SCHRADER, S. and SMITH, S.T.
2022 *Status and diet in Ancient Nubia: New insights from Abu Fatima*. Presented at the 15th International Conference for Nubian Studies, Warsaw.

SIMONETTI, A., BUZON, M.R., CORCORAN, L., BREIDENSTEIN, A.M. and EMBERLING, G.
2021 Trace element and Pb and Sr isotope investigation of tooth enamel from archaeological remains at El-Kurru, Sudan: Evaluating the role of groundwater-related diagenetic alteration, *Applied Geochemistry* 132, 105068.

SIMONETTI, A., BUZON, M.R., SIMONETTI, S.S., GUILBAULT, K.A., KORDOFANI, M.A. and MILLER, N.F.
2023 Assessing the impact of Holocene climate change on bioavailable Sr within the Nile River Valley: Geochemical and radiogenic isotope perspectives, *Bioarchaeology International* Vol. 7, No. 3, 211–233, https://doi.org/10.5744/bi.2022.0024.

SMITH, B.N. and EPSTEIN, S.
1971 Two categories of $^{13}C/^{12}C$ ratios for higher plants, *Plant Physiology* 47 (3), 380–384.

SMITH, S.T.
1998 Nubia and Egypt: Interaction, acculturation, and secondary state formation from the Third to First Millennium B.C., in: J.G. CUSICK (ed.), *Studies in Culture Contact: Interaction, Culture Change and Archaeology*, Carbondale, 256–287.
2003 *Wretched Kush: Ethnic Identities and Boundaries in Egypt's Nubian Empire*, London.

SMITH, S.T. and BUZON, M.R.
2014 Identity, commemoration, and remembrance in colonial encounters: burials at Tombos during the Egyptian New Kingdom Nubian empire and its aftermath, in: B.W. PORTER and A.T. BOUTIN (eds.), *Remembering the Dead in the Ancient Near East: Recent Contributions from Bioarchaeology and Mortuary Archaeology*, Boulder, 185–216.
2018 The fortified settlement at Tombos and Egyptian colonial strategy in New Kingdom Nubia, in: J. BUDKA and J. AUENMÜLLER (eds.), *From Microcosm to Macrocosm: Individual Households and Cities in Ancient Egypt and Nubia*, Leiden, 205–225.

SPENCER, N., BINDER, M., BUZON, M.R., WOODWARD, J., MACKLIN, M. and SIMONETTI, A.
In rev Maintaining empire: Isotopic evidence for elite mobility in Nubia under pharaonic rule, *Journal of African Archaeology*.

STANTIS, C., NOWELL, G.M., PRELL, S. and SCHUTKOWSKI, H.
2019 Animal proxies to characterize the strontium biosphere in the northeastern Nile Delta, *Bioarchaeology of the Near East* 13, 1–13.

STANTIS, C., KHAROBI, A., MAARANEN, N., NOWELL, G.M., BIETAK, M., PRELL, S. and SCHUTKOWSKI, H.
2020 Who were the Hyksos? Challenging traditional narratives using strontium isotope ($^{87}Sr/^{86}Sr$) analysis of human remains from ancient Egypt, *PLOS ONE* 15 (7), e0235414.

STANTIS, C., KHAROBI, A., MAARANEN, N., MACPHERSON, C., BIETAK, M., PRELL, S. and SCHUTKOWSKI, H.
2021 Multi-isotopic study of diet and mobility in the Northeastern Nile Delta, *Archaeological and Anthropological Sciences* 13 (6), 105.

THOMPSON, A.H., RICHARDS, M.P., SHORTLAND, A. and ZAKRZEWSKI, S.R.
2005 Isotopic palaeodiet studies of ancient Egyptian fauna and humans, *Journal of Archaeological Science* 32 (3), 451–463.

THOMPSON, A.H., CHAIX, L. and RICHARDS, M.P.
2008 Stable isotopes and diet at Ancient Kerma, Upper Nubia (Sudan), *Journal of Archaeological Science* 35 (2), 376–387.

TIESZEN, L.L. and FAGRE, T.
1993 Effect of diet quality and composition on the isotopic composition of respiratory CO_2, bone collagen, bioapatite, and soft tissues, in: J.B. LAMBERT and G. GRUPE (eds.), *Prehistoric Human Bone: Archaeology at the Molecular Level*, Berlin, 121–155.

TOUZEAU, A., AMIOT, R., BLICHERT-TOFT, J., FLANDROIS, J.-P., FOUREL, F., GROSSI, V., MARTINEAU, F., RICHARDIN, P. and LÉCUYER, C.
2014 Diet of ancient Egyptians inferred from stable isotope systematics, *Journal of Archaeological Science* 46, 114–124.

TOUZEAU, A., BLICHERT-TOFT, J., AMIOT, R., FOUREL, F., MARTINEAU, F., COCKITT, J., HALL, K., FLANDROIS, J.-P. and LÉCUYER, C.
2013 Egyptian Mummies Record Increasing Aridity in the Nile Valley from 5500 to 1500yr before Present, *Earth and Planetary Science Letters* 375, 92–100.

TURNER, B.L., KAMENOV, G.D., KINGSTON, J.D. and ARMELAGOS, G.J.
2009 Insights into immigration and social class at Machu Picchu, Peru based on oxygen, strontium, and lead isotopic analysis, *Journal of Archaeological Science* 36 (2), 317–332.

VAIGLOVA, P., LAZAR, N.A., STROUD, E.A., LOFTUS, E. and MAKAREWICZ, C.A.
2023 Best practices for selecting samples, analyzing data, and publishing results in isotope archaeology, *Quaternary International* 650, 86–100.

WHITE, C.D.
1993 Isotopic determination of seasonality in diet and death from Nubian mummy hair, *Journal of Archaeological Science* 20 (6), 657–666.

WHITE, C.D., LONGSTAFFE, F.J. and LAW, K.R.
2004 Exploring the effects of environment, physiology and diet on oxygen isotope ratios in ancient Nubi-

an bones and teeth, *Journal of Archaeological Science* 31 (2), 233–250.

WHITEMAN, A.J.
1971 *The Geology of the Sudan Republic*, Oxford.

WICKHAM, H.
2016 *Ggplot2: Elegant Graphics for Data Analysis*, New York.

WRIGHT, L.E. and SCHWARCZ, H.P.
1998 Stable carbon and oxygen isotopes in human tooth enamel: Identifying breastfeeding and weaning in prehistory, *American Journal of Physical Anthropology* 106 (1), 1–18.

XIA, Y., ZHANG, J., YU, F., ZHANG, H., WANG, T., HU, Y. and FULLER, B.J.
2018 Breastfeeding, weaning, and dietary practices during the western Zhou Dynasty (1122–771 BC) at Boyangcheng, Anhui Province, China, *American Journal of Physical Anthropology* 165 (2), 343–352.

Chapter 9

Foodways and cultural entanglements in New Kingdom Nubia

Stuart Tyson Smith[1]

Abstract

Foodways play an important role in both ancient and modern societies, particularly in the context of imperial expansions like the New Kingdom Egyptian occupation of Nubia after the conquest of Kush. On the one hand, access to certain foods and knowledge of and the means to properly deploy dining etiquette provide ways to emphasise the differential status of members of the colonial regime and its local collaborators. But in both elite and non-elite contexts, foodways also provide insights into the logics of adoption, adaptation, and rejection that characterise Dietler's consumption-based model of cultural entanglement. Entanglement complicates the binary dichotomy of Egyptian dominance and Nubian or Kushite subordination, instead allowing us to document mutual influence by tracing the different cultural threads that entangled to produce a new fabric that was itself dynamic, evolving over time as individual tastes shifted over the course of the colonial encounter. This paper focuses on domestic foodways, while also considering funerary and religious evidence. An ongoing re-analysis of data on intercultural interaction between colonists and local populations from Askut in Lower Nubia and recent excavation at Tombos in Upper Nubia informs a discussion of the intercultural social role and politics of taste within the colony.

Keywords:

Practice theory, colonialism, meals, feasting, taste, Askut, Tombos, Nubia

"Each meal carries something of the meaning of other meals; each meal is a structured social event which structures others in its own image." (Mary Douglas)

Foodways play an important role in both ancient and modern societies. In particular, the commensal character of food and feasting plays an important role in establishing and maintaining social relations, as the quote above illustrates.[2] Cultural entanglements are generally framed in terms of the circulation of objects and practices connected with the elite, in particular imagery, material culture, and practices surrounding funerary traditions.[3] These entanglements had a multi scalar dimension, with adoption and adaptations of burial practices and funerary material culture reflecting the interpenetration of cultural features from simple burials to the elaborate tombs of the colonial elite.[4] This cultural interchange extended into daily life in the form of a variety of cultural practices, including a range of foodways from the elite to common contexts.[5] This paper focuses on domestic foodways in New Kingdom Nubia, while also considering funerary and religious evidence. An ongoing re-analysis of data on intercultural interaction between colonists and local populations from Askut in Lower Nubia and recent excavation at Tombos in Upper Nubia will inform the discussion.

Theory, foodways and entanglement, taste and Bourdieu's distinction

Foodways are central to the process of enculturation and in the context of colonialism play a central role in negotiations of identity and power between and among coloniser and colonised populations. Their communal character constructs and reinforces a shared habitus, or set of cultural predispositions, creating a social context for children to observe adults acting in appropriate roles centered around meals. More generally, shared dining experiences produce and reinforce bonds of friendship and mutual obligation.[6] For example, Bourdieu points out that a "bon vivant in not just someone who enjoys eating and drinking; he is someone capable of entering into the generous and familiar – that is, both simple and free – relationship that is encouraged and symbolised by eating and drinking together, in a conviviality which sweeps away restraints and reticence."[7] Ancient Egyptian "wisdom" literature plays upon this theme. For example, the Instruction of Ptahhotep says: "Sustain your friends with what you have..." and "... friends will say 'Welcome!'"[8] This advice on dining etiquette and other aspects of "proper" social relations remained a part of the cannon in scribal schools for around thousand years after its composition.[9] At the

1 University of California, Santa Barbara; stsmith@anth.ucsb.edu.

2 Douglas 1971, 69; Goody 1982; Goody 1998; Wood 1995.

3 van Pelt 2013; Smith and Buzon 2017; Lemos and Budka 2021.

4 Smith 2015; Grajetzki 2022.

5 Smith 2003a; Spencer 2014.

6 Goody 1982; Wood 1995; Bourdieu 1977.

7 Bourdieu 1984, 179.

8 Lichtheim 1973, 69.

9 Eyre 2013, 57; Lichtheim 1973.

same time, foodways are not static, but dynamic. Meals are structured social events providing continuities that bridge previous and later meals. But they also adapt to the different social contexts in which they occur in dynamic ways through improvisations that allow for both cultural continuity and negotiations that structure relations within a family group and between that group and others. Who eats what, who is invited to join and who is included and who excluded, and how food is consumed in a meal play a fundamental role in constructions and maintenance of identity and community.[10]

In addition to their importance in everyday life, meals play a role in the creation and reinforcement of social status and roles through commensal politics, a dynamic that often takes place in the context of feasting.[11] Host and guest can demonstrate social competence and position to each other and potentially onlookers through the choice of foods. Food represents an embodied material culture through its consumption during dining, transformed by being ingested directly into the body. Food and the material culture and practices surrounding dining become embodied through life experiences within different social contexts, in particular the demonstration of status through access to "exotic" resources, and the creation of etiquettes surrounding dining, and the preparation and serving of different dishes.[12] Hayden and Villeneuve point out that "feasts play important roles in establishing social identities and memories, creating political power and inequalities, gender identities, accomplishing work, and developing prestige technologies..."[13] The distinctive tastes that mark different social classes and factions within them are not static but dynamic, the dominant aesthetic defined and negotiated through a nuanced and flexible intersection of symbolic oppositions, inversions, and imitations. Drawing on Bourdieu, Dietler sees this embodied process as a structured improvisation where cross cultural consumption that deals with alien objects and practices through transformative appropriations, assimilation, or rejection.[14] Texts, artistic representations, and material remains all point towards an elaborate and layered set of practices and etiquette, from reified to mundane, surrounding dining in ancient Egypt. [15] Different types of food could have played a role in social signaling. Used for scribal training from the late Ramesside Period into the Third Intermediate Period, the Onomasticon of Amenemope lists a variety of foodstuffs, including over 40 types of bread and cake, 23 types of beer, and 29 cuts of beef prepared with a variety of spices and pickled or salted.[16] Meat, especially from cattle, was expensive compared to fish, which are often overlooked as a source of animal protein. Similarly, while a basic type of beer was a staple, more elaborate brews also existed, some with a high enough alcoholic content for teachers to criticise student excesses in its consumption. Wine represents another alcoholic beverage that was associated with elite cuisine and royal feasting in Egypt, Nubia, and the Mediterranean world.[17] Labelled pottery provides evidence at Malqata for consumption of a variety of imported prestige foodstuffs, including wine, on a massive scale during the Heb-Sed festival of Amenhotep III.[18]

Foodways play a particularly important role in empires, like the New Kingdom occupation of Nubia under consideration here. On the one hand, access to certain foods and knowledge of and the means to properly deploy dining etiquette provide ways to emphasise the differential status of members of the colonial regime and its local collaborators. But in both elite and non-elite contexts, foodways also provide insights into the logics of adoption, adaptation, and rejection that characterise Dietler's consumption based model of cultural entanglement. Entanglement complicates the binary dichotomy of Egyptian dominance and Nubian or Kushite subordination, instead allowing us to document mutual influence by tracing the different cultural threads that entangled to produce a new fabric that was itself dynamic, evolving over time as individual tastes shifted over the course of the colonial encounter. Stockhammer's top down approach to entanglement emphasises the creation of a generalised hybrid, a strategy applied by van Pelt and emphasised as a way to move forward by Langer and Matić, but hybridity as a generalised concept has come under a sustained critique because of its biological underpinnings and homogenising effect.[19] Dietler takes a bottom up practice approach to entanglement that emphasizes the role that accumulated choices in the consumption of foreign cultural elements played in determining the outcomes of cultural encounters, particularly in a colonial context. Tracking the different threads that are interwoven into new fabrics provides a powerful tool for examining the intersection of the different social and cultural logics of the parties

10 Douglas 1971; Bourdieu 1977; O'Connor 2015.

11 Wiessner and Schiefenhövel 1996; Dietler and Hayden 2001; Bray 2003; Hastorf 2017.

12 Bourdieu 1984, 169–225; Dietler 2006; Dietler 2010a.

13 Hayden and Villeneuve 2011, 433.

14 Dietler 2010a, 217–218; Bourdieu 1984, 169–225.

15 Goody 1982; Ikram 1995; Smith 2003a; e.g., Schiaparelli 1927.

16 Gardiner 1947.

17 McGovern 2003; McGovern 2009.

18 Dietler 1990; Hayes 1951.

19 For a critique of Stockhammer 2012; see Lemos and Budka 2021. And for critiques of the concept of hybridity in archaeology see Dietler 2010b, 50–53; Reger 2014; Silliman 2015; Liebmann 2015. Langer and Matić 2023 in particular seem to be unaware of the literature critiquing hybridity. For a more nuanced approach to entanglement and hybridity applied to Nubia see Smith and Buzon 2017.

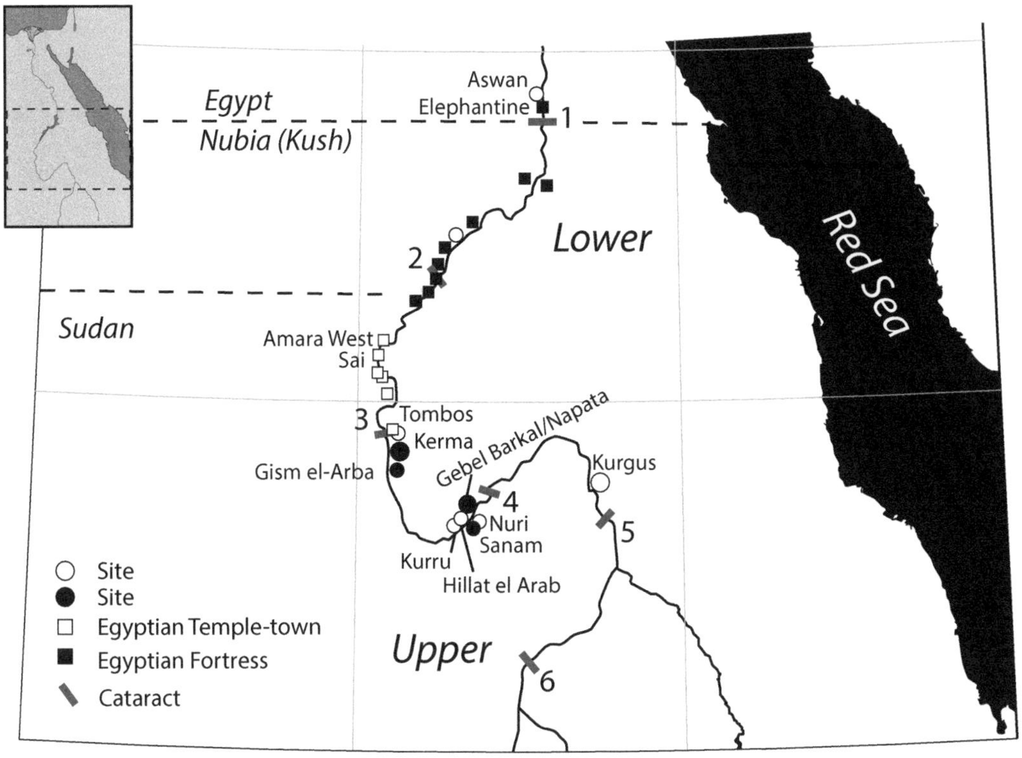

Fig. 1 Map (prepared by author).

involved. In this way, agency is both potentially discernible and historically crucial to understanding larger developments.[20]

Background: New Kingdom Nubia

The New Kingdom Egyptian empire in Nubia lasted half a millennium and included the immigration of Egyptians in a pattern of settler colonialism that unlike modern examples of the phenomenon did not have the goal of displacing local populations. Instead, there is evidence for cultural and biological entanglement in spite of the power differences inherent in imperial domination (Fig. 1).[21] These colonial establishments provided a direct conduit for Egyptian practices, but also allowed countervailent Kushite influences to penetrate and entangle with colonial society. Egyptian material culture and practices also entangled with Kushite in complex patterns resulting in a series of differing cultural configurations reflecting the importance of localised social contexts against a broader pattern of cultural interweavings.[22] As Goody points out, foodways are also embedded in the structures of colonial power and labor exploitation, particularly with the circulation of exotic foodstuffs, preparation, and culinary equipment.[23] Foodways can be reconstructed through multiple lines of evidence, including a direct reconstruction of what people ate through paleoethnobotanical and zooarchaeological studies of food remains, chemical analysis of food residues, and isotopic analysis of human remains. As with Dietler's case study in southern France, there is considerable overlap in the different plants and animals consumed in Egypt and Nubia, so the preferences of taste and the material aspects of cuisine in the form of pottery and other objects associated with food preparation, transport, and consumption play an important role.[24]

This study will draw upon the legacy collection from the late Alexander Badawy's excavation at Askut during the Aswan High Dam Salvage Campaign and recent work at Tombos. Askut was founded in the Middle Kingdom as a part of the second cataract fort system, likely under Senwosret III (c. 1850 BC) and was occupied continuously through at least the Ramesside Period, perhaps extending into the early Napatan/Third Intermediate Period. Tombos was founded just north of Kerma at the headwaters of the third cataract about half a century after the conquest of Kush at the beginning of the New Kingdom, around the reign of Hatshepsut/Thutmose III (c. 1450 BC). A

20 Dietler 2010b, 55–56; applied for later periods in Nubia in Smith 2014a; Buzon, Smith and Simonetti 2016.

21 Buzon, Smith and Simonetti 2016.

22 Smith 2020b; Lemos 2023.

23 Goody 1982; Dietler 2010a.

24 Hastorf 2017; Dietler 2010b; Bourdieu 1984.

massive dry moat fortification enclosing an area of over 6 hectares was established on the Nile riverbank, from which much of the settlement pottery derives. A large cemetery nearby was in use through at least the Napatan Period and contains a mixture of elite and non-elite tombs and burials (c. 650 BC).[25]

Nubian style handmade pottery appears as a part of the ceramic assemblages at New Kingdom colonial sites in Nubia, although Egyptian wares dominate.[26] The same appears to be the case for indigenous sites like Gism el-Arba, an earlier Kushite site where Egyptian pottery dominates but Nubian wares continue after the transition to colonial rule.[27] Nubian style cooking pottery plays an outsized role at these sites, but with varying percentages.[28] The overall proportions of Egyptian vs Nubian style pottery only show a general pattern of entanglement. For example, the earliest contexts at Amara West contained only about 1% in Nubian style, increasing to 10% in the later phases. This pattern may reflect initial settler colonialism at the founding of the site with increasing local entanglements over the site's history. In a similar way, the proportion of Nubian pottery at Askut starts at only around 3% in the Middle Kingdom, rising to 12% in the Second Intermediate Period when the kingdom of Kush controlled the region, declining slightly after the New Kingdom reconquest to 10%, and increasing to 13% in the Ramesside period.

Food preparation

Separating the assemblages into different functional categories offers a more nuanced view of culinary entanglements. The Egyptian and Nubian style cooking pots that appear at Askut and Tombos align in shape and decoration with those from other sites, including Sai, Amara West, and Gism el-Arba (Fig. 2). Nubian mat impressed wares dominate, also appearing in New Kingdom funerary contexts in the Western Cemetery at Kerma,[29] but incised wares are very similar to those found at Sai and in domestic and New Kingdom funerary contexts at Kerma. Patterns of incising with straight lines and hatching below a rim band are also similar at Askut, Tombos, and Sai, and resonate with domestic pottery at Kerma as well as other Nubian groups. The frequency and variety of incised wares are notably higher at Askut than Tombos or Sai, perhaps reflecting a Lower Nubian dynamic. Diachronically, the Askut Middle Kingdom assemblage shows greater affinities to styles from the Kerma Moyen, ceramics with C-Group affinities being very rare, while Second Intermediate Period contexts reflect a mix of Kerma Classique and decorative motifs associated with the so called "Pan Grave". Consistent with the pattern at other New Kingdom sites, Egyptian cooking pots were also used, again with similar shapes and sizes to those found elsewhere, notably similar to the open carinated forms at Sai (Fig. 3D) and somewhat later at Amarna (Fig. 3C).[30]

In contrast to the overall fluctuations in the proportions of Nubian vs Egyptian pottery at Askut, the percentage of Nubian style cooking pots steadily increases over time, apparently not responding to political changes. By the New Kingdom, Nubian style cooking pottery makes up over 80% of the cooking assemblage, pointing towards a deeper entanglement in the preparation of food at the site. The percentages are, however, variable across the site (Fig. 4), reflecting the complex web of choices underlying domestic cultural entanglements during the New Kingdom. Nubian cooking pottery still dominates in Meryka's house, but only at around 70%, rising to 93% in the more modest houses nearby, and in between at 84% in the two large houses or mansions that remained within old fortifications.

In addition to cooking pots, culinary equipment tied to Egyptian ways of preparing food include beer jars, "flowerpots," "fish bowls," firedogs, and bread plates and moulds (Fig. 5).[31] "Fish bowls" with their functional cross hatched design appear at both Askut and Tombos, as well as other sites like Sai. The type already appears in Egyptian colonial establishments in Lower Nubia.[32] Also introduced during the Middle Kingdom, bread trays and bread moulds point towards the introduction of Egyptian style baking. The latter were designed to produce a distinctive conical loaf of bread. They were relatively common during the Middle Kingdom at Askut, distributed throughout domestic contexts at about 5% of the ceramic assemblage. By the New Kingdom they accounted for only around 1% of the assemblage and appear to be associated with religious structures, in particular the mud brick chapel complex built against the old fortifications. At Tombos they also appear in limited contexts, rarely in the cemetery and to the southeast in settlement dumps into the dry moat fortification ditch. Whether or not their distribution correlates with religious contexts or is more generalised must await further excavation.

So called "flowerpots" and beer bottles are also widespread in both funerary and domestic contexts within Egyptian colonies as well as indigenous

25 Badawy 1964; Badawy 1965; Smith 1995; Smith and Buzon 2018.

26 Smith 2003b; Spence et al. 2011; Spencer 2014; Budka 2017; Budka 2020.

27 Miellé 2016.

28 Smith 2003a; Spencer 2014.

29 Bonnet 1990, 234, cat. no. 338.

30 Cf., Lacovara 2003; Budka 2020, 202–204, 221–222, figs. 71, 92, and 93; Privati 1999; Sadr 1987. For Nubian pottery at Askut during the Middle Kingdom, see Smith 2012.

31 Budka 2020, 221–225, figs. 91–95.

32 Smith 2012.

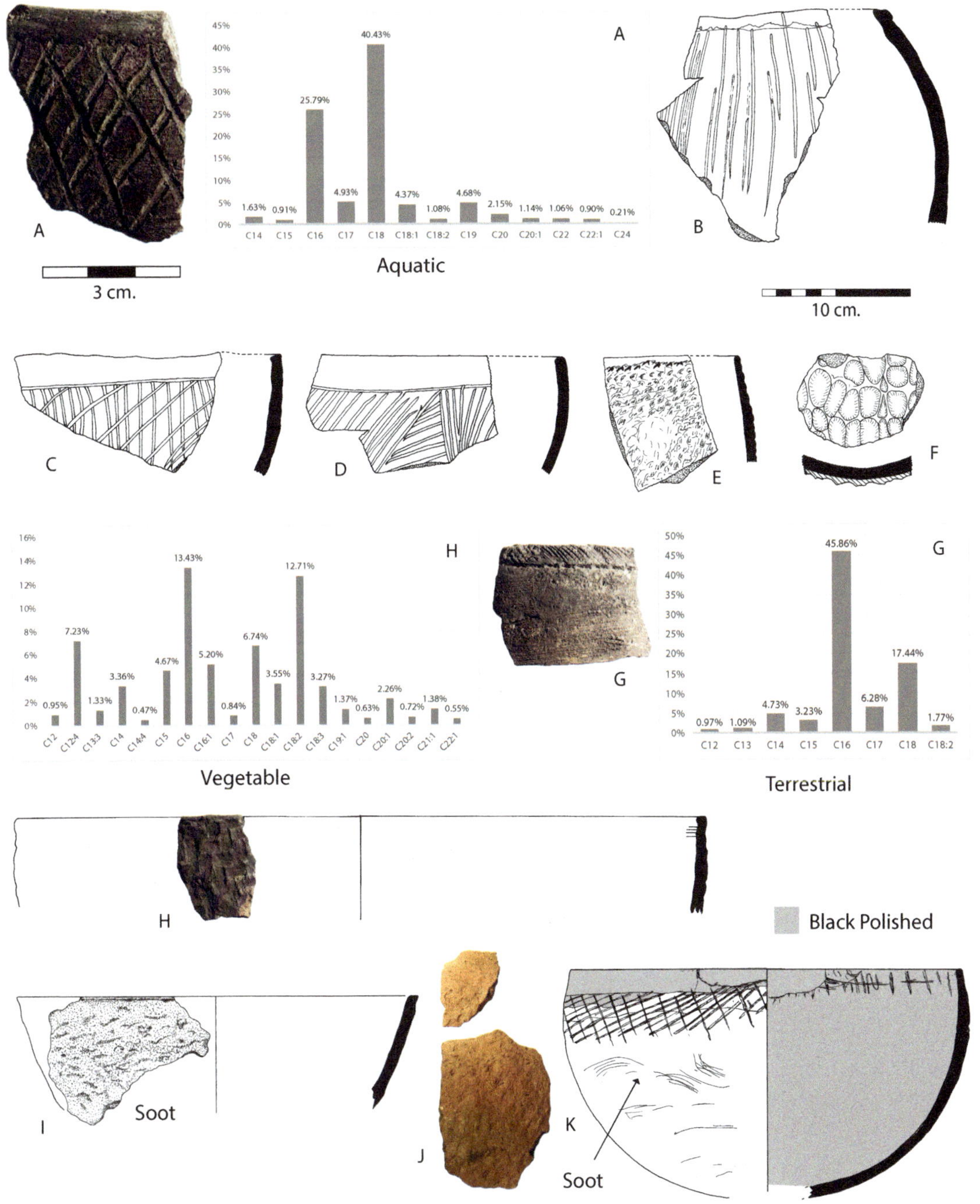

Fig. 2 Nubian cooking pottery from Askut (A–H) and Tombos (I–K) with examples of fatty acid proportions from GC/MS analysis (prepared by author).

sites like Gism el-Arba. Both are highly utilitarian in nature, simply finished with a heavy rilling pattern that must have been deliberate, as well as a distinctively finished base with indentations (Fig. 5). These features would have helped the user to maintain a firm grip on the pots. They are also often associated together, again pointing towards a specialised use.[33] They have generally been seen as symbolic of bread and beer offerings, which makes sense when they appear in a funerary context, but is less satisfactory in a domestic context. The base is often, but not always, pierced, another feature suggestive of a

33 Budka 2020, 211; Miellé 2016.

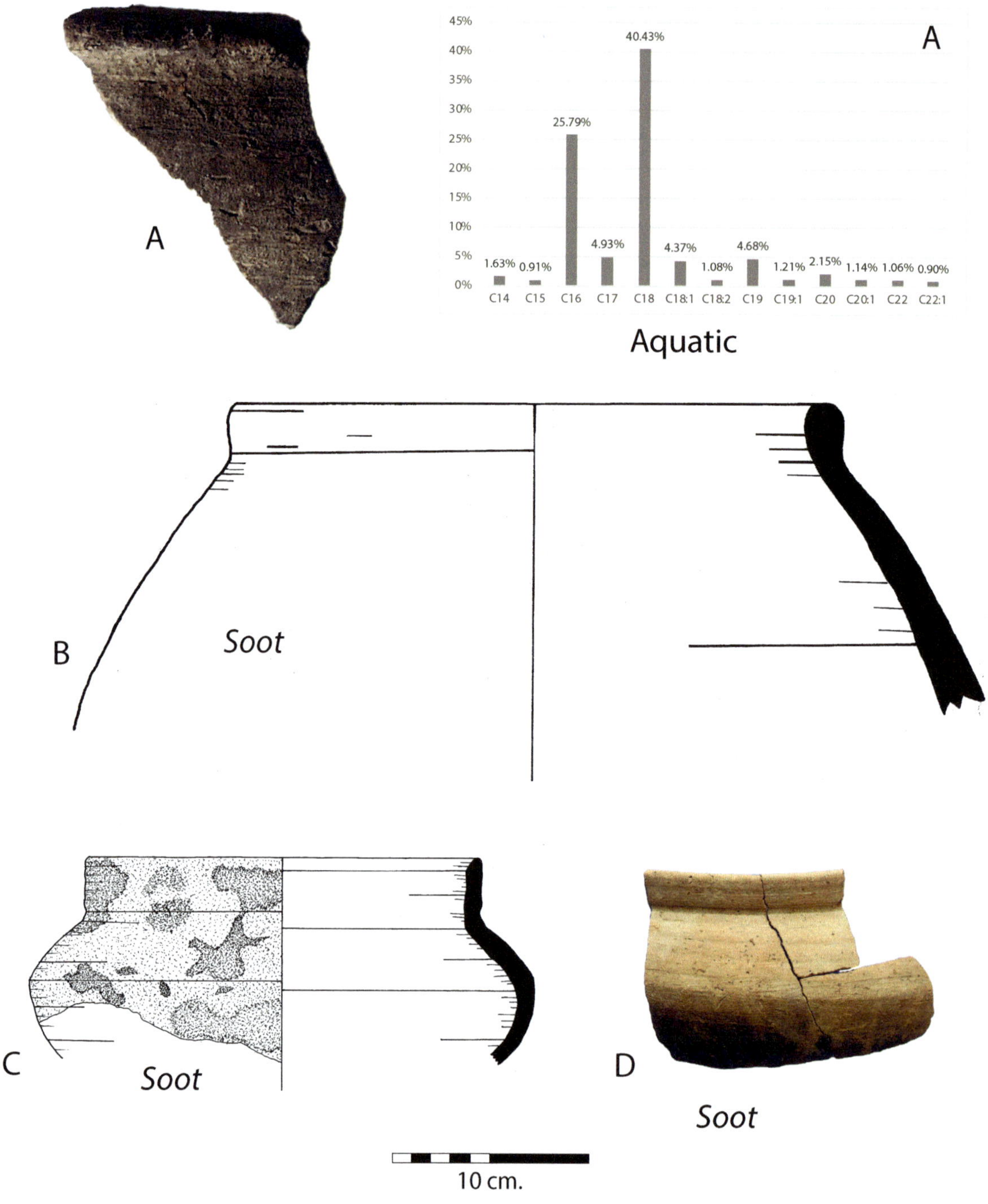

Fig. 3 Egyptian cooking pottery from Askut (A–C) and Tombos (D) with an example of fatty acid proportions from GC/MS analysis (prepared by author).

specialised use. Holthoer likened the "flowerpots" to Old Kingdom two part bread moulds, concluding that the lack of sooting pointed towards a symbolic rather than practical use.[34] Miellé suggests a tendency for "flowerpots" without holes in the base to appear in settlement contexts and those with holes in cemetery contexts,[35] but the pattern at both Askut and Tombos contradicts this idea, since both types appear in both contexts, which is also the case at Sai and Elephantine.[36] "Flowerpots" and beer bottles,

34 Holthoer 1977, 86.

35 Miellé 2016.

36 Budka 2020, 210, fig. 79.

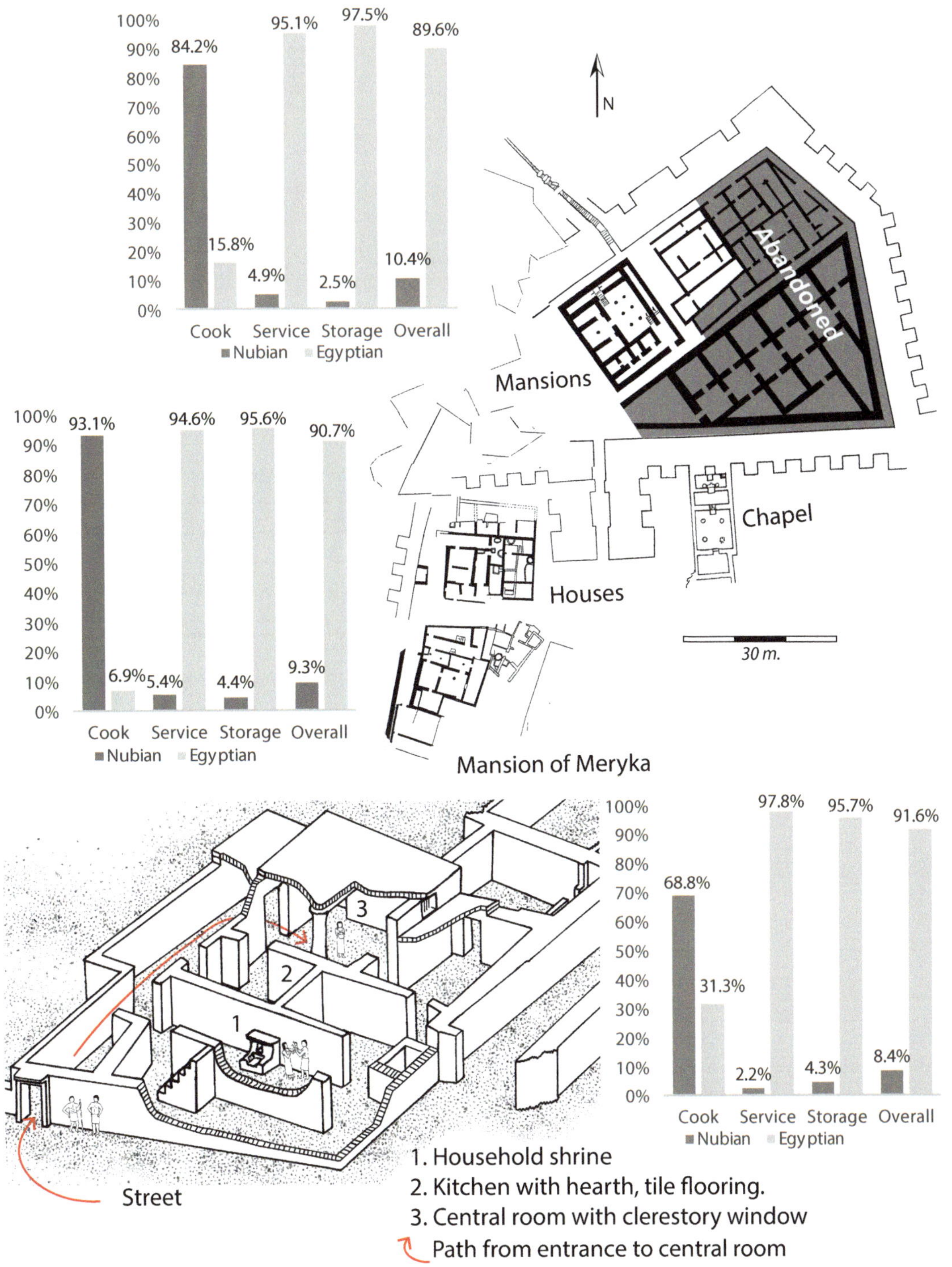

Fig. 4 Proportions of Nubian and Egyptian style pottery at Askut (prepared by author, reconstruction of Meryka's mansion by Dustin Maxam).

typically with pierced bases, also appear in domestic contexts in the Levant at sites with an Egyptian presence or influence. After a careful consideration of the different explanations for their use, Martin makes a plausible argument for adopting Petrie's original suggestion that "flowerpots" were used as a funnel and strainer for pressing barley mash when brewing beer. He suggests a similar function for beer bottles, which replace "flowerpots" after the 18th Dynasty.[37] If this is

37 Martin 2011, 47–49, 51–57. Unfortunately, tests for calcium oxalate, commonly known as beer stone, were unsuccessful. Several likely sherds from Tombos have been set aside for testing in the future.

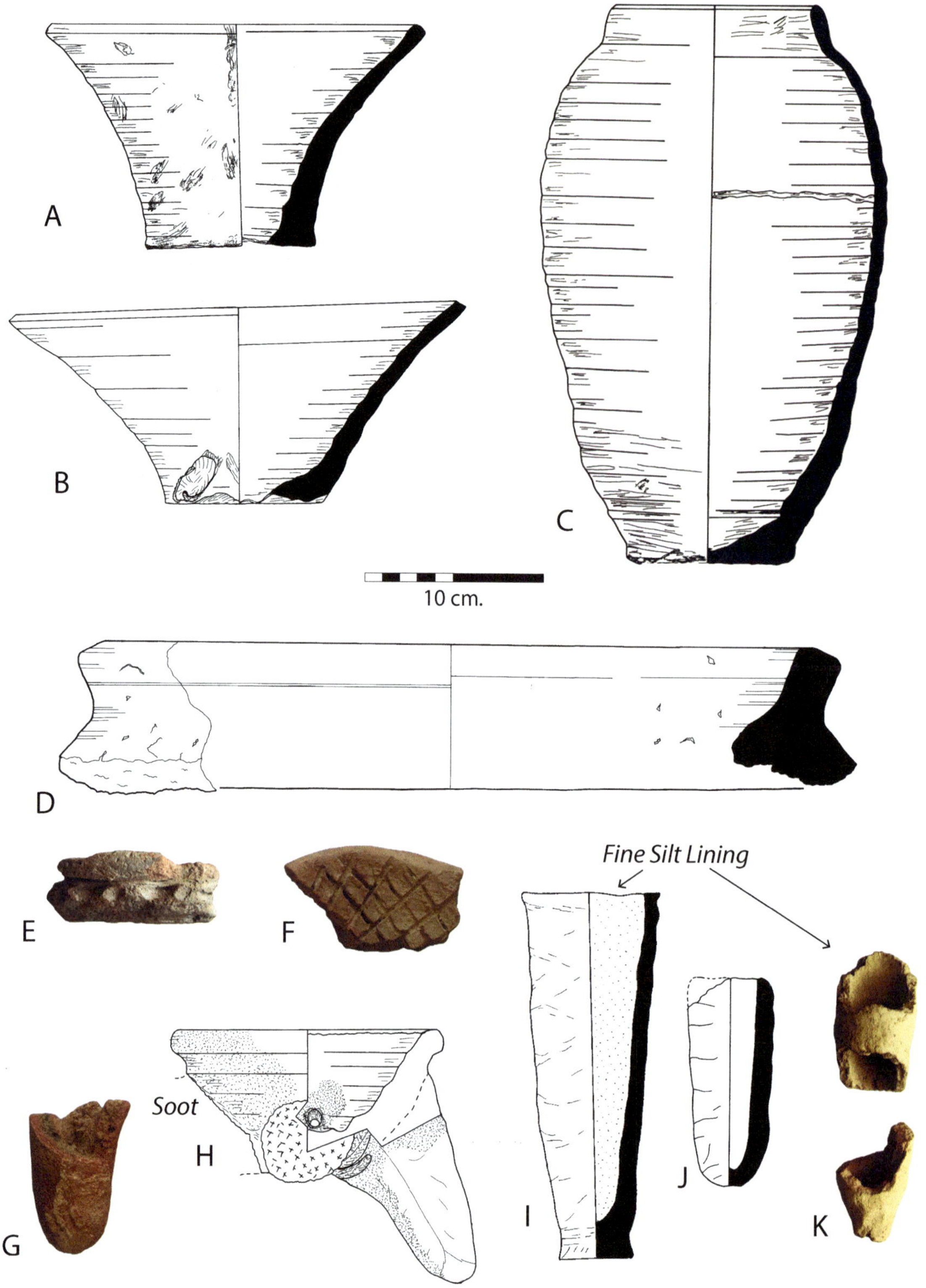

Fig. 5 Egyptian ceramic culinary equipment (prepared by author): "Flowerpots" from Tombos (A) and Askut (B) with pierced bases; (C) beer bottle from Tombos; Middle Kingdom bread tray from Askut (D, similar to New Kingdom examples) and smaller decorated New Kingdom example from Tombos (E); a New Kingdom "fishplate" from Tombos (F); New Kingdom "fire dogs" from Tombos (G) and Askut (H), and Middle Kingdom (I) and New Kingdom (J) bread moulds from Askut and Tombos (K).

the case then the related production of bread and beer in Egyptian controlled Nubia would have followed Egyptian patterns in contrast to the dominance of Nubian cooking pottery.

Food preferences: Chemical analysis, zooarchaeology and paleoethnology

The chemical analysis of organic compounds from archaeological excavations is an endeavour that goes back to the beginnings of modern archaeology in Egypt.[38] Recent efforts began sporadically in the 1960's and 70's, with increasing interest and collaboration between scientists and archaeologists through the present. Archaeologically significant organic compounds have been extracted and analysed from a variety of materials, including ceramics, flaked stone, bone, coprolites, cooking stones, grinding stones, pigments, and wood from shipwrecks, although pottery has provided the focus for the bulk of research.[39] Food residues appear both as visible deposits on pottery (or other artifacts) and are absorbed into the walls of serving, storage, and cooking vessels. The most common methodology employs a combination of Gas Chromatography with Mass Spectrometry (GC/MS) to yield profiles of the different lipids that make up organic residues,[40] with a view toward recognizing both broad associations with different kinds of food, as well as making more specific identifications. In modern samples, ratios of common fatty acids, along with some biomarkers, are linked to specific plants and animals, allowing for both gross determinations (grain/vegetable; plant/animal; terrestrial/aquatic animal) as well as the identification of specific species in food residues.

A pilot study of cooking pottery from Askut tentatively identified fatty acid signatures reflecting different meats, including deer/cattle/mutton (herbivores), and possibly pork and fish, as well as vegetable sources. Ratios of medium chain fats gained a certain acceptance as a biomarker for different food sources. However, the effects of heating and age result in the decomposition of fatty acids through oxidation and hydrolysis, posing difficulties in the chemical characterization of organic residues. Whelton et al.[41] have recently argued that ratios are an unreliable method for specific identifications.[42] They also note an over confidence in the identification of biomarkers that are often not distinctive enough to be tied to specific plants and animals. This is especially problematic when making dramatic claims, like the recent study of embalming materials identifying a southeast Asian ingredient, dammar, based upon a plausible but superficial resemblance in fatty acid profile from a single sample.[43] This problem was highlighted in a multi-lab experimental study, where none of the labs were able to correctly identify the exact source of a modern sample from Egypt containing Camel's milk.[44] As a result, GC/MS analysis has increasingly been combined with Carbon isotopic analysis (since fatty acids consist of chains of Carbon atoms) with successful results in identifying specific food sources.[45]

As a follow up to the earlier pilot study, a larger sample of 60 Nubian style and 38 Egyptian style cooking pots were selected for GC/MS analysis, reflecting their relative proportions within each period, Middle Kingdom, Second Intermediate Period, early New Kingdom, and later New Kingdom (possibly extending into the early Third Intermediate/ Period). Cooking pottery at Askut was identified through a combination of form and sooting patterns (Figs. 2, 3). The number of sherds from the Second Intermediate period was too small to draw any separate conclusions, so they are not considered here. For similar reasons, sherds from 18th Dynasty contexts are combined in the tabulations presented here with those from Ramesside and Late Ramesside contexts—the last potentially extending into the early Napatan/ Third Intermediate Period (Fig. 6). Most had strong fat signatures with remarkably good preservation of both saturated and unsaturated fats in many cases, confirming the patterns identified in the pilot study. As noted in the tables, a small percentage had very low results that might either indicate a food source with a lower fat content, which characterises many vegetable ingredients, or that the pot was not used for cooking in spite of the shape and/or sooting pattern. Given the concerns over specific identifications using GC/MS alone, conclusions regarding specific plants and animals must await isotopic analysis. But identifications can be made with some confidence for the larger categories of terrestrial mammal (including wild animals like gazelle and domesticates like cattle, sheep, and pig), freshwater aquatic (fish and shellfish), and plants and the oils derived from them (for example

38 E.g., Lucas 1911; Lucas 1926.

39 E.g., Condamin et al. 1976; Skibo 1992; Barnard and Eerkens 2007.

40 Fatty acids are characterised by the number of carbon atoms and double bonds between those atoms (e.g., C18:1 = eighteen carbon atoms with a single double bond). Fats without double bonds are saturated and tend to be stable over time. Unsaturated fats have multiple bonds and are less stable. Palmitic Acid (C16:0) and Oleic acid (C18:0) are ubiquitous. The others vary by food source but are overlapping, especially after heating and/or decay.

41 Whelton et al. 2021.

42 Monroe 2021.

43 Rageot et al. 2023.

44 Barnard et al. 2007.

45 E.g., Grillo et al. 2020; Outram et al. 2009, who were able to distinguish between fish, ruminant, equine, and porcine meat and milk fats through the Carbon isotopic ratios of C16:0 and C18:0. Hopefully a future analysis of this kind for Askut can help to clarify and extend earlier findings.

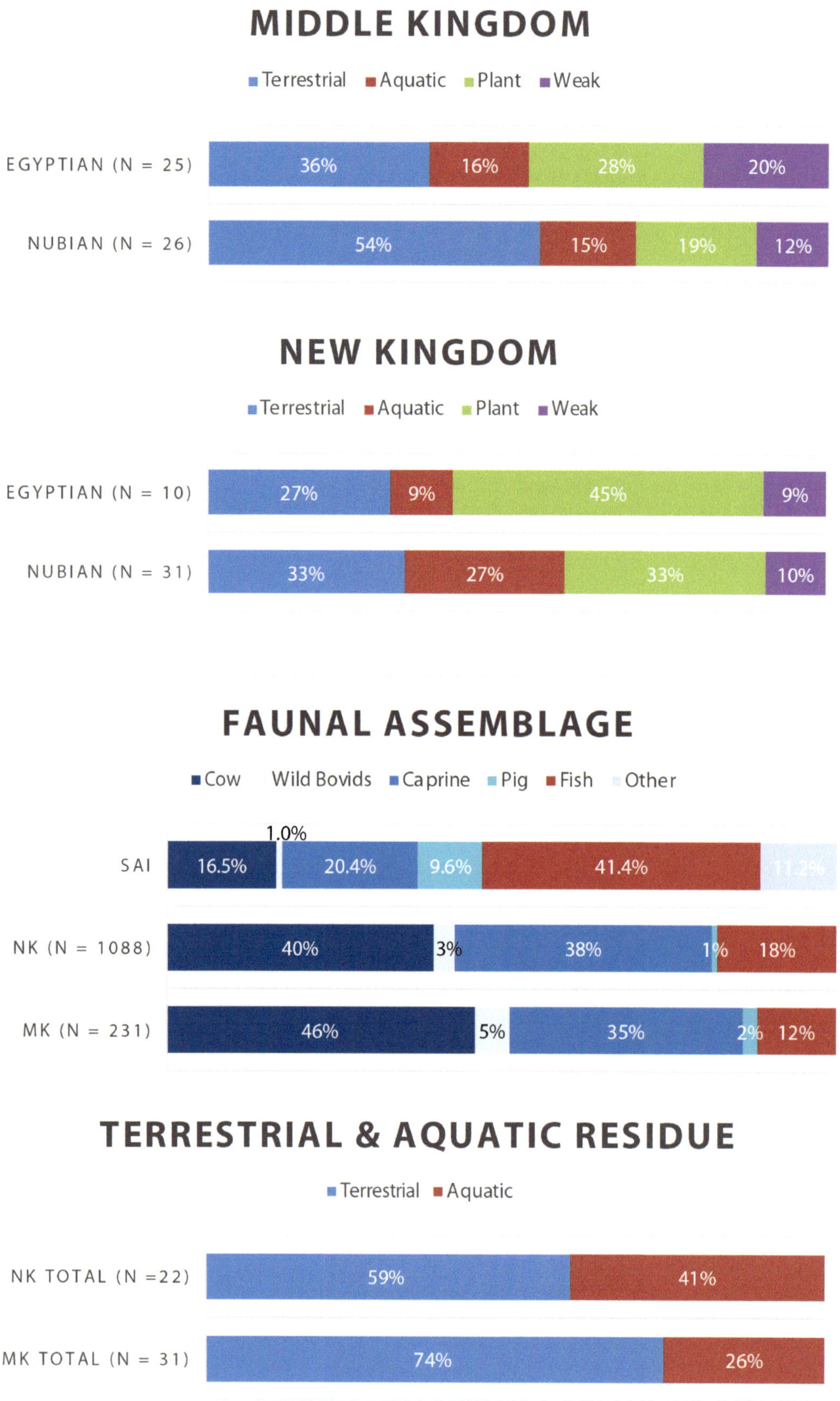

Fig. 6 Results of GC/MS study of Askut cooking pots and comparison of faunal analyses from Askut and Sai (prepared by author).

beans and olive oil). The presence of abundant medium chain fats (C:14 through C:19) and high amounts of C16 and C18 in the absence of long chain fats (higher than C:20) point towards terrestrial animal sources. Freshwater fish can be identified through the presence of the common medium chain fats C16 and 18, with long chain fats C20 and 22 (Figs. 2, 3). A specific set of biomarkers that correspond to aquatic resources also appear sporadically in the samples, including Phytanic Acid (3,7,11,15-tetramethyl-Hexadecenoic acid), 4,8,12-trimethyl-Tridecanoic acid, and 3,7,11,15 tetramethyl-Hexadecenoic acid. The presence of monounsaturated C18:1 (Oleic) in combination with the other fats mentioned above would provide further support of an identification of freshwater aquatic resources, but if polyunsaturated fats C18:2 (Linoleic) and 18:3 (Linolenic) appear in large amounts then vegetable, not aquatic or terrestrial sources would be indicated (Fig. 3).[46]

Cooking pots only represent a part of the diet, dishes like stews, beans, and porridges, but the cultural associations of the pottery allow us to draw conclusions about food preferences that is not possible in faunal and botanical assemblages, particularly in multiethnic/cultural contexts. The fatty acid profiles from Nubian and Egyptian cooking pots are overlapping, but the proportions of food sources reflect preferences as well as chronological trends for the broad categories noted above (Figs. 2, 3, and 6). In both the Middle and New Kingdom, the sherds reflect a general preference for meaty stews that is greater in Nubian style pottery. Fatty acid signatures indicating meat decline slightly between the Middle and New Kingdom for Nubian style sherds (from 69-52%), more dramatically for Egyptian style sherds (from 60% to 36%), which make up an increasingly smaller proportion of the overall cooking assemblage. The proportion of pots in which terrestrial meat was cooked declines from the Middle to New Kingdom (from 44% to 34% overall), with the most dramatic decline in Nubian pottery (from 54 to 33%). At the same time, the proportion of pottery in which fish was cooked increases dramatically in the New Kingdom for Nubian pottery (from 15% to 27%), perhaps indicating a developing taste for fish contrasting with a corresponding decline in Egyptian style pottery (from 16% to 9%). There is an overall jump in vegetable fats, most markedly in Egyptian (from 28% to 45%), which had already had a higher ratio compared to Nubian cooking pottery during the Middle Kingdom (28% vs. 19%). If ceramics with weak fatty acid signatures were indeed used for cooking non-fatty vegetables, then the percentages would be higher for both Nubian and Egyptian cooking pots, but especially the latter. This pattern suggests an increasing specialization in cooking for the decreasing numbers of Egyptian style pots, perhaps amplifying an earlier preference compared to Nubian style cookware.

The pattern for meats is broadly consistent with Monroe's analysis of Askut's faunal assemblage (Fig. 6),[47] where there is also an increase in fish from the Middle to New Kingdom (12% to 18%), although the increase in the proportion of aquatic resources is much higher in the cooking pottery (26% to 41%). This could either reflect the manner of preparation, grilling or roasting vs. stews, or a bias in the survival or collection of fish bone during excavation.[48] Pigs also appear in small numbers, a reflection of Egyptian influence at the site, hinted at in the residues, but one that is hard to confirm without isotopic analysis. The large proportion of aquatic resources aligns with the faunal analysis at Sai at around 41%.[49] In contrast to the inhabitants of Sai's apparent preference for sheep rather than cattle, cattle outnumber sheep at Tombos, although the gap narrows considerably from the Middle to New Kingdom. Hunting was also more common at Tombos than Sai, although only accounting for a very small percentage of the faunal assemblage, at Tombos declining from 5%-3% over time and only making up around 1% of fauna at Sai. This could have been opportunistic but may also reflect a somewhat stronger emphasis at Askut of long tradition in Nubia of hunting small bovids like gazelle.[50]

The emphasis on cooking fish in Nubian pottery can be seen as an example an Egyptian entanglement that was amplified in Nubian cuisine. Budka and Doyen note that inscribed sherds from transport vessels found at Sai and Buhen indicate that they contained preserved fish, presumably an Egyptian delicacy.[51] Cattle and sheep had a strong symbolic prominence in Kushite society, while the importance of fish and fishing is well attested in Egypt, although sheep and cattle were also prominent. Carbon and Nitrogen isotopic analysis of human remains can provide another line of direct evidence for the consumption of certain kinds of food, in particular terrestrial vs. aquatic animals through Nitrogen and for Carbon temperate/wet vs. tropical/dry vegetation (e.g., C_3 plants like wheat vs. C_4 plants like sorghum). Humans consuming a significant proportion of food from freshwater aquatic sources should have $d^{15}N$ values of at least 13‰.[52] The high $d^{15}N$ values at Kerma suggest that fish did make up a component

46 For animal fats see, Grillo et al. 2020; for aquatic resources and plants, Cramp and Evershed 2014; for the aquatic biomarkers, Bondetti et al. 2021; and for vegetable oils, Tanasi et al. 2018.

47 Monroe 2021.

48 Mollusks appear at Askut but were not considered in the faunal analysis. In residues, they would add to the aquatic category, but their contribution would be small, as at Sai (not more than about one percent in the "other" category in the chart, which includes birds, reptiles, and cats—the last were not consumed as food).

49 Budka 2020, 350–357.

50 Monroe 2021.

51 Budka and Doyen 2012/2013.

52 Touzeau et al. 2014.

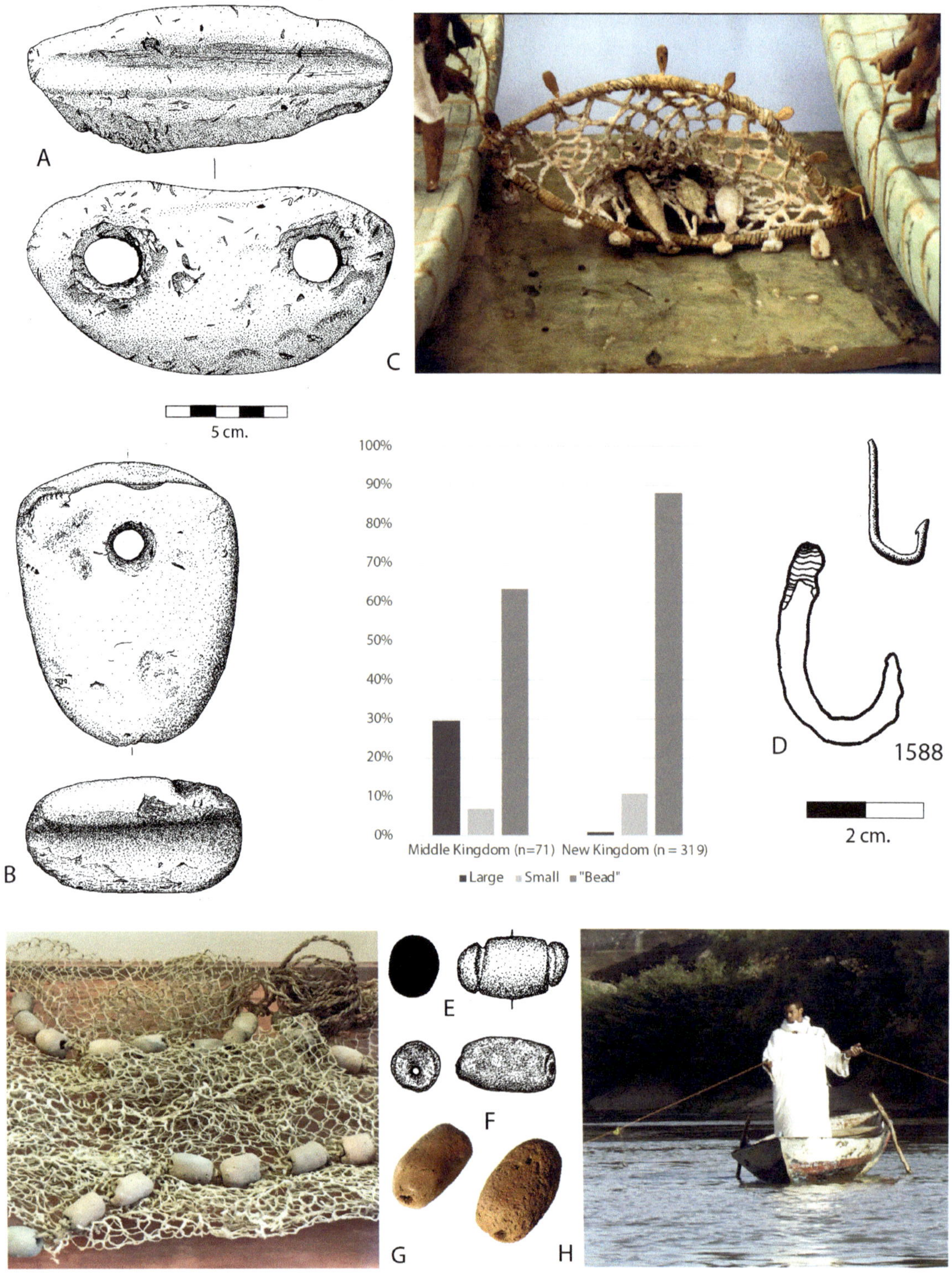

Fig. 7 Fishing equipment from Askut (prepared by author): Large Middle Kingdom net weights from Askut (A, B); (C) model showing arrangement of similar weights from the tomb of Meketre (Cairo JE 46715, photo by author); (D) copper fish hooks from Askut; stone (E) and ceramic "bead" (F) net weights from Askut; (G) "bead" net weights on a net from Deir el Medina (Louvre E 286, photo by author); fisherman at Tombos using a similar kind of cast net (H, photo by author).

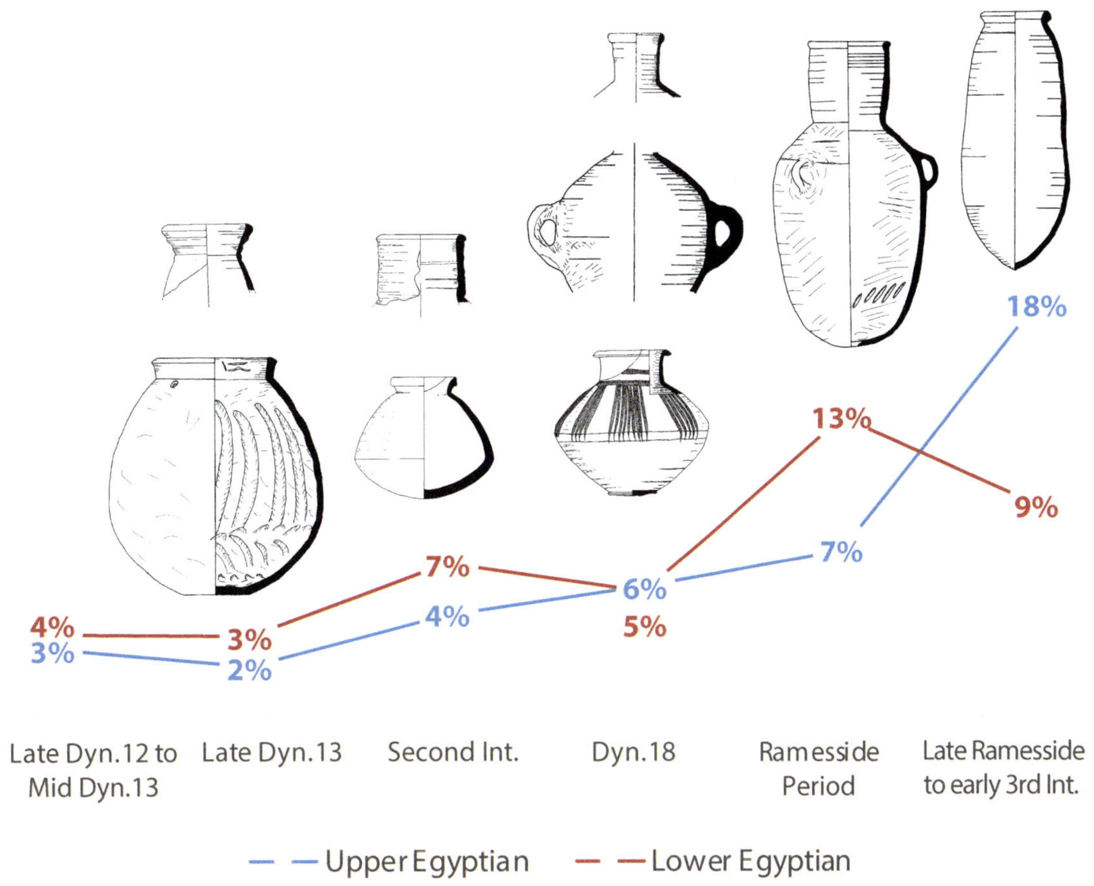

Fig. 8 Proportion of Upper and Lower Egyptian marl jars at Askut from the Middle through New Kingdom with select examples from each period (prepared by author).

in the diet at Kerma.[53] However, citing the paucity of fish in the Kerma faunal assemblages, a more recent study suggested that higher d[15]N values were due to the well-known enrichment effect of a terrestrial diet in arid environments. At the nearby site of Gism el-Arba, which was occupied through the early New Kingdom, fish account for more than 10% of the faunal assemblage, much less than at New Kingdom Sai or as indicated in cooking residues at Askut and to a lesser extent in the faunal assemblage, where fish were more abundant, especially in the New Kingdom.[54] Thus, while the emphasis on fish does not conflict with Kushite practices, the larger proportions at Askut and Sai do stand out in comparison, perhaps pointing towards Egyptian influence. As a caveat, it is not clear whether/what kind of sieving was undertaken at Gism el-Arba, a factor that could explain the lower numbers. The lack of sieving at Askut also means that fish is likely underrepresented in the assemblage, perhaps closer to the percentages indicated in the residues.

There is also ample evidence for fishing at Askut in all periods. Net weights are abundant from the Middle Kingdom through the New Kingdom. They are most commonly made of ceramic material. They include both large weights for nets towed by boats and small weights for cast nets (Figs. 7A, E–H). The former have a groove and holes for lashing to the bottom of a large drag net. As Budka points out, these objects are often misidentified as "axes," but appear clearly in Middle Kingdom models like the pair of boats dragging at net from the tomb of Meketre (JE 46715, Fig. 7C).[55] Small net weights consist primarily of clay "beads," which are often misidentified as pieces of jewellery (Fig. 7F), but their use as net weights is clear from an example, now in the Louvre, found at Deir el-Medina (E 286, Fig. 7G).[56] Unlike Sai, the large "axe" shaped weights appear overwhelmingly in Middle Kingdom contexts

53 Iacumin et al. 1998.

54 Thompson, Chaix and Richards 2008; Chaix 2006.

55 The large weights are also sometimes misinterpreted as loom weights. Very small examples also appear at Sai, Buhen, and Kerma, for examples and discussion see Budka 2020, 192; Winlock 1955; Smith 2003b; Smith 2013; Bonnet 1990, 162, #61.

56 E.g., Giddy 1999, pl. 25; Budka 2020, 186, fig. 55.

at Askut, the three examples from New Kingdom contexts are probably intrusive. In any case, solid weights of stone and ceramic and especially pottery "beads" replace these larger weights. In contrast to Sai, this shift appears to indicate a transition from a more centrally organised drag fishing industry to a small scale household/individual cast net fishing strategy, still practiced today at Tombos (Fig. 7H), that may have accompanied the site's shift from an imperial fortress to simply a small village by the New Kingdom. Their ubiquity aligns with the increasing importance of fish in the New Kingdom diet seen in the residues and faunal assemblage. Two copper fishhooks consistent with Egyptian line fishing round out the assemblage of fishing tackle (Fig. 7D).

Fruit attested at Askut include watermelon, grape, numerous dates, dôm palm nuts, fig, carob, and nabq fruit (jujube) although as at Sai some of the largest deposits are from Christian contexts.[57] All four plants appear in Egypt but have particular symbolic and economic associations with Nubia. The tomb of the Prince of Tehkhet Djehutyhotep depicts the tomb owner supervising the harvest of dates, dôm nuts, and perhaps carob and/or nabq, a contrast with agricultural motifs in Egyptian tomb scenes,[58] pointing towards their symbolic importance in the New Kingdom colony. Similarly, the Viceroy Huy's scene showing the offerings from Wawat and Kush during Presentation of Inu includes an elaborate piece of goldwork depicting idealised Nubians and branching dôm palms.[59] *P3-nbs*, the name of the New Kingdom town at Kerma-Dokki Gel, means "The Jujube Tree," which at least attests to its local symbolic importance.[60] Watermelon and figs also appear at Askut and other New Kingdom sites, but were a part of the diet in both regions, although watermelon likely was domesticated in Sudan and spread north into Egypt at an early date. Part of a grape vine comes from a secure Middle Kingdom context at Askut, providing very early evidence for its introduction from Egypt and local cultivation. Grapes are attested from the Middle Kingdom onwards in Egypt and seeds appear in New Kingdom contexts at Semna West and Sai in Nubia.[61] Transport amphorae are common at New Kingdom sites and at least some probably contained wine. Jars made of Upper and Lower Egyptian marls increase as a percentage of the assemblage over time at Askut, gradually through the 18th Dynasty and dramatically in the Ramesside Period, suggesting an increasing taste for Egyptian delicacies (Fig. 8). An amphora from the tomb of the Lector Priest Hapy at Tombos contained an amphora with the remains of a distinctive conical mud closure associated with tall necked transport vessels. A large seal for stamping these closures was found at Buhen, which might indicate at least some local production of wine and reuse and/or filling of locally made amphorae in Nile silt clays, although locally sealed vessels could have been used for other commodities, including oils and preserved meats, as noted above for fish.[62]

Paleoethnobotanical analysis at Sai and Amara West shows a reliance on varieties of wheat and barley and no evidence for cultivated sorghum.[63] Wheat and barley were introduced into the region from Western Asia, appearing very early in Nubia, for example in storage pits on Sai Island during the Pre-Kerma phase.[64] Sorghum was particularly important symbolically and as a crop by the Meroitic Period but appears only in wild form in the north. The crop was domesticated farther to the south, appearing as early as c. 1500 BC with the Jebel Mokram Group, which was located east of the colony.[65] There are indications of contact with Egypt, so transmission would have theoretically been possible if domesticated sorghum was available, but the crop appears to have only spread into northern Nubia long after the New Kingdom. A comparison of d^{13}C values from selected sites in the Scandinavian Joint Concession points towards a C_3 based plant diet for the "Pharaonic" sites, but a more mixed C_3/C_4 diet for the C-Group sites. An isotope study of Egyptian individuals similarly reflected a preference for C_3 derived foods.[66] Given the lack of evidence for sorghum, the C_4 component of the diet may have arrived through animals foraging on C_4 plants, perhaps indicating a contrast in grazing locations, with a more transhumant pattern with the C-Group affiliated sites transitioning to a more sedentary pattern with colonization.

Material culture and dinning etiquette

While the foods consumed provide insights into cultural entanglements in terms of preparation and preferences, information about dining etiquette can also be recovered from texts, art, and archaeologically in material culture used during meals. Decorated fine wares provide a particular avenue for overt social signaling in the context of dining etiquette (Fig. 9). Unlike the cooking pots from Askut, Egyptian types

57 Like Sai, the Pharaonic fortress at Askut was overlain by a late Christian settlement, see Badawy 1964; Badawy 1965; Budka 2020. A large botanical collection exists for Askut, and analysis is ongoing.

58 Säve-Söderbergh 1960.

59 Davies and Gardiner 1926, pl. XXVI.

60 Säve-Söderbergh and Troy 1991; Valbelle 2003.

61 For a thorough discussion of these crops, see Heinrich and Hansen 2020, 343.

62 Smith 1976; Smith 2018.

63 Heinrich and Hansen 2020, 337–341; Ryan, Cartwright and Spencer 2012.

64 See Garcea this volume.

65 Chaff from a wild variety was identified, likely just a part of the local ecology, see Heinrich and Hansen 2020, 338–339; Geus 2003; Manzo 2012; Manzo 2022.

66 Touzeau et al. 2014.

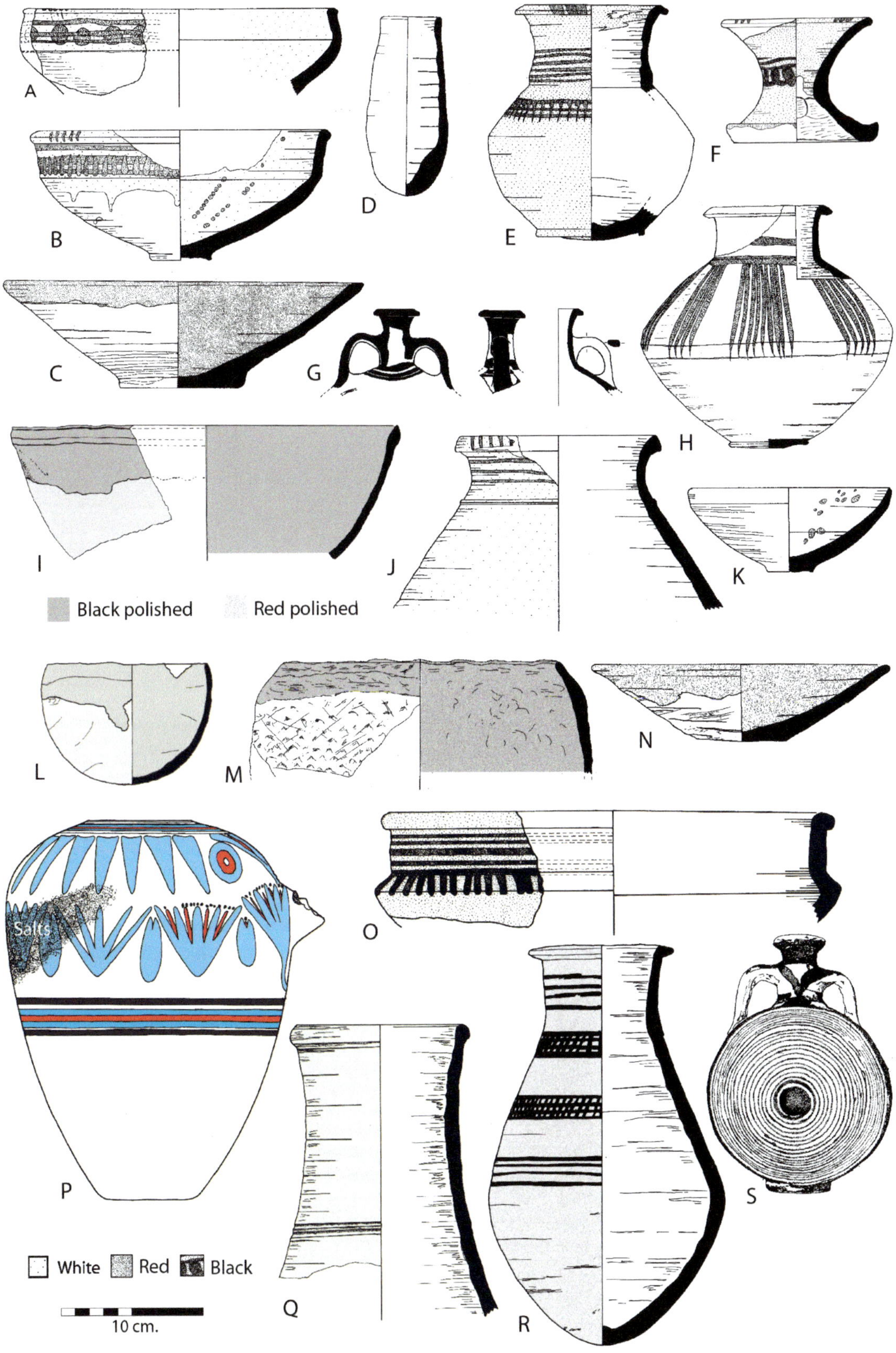

Fig. 9 Examples of New Kingdom decorated pottery from Askut (A–K) and Tombos (L–S) in Egyptian and Nubian Style (I, L, M) and including imported Mycenean flasks (G, S) and blue painted ware (P) (prepared by author).

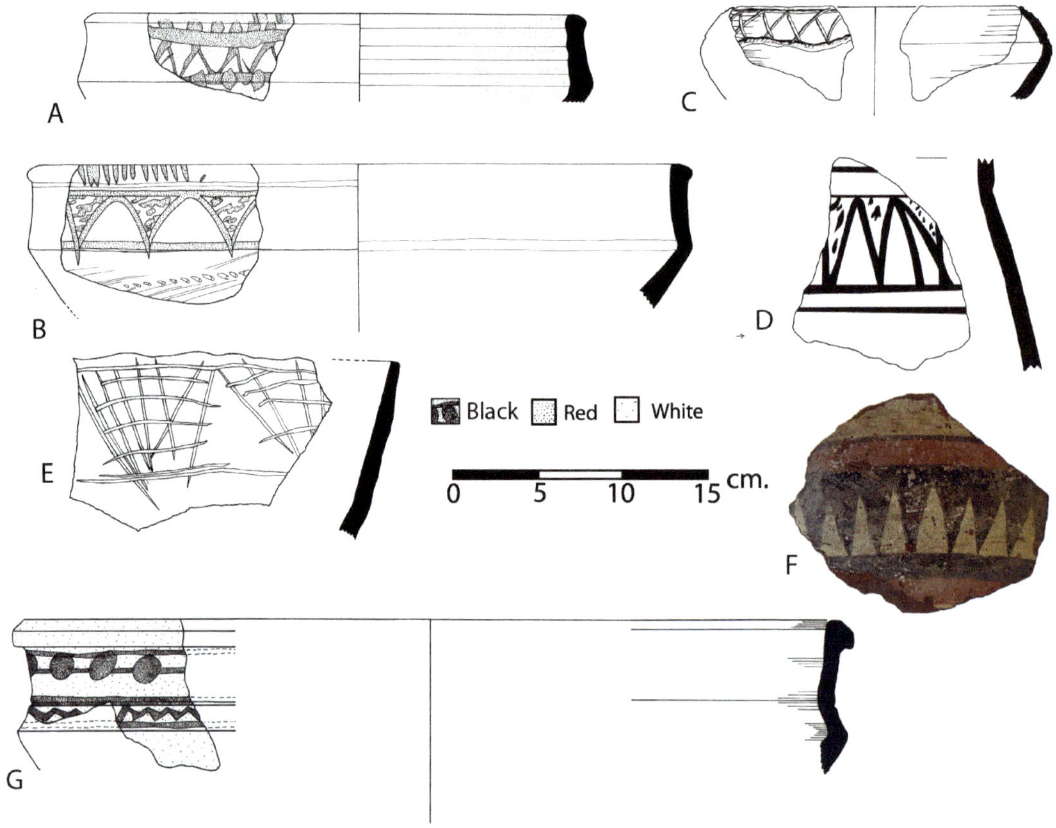

Fig. 10 Bowls with potentially Nubian influenced motifs from Askut: a New Kingdom carinated bowl combining a line and dot and triangular motif (A); a triangular petal motif similar to D; a Middle Kingdom bowl with triangular motif (C); and an incised handmade Nubian style cooking pot with triangular motif (E). Similar pottery from Tombos: the shoulder of a storage jar decorated with a petal motif (D) similar to B; a bichrome painted jar shoulder with a more conventional triangular petal motif (F); and a carinated bowl with line and dot and sharp wavy line (G; prepared by author).

dominate the serving and storage assemblages during the New Kingdom (Fig. 4), but Nubian style serving and storage vessels appear regularly if in small numbers at Askut, Tombos, and Sai.[67] One explanation for the Nubian pottery is simply expedience in the absence of a local Egyptian ceramic industry. However, there is amble evidence of pottery production in connection with Egyptian colonialism in Nubia starting in the Middle Kingdom and continuing into the New Kingdom at Askut and other sites.[68] A Neutron Activation Analysis study of pottery from Askut, Tombos, and other third cataract sites suggests the presence of a standardised workshop industry connected with Egyptian style Nile silt wares and a decentralised, probably household, industry related to Nubian wares.[69] Thus, choices in consumption were not only possible but potentially affected the intercultural social dynamics surrounding dining within the colony.

The shapes and decorative motifs from Askut and Tombos align well with pottery found on both colonial and indigenous sites (Fig. 8).[70] As at other sites, a red or white slip or coating provided a background for red or black lined geometric decorative motifs, with line and dot, hatching, and rim ticks particularly common. The use of pot stands of various sizes, sometimes decorated, also reflect Egyptian practices that would have been visible during meals. As noted above, pottery imported from Egypt and the Mediterranean may have contained exotic foodstuffs and would in any case signal access to distant valuables, enhancing prestige in the context of dining.[71] Although pottery made from Nile silt clays is notoriously hard to source, a variety of vessels in Upper and Lower Egyptian marls appear throughout Nubia during the New Kingdom, some elaborately decorated, including monochrome, bichrome, and more rarely

67 Smith 2003c; Smith and Buzon 2018; Budka 2020.
68 Smith 2014b; Budka 2020.
69 Carrano et al. 2009.
70 Cf., Miellé 2016; Budka 2020.
71 Sensu Helms 1992.

polychrome small to medium sized vessels. As noted above, large often undecorated or white slipped transport vessels, in particular amphorae, would have originally contained products like wine, olive oil, preserved meat, or rendered fats (Figs. 7, 8).[72] Carinated small to medium sized jars in marl clays have been found in tombs containing honeycombs and fruit, although it is not clear whether these smaller vessels were imported for their own sake or with contents (or both).[73] A more distant entanglement is reflected in the presence of Mycenean pottery as far south as Gism el-Arba.[74] Small upright flasks would have held valuable oils, usually thought to be scented perfume,[75] but perhaps also specially flavored for dining. Blue painted ware, found as far south as Tombos, represents a special category of pottery that only rarely appears in Nubia.[76] The spouted jar from Tombos with an elaborate lotus motif showed wear pointing towards domestic use, including a broken spout. This unusual vessel might have signaled the status and political connections of the owner in both small-scale dining and larger scale feasting. Its final deposition in a mortuary context, reused as a container for a burnt offering, would have similarly marked the status of the deceased and their family during the funeral.

The presence of comparatively small amounts of Nubian style handmade pottery in New Kingdom contexts reflects a more explicit cultural entanglement connected with dining. In addition to cooking pots, serving and storage vessels appear regularly in ceramic assemblages in New Kingdom Nubia. This includes initially Kerma Classique style vessels, which are replaced by somewhat cruder vessels in a post-Kerma style with a high polish and blacktopped red ware decoration (Fig. 9).[77] The popularity of carinated bowls in Nile silt clays with a variety of decorative motifs running across the panel below the rim is a distinctive characteristic of the Egyptian ceramic assemblage that likely reflects Nubian influence. Many of these motifs, including line and dot and triangular petal designs, can be found in Egypt on jars, which might be interpreted as just a regional difference when applied to bowls. However, the long tradition of decorated bowls and cooking pottery in Nubia points towards a subtle entanglement with older Kushite decorative traditions (Figs. 9, 10).[78] Triangular, wavy line and dot patterns appear in very similar motifs at Askut and Sai, and with some differences at Tombos likely due to the somewhat later founding of the site and nature of deposition (Fig. 10). An unfired white slipped rim sherd from Askut demonstrates that this type of slipped carinated vessel was locally produced.[79] The triangular motifs resonate with decoration on earlier Kushite pottery, where incised and impressed triangles were very common.[80] At Askut, a small restricted bowl from the Middle Kingdom with a triangular incised motif provides an early example of Kushite influence on local Egyptian potters that is quite similar to a somewhat more elaborate pattern in red paint on a larger New Kingdom carinated bowl (Figs. 10A–B). Similarly, the use of painted triangles with a dashed infill on carinated bowls is reminiscent of some roughly contemporary triangular incised Nubian style cooking pots at Askut (and elsewhere).[81] These unique combinations of motifs on bowls, appearing in ways not present in Egypt, points towards a kind of Nubian sensibility in the creation of an entangled localised ceramic tradition.

Discussion: Entanglements, intersectionality and empire

Foodways in New Kingdom Nubia were deeply entangled through an accumulation of individual decisions about consumption in the context of empire and an embodied set of practices in an interplay with various axes of identity, including ethnicity, class, religion, and gender. As the quote at the beginning illustrates, what dishes were created and how they are consumed within and between households play an important role in enculturation, structuring and structured by the identities and social relationships of the participants. Foodways not only reflect intercultural interaction in a colonial encounter, but tastes and preferences can serve as an agent of change in both the enactment of colonial regimes but also the reaction to them.[82] This dynamic is multi-scalar, beginning with the individual and moving upwards to larger social groupings. Bourdieu is clear that his concept of habitus is not a homogenous structural machine that produces outcomes but is rather a set of social predispositions that individuals draw upon while interacting in different social contexts. While there is a tendency to simply follow these predispositions, each encounter is a kind of improvisation, allowing for both subtle changes at the individual and collective level, but

72 Hayes 1951.
73 Brovarski, Doll and Freed 1982, 80; Schiaparelli 1927.
74 Miellé 2016.
75 Bourriau 1981, 124–126.
76 Hope 1982; Smith and Buzon 2018; Budka 2020.
77 Smith 2003b; Smith and Buzon 2017; Miellé 2014; Budka 2020.
78 Miellé 2014; Smith 2014b.
79 Smith 2014b.
80 Miellé 2014, cf.; Gratien 1986; Lacovara 1987; Lacovara 2003; Privati 1999.
81 Cf. Miellé 2014.
82 Dietler 2010b, 183–256; Stahl 2002; see Jones 1997; and Smith 2003b for ethnicity.

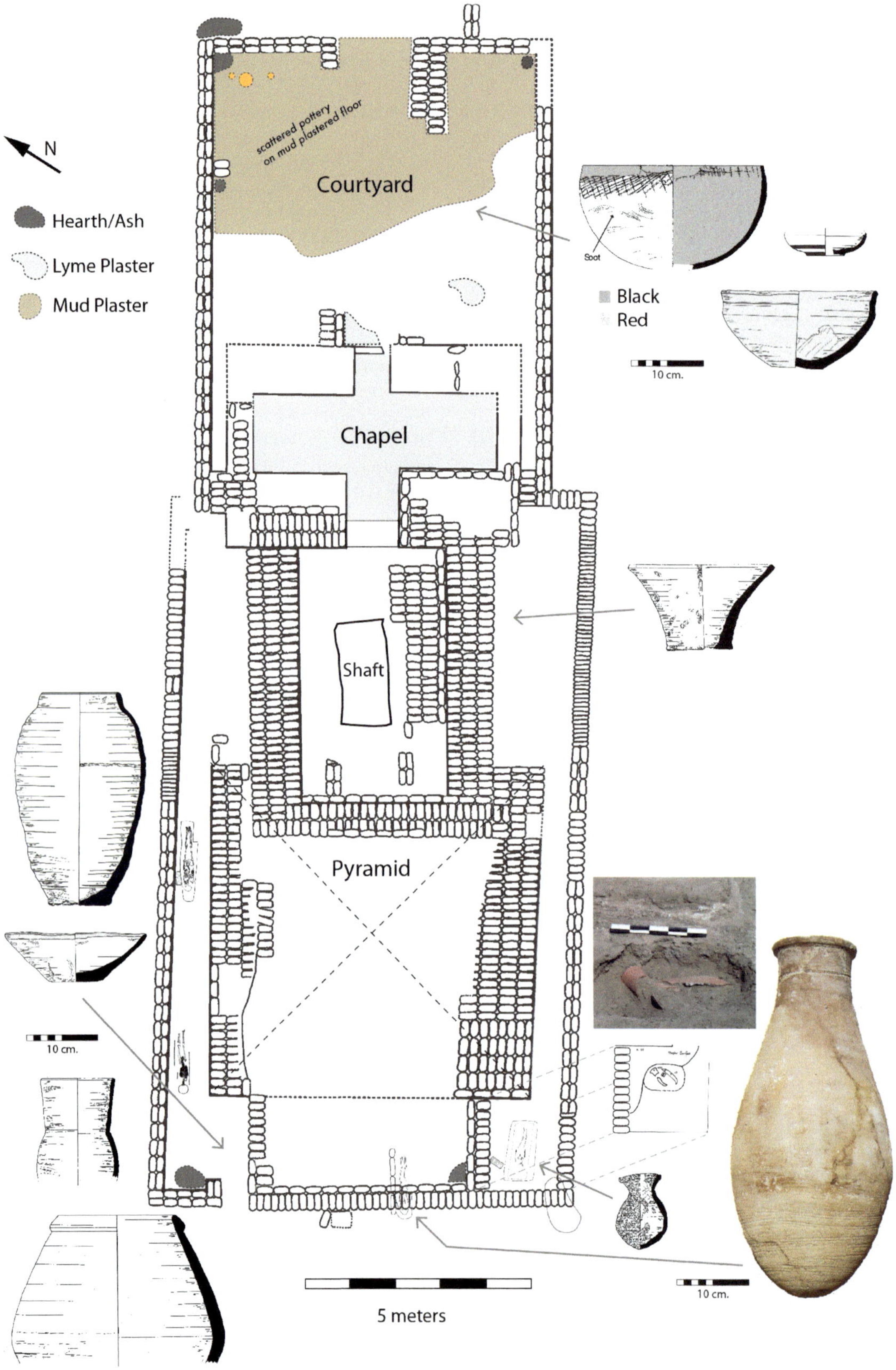

Fig. 11 The pyramid complex of Siamun with associated pottery (prepared by author, plan of the tomb by Ian Lindsay and author).

also innovations that can significantly change an individual and group's habitus. Habitus operates primarily at a subconscious level, but individuals can become conscious of their predispositions in certain social contexts, especially when confronted by or in the creation of difference.[83] Intercultural/ethnic encounters like Egyptian colonialism in Nubia provides a clear example of a social context where habitus surrounding foodways and other cultural practices might rapidly change in response to personal and political encounters in the context of the relations of power between individuals, although ultimately still conditioned by the predispositions of the participants.

Since funerals represent an act of commemoration, foodways expressed in a funerary context through feasts and grave goods provide a social context where overt signaling of identity is more likely given the public nature of the event. At Tombos, the preparation of funeral feasts is attested by the presence of hearths and cooking pottery, particularly in the pyramid complex of Siamun with its large courtyard. In addition to a range of Egyptian vessels, including "flowerpots" and beerbottles symbolic of or perhaps used for beer production (Fig. 11). Nubian pottery also appears, including a very fine quality pot used for cooking and decorated in Nubian style with incising and a highly polished blacktopped red design, a vessel that would have stood out against the monumental Egyptian backdrop of the pyramid tomb and chapel during funeral ceremonies. Similarly, a highly polished cup in a Kerma Recent style was directly associated with the burial of two women in Kushite flexed position and placed upon a bed in an otherwise communal Egyptian style chamber tomb (Figs. 9L, 12). In contrast, the blue painted spouted vessel mentioned above came from the same tomb (Figs. 9P, 12), again complicating identity signaling and reflecting cultural entanglements in the context of a shared burial complex. Imported amphorae were common in the cemetery and Mycenean pottery also appears, both associated with wealthier tombs or contexts. The display of these vessels would have served to demonstrate the cultural affiliations and status of the deceased through cooking, consumption, display, and access to exotic foodstuffs, delicacies to fuel a kind of Egyptian haute cuisine in demonstration of social status within the colony.

Based on the Egyptian emphasis on feminine control over households in texts like Ptahhotep, I have argued that the prevalence of Nubian cooking pottery reflects the influence and preferences of Nubian women who entered into colonial contexts, transforming the way in which foods were cooked.[84] Women are often

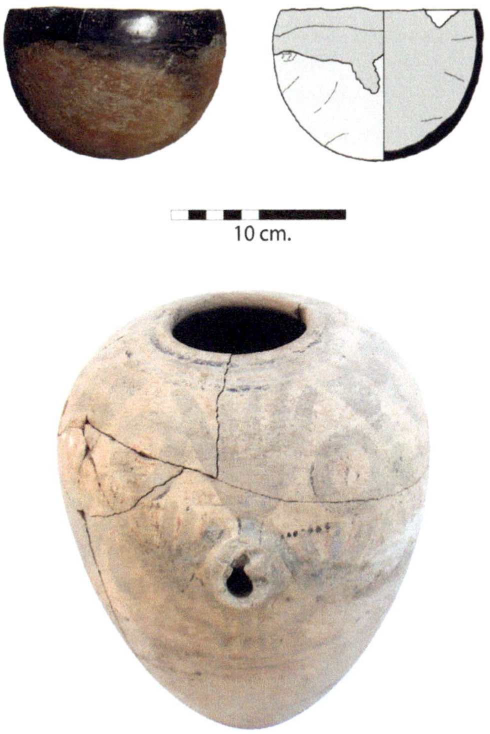

Fig. 12 Kerma Recent cup and blue painted ware spouted jar from the same tomb at Tombos (prepared by author).

neglected in studies of empires, given at best a passive role in intercultural interactions. But they commonly enter into colonial communities, crossing cultural boundaries and creating complicated entanglements.[85] The disproportionate representation of Nubian cooking pottery at Askut and other sites resonates with the gendered patterning in funerary practice at Tombos, where only women were buried in Kushite styles attested previously at nearby Kerma. This pattern highlights the central role that women played in New Kingdom Nubia in negotiating intercultural borrowing in both the funerary and domestic sphere. However, gendered and sexual relationships in colonial contexts are complex and variable. As Barbara Voss points out, a gendered pattern of domestic influence in colonial contexts should not be assumed or universalized.[86] However, the admonition of Ptahhotep, which still had currency in the New Kingdom, combined with the use of the title "Mistress of the House" for elite women

83 Bourdieu 1977; Bourdieu 1984.

84 Lichtheim 1973, 143; Smith 2003b, 183–206.

85 E.g., Lightfoot, Martinez and Schiff 1998; for Nubia see Smith 2020a.

86 Voss 2008. Contrary to Matić 2020, 41–42, I have never "assumed" a gendered pattern, but instead have argued for it based upon multiple lines of evidence, e.g., Smith 2003b, 183–206. He also misinterprets how Bourdieu's conception of *habitus* operates and in particular fails to acknowledge how I have framed it, inspired by the practice approach to ethnicity in Jones 1997.

attested at Tombos and elsewhere in New Kingdom Nubia, explicitly signals this gendered role. These and other points of evidence demonstrate the emphasis that Egyptians placed on the gendered construction of household responsibilities, which would include foodways.[87]

In the context of colonial domination, the use of Nubian style pottery in both a funerary and domestic context of dining and especially public feasting is more likely to reflect an assertion of the owners ethnic Nubian affiliations, whether as a matter of solidarity within colonial communities or as a kind of active resistance to Egyptian cultural hegemony. Kushite polished wares also have an inherent attraction with their colorful appearance and the sensual appeal of their smooth surface when held. This tactile appeal would apply especially to earlier Kushite pottery, especially Kerma Classique beakers, with a developing taste for the pottery helping to explain their appearance in Egypt. Even the simpler Kerma Recent pottery in a similar style might have had a similar appeal that transcended the original cultural affiliations of the owners (Fig. 12). Their use might also reflect the maintenance of social and political relationships with local peoples.[88] Goody notes that conservatism in traditional cuisine can provide a thread of continuity in times of dramatic change like that which characterised New Kingdom Nubia. Familiar Egyptian elements of everyday cuisine like bread and beer would have helped colonists to adjust to the new physical and social environments with the founding of imperial outposts like Tombos and the continuing emigration to them over the course of the empire.[89] In a similar way, elements reflecting Nubian tastes in the preparation of dishes like stews would have provided comfort to the Nubian women and men who entered into New Kingdom colonial communities. Goody also notes that foodways can become entangled with larger sociopolitical systems. These different dynamics are not mutually exclusive but can operate simultaneously, with longstanding food preferences continuing while other aspects of the cuisine changed dramatically. This is especially true in colonial contexts where negotiations of identity and power within and between different communities are heightened.[90]

Internal variability at Askut highlights the role played by individual choices in consumption, as well as intersections of gender and class at the site. The association of sherds from peripheral trash disposal around different domestic complexes suggests that Nubian cuisine was strongest in modest houses outside the old fortifications, somewhat weaker in the large mansions remaining within the original enclosure, and strongest in the mansion closest to the riverbank, where Meryka was venerated in a household shrine (Fig. 4). The variability in proportions of Nubian pottery between households could be the result of the different histories and relationships of their inhabitants but may also correspond to their ties to the larger social and political structure. The greater emphasis on Egyptian ceramics used in the preparation and consumption of food by a prominent family at Askut might correspond to Goody's observation that normally conservative culinary practices can be impacted by larger political contingencies, for example when hosting meals with colonial officials.[91] Given the overwhelming role of men in the Egyptian bureaucracy in both Egypt and Nubia, this pattern could reflect a male strategy towards feasting. In a similar way, the dominance of Nubian cooking pottery and continuing use of vessels for service and storage might represent a strategy of solidarity within and between households, a subtle countervailing signal of local identity in the context of imperial power and cultural hegemony. This may have operated primarily at a very intimate scale, but it is interesting to note that as they made their way from the entrance to the central hall, visitors to Meryka's mansion would have passed by the Egyptian style household shrine, followed by the kitchen, which also had direct access to the hall, complicating identity signaling and perhaps juxtaposing Egyptian and Nubian cultural threads in a similar way to ethnic signaling through the use of Kushite practices during funerals at Tombos.[92]

The proportions of Egyptian transport vessels made from Egyptian marl clays that indicate a taste for "exotic" foodstuffs also vary at Askut by social context, with the mansions in the main fort having the highest proportions, followed by Meryka, with the nearby modest houses having the least. Beer was made locally all across the site but may also have followed Egyptian tastes. As Dietler points out, drinking plays an important role in societies cross culturally, facilitating social ties but also distinctions through inclusion and exclusions in the formation of drinking groups, especially in colonial contexts.[93] At Askut and Tombos, the elite apparently dominated consumption of imported beverages (and other foodstuffs) in a longstanding cultural entanglement that goes back to the early kingdom of Kush with their appearance in increasing numbers at Kerma.[94]

87 Robins 1993; Smith 2003b.
88 Walsh 2018; Smith 2003b.
89 Buzon, Smith and Simonetti 2016.
90 Goody 1982, 152, 183–184.
91 Goody 1982, 151–152.
92 Smith 2003b, 188–206.
93 Dietler 1990; Dietler 2006; O'Connor 2015.
94 Lacovara 1987.

Conclusion

New kinds of foods and the ways in which they are prepared and consumed can be used by leaders to create prestige through feasting, but foodways can conversely play a role in the maintenance and spread of indigenous practices, complicating the binary oppositions that tend to characterise colonial encounters both in antiquity and modern times.[95] Foodways provide a particularly important example of the interpenetration of colonial and indigenous society beyond elite politics, especially in domestic contexts where local women (and men) enter into colonial communities. One way of capturing the complexities of foodways is by tracing the different threads and the ways in which they become entangled to form new cultural fabrics that vary between and within sites like Askut and Tombos rather than producing a generalised hybrid.

Acknowledgements

The late Alexander Badawy directed the UCLA excavations from 1962–64 as a part of the Aswan High Dam Salvage Project and was ably assisted by Ernest Chandonet. Particular thanks to the late May Trad from the Egyptian Museum, Cairo, and Wendy Giddens Teeter from the Fowler Museum of Cultural History at UCLA, where the collection is curated. The joint UCSB-Purdue University project at Tombos is directed by me, bioarchaeologist Michele Buzon (Purdue), and Mohamed Faroug Abdelrahman Ali (International University of Africa). Principle funding has been provided by the National Geographic Society, National Science Foundation (BCS-0917824, 0907815, 0313247, 1916719) and the Brennan and Schiff Giorgini Foundations. We appreciate the support of the Sudan National Corporation for Antiquities and Museums and in particular Dr. El-Hassan Mohamed Ahmed. Personal thanks to Emily Smith on foodways, Drs. Julie Anderson, Bruce Williams, David Edwards, Ali Osman M. Salih and the Faculty of Archaeology at the University of Khartoum, the late George Pagoulatos and his family and staff at the Acropole Hotel in Khartoum, and last but not least the people of Tombos.

95 Bhabha 1994.

Bibliography

Badawy, A.
1964 Preliminary report on the excavations by the University of California at Askut (First Season, October 1962–January 1963), *Kush* 12, 47–53.
1965 Askut: A Middle Kingdom fortress in Nubia, *Archaeology* 18, 124–31.

Barnard, H.and Eerkens, J.W.
2007 *Theory and Practice of Archaeological Residue Analysis*, Oxford.

Barnard, H., Ambroase, S.H., Malainey, M.E., Parr, R.E., Rider, M., Solazzo, C.and Yohe II, R.M.
2007 Mixed results of seven methods for Organic Residue Analysis applied to one vessel with the residue of a known foodstuff, *Journal of Archaeological Science* 34, 28–37.

Bhabha, H.K.
1994 *The Location of Culture*, London.

Bondetti, M., Scott, E., Courel, B., Lucquin, A., Shoda, S., Lundy, J., Labra-Odde, C., Drieu, L. and Craig, O.E.
2021 Investigating the formation and diagnostic value of ω-(o-alkylphenyl)alkanoic acids in ancient pottery, *Archaeometry* 63, 594–608.

Bonnet, C.
1990 *Kerma, Royaume de Nubie*, Geneva.

Bourdieu, P.
1977 *Outline of a Theory of Practice*, Cambridge.
1984 *Distinction: a Social Critique of the Judgement of Taste*, Cambridge, MA.

Bourriau, J.
1981 *Umm el-Ga'ab. Pottery from the Nile Valley before the Arab Conquest*, Cambridge.

Bray, T.L. (ed.)
2003 *The Archaeology and Politics of Food and Feasting in Early States and Empires*, New York.

Brovarski, E., Doll, S.K. and Freed, R.E. (eds.)
1982 *Egypt's Golden Age: the Art of Living in the New Kingdom 1558–1085 B.C*, Boston.

Budka, J.
2017 *AcrossBorders I: The New Kingdom town of Sai Island, Sector SAV1 North*, Contributions to the Archaeology of Egypt, Nubia and the Levant 4, Vienna.
2020 *AcrossBorders 2: Living in New Kingdom Sai*, With contributions by Johannes Auenmüller, Annette M. Hansen, Frits Heinrich, Veronica Hinterhuber, Ptolemaios Paxinos, Nadja Pöllath, Helmut Sattmann, Sara Schnedl and Martina Ullmann, Archaeology of Egypt, Sudan and the Levant 1, Vienna.

Budka, J. and Doyen, F.
2013 Life in New Kingdom towns in Upper Nubia – New evidence from recent excavations on Sai Island, *Ägypten & Levante* 22/23, 167–208.

Buzon, M.R., Smith, S.T. and Simonetti, A.
2016 Entanglement and the formation of the ancient Nubian Napatan State, *American Anthropologist* 118, 284–300.

Carrano, J., Smith, S.T., Girty, G.A., Carrano, C.J. and Fergeson, J.R.
2009 A chemical analysis of ancient Nubian and Egyptian style ceramics: evaluating the substance of style, *Mitteilungen des Deutschen Archäologisches Instituts, Abteilung Kairo* 64, 35–61.

Chaix, L.
2006 New data about rural economy in the Kerma culture: the site of Gism el-Arba (Sudan), in: K. Kroeper, M. Chłodnicki and M. Kobusiewcz (eds.), *Archaeology of Early Northeastern Africa. In Memory of Lech Krzyżaniak*, Studies in African Archaeology 9, Poznań, 25–38.

Condamin, J., Formenti, F., Metais, M.O., Michel, M. and Blond, P.
1976 The application of gas chromatography to the tracing of oil in ancient amphorae, *Archaeometry* 18, 195–201.

Cramp, L. and Evershed, R.P.
2014 14.20 - Reconstructing aquatic resource exploitation in human prehistory using lipid biomarkers and stable isotopes, in: H.D. Holland and K.K. Turekian (eds.), *Treatise on Geochemistry* (Second Edition), Oxford, 319–339.

Davies, N. de Garis and Gardiner, A.H.
1926 *The Tomb of Huy, Viceroy of Nubia in the Reign of Tutankhamun (no. 40)*, London.

Dietler, M.
1990 Driven by drink: the role of drinking in the political economy and the case of early Iron Age France, *Journal of Anthropological Archaeology* 9, 352–406.
2006 Alcohol: anthropological/archaeological perspectives, *Annual Review of Anthropology* 35, 229–249.
2010a Consumption, in: D. Hicks and M.P. Beaudry (eds.), *The Oxford Handbook of Material Culture Studies*, Oxford, 207–226.
2010b *Archaeologies of Colonialism: Consumption, Entanglement, and Violence in Ancient Mediterranean France*, Berkeley.

Dietler, M. and Hayden, B.
2001 *Feasts: Archaeological and Ethnographic Perspectives on Food, Politics, and Power*, Washington, D.C.

Douglas, M.
1971 Deciphering a meal, in: C. Geertz (ed.), *Myth, Symbol and Culture*, New York, 61–68.

Eyre, C.
2013 *The Use of Documents in Pharaonic Egypt*, Oxford.

Gardiner, A.H.
1947 *Ancient Egyptian Onomastica*, London.

Geus, F.
2003 Two seasons in Saï Island (1996–1997), *Kush* 18, 61–79.

GIDDY, L.
1999 *The Survey of Memphis II: Kom Rabi'a: the New Kingdom and Post-New Kingdom Objects*, London.

GOODY, J.
1982 *Cooking, Cuisine, and Class: a Study in Comparative Sociology*, Cambridge; New York.
1998 *Food and Love: a Cultural History of East and West*, London; New York.

GRAJETZKI, W.
2022 *The Archaeology of Egyptian Non-Royal Burial Customs in New Kingdom Egypt and Its Empire*, Cambridge Elements: Ancient Egypt in Context, Cambridge.

GRATIEN, B.
1986 *Saï I: la nécropole Kerma*, Paris.

GRILLO, K.M., DUNNE, J., MARSHALL, F., PRENDERGAST, M.E., CASANOVA, E., GIDNA, A. O., JANZEN, A., KAREGA, M., KEUTE, J., MABULLA, A.Z.P., ROBERTSHAW, P., GILLARD, T., WALTON-DOYLE, C., WHELTON, H.L., RYAN, K. and EVERSHED, R.P.
2020 Molecular and isotopic evidence for milk, meat, and plants in prehistoric eastern African herder food systems, *Proceedings of the National Academy of Sciences* 117, 9793.

HASTORF, C.A.
2017 *The Social Archaeology of Food: Thinking About Eating from Prehistory to the Present*, New York.

HAYDEN, B. and VILLENEUVE, S.
2011 A century of feasting studies, *Annual Review of Anthropology* 40, 433–449.

HAYES, W.C.
1951 Inscriptions from the palace of Amenhotep III, *Journal of Near Eastern Studies* 10, 82–112.

HEINRICH, F.B.J. and HANSEN, A.M.
2020 Mud bricks, cereals and the agricultural economy. Archaeobotanical investigations at the New Kingdom town, in: J. BUDKA, *AcrossBorders 2. Living in New Kingdom Sai,* Archaeology of Egypt, Sudan and the Levant 1, Vienna, 275–349, 480–488 (plates).

HELMS, M.W.
1992 Long distance contacts, elite aspirations, and the age of discovery in cosmological context, in: E.M. SCHORTMAN and P.A. URBAN (eds.), *Resources, Power and Interregional Interaction*, New York, 157–74.

HOLTHOER, R.
1977 *New Kingdom Pharaonic Sites. The Pottery*, Scandinavia Joint Expedition 5:1, Stockholm; Copenhagen.

HOPE, C.A.
1982 Blue-painted pottery, in: E. BROVARSKI, S.K. DOLL and R.E. FREED (eds.), *Egypt's Golden Age. The Art of Living in the New Kingdom 1558–1085 B.C.*, Boston, 88–100.

IACUMIN, P., BOCHERENS, H., CHAIX, L. and MARIOTH, A.
1998 Stable carbon and nitrogen isotopes as dietary indicators of ancient Nubian populations (Northern Sudan), *Journal of Archaeological Science* 25, 293–301.

IKRAM, S.
1995 *Choice Cuts: Meat Production in Ancient Egypt*, Orientalia Lovaniensia Analecta 69, Leuven.

JONES, S.
1997 *The Archaeology of Ethnicity: Constructing Identities in the Past and Present*, London; New York.

LACOVARA, P.
1987 The internal chronology of Kerma, *Beiträge zur Sudanforschung* 2, 51–74.
2003 A deposit of "domestic" pottery at Kerma, in: C. REDMOUNT and C.A. KELLER (eds.), *Egyptian Pottery: Proceedings of the 1990 Pottery Symposium at the University of California, Berkeley*, Berkeley, 80–86.

LANGER, C. and MATIĆ, U.
2023 Postcolonial theory in Egyptology: key concepts and agendas, *Archaeologies: Journal of the World Archaeological Congress*, DOI 10.1007/s11759-023-09470-9.

LEMOS, R.
2023 Can we decolonize the ancient past? Bridging postcolonial and decolonial theory in Sudanese and Nubian Archaeology, *Cambridge Archaeological Journal* 33 (1), 19–37.

LEMOS, R. and BUDKA, J.
2021 Alternatives to colonization and marginal identities in New Kingdom colonial Nubia (1550–1070 BCE), *World Archaeology* 53, 401–418.

LICHTHEIM, M.
1973 *Ancient Egyptian Literature; A Book of Readings, vol. I: The Old and Middle Kingdoms*, Berkeley.

LIEBMANN, M.
2015 The Mickey Mouse kachina and other "Double Objects": Hybridity in the material culture of colonial encounters, *Journal of Social Archaeology* 15, 319–341.

LIGHTFOOT, K.G., MARTINEZ, A. and SCHIFF, A.M.
1998 Daily practice and material culture in pluralistic social settings: an archaeological study of culture change and persistence from Fort Ross, California, *American Antiquity* 63, 199–222.

LUCAS, A.
1911 *Preservative Materials Used by the Ancient Egyptians in Embalming*, Cairo.
1926 *Ancient Egyptian Materials*, New York; London.

MANZO, A.
2012 From the sea to the deserts and back: New research in Eastern Sudan, *British Museum Studies in Ancient Egypt and Sudan* 18, 75–106.
2022 *Ancient Egypt in its African Context: Economic Networks, Social and Cultural Interactions*, Cambridge Elements: Ancient Egypt in Context, Cambridge.

MARTIN, M.A.S.
2011 *Egyptian-type Pottery in the Late Bronze Age Southern Levant*, Contributions to the Chronology of the Eastern Mediterranean 29, Vienna.

MATIĆ, U.
2020 *Ethnic Identities in the Land of the Pharaohs: Past and Present Approaches in Egyptology*, Cambridge Elements: Ancient Egypt in Context, Cambridge.

MCGOVERN, P.E.
2003 *Ancient Wine: the Search for the Origins of Viniculture*, Princeton, N.J.; Oxford.
2009 *Uncorking the Past: the Quest for Wine, Beer, and Other Alcoholic Beverages*, Berkeley.

MIELLÉ, L.
2014 Nubian traditions on the ceramics found in the pharaonic town on Sai Island, in: J.R. ANDERSON and D.A. WELSBY (eds.), *The Fourth Cataract and Beyond. Proceedings of the 12th International Conference for Nubian Studies*, British Museum Publications on Egypt and Sudan 1, Leuven, 387–392.
2016 Eighteenth Dynasty pottery from Gism el-Arba (Sudanese Nubia) in: B. BADER, C. KNOBLAUCH and E.C. KÖHLER (eds.), *Vienna 2 – Ancient Egyptian Ceramics in the 21st Century. Proceedings of the International Conference held at the University of Vienna, 14th-18th of May, 2012*, Orientalia Lovaniensia Analecta 245, Leuven, 423–434.

MONROE, S.L.
2021 *Colonizing Cattle: The Zooarchaeology of a Military Frontier in the Egyptian-Nubian Borderlands*, PhD dissertation, University of California, Santa Barbara.

O'CONNOR, K.
2015 *The Never-Ending Feast: the Anthropology and Archaeology of Feasting*, London; New York.

OUTRAM, A.K., STEAR, N.A., BENDREY, R., OLSEN, S., KASPAROV, A., ZAIBERT, V., THORPE, N. and EVERSHED, R.P.
2009 The earliest horse harnessing and milking, *Science* 323, 1332–1335.

PRIVATI, B.
1999 La céramique de la nécropole orientale de Kerma (Soudan): essai de classification, *Cahiers de Recherches de l'Institut de Papyrologie et d'Égyptologie de Lille* 20, 41–69.

RAGEOT, M., HUSSEIN, R.B., BECK, S., ALTMANN-WENDLING, V., IBRAHIM, M.I.M., BAHGAT, M.M., YOUSEF, A.M., MITTELSTAEDT, K., FILIPPI, J.-J., BUCKLEY, S., SPITERI, C. and STOCKHAMMER, P.W.
2023 Biomolecular analyses enable new insights into ancient Egyptian embalming, *Nature* 614, 287–293.

REGER, G.
2014 Ethnic identities, borderlands, and hybridity, in: J. MCINERNEY (ed.), *A Companion to Ethnicity in the Ancient Mediterranean*, Oxford, 112–126.

ROBINS, G.,
1993 *Women in Ancient Egypt*, Cambridge.

RYAN, P., CARTWRIGHT, C. and SPENCER, N.
2012 Archaeobotanical research in a pharaonic town in ancient Nubia, *British Museum Technical Research Bulletin* 6, 97–107.

SADR, K.
1987 The territorial expanse of the Pan-Grave culture, *Archéologie du Nil Moyen* 2, 265–291.

SÄVE-SÖDERBERGH, T.
1960 The paintings in the tomb of Djehuty-hetep at Debeira, *Kush* 8, 25–43.

SÄVE-SÖDERBERGH, T. and TROY, L.
1991 *New Kingdom Pharaonic Sites: The Finds and the Sites*, Scandinavian Joint Expedition 5:2 and 5:3, Uppsala.

SCHIAPARELLI, E.
1927 *Tomba Intatta dell' Architetto Cha*, Turin.

SILLIMAN, S.W.
2015 A requiem for hybridity? The problem with Frankensteins, purées, and mules, *Journal of Social Archaeology* 15, 277–298.

SKIBO, J.M.
1992 *Pottery Function: A Use-Alteration Perspective*, New York.

SMITH, H.S.
1976 *The Fortress of Buhen: The Inscriptions*, London.

SMITH, S.T.
1995 *Askut in Nubia: The Economics and Ideology of Egyptian Imperialism in the Second Millennium BC*, London.
2003a Pharaohs, feasts, and foreigners: cooking, foodways, and agency on ancient Egypt's southern frontier, in: T.L. BRAY (ed.), *The Archaeology and Politics of Food and Feasting in Early States and Empires*, New York, 39–64.
2003b *Wretched Kush: Ethnic Identities and Boundaries in Egypt's Nubian Empire*, London; New York.
2003c Pots and politics: ceramics from Askut and Egyptian colonialism during the Middle through New Kingdoms, in: C. REDMOUNT and C.A. KELLER (eds.), *Egyptian Pottery: Proceedings of the 1990 Pottery Symposium at the University of California, Berkeley*, Berkeley, 38–79.
2012 Pottery from Askut and the Nubian fortresses, in: R. SCHIESTL and A. SEILER, (eds.), *Handbook of the Pottery of the Middle Kingdom, Volume II: The Regional Volume*, Contributions to the Chronology of the Eastern Mediterranean 28, Vienna, 377–405.
2013 The garrison and inhabitants: a view from Askut, in: F. JESSE and C. VOGEL (eds.), *The Power of Walls – Fortifications in Ancient Northeast Africa. Proceedings of the International Workshop held at the University of Cologne 4th–7th August 2011*, Cologne, 269–291.
2014a Desert and river: consumption and colonial entanglements in Roman and Late Antique Nubia, in: J.H.F. DIJKSTRA and G. FISHER (eds.), *Inside and Out: Interactions Between Rome and the Peoples on the Arabian and Egyptian Frontiers in Late Antiquity*, Leuven, 89–107.

2014b A potter's wheelhead from Askut and the organization of the Egyptian ceramic industry in Nubia, *Journal of the American Research Center in Egypt* 50, 103–121.

2015 Hekanefer and the Lower Nubian princes: entanglement, double identity or topos and mimesis?, in: H. Amstutz, A. Dorn, M. Müller, M. Ronsdorf and S. Uljas (eds.), *Fuzzy Boundaries (Festschrift Loprieno) II*, Hamburg, 767–779.

2018 Middle and New Kingdom sealing practice in Egypt and Nubia: a comparison, in: G. Jamison, M. Ameri, S.J. Scott and S.K. Costello (eds.), *Seals and Sealing in the Ancient World: Case Studies from the Near East, Egypt, the Aegean, and South Asia*, Cambridge, 302–324.

2020a Colonial entanglements: imperial dictate, individual action and intercultural interaction in Nubia, in: A.L. Boozer, B.S. Düriing and B.J. Parker (eds.), *Archaeologies of Empire: Local Participants and Imperial Trajectories*, Santa Fe; Albuquerque, 21–56.

2020b The Nubian experience of Egyptian domination during the New Kingdom, in: G. Emberling and B.B. Williams (eds.), *The Oxford Handbook of Ancient Nubia*, Oxford, 369–394.

Smith, S.T. and Buzon, M.R.

2017 Colonial encounters at New Kingdom Tombos: Cultural entanglements and hybrid identity, in: N. Spencer, A. Stevens and M. Binder (eds.), *Nubia in the New Kingdom: Lived Experience, Pharaonic Control and Indigenous Traditions*, British Museum Publication on Egypt and Sudan 3, Leuven, 613–628.

2018 The fortified settlement at Tombos and Egyptian colonial strategy in New Kingdom Nubia, in: J. Budka and J. Auenmüller (eds.), *From Microcosm to Macrocosm. Individual Households and Cities in Ancient Egypt and Nubia*, Leiden, 205–226.

Spence, K., Rose, P.J., Bradshaw, R., Collet, P., Hassan, A., MacGinnis, J., Masson, A. and van Pelt, P.

2011 Sesebi 2011, *Sudan and Nubia* 15, 34–38.

Spencer, N.

2014 Creating and re-shaping Egypt in Kush: responses at Amara West, *Journal of Ancient Egyptian Interconnections* 6, 42–61.

Stahl, A.B.

2002 Colonial entanglements and the practices of taste: an alternative to logocentric approaches, *American Anthropologist* 104, 827–845.

Stockhammer, P.W.

2012 Conceptualizing cultural hybridization in archaeology, in: P.W. Stockhammer (ed.), *Conceptualizing Cultural Hybridization: A Transdisciplinary Approach*, Heidelberg, 43–58.

Tanasi, D., Greco, E., Noor, R.E., Feola, S., Kumar, V., Crispino, A.and Gelis, I.

2018 1H NMR, 1H–1H 2D TOCSY and GC-MS analyses for the identification of olive oil in Early Bronze Age pottery from Castelluccio (Noto, Italy), *Analytical Methods* 10, 2756–2763.

Thompson, A.H., Chaix, L and Richards, M.P.

2008 Stable isotopes and diet at Ancient Kerma, Upper Nubia (Sudan), *Journal of Archaeological Science* 35, 376–387.

Touzeau, A., Amiot, R., Blichert-Toft, J., Flandrois, J-P., Fourel, F., Grossi, V., Martineau, F., Richardin, P. and Lécuyer, C.

2014 Diet of ancient Egyptians inferred from stable isotope systematics, *Journal of Archaeological Science* 46, 114–124.

Valbelle, D.

2003 L'Amon de Pnoubs, *Revue d'Égyptologie* 54, 191–217, Pls. X–XII.

van Pelt, P.

2013 Revising Egypto-Nubian relations in New Kingdom Lower Nubia: From Egyptianization to cultural entanglement, *Cambridge Archaeological Journal* 23, 523–550.

Voss, B.L.

2008 *The Archaeology of Ethnogenesis: Race and Sexuality in Colonial San Francisco*, Berkeley.

Walsh, C.

2018 Kerma ceramics, commensality practices, and sensory experiences in Egypt during the Late Middle Bronze Age, *Journal of Ancient Egyptian Interconnections* 20, 31–51.

Whelton, H.L., Hammann, S., Cramp, L.J.E., Dunne, J., Roffet-Salque, M. and Evershed, R.P.

2021 A call for caution in the analysis of lipids and other small biomolecules from archaeological contexts, *Journal of Archaeological Science* 132, 105397, https://doi.org/10.1016/j.jas.2021.105397.

Wiessner, P.W. and Schiefenhövel, W.

1996 *Food and the Status Quest: an Interdisciplinary Perspective*, Providence, RI.

Winlock, H.E.

1955 *Models of Daily Life in Ancient Egypt*, Cambridge, MA.

Wood, R.C.

1995 *The Sociology of the Meal*, Edinburgh.

Part IV

Circulating products, society and ritual landscapes

Introduction

Nubian material resources between indigenous diversity and colonial impositions

Rennan Lemos

Nubia in the Bronze Age has been mostly identified as a source of Egypt's wealth, especially in the New Kingdom. At the same time, Kerma's engagement with its natural landscape has been mostly overlooked, despite exquisite material culture from Kerma cemeteries, which work as evidence for Nubian extraction of natural resources and their transformation into fine objects. Looking at resource management and how the objects made out of various materials behaved in the local contexts where they were adopted can reveal hidden aspects of Nubian society in the Bronze Age, especially indigenous utilisations of resources and material culture to shape complex social relations out of the shadow of Egypt.

Materials and production across borders

Gold plays a major role within the generalised Egyptological perception of Nubia as the origin of many of the resources desired by the ancient Egyptians. Gold was at the core of the Egyptian enterprise in Nubia, although a series of other circulating materials also played a major role in Egypto-Nubian interactions in the Bronze Age. Ivory was among a set of crucial materials that played a major role in Bronze Age cross-cultural interactions in Northeast Africa. Ivory was a material traditionally connected with various Nubian forms of expressing identity, which is attested in the material assemblages of various cemeteries belonging to C-Group, Pan-grave and Kerma communities.[1] Ivory bangles and penannular earrings were typical of Nubian cultural and bodily expressions.[2] Other objects made of ivory worked as symbols of power shared across Kerma centres and peripheries that later on were appropriated by the Egyptian state of the 18th Dynasty as symbols of distinction and military bravery (Fig. 1).[3] Despite being a material historically connected to Nubian cultural expressions, ivory was highly valued by the Egyptians, which materialises as representations of Nubians carrying ivory tusks in tribute processions on tomb walls.[4]

Other Nubian materials valued by the Egyptians appear on tomb scenes, for instance, at TT40, where Nubians are depicted bringing, among other materials, carnelian.[5] A main source of carnelian was the Jebel el-Asr area in Nubia.[6] Carnelian mining is usually seen as a typical Egyptian enterprise.[7] However, numerous objects from Kerma sites suggest indigenous engagements with carnelian as an object-manufacturing material, both in the third cataract area and peripheries of the Kerma state.[8]

Egyptocentric perspectives have also impacted the way we see other materials, especially gold and faience. Egyptian-style objects in New Kingdom colonial Nubia have been historically seen as imports from Egypt.[9] Such perspectives mask indigenous inputs to management of resources in colonised Nubia and can be connected to underlying epistemologies that considered Nubia as unable of producing wealth on its own.[10] There is evidence from various parts of New Kingdom Nubia that strongly suggest that small faience objects were produced locally. For example, at Sesebi, several moulds for pendants were found inside 'houses' during the Egypt Exploration Society's excavations at the site. One fragmented faience shabti was also excavated in the urban area at Sesebi, an unusual findspot for funerary objects in New Kingdom colonial Nubia. This, together with the presence of various moulds, allows us to suggest that local production of faience objects took place at the site.[11] More recent evidence from Amarna West also points to the complexity of spaces in the town, with 'houses' both working as domestic spaces and spaces for manufacturing funerary goods.[12]

The local production of faience objects in New Kingdom colonial Nubia stems out of a long history of faience production in the Middle Nile at Kerma.[13] This long history was shaped by indigenous experiences, but also interactions with Egypt.[14] In a colonial situation, locally (re)producing global

1 Welsby 2013; Budka 2023.
2 Lemos 2020a.
3 Manzo 2016; see Binder 2008.
4 Davies 1943; see also Anthony 2017.
5 Davies and Gardiner 1926.
6 Engelbach 1938.
7 Aston, Harrell and Shaw 2000, 26–27; Bloxam 2010; Minor 2012, 150.
8 Markowitz and Doxey 2014, 94, 101; Budka 2023, 48.
9 E.g., Steindorff 1937, 75.
10 See Lemos 2023; Lemos and Tipper 2021; Ambridge 2013; Minor 2018.
11 Lemos 2020b; in press a.
12 Spencer, Dalton and Lehmann 2022.
13 Lacovara 2021; see Markowitz and Doxey 2014.
14 Lacovara this volume.

Fig. 1 *In situ* ivory fly pendants excavated in a Classic Kerma grave at Ginis East (photo by J. Budka, ©DiverseNile Project).

styles originating from the coloniser also offers an opportunity to innovate. This is the case for a number of New Kingdom faience shabtis from Aniba, which seem to bear unique decorative elements.[15] No scientific investigations of New Kingdom faience from colonised Nubia have been systematically carried out yet, but observations of the Aniba material might also point to local technical variability.[16]

Recent work on pottery manufacture has also been unveiling indigenous technical complexity and relationships between techniques and identities.[17] The application of scientific methods to the study of clays and ceramic objects holds an immense potential to shed light onto obscure dynamics of production and consumption of goods in Bronze Age Nubia.[18]

The circulation of materials and finished products to and within Bronze Age Nubia is only now becoming a central part of current discussions. This is especially true as the results of excavations at H25 are progressively coming out.[19] The study of objects such as scarabs and other seals can also reveal further patterns of circulation of both imported and locally produced objects. The occurrence of the same iconographic patterns on scarabs and other types of seals found at different sites might point towards the existence of complex circulation networks, which included object flows from Egypt to Nubia, but also within Nubia and, potentially, networks between Nubia and other parts of the Late Bronze Age globalising world.[20] The combined study of local technology and the internal circulation of artefacts within colonial Nubia, especially in the New Kingdom colonial period, opens space for the investigation of local Nubian inputs to broad networks of exchange, which consists of one of the major research topics in need of further investigation.[21]

15 Lemos 2020b, 259.
16 Lemos 2020b, 262–263.
17 D'Ercole this volume.
18 The study by Dellefant et al. 2023 advances to a great extent our knowledge of the differentiation of Nile clays from Egypt and Sudan, which represents a major step forward. My current British Academy-funded project also explores the local production of clay vessels and figurines from Aniba. See Lemos 2020b.
19 Porter 2019; Kilroe 2019; Kilroe this volume.
20 Lemos 2020b, 112–121.
21 E.g., Fulcher and Budka 2020; Lemos et al. 2023.

Indigenous inputs to resource management and processing in ancient Nubia

Indigenous inputs to resource exploitation and management in Bronze Age Nubia are only now becoming a major focus within the archaeology of the Middle Nile. Understanding the role played by local Nubian communities in the extraction of locally available resources is key to understanding the manufacturing of goods that later circulated throughout northeast Africa.

Cooper recently suggested that desert dwellers were the hidden hands behind the Egyptian gold extraction and processing in the Nubian deserts in the Late Bronze Age.[22] Acknowledging the existence of alternative modes of social organisation with which the Egyptians interacted is key to advancing our knowledge of indigenous inputs to resource management and processing, and consumption patterns of finished goods. Opening space for the hands who perform the work behind the fine objects that circulate and shape social relations is crucial,[23] and excavations at Hosh el-Guruf and H25 present opportunities to diachronically compare the experiences of those who produce social wealth, but nonetheless remain invisible in the archaeological record and/or scholarly narratives emphasising Egyptian social relations as model.[24]

The potential from the peripheries

The current focus on the interactions between model states and peripheries is shedding new light on a diversity of modes of social organisation in Northeast Africa and how those were impacted and shaped by object flows throughout history.[25] The archaeology of the Middle Nile in the Bronze Age has been key to understanding such dynamics. Exploring the role played by circulating objects – imported and locally produced – in the shaping of alternative social relations in New Kingdom colonial Nubia has been opening new research directions on Nubia's internal diversity stemming from how different groups placed in distinctive hierarchical spaces engage with globalising objectscapes.[26]

Object manufacture and circulation within and across borders helped shape diverse interactions and modes of social organisation in the Nile valley.[27] Emberling's pastoral state model for Kerma has been used to understand object circulation from Egypt to Kerma and the cultural practices attached to these objects.[28] The available material, especially from provincial sites, offers opportunities to investigate how different social relations emerge from alternative uses of circulating material culture.[29] Recent excavations at Ginis East also contribute to ongoing discussions on the centrality of Kerma peripheries, where high-status objects and a relative abundance of wealth characterised somewhat collaborative interactions with the centre in the Third Cataract.[30]

22 Cooper 2021, 7; See also Budka this volume (Chapter 4).
23 Lemos in press b.
24 Williams this volume; Kilroe this volume.

25 See González-Ruibal 2021; González-Ruibal et al. 2022; Cooper 2021; Cooper 2022; Manzo 2022.
26 Lemos 2020b; Lemos 2021a; Lemos and Budka 2021.
27 See, for example, Emberling 2014.
28 Walsh 2021.
29 E.g., Walsh 2022.
30 Lemos 2022; Budka 2023.

Bibliography

AMBRIDGE, L.
2013 Imperialism and racial geography in James Henry Breasted's *Ancient Times, a History of the Early World*, in: T. SCHNEIDER and P. RAULWING (eds.), *Egyptology from the First World War to the Third Reich*, Leiden, 12–33.

ANTHONY, F.B.
2017 *Foreigners in Ancient Egypt: Theban Tomb Paintings from the Early Eighteenth Dynasty*, London.

ASTON, B., HARRELL, J. and SHAW, I.
2000 Stone, in: P. NICHOLSON and I. SHAW (eds.), *Ancient Egyptian Materials and Technology*, Cambridge, 5–77.

BINDER, S.
2008 *The Gold of Honour in New Kingdom Egypt*, Oxford.

BLOXAM, E.
2010 Quarrying and mining (stone). *UCLA Encyclopedia of Egyptology*, 1(1). Retrieved from https://escholarship.org/uc/item/9bb918sd.

BUDKA, J.
2023 Investigating Nubian funerary practices of marginal communities: new evidence from a Kerma cemetery at Ginis, *Egitto e Vicino Oriente* 45 (2022), 37–62.

COOPER, J.
2021 Between the Nile and the Red Sea: Medjay desert polities in the third to first millennium BCE, *Old World: Journal of Ancient Africa and Eurasia*, 1–22.
2022 Beyond the Nile: Long term patterns in nomad-state interactions across Northeast Africa, *Mare Nostrum* 13 (1), 37–86, https://doi.org/10.11606/issn.2177-4218.v13i1p37-86.

DAVIES, N. DE GARIS and GARDINER, A.H.
1926 *The Tomb of Huy, Viceroy of Nubia in the Reign of Tutankhamun (no. 40)*, London.

DAVIES, N. DE GARIS
1943 *The Tomb of Rekh-mi-Rēʿ at Thebes*, New York.

DELLEFANT, F., D'ERCOLE, G., KALIWODA, M. and BUDKA, J.
2023 Differentiation of Late Bronze Age Nubian- and Egyptian-style ceramics from northern Sudan by manufacturing firing temperatures using Raman spectroscopy, *Journal of Archaeological Science: Reports* 52, 104233, https://doi.org/10.1016/j.jasrep.2023.104233.

EMBERLING, G.
2014 Pastoral states: Toward a comparative archaeology of Early Kush, *Origini* 36, 125–156.

ENGELBACH, R.
1938 The quarries of the Western Nubian desert and the ancient road to Tushka, *Annales du Service des Antiquités de l'Égypte* 38, 369–390.

FULCHER, K. and BUDKA, J.
2020 Pigments, incense, and bitumen from the New Kingdom town and cemetery on Sai Island in Nubia, *Journal of Archaeological Science: Reports* 33, https://doi.org/10.1016/j.jasrep.2020.102550.

GONZÁLEZ-RUIBAL, A.
2021 Subaltern assemblages. The archaeology of marginal places and identities, *World Archaeology* 53 (3), 369–383, https://doi.org/10.1080/00438243.2021.2040127.

GONZÁLEZ-RUIBAL, A., DE TORRES, J., BARRIO, C.M., FERNÁNDEZ, M.A.F., FERNÁNDEZ, A.F., DE LEÓN JUBERÍAS, P.G., SAINZ DE LOS TERREROS, J.Y., GAUDIELLO, M. and DUALEH, A.J.
2022 Nomads trading with empires: Intercultural trade in ancient Somaliland in the first to seventh centuries CE, *American Journal of Archaeology* 126 (1), 103–138, https://doi.org/10.1086/718184.

KILROE, L.
2019 H25: the ceramics, *Sudan & Nubia* 22, 81–84.

LACOVARA, P.
2021 The faience industry at Kerma, *Journal of Ancient Egyptian Interconnections* 29, 32–38.

LEMOS, R.
2020a Material culture and colonization in ancient Nubia: Evidence from the New Kingdom cemeteries, in: C. SMITH (ed.), *Encyclopedia of Global Archaeology*, Cham, https://doi.org/10.1007/978-3-319-51726-1_3307-1.
2020b *Foreign Objects in Local Contexts: Mortuary Objectscapes in Late Colonial Nubia (16th–11th centuries BCE)*, PhD thesis, University of Cambridge, https://doi.org/10.17863/CAM.71911.
2022 *Mortuary archaeology in the cracks of empires: Bronze Age evidence from the region between Attab and Ferka*. Presented at the 15th International Conference for Nubian Studies, Warsaw.
2023 Can we decolonize the ancient past? Bridging postcolonial and decolonial theory in Sudanese and Nubian archaeology, *Cambridge Archaeological Journal* 33 (1), 19–37, https://doi.org/10.1017/S0959774322000178.
in press a Connections to the south: Religious connectivity and fragmentation in the Middle Nile valley during the Late Bronze Age (c. 1550–1070 BCE), in: C.E. BARRETT (ed.), *The Routledge Handbook of Ancient Mediterranean Religions*, London.
in press b Beyond cultural entanglements: Experiencing the New Kingdom colonization of Nubia 'from below', in: S. ASHBY and A. BRODY (eds.), *New Perspectives on Ancient Nubia*, Piscataway, NJ, 53–94.

LEMOS, R. and BUDKA, J.
2021 Alternatives to colonization and marginal identities in New Kingdom colonial Nubia (1550–1070 BCE), *World Archaeology* 53, 401–418, https://doi.org/10.1080/00438243.2021.1999853.

LEMOS, R. and TIPPER, S.
2021 Sudanese and Nubian archaeology: Scholarship past and present, in: R. LEMOS and S. TIPPER (eds.), *Current Perspectives in Sudanese and Nubian*

Archaeology: A Collection of Papers Presented at the 2018 Sudan Studies Research Conference, Cambridge, Oxford, 1–12.

Lemos, R., Fulcher, K., Abdllatief, I., Werskтröm, L. and Hocker, E.
2023 Reshaping Egyptian funerary ritual in colonized Nubia? Organic characterization of unguents from mortuary contexts of the New Kingdom (c. 1550–1070 BCE), *Archaeological and Anthropological Sciences* 15, 73, https://doi.org/10.1007/s12520-023-01769-6.

Manzo, A.
2016 Weapons, ideology and identity at Kerma (Upper Nubia, 2500–1500 BC), *Annali Sezione Orientale* 76, 3–29.
2022 *Ancient Egypt in its African Context: Economic Networks, Social and Cultural Interactions*, Cambridge Elements: Ancient Egypt in Context, Cambridge.

Markowitz, Y. and Doxey, D.
2014 *Jewels of Ancient Nubia*, Boston.

Minor, E.
2012 *The Use of Egyptian and Egyptianizing Material Culture in Nubian Burials of the Classic Kerma Period*, PhD Thesis, University of California, Berkeley.
2018 Decolonizing Reisner: a case study of a Classic Kerma female burial for reinterpreting early Nubian archaeological collections through digital archival resources, in: M. Honegger (ed.), *Nubian Archaeology in the XXIst Century: Proceedings of the Thirteenth International Conference for Nubian Studies*, Leuven, 251–262.

Porter, S.
2019 Excavations at H25 in the Northern Dongola Reach, *Sudan & Nubia* 23, 77– 80.

Spencer, N., Dalton, M. and Lehmann, M.
2022 *Beyond the "temple-town": changing lifeways and production at Amara West (1300–1000 BC)*. Presented at the 15th International Conference for Nubian Studies, Warsaw.

Steindorff, G.
1937 *Aniba.* Zweiter Band, Service des Antiquités de l'Egypte. Mission archéologique de Nubie 1929–1934, Glückstadt.

Walsh, C.
2021 Techniques for Egyptian eyes: Diplomacy and the transmission of cosmetic practices between Egypt and Kerma, *Journal of Egyptian History* 13, 295–332, https://doi.org/10.1163/18741665-12340064.
2022 Marginal communities and cooperative strategies in the Kerma pastoral state, *Journal of Ancient Near Eastern History* 9 (2), 195–220, https://doi.org/10.1515/janeh-2021-0014.

Welsby, D.
2013 Kerma and Kush and their neighbours, in: P. Mitchell and P. Lane (eds.), *The Oxford Handbook of African Archaeology*, Oxford, 751–764.

Chapter 10

Material meanings, technology and cultural choices: Pottery production in Late Bronze Age Nubia

Giulia D'Ercole[1]

Abstract

This chapter tackles the concepts of materiality and style in relation to the manufacturing sequence of the production of Egyptian-style and Nubian-style vessels in Nile clay, presenting case studies from the two colonial sites of Sai Island and Dukki Gel (Kerma) in Late Bronze Age Nubia. Through a combined macroscopic and microscopic analysis of the ceramic assemblages, it was possible to determine in which stages of the *chaîne opératoire* the influence of the Egyptian and Nubian cultures, and associated pottery traditions, were the most emphasised. This demonstrates the potential of integrating a multi-analytical approach to the study of material evidence with the aim of expanding our knowledge of the interplay between the system of production and use of vessels, as well as the surrounding cultural and environmental landscape.

Keywords:

Materiality, *chaîne opératoire*, Late Bronze Age, Sudan, Nubian-style pottery, Egyptian-style pottery

Introduction

Humans have an intrinsic relationship with objects, we witness their entry and exit from our lives sometimes regardless of our will. Through objects we build relationships with ourselves, with other humans, with animals, the landscape, and eventually with time. We live surrounded by objects. Every day we create, use, and destroy objects. Humans do not only produce tools, but also objects which are purely aesthetic or symbolic, such as luxury goods or amulets, through which we constitute a social status of belonging. Objects encounter our body in life, and after death, and they paradoxically survive us. This is especially the case for objects we use every day, such as tools or tableware, which become part of our daily routines, culinary practices, activities, and verbal expressions. These objects become so ingrained in our daily lives and we talk about them so much that every family, as well as culture group more broadly, develops its own "family lexicon" to refer to them.[2]

The material culture of the region of ancient Nubia during the New Kingdom colonial Period (1550–1070 BC), appears as an intertwined composite assortment of objects, among which ceramics, which relate in different ways to both the foreign Egyptian culture and to the Nubian and Sudanese tradition. Notably, the various temple towns, cemeteries and settlements built by the Egyptians in colonial Nubia during the New Kingdom provide archaeological evidence for the interesting coexistence of Egyptian-style ceramic objects – produced locally in Nubia, possibly by local Nubian artisans and with local Nubian raw materials but according to the Egyptian fashion and style – with objects produced entirely according to the Nubian style in Nubian raw materials, and eventually imported Egyptian objects. There is also evidence of so-called hybrid products, designed with a mixture of Egyptian- and Nubian-styles and most likely made in Nubia.[3]

The presence of such a rich and varied repertoire of Egyptian material culture, which at places like Sai Island and Dukki Gel (Kerma) is much higher in quantity than the local Nubian material culture, is most likely a consequence of the colonisation of Nubia by Egypt, a process that had already started during the Middle Kingdom (2025–1700 BC) and progressively affected, alongside material culture, architectural and funerary customs, and eventually most aspects of social, economic and cultural life in Nubia.[4]

Such tangible movement of objects – and with them of traditions, cultural meanings and social implications – from one region to another, in a relatively short period of time, and concurrently the intersection of foreign objects with local material culture is a rather common phenomenon in the history of human populations. This can be observed in different geographical and cultural contexts that face significant processes of

1 Ludwig-Maximilians-Universität München, ERC DiverseNile Project; Giulia.Dercole@aegyp.fak12.uni-muenchen.de.

2 *Sensu* Ginzburg 1963.

3 Budka 2017, 126 with references. On the topic of hybridity, see also de Souza 2020. Cf. also above, Introduction to Part I and Smith this volume; Kilroe this volume.

4 On the topic of material culture and cultural entanglement in New Kingdom colonial Nubia, see Lemos and Budka 2021. See also Lemos 2020.

colonisation.[5] Generally speaking, both colonisation and globalisation should not be understood as merely one-directional phenomena of cultural *acceptance* but as more complex forms of "synergical reflexive interaction and connectivity."[6] Furthermore, these scenarios – for a long time understood mainly from an humancentric perspective – have been recently re-evaluated through the concept of objectscapes, that is from the point of view of the objects, thereby benefiting from their active role in the establishment of social and cultural meanings.[7]

This chapter sheds new light on the interplay between material practices (specifically pottery making), human cultural traditions, and natural landscapes in site-specific contexts. In particular, it aims to explore the concepts of materiality and style, as well as the tangible entanglement of Nubian and Egyptian material culture through the example of the production of Egyptian-style and Nubian-style ceramic objects in Nile clay, offering case studies from the New Kingdom colonial sites of Sai Island and Dukki Gel in Upper Nubia.

From material culture to materiality and the chaîne opératoire approach

By definition, an "object is a thing that you can see or touch but is not usually a living animal, plant or person", which is how archaeologists normally conceive of objects: an artefact which differs from an ecofact or biofact.[8] Furthermore, the etymology of the word object comes from the Medieval Latin *obiectum* "thing put before (the mind or sight)" from which derives the idea of the object as everything that the subject (human/culture) perceives as different from themselves. Hence, the existence of a long tradition of philosophical and linguistic studies of Aristotelian and Cartesian derivation in which objects, and material culture, in its broader sense, have often been interpreted, through an anthropocentric one-way perspective, mainly as static representations of the *human* subject.[9]

In archaeology, the definition of object or thing is often replaced with that of *material culture*, however the origin of the term and its exact meaning is still debated.[10] Possibly, because "the terms 'material culture' and 'material culture studies' emerged one after the other during the twentieth-century in the disciplines of archaeology and socio-cultural anthropology, and especially at intersection of the two: anthropological archaeology."[11]

Lewis Binford and Processual Archaeology of the 1960s considered culture as an extrasomatic means of adaptation (to the environment) within which material categories were mainly understood in functional terms as components of behavioural categories, functionally determined by the social and biological systems in which they operated.[12] Thus, during the 1980s, Post-Processual archaeologists introduced for the first time the concept of *agency* in relation to material culture. Through Post-Processualism, material culture was freed from being only a static representation (or *significant* – borrowing a term from linguistic semiotics) of the social and human system to which it belongs, being newly recognised as a constituent entity in itself, constituting social relations in the creation of meanings.[13] It was in those years – as a result of the combination of new theories of French structural Marxism, ethnoarchaeological approaches introduced by Processual Archaeology and modern material cultural studies developed in American historical archaeology – that "the terminological shift from 'technology' to 'material culture' was completed," culminating in what has been called the "Material-Cultural Turn."[14]

In the last few decades, the approach to materiality and the study of material culture has increasingly become a central aspect of archaeological research

5 Well-known examples from the past are the traditionally called phenomena of *'Hellenisation'* or *'Romanisation'* while an even greater impact in this direction has occurred in modern times as a result of globalisation (e.g., the globalisation by *'Americanisation'* that occurred in Europe after the Second World War). However, it is worth mentioning that as much as the term and idea of the Egyptianisation of Nubia has been questioned, so have the notions of *'Hellenisation'* and *'Romanisation'*. In general, these labels have now been broadly dismissed in favour of a new picture of transformation in which "new configurations of people and things are central" (Pitts and Versluys 2021, 378).

6 Robertson 2017, 55.

7 On the subject of objectscapes see Pitts and Versluys 2021; see also Versluys 2017; Pitts 2019; Lemos 2020; Lemos and Budka 2021 (cf. also the Introduction to Part I in this volume).

8 For an overview see e.g., Knappett 2014 with references.

9 As summarised by Tsoraki et al. 2020, 494–495: "Representation captures the dominant Western ontology, that human beings are separated from the world, and have to 'represent' it in their minds. From Plato's cave via Descartes dualisms to Kant's phenomena and noumena, a gap has been posited between the world 'as it is' and the world that human beings represent to themselves." See also McFadyen and Hicks 2020, 3.

10 Fahlander 2008, 129 with references.

11 Hicks 2010, 25. For a recent overview on the subjects of materiality, objects, and agency in archaeology and anthropology, see also Lunn-Rockliffe, Derbyshire and Hicks 2019.

12 According to Processual Archaeology, artefacts have a primary utilitarian (performative) function and a secondary stylistic function, this latter referring to the social context of production and use of material culture. See Binford 1962; Binford 1965. For recent reviews see Barret 2001; Shriver-Rice 2009.

13 Hodder 1982; see also Bourdieu 1977; Gell 1998.

14 This definition was proposed by Hicks 2010, 45.

and new important cognitive theories have developed around this concept. We have also witnessed a gradual change in terminology: the use of the words *things* and *materiality* replacing that of material culture.[15] In 2012, Bjornar Olsen and colleagues defined archaeology as "the discipline of things," that is the science of objects which "obliged the archaeologists to be bricoleurs, who collect bits and pieces, not because of an erratic whim but because of a commitment, a fidelity to the materials we engage."[16] Moreover, in those years, two other key volumes were published: "How things shape the mind" by Lambros Malafouris[17] and "Entangled. An Archaeology of the Relationships between humans and things" by Ian Hodder.[18]

If for Hodder, the focus still remained mainly on the relationship between things and humans, New Materialism newly and provocatively suggests shifting away from an emphasis on representation, exploring a more-than representational version of material meanings, and embracing a systemic (and relational), rather than dualistic, vision of reality.[19] It considers a more complex system of relationships where things, humans, landscape – and in a broader sense whatever forms part of it – are dynamically interconnected and linked to each other. Hence, the study of material culture potentially expands beyond the human context – imbued as it is with its symbolic, aesthetic, or functional meanings – and embraces the much wider space of ecology.[20]

Remarkably, the study of things is more fluid and dynamic when it is incorporated into the concept of the chaîne opératoire, this being the most suitable and powerful analytical tool for an effective analysis of past material objects as embedded in a network of diverse and intertwined human and non-human actions. The chaîne opératoire in fact "imposes systematization in data collection, as well as the acknowledgement of a variety of elements that are invariably brought together in the conduct of technical activities."[21] Style is, here, intended in its broader sense of "technological style"[22] and "potentially resides in every phase of the manufacturing sequence or chaîne opératoire" from raw material procurement to production, including the stages of use and discard of the object.[23] Hence, the chaîne opératoire approach makes it possible, in a way, to connect the natural world with the anthropocentric world.

The chaîne opératoire approach in Upper Nubia

In the geographical framework of Upper Nubia, the concept of *chaîne opératoire* has already been applied to the study of both ceramics and other types of artefacts by a number of scholars.[24] Furthermore, technological and interdisciplinary laboratory analyses on Nubian- and Egyptian-style ceramics have been successfully conducted, especially around the main centres of the New Kingdom empire like Amara West[25] and Sesebi,[26] as well as upstream of the Nile, in the region of the Third Cataract, at the sites of Askut, Tombos, and Hannek.[27] In northern Sudan, studies on pottery provenance and production technology span from Late Prehistory[28] to the mid-second millennium BC[29] and up to the Meroitic Period.[30]

Regardless of the chronological or geographical time frame, these studies consistently demonstrate that ceramic manufacture needs to be understood as more than a finished product. This product may be the result of human action and have a specific function, but it is also the outcome of a direct initial contact with the environment thorough the choice and manipulation of raw materials. As a result, we can think in terms of a new multi-scale perspective,

15 E.g., see Tilley 2004, "The Materiality of Stone." In 2004, Renfrew and Malafouris developed the so-called *'Material Engagement Theory (MET)'*, from which comes the notion of creative *'thinging'* which refers to the capacity of humans to feel/think through and about things. See e.g., Renfrew 2004; Malafouris 2004; Malafouris 2019a; 2019b.

16 Olsen et al. 2012.

17 Malafouris 2013.

18 Hodder 2012; see also Hodder 2014, 19–20 defined "entanglement as the sum of four types of relationships between humans and things: humans depend on things (HT), things depend on other things (TT), things depend on humans (TH), humans depend on humans (HH). Thus entanglement = (HT) + (TT) + (TH) + (HH)."

19 Tsoraki et al. 2020, 497; see also McFadyen and Hicks 2020, 3.

20 This was also partly anticipated by the anthropologist Tim Ingold (see among others, Ingold 2000a, 2000b, 2007a, 2007b) in his critique on the notion of agency being in general a too human-centric and static vision of material culture to which he contrasts the concept of *meshwork* of (humans and non-humans) and the idea that objects and organic matter are variable, transformative and constantly in flux. See also Hicks 2010, 78, 80 with references.

21 Gosselain 2012, 246.

22 Following the concept of Lechtman 1977.

23 Sillar and Tite 2000. See also Roux 2020.

24 The *chaîne opératoire* approach has been used for the study of Khartoum Variant, Abkan, and Pre-Kerma ceramic material from Sai Island by D'Ercole 2017; D'Ercole et al. 2017a. Also, for an application of the *chaîne opératoire* concept on painting materials, see Fulcher 2022.

25 Spataro et al. 2015; Gasperini 2023.

26 Rose 2012; Rose 2017.

27 Carrano et al. 2008; 2009.

28 D'Ercole 2017; D'Ercole et al. 2017b.

29 See e.g., the study by de Souza and Ownby 2022 on the Middle Nubian cultures (C-Group, Pan-Grave, and Kerma ceramic traditions).

30 McCarthy 2022/2023.

Fig. 1 Location of the two New Kingdom colonial sites of Sai Island and Dukki Gel (Kerma) (map by K. Rose, ©DiverseNile Project).

beyond one that is purely anthropocentric (i.e., objects *vs.* humans), which includes an environmental dimension made up of vegetation, animals, and various natural materials – such as clay, water, or sand.[31]

Case study from Upper Nubia: Sai Island and Dukki Gel

In the following, the *chaîne opératoire* of two sets of ceramic samples are presented and compared: one from the Egyptian temple town of Sai Island and the other from Dukki Gel (Kerma) (Fig. 1). This set of samples consists of both Nubian-style (Figs. 2a–c) and Egyptian- style pottery (Figs. 2d–f) made in different Nile clay fabrics and dated to the 18th Dynasty of the New Kingdom colonial Period in Nubia.

The ceramic material from Sai Island comes from three sectors of the fortified town located on the eastern bank of the island, namely SAV1 North, SAV1 East and SAV1 West, all of which were excavated between 2013 and 2017 through the ERC AcrossBorders Project.[32] Overall, during the AcrossBorders Project, a total of 253 ceramics were selected from the Pharaonic town and submitted for laboratory analyses. For comparative purposes, 43 prehistoric ceramic samples from other sites on Sai Island, 33 samples from natural soils, modern ceramics and clay-rich material, and 6 oven fragments and unfired sherds were also analysed, although they will not be discussed in this article.[33] It is worth mentioning that among the 253 New Kingdom samples, are also classes of ceramics other than Nile clay ware, such as Egyptian Marl clays, Oasis clays, and other imports from the Levant. These latter are not, however, the subject of this chapter which focuses exclusively on the set of Nile clay samples. The ceramic material from Dukki Gel (Kerma) – kindly provided by the site's excavator, Charles Bonnet, and the responsible ceramicist Philippe Ruffieux – includes ceramic specimens from Nubian-style or Egyptian-style Nile

31 On this subject, see Tsoraky et al. 2020.

32 Budka 2017; Budka 2020; Budka forthcoming.

33 Sterba and D'Ercole forthcoming.

Fig. 2 Examples of Nubian-style (a–c) and Egyptian-style (d–f) ceramic ware in Nile clay selected as samples from the colonial town of Sai Island and Dukki Gel (photos by G. D'Ercole).

Site	Total No. of Ceramics analysed by INAA	No. of Nile clay ware analysed by INAA	Total No. of Ceramics analysed by OM	No. of Nile clay ware analysed by OM
Sai Island	253	Nubian-style (=55) Egyptian-style (=118)	84	Nubian-style (=20) Egyptian-style (=19)
Dukki Gel (Kerma)	52	Nubian-style (=20) Egyptian-style (=32)	21	Nubian-style (=18) Egyptian-style (=3)
Total	305	225	105	60

Table 1 Site, number of ceramic sherds sampled per type of analysis (INAA/OM), cultural tradition (Nubian/Egyptian), and the total number of specimens sampled per site.

clay pottery which were selected from different sectors and all dated to the 18th Dynasty.[34] Nine of the samples from Dukki Gel were previously analysed during the ERC AcrossBorders Project. Additional reference material was provided by new samples in 2020 and 2021 within the scope of the ERC DiverseNile Project (Table 1).

Materials and methods

This study involved a multi-analytical approach which started with an autoptic assessment of the ceramic samples combined with targeted laboratory investigations – including optical microscopy (OM) and bulk compositional analyses by Instrumental Neutron Activation Analysis (INAA).

As a first step, all samples were macroscopically documented according to their visual stylistic and morphometric features, and state of preservation. For

34 The ceramics sampled from Dukki Gel (from sectors 1/36, 23D, and 45C) date mostly to the first half of the 18th Dynasty, that is from the reign of Thutmose I up to Thutmose III (Phases II and III at Dukki Gel). Samples from sectors 3, 12, 79 and 82 date to Phases IV and V, that is from Thutmose III-Amenhotep II to the end of the 18th Dynasty. The material from Sector 45C is especially interesting as it comes from a Nubian religious complex with very peculiar architecture. For details, see Ruffieux 2016, 516; see also Ruffieux 2018.

Sai Island, the autoptic assessment of the Egyptian-style pottery is based on the macroscopic site-specific fabric corpus established by Julia Budka for the ceramic assemblage of the town. The macroscopic analysis of the Nubian fabrics was undertaken by the author.[35] The ceramic material from Dukki Gel (Kerma) was stylistically and morphometrically classified by Philippe Ruffieux.[36]

Next, a selection of specimens was submitted to OM and INAA. For Sai Island, 173 Nubian- and Egyptian-style Nile clays underwent INAA, out of a total of 253 New Kingdom ceramic samples; optical microscopy was performed on 84 of the samples, out of which 39 were Egyptian and Nubian vessels in Nile clay. From Dukki Gel, 52 samples underwent INAA and 21 were selected for OM (Table 1).

Petrographic observations were carried out by the author at the Department of Geodynamics and Sedimentology, University of Vienna, for the Sai Island samples, and at the Department of Earth and Environmental Sciences, Ludwig-Maximilians University Munich, for the Dukki Gel samples. The microscopic analysis of thin sections provided information on the following aspects: a) the groundmass or clay matrix of the ceramic body (i.e., colour, homogeneity and optical activity); b) non-plastic inclusions (i.e., sorting, dominant grain size, maximum grain size, abundance, and mineral composition); c) plastic inclusions (i.e., clay pellets, argillaceous rock fragments etc.); d) porosity (i.e., voids abundance, type, dominant size, iso-orientation); e) organics (i.e., abundance, type, dominant size). The firing process of the ceramic sample (i.e., oxidised, reduced, reduced with narrow oxidised margins, dark core due to insufficient oxidisation, oxidised to reduced), and other relevant information relating to the stages of raw material procurement, preparation, forming and production of the vessels were also recorded through optical microscopy. Instrumental Neutron Activation Analysis was performed at the Atominstitut of Vienna by J.H. Sterba. Ceramic samples (approx. 100 mg milligrams of powder) were run in sets of 43 samples each and were irradiated together with five internationally certified reference materials. INAA meant that measuring the composition of 28 major, minor and trace elements was possible. For statistical analysis, a multivariate statistical filter method was applied.[37]

Results: the chaîne opératoire of the Nubian-style and Egyptian-style Nile clay ceramics from the New Kingdom sites of Sai Island and Dukki Gel

Raw material procurement

What is macroscopically referred to as a Nile clay, appears under the microscope as a non-calcareous ferruginous and micaceous clay with a moderate to high optically active groundmass and a fired colour ranging from black to red-brown. The mineral composition is mainly of silicate minerals ranging from silt to very fine up to fine sand which includes grains of quartz, alkali feldspar, plagioclase, and micas, together with epidote and amphibole, and a few to common rock lithic fragments derived from metamorphic (e.g., schist, quartzite), carbonate (micrite) and volcanic rocks (volcanic tephra). The frequency and sorting of the non-plastic inclusions, as well as other specific technological characteristics of the fabrics vary from sample to sample, which parallels the macroscopic groups identified (Fig. 3).[38]

Chemically, the Nubian-style and Egyptian-style ceramics are almost indistinguishable, forming a single compositional group (i.e., the Nile clay group) which was statistically the largest amongst all recognised chemical groups. This group could be further separated into eleven subgroups which were chemically highly similar, except for the behavior of specific elements (Fig. 4).[39]

All in all, the petrographic and compositional data suggest that most of the Egyptian- and Nubian-style ceramics examined from the sites of Sai Island and Dukki Gel were manufactured using a very similar clay raw material, probably of local (Upper Nubia) origin. Despite the significant distance between the sites, the chemical fingerprint of the clay used at Sai Island and Dukki Gel is almost identical, apart from minor differences likely due to local changes in the Nile and/or the specific formula used by the potters to prepare their ceramic mix. An exception to this is represented by a small group of Egyptian cooking pots (Fig. 2f) forming a chemical cluster noticeably distinct from the other samples, which suggests an allochthonous origin from Egypt.[40]

Preparation of the paste

If the base clay raw material selected for the preparation of the Egyptian and Nubian ceramics at the sites of Sai Island and Dukki Gel turned out to be petrographically and chemically very similar, the recipe used to make the pastes incorporates specific traditions and technological choices. There are clear differences between the Nubian and Egyptian

35 Budka 2017, 120.

36 Ruffieux 2018.

37 For details see D'Ercole forthcoming; Sterba and D'Ercole forthcoming.

38 D'Ercole forthcoming; D'Ercole and Sterba 2018.

39 Sterba and D'Ercole forthcoming.

40 D'Ercole and Sterba 2018; Sterba and D'Ercole forthcoming.

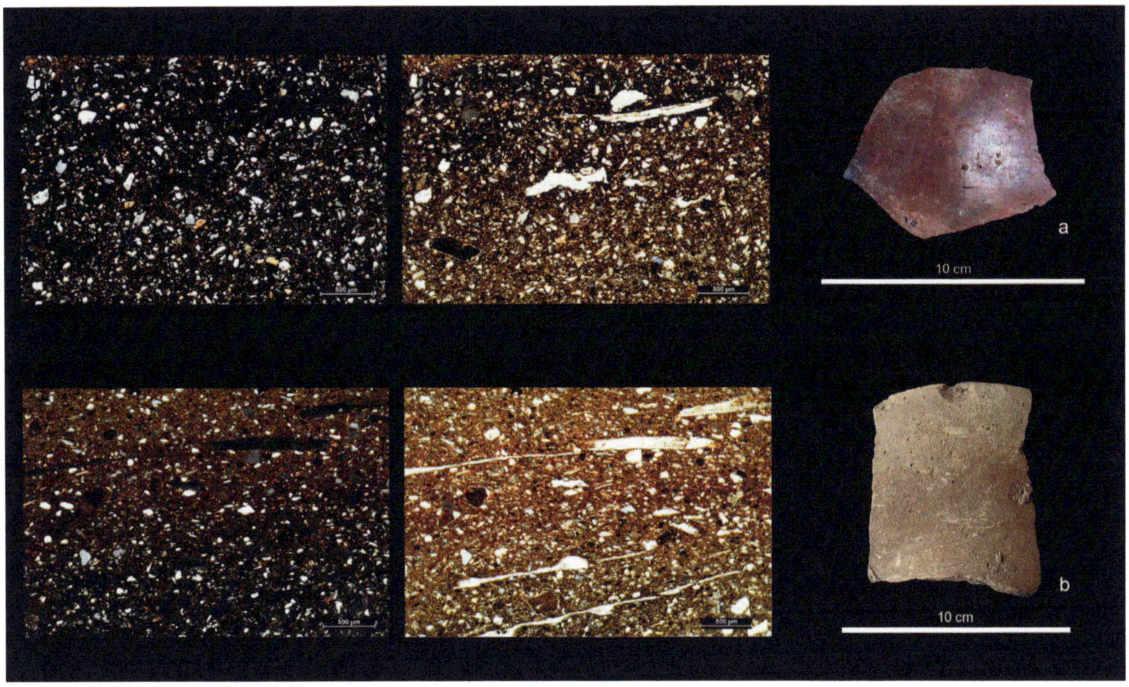

Fig. 3 Thin sections taken in cross polarised light (left) and in plane polarised light (right) showing the characteristic ferruginous optically active clay matrix and the overall mineral framework of a red burnished Nubian-style pot (a, photographed on top) and of a wheel made dish according to the local Egyptian-style (b, photographed below). Note that although the two samples belong macroscopically to two clearly different styles and technological traditions (respectively Nubian and Egyptian), they look almost identical under the microscope (photos by G. D'Ercole).

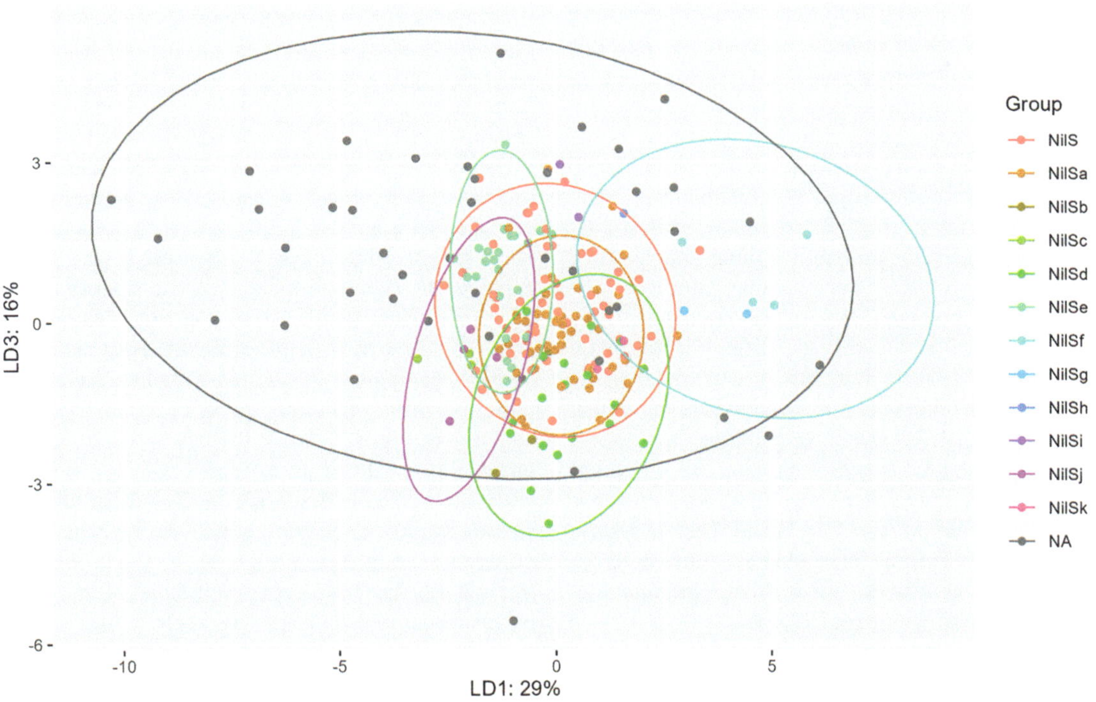

Fig. 4 Discriminant analysis chart, showing the eleven Nile clays subgroups identified from Sai Island (NilSa – NilSk, in colours). The NilS samples, in orange, are those we could not reliably assign to any of the 11 subgroups. The dark grey circles are the Dukki Gel samples. Note the significant overlap between the different groups (figure by J.H. Sterba).

production, as well as within the various ware types. Overall, the Egyptian-style samples show a slightly coarser texture than the Nubian-style samples and normally contain a larger amount of medium sand sized quartz and feldspar inclusions, as well as more common lithic fragments. For some Egyptian fabrics (in Nile clay B2), we cannot exclude the possibility that the potters intentionally added a quartz and quartzite component to the base clay. The presence of grains of microcrystalline calcite (micrite) in some samples – although ubiquitous in most of the analysed ceramics from Sai Island and Dukki Gel – also seems to indicate that they could be used as tempering material together with quartz. Chemically, the Egyptian-style samples analysed from Sai Island contained higher potassium levels than the Nubian-style samples.[41]

Another aspect in which Egyptian and Nubian ceramics differ is the content and type of organic matter. In general, the Nubian-style samples contain more organic inclusions than the Egyptian-style pottery, although the very fine Nubian wares (e.g., Kerma beakers and some fine Black-topped cups and bowls) are mainly sandy and micaceous in composition. However, it is not so much the amount of organic matter that differs but rather the type of inclusions added. For the Egyptian-style samples, chaff (mostly in the form of elongate rectangular charred pieces derived from stems or grassy species) was the preferred vegetal type intentionally added to the clay pastes. The Nubian-style ceramics were tempered with a greater variety of organic matter, including silica skeletons composed of multiple morphotypes and possibly also herbivore dung, finely divided vegetal remains, and carbonised straw ash. The Black-topped wares, cups, beakers and bowls with burnished or wet smoothed surfaces, assigned mainly to the macroscopic Nubian fabric 2 (and secondary to fabric 1/2), were tempered with a finer organic component (probably animal dung, straw ash, or small divided plant remains). Otherwise the cooking pots and the coarse wares assigned to the Nubian fabric 3 were tempered with abundant plant inclusions of variable size and sorting, most likely chaff remains (i.e., diverse by-products of cereal processing).[42] It is worth mentioning that some Nubian-style cooking pots from the site of Dukki Gel, although containing abundant heterogeneous organics similar to the Sai Island Nubian fabric 3, also showed frequent carbonate inclusions of microcrystalline calcite, most likely intentionally added as tempering material.

Production

With some exceptions (e.g., the bread plates and bread moulds), the majority of the Egyptian-style pottery is wheel-made,[43] as opposed to the Nubian-style ceramics which are hand-made. Under the microscope, the orientation of the voids left by the combustion of the organic matter into the paste could be used to determine more information on the use of different manufacturing techniques. Where the organics show a poor alignment and a specific orientation indicative of the 'relict' coil features, it is likely that the pot was handmade using the coiling technique (Fig. 5a). On the other hand, when the organics appear moderately to well aligned with a prevalent presence of longitudinal features, such as stems or plant stalks, this suggests the use of a wheel, or, in the case of the Nubian cooking pots with basketry impressions, that the pot was, at least in part, built on a mat (Fig. 5b). The burnishing or polishing treatments of vessels may also influence the orientation of the inclusions (see below). In some Nubian sherds the smoothing treatment applied to the inner surface of the vessel seems to have been intentionally made to imitate the Egyptian wheel.

Finishing

Nubian-style pottery is typically uncoated, smoothed/wet-smoothed (e.g., by using fingers, with grass or with a dump cloth) – this includes common medium and coarse ware such as bowls, cooking pots and jars (Figs. 2b–c) – and burnished such as fine to very fine ware (e.g., Kerma beakers, Black-topped vessels and cups) (Fig. 2a). Burnishing is quite a complex treatment that can be applied in a large number of different ways, styles and quality standards (from poor burnishing which leaves traces of visible strikes, striations or scratches, to a medium quality burnish characterised by an overall average lustre, up to a highly fine and homogeneous burnishing). High quality burnishing was likely achieved by rubbing a pebble with a smooth, well-rounded or oval surface, from the rim of the vessel and then progressing towards the body and the bottom, having taken care to previously wet and wipe the walls of the pot so as to avoid scratches and stroke marks. Under the optical microscope, burnishing produces an even and compact surface, with small-sized irregularities and a glossy/lustrous surface due to the specular reflection of light (the clay minerals tend in fact to align due to the burnishing treatment). Thus, two separate individual levels ("a burnish peel and a subsurface layer"[44]) are clearly

41 D'Ercole and Sterba 2018; Sterba and D'Ercole forthcoming.

42 D'Ercole forthcoming. See also Budka and D'Ercole 2022.

43 For details, see Nordström and Bourriau 1993.

44 Ionescu and Hoeck 2020, 204, fig. 6d.

a

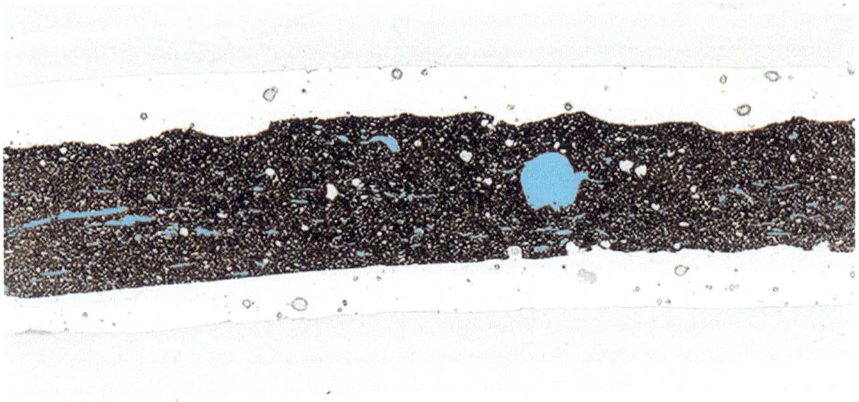

b

Fig. 5 Thin section scans of two Nubian ceramic samples from Dukki Gel (Kerma). In the image on top (a) the specific concentric alignment of the pores structures and of the voids and relicts left by the combustion of the organics indicates that this vessel was manufactured using the coiling technique. In the image below (b), the good alignment of the pores structures and of the voids and relicts left by the combustion of the organics indicates that this vessel was built on a mat (figure by G. D'Ercole).

visible. Otherwise, a smoothed surface "has small and numerous irregularities, in particular parallel-oriented striations, which diffusely reflect the light and produce a characteristic matte or dull luster."[45] Smoothed and burnished wares characterise the majority of the Nubian-style samples analysed from Sai Island and Dukki Gel. Both treatments could be recognised with the naked eye, however the difference between the two became even clearer under the microscope. Nubian-style pottery from Sai Island and Dukki Gel was also occasionally decorated with simple impressions and/or incisions (Fig. 6a).

The Egyptian-style pottery shows a wider range of finishing and decorative surface treatments which, depending on the different ceramic ware and type, may include uncoated, washed (white and red), polished, and even painted (monochrome and bichrome) ware (Figs. 2d–f).[46] Unlike burnishing, which results merely in some compression and alignment of the clay particles at the surface, a coating such as a paint or "an applied slip is associated with a clearly visible layer of more finely textured and less porous clay"[47] (Fig. 6b).

The Nubian-style samples are commonly characterised by a reduced core and more or less

45 Ionescu and Hoeck 2020, 204.

46 See e.g., Budka 2017; Ruffieux 2016.

47 Ionescu and Hoeck 2020, 204 with references.

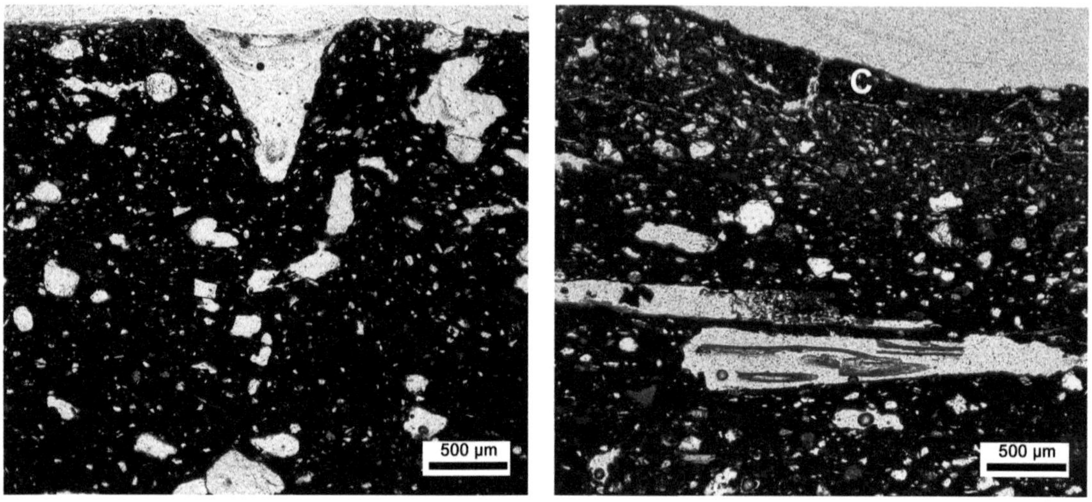

Fig. 6 Photomicrographs of thin sections taken with plane polarised light showing a Nubian-style sample from Dukki Gel (Kerma) with incised decorations on an smoothed surface (a) and an Egyptian-style sample from Sai Island with a red coating (b); the letter c marks the coating in the photo (photos by F. Dellefant).

wide to tiny oxidised external margins. They were most likely fired upside down using biomass as combustible (e.g., wood, straw, dung) so as to produce the reducing atmosphere and to achieve the black top and black interior.[48] Otherwise, the Egyptian-style specimens show, in most cases, an orange-brown to red fracture throughout and on the external surface, with some samples having a zoned fracture consisting of a dark core and oxidised surfaces. For the Nubian ceramics proposed firing temperatures are around 850°C, while temperatures were occasionally slightly higher for the Egyptian samples.[49] No kilns or pottery workshops have been identified so far from the New Kingdom town on Sai Island.[50]

Use

From both sites, the Egyptian samples typically include beakers/drop pots, beer jars, bowls, dishes, cooking pots and *zir* vessels. Sherds from bread plates and bread moulds were also analysed. The Nubian samples generally consist of Black-topped beakers, cups, bowls, cooking pots with characteristic basketry impressions and a small amount of *zirs* and storage vessels. All in all, these ceramics were mostly intended for food preparation, cooking, baking, storing and consumption. At sector SAV1 North on Sai Island, the presence, among the Egyptian-style vessels, of spinning bowls, beer jars and incense burners also suggests complementary spinning and ritual activities.[51]

48 Budka et al. 2019.
49 D'Ercole forthcoming; Dellefant et al. 2023.
50 Budka 2017, 127 with references.
51 Budka 2017. The same set of ceramics, including spinning bowls, is also attested at sector SAV1 West, see Budka 2020, 220.

Discussion

In ceramic studies, "the *chaîne opératoire* is a privileged qualitative approach used to reconstruct multi-scalar networks linking either the different steps of the manufacturing tasks [...], producers [...], producers and distributors [...], producers and users [...], and users [...]".[52] Further, "*chaînes opératoires* are not a 'closed package' but they are made of components which can be modified through encounters with other practitioners."[53] In general, among the various stages of the *chaîne opératoire*, forming is recognised as the most stable and less likely to be influenced after contacts with other traditions.[54] The stages of clay preparation and finishing are those most likely to change from direct or indirect transmission.[55]

As a result of our multi-scale combined macroscopic and microscopic analysis it is clear that most of the ceramics found at Sai Island and Dukki Gel, either in Egyptian- and Nubian-style, do not significantly differ in their chemical composition (the stage of raw material procurement), although a different chemical fingerprint has been identified at Sai Island for specific imported Egyptian ware (i.e., the Egyptian cooking pots manufactured in a Nile clay E var. and in a sandy version of the Nile clay B2 in the "Vienna System") (Table 2). This suggests that the ceramic manufacture of both the Nubian-style and Egyptian-style vessels in Nile clay took place, for the most part, locally in Upper Nubia, using raw materials and tempers found opportunistically within, or nearby,

52 Roux 2020, 16.
53 Gosselain 2011, 219, cited in Roux 2020, 21.
54 Gosselain 2000.
55 Roux 2020, 20. See also Gosselain 2008; Roux 2015.

Nubian-style	Chaîne Opératoire	Egyptian-style
Local clay raw material (Nubian Nile clay)	Procurement	Local clay raw material (Nubian Nile clay)
Organic temper (i.e., ash, dung, very fine to coarse chaff, combination of these)	Preparation	Mineral temper (i.e., quartz, quartzite); organic temper (mainly coarse chaff)
Hand-made pottery (coiling and built on a mat)	Production	Wheel-made pottery
Uncoated, burnished (wet) smoothed surfaces; non-oxidizing atmosphere; firing up to circa 850 °C	Finishing	Uncoated, washed, polished, painted surfaces; oxidizing atmosphere with reduced domains; firing up to circa 1000 °C
Food preparation, cooking, storing and consumption	Use	Food preparation, cooking, storing and consumption, spinning, ritual activities

Table 2 Comparison between the most important technological choices characterising the *chaîne opératoire* of the Nubian-style and the Egyptian-style ceramic manufacture from Sai Island and Dukki Gel (Kerma).

the main colonial sites where the pottery workshops were also possibly located. Moreover, the fact that there are no significant differences in the clay raw material used, either in its composition or its tactile and visual characteristics, may indicate that the same – most likely Nubian – potters collected (and possibly also prepared) the clay both for the manufacture of their own ceramics and for those produced according to the Egyptian-style. Moreover, this data points to an in-depth and shared knowledge of the surrounding geomorphological and hydrological landscape and of its available raw materials and resources, as well as to a drive from the side of the Egyptians in accepting and incorporating, at least in part, some of the local Nubian traditions.

Otherwise, within New Kingdom Nubia, regional ceramic style was mostly expressed through surface treatment and decoration, that is within the manufacturing stages of production, including forming (wheel-made *vs.* hand-made), and finishing. Other differences were also recognised in the so-called preparation stage, i.e., the formula or recipe used for making the pastes. Here the main variation is in the use of organic tempers, with the Egyptian-style ceramics being mostly chaff-tempered while the Nubian-style both chaff and dung-tempered (Table 2).

On the use of the vessels, some functions seem to be exclusive to Egyptian or Nubian pots, while for others we observe overlaps even if, regardless of the nominal function (e.g., cooking pots), the specific content[56] of the vessel could vary (Table 2).

In general, it is possible that, even if not all, at least some of the *gestures* and stages of the manufacturing sequences took place simultaneously in the same workshop without a rigid separation between Egyptian and Nubian manufacture. That is, that the same potter/s possibly prepared and fired Nubian- and Egyptian-style vessels together and that only some stages of the manufacturing sequence took place separately, on the basis of specific technological skills and regional traditions. It seems plausible that so-called hybrid vessels, showing a mixture of Egyptian and Nubian stylistic aspects and technologies, were developed in such contexts, perhaps accidently at first but becoming more widespread based on demand. This reflects shared used of the same region and of the, mostly, progressive entanglement between Egyptian and Nubian cultures.

All in all, this picture – social groups sharing, at least in part, their technological traditions – points to overall effective communications and "*social learning*" between the two cultural parts (Egyptians and Nubians), although a certain degree of "*polarization*" and "*sense of groupness*"[57] still persisted and is clearly visible in some stages of the *chaîne opératoire* (in particular, forming and finishing).

It seems apparent that Sackett's traditional definition of style[58] as "something always peculiar to a specific time and place" is a useful starting point but is far from the full answer. When studying ceramic assemblages, especially in such complex, dynamic and multicultural contexts, it is crucial to approach them from a

56 Organic Residues Analysis studies hold much potential here; see also Smith this volume.

57 Following Roux et al. 2017.

58 Sackett 1977.

multiscale perspective, in other words to think in terms of *chaîne opératoire* and of technological style.

Style and the meaning that we attribute to the objects has contingent value, this is not personal, but based on a specific *"community of practice."*[59] Style can also transform continuously and take on different meanings depending on the place (and time) but most importantly on contemporary social and cultural relationships.

From our compositional analyses, it is clear that "the Nile clay chemistry is not a set of distinct signatures but rather a slow progression of variations/changes in a common chemistry."[60] Possibly, the idea of very distinctive specific ceramic traditions *and* a common fingerprint (due to the fact that these people were actually sharing the same landscape), reflected in a similar fluid progression in ceramic style/s – could also apply to the system of relationships and encounters that we are here trying to understand and reconstruct between Nubians and Egyptians.[61]

Eventually, the new ceramic material selected from the Attab to Ferka region[62] will shed new light on the complex system of socio-cultural, economical, and ecological dynamics that took place during the Bronze Age in the various sectors of Nubia.

Acknowledgements

This text was written during the ERC DiverseNile Project. The project received funding from the European Research Council (ERC) under the European Union's Horizon 2020 research and innovation programme (grant agreement No. 865463). I would like to deeply thank Julia Budka and Rennan Lemos who during the hardest period of the Covid-19 pandemic and remote working had the optimism and foresight to organize the splendid DiverseNile Seminar Series "Landscape and resource management in Bronze Age Nubia: Archaeological perspectives on the exploitation of natural resources and the circulation of commodities in the Middle Nile", and kindly invited me to offer my contribution to that and then to this volume. Further, I am deeply grateful to Philippe Ruffieux who kindly provided the ceramic sample from the site of Dukki Gel. Eventually, I thank my colleague Kate Rose for preparing the map in Figure 1.

59 Roux 2020 with references.

60 Sterba and D'Ercole forthcoming.

61 See also the concept of *"community of style"* by M.H. Feldman discussed in Budka 2022, with references.

62 This area, which is part of the research concession of the Munich University Attab to Ferka Survey Project (MUAFS), is presented in Budka 2022.

Bibliography

Barrett, J.C.
2001 Agency, the duality of structure, and the problem of the archaeological record, in: I. Hodder (ed.), *Archaeological Theory Today*, London, 141–164.

Binford, L.R.
1962 Archaeology as anthropology, *American Antiquity* 28 (2), 217–225.
1965 Archaeological systematics and the study of culture process, *American Antiquity* 31 (2), 203–210.

Bourdieu, P.
1977 *Outline of a Theory of Practice* (trans. R. Nice), Cambridge.

Budka, J.
2017 Pottery from SAV1 North, in: J. Budka (ed.), *AcrossBorders I. The New Kingdom Town of Sai Island, Sector SAV1 North*, Contributions to the Archaeology of Egypt, Nubia and the Levant 4, Vienna, 119–156.
2020 *AcrossBorders 2. Living in New Kingdom Sai.* With contributions by Johannes Auenmüller, Annette M. Hansen, Frits Heinrich, Veronica Hinterhuber, Ptolemaios Paxinos, Nadja Pöllath, Helmut Sattmann, Sara Schnedl and Martina Ullmann,, Archaeology of Egypt, Sudan and the Levant 1, Vienna.
2022 Early New Kingdom settlement activities in the periphery of Sai Island: towards a contextualisation of fresh evidence from Attab West, *Der antike Sudan. Mitteilungen der Sudanarchäologischen Gesellschaft zu Berlin e.V.* 33, 45–61.
Forthc. *AcrossBorders 3: Vessels for the Home Away from Egypt. The Pottery Corpus from the New Kingdom Town of Sai Island.* With contributions by Giulia D'Ercole, Johannes Sterba and Philippe Ruffieux, Archaeology of Egypt, Sudan and the Levant, Vienna.

Budka, J., Geiger, C., Heindl, P., Hinterhuber, V. and Reschreiter, H.
2019 The question of fuel for cooking in ancient Egypt and Sudan, *EXARC Journal* 2019/1, https://exarc.net/ark:/88735/10398.

Budka, J. and D'Ercole, G.
2022 An experimental approach to assessing the tempering and firing of local pottery production in Nubia during the New Kingdom Period, *EXARC Journal* 2022/2, https://exarc.net/ark:/88735/10638.

Carrano, J., Ferguson, J.R., Girty, G.H., Smith, S.T. and Carrano, C.J.
2008 A chemical and mineralogical comparison of Nubian and Egyptian style ceramics and the implications for culture contact: preliminary report, *Sudan & Nubia* 12, 90–98.

Carrano, J.L., Girty, G.H. and Carrano, C.J.
2009 Re-examining the Egyptian colonial encounter in Nubia through a compositional, mineralogical, and textural comparison of ceramics, *Journal of Archaeological Science* 36, 785–797.

D'Ercole, G.
2017 *Ceramic Manufacturing Techniques and Cultural Traditions in Nubia from the 8th to the 3rd Millennium BC. Examples from Sai Island*, Cambridge Monographs in African Archaeology 96, Oxford.
Forthc. Petrography of the pottery from the New Kingdom town of Sai, in: J. Budka, *AcrossBorders 3: Vessels for the Home Away from Egypt. The Pottery Corpus from the New Kingdom Town of Sai Island.* With contributions by Giulia D'Ercole, Johannes Sterba and Philippe Ruffieux, Archaeology of Egypt, Sudan and the Levant, Vienna.

D'Ercole, G. and Sterba, J.H
2018 From macro wares to micro fabrics and INAA compositional groups: the pottery corpus of the New Kingdom town on Sai Island (northern Sudan), in: J. Budka and J. Auenmüller (eds.), *From Microcosm to Macrocosm: Individual Households and Cities in Ancient Egypt and Nubia*, Leiden, 171–183.

D'Ercole, G., Garcea, E.A.A., Eramo, G. and Muntoni, I.M.
2017a Variability and continuity of ceramic manufacturing of prehistoric pottery from Upper Nubia, Sudan: An ethnographic comparison, *Journal of Archaeological Science: Reports* 16, 553–563.

D'Ercole, G., Budka, J., Sterba, J.H., Garcea, E.A.A. and Mader, D.
2017b The successful 'recipe' for a long-lasting tradition: Nubian ceramic assemblages from Sai Island (northern Sudan) from prehistory to the New Kingdom, *Antiquity* 91, 24–42.

Dellefant, F., D'Ercole, G., Kaliwoda, M. and Budka, J.
2023 Differentiation of Late Bronze Age Nubian- and Egyptian-style ceramics from northern Sudan by manufacturing firing temperatures using Raman spectroscopy, *Journal of Archaeological Science: Reports* 52, 104233, https://doi.org/10.1016/j.jasrep.2023.

Fahlander, F.
2008 Differences that matter. Materialities, material culture and social practice, in: H. Glørstad and L. Hedeager (eds.), *Six Essays on the Materiality of Society and Culture*, Lindom, 127–154.

Fulcher, K.
2022 *Painting Amara West: The Technology and Experience of Colour in New Kingdom Nubia*, Amara West Research Project Publications 1, British Museum Publications on Egypt and Sudan 13, Leuven.

Gasperini, V.
2023 *Amara West: The Pottery from Cemeteries C and D*, Amara West Research Project Publications 2, British Museum Publications on Egypt and Sudan 17, Leuven.

Gell, A.
1998 *Art and Agency*, Oxford.

Ginzburg, N.
1963 *Lessico Familiare (Family Lexicon)*, Torino.

GOSSELAIN, O.P.
2000 Materializing identities: An African perspective, *Journal of Archaeological Method and Theory* 7, 187–217.
2008 Mother Bella was not a Bella. Inherited and transformed traditions in Southwestern Niger, in: M. STARK, B. BOWSER and L. HORNE (eds.), *Cultural Transmission and Material Culture. Breaking Down Boundaries*, Tucson, 150–177.
2011 Fine if I do, fine if I don't. Dynamics of technical knowledge in Sub-Saharan Africa, in: B.W. ROBERTS and M. VANDER LINDEN (eds.), *Investigating Archaeological Cultures: Material Culture, Variability, and Transmission*, New York, 211–227.
2012 Technology, in: T. INSOLL (ed.), *Oxford Handbook of the Archaeology of Ritual and Religion*, Oxford, 243–260.

HICKS, D.
2010 The material-cultural turn: event and effect, in: D. HICKS and M.C. BEAUDRY (eds.), *The Oxford Handbook of Material Culture Studies*, Oxford, 25–98.

HODDER, I.
1982 *Symbols in Action*, Cambridge.
2012 *Entangled: An Archaeology of the Relationships between Humans and Things*, Oxford.
2014 The entanglements of humans and things: a long-term view, *New Literary History* 45 (1), 19–36.

IONESCU, C. and HOECK, V.
2020 Ceramic technology. How to investigate surface finishing, *Archaeological and Anthropological Sciences* 12, 204, https://doi.org/10.1007/s12520-020-01144-9.

INGOLD, T.
2000a *The Perception of the Environment of the Environment: Essays on Livelihood, Dwelling and Skill*, London.
2000b Making culture and weaving the world, in: P.M. GRAVES-BROWN (ed.), *Matter, Materiality and Modern Culture*, London, 50–71.
2007a Materials against materiality, *Archaeological Dialogues* 14(1), 1–16.
2007b *Lines: A Brief History*, London.

KNAPPETT, C.
2014 Materiality in Archaeological Theory, in: C. SMITH (ed), *Encyclopedia of Global Archaeology*, Cham, https://doi.org/10.1007/978-1-4419-0465-2_292.

LECHTMAN, H.
1977 Style in technology: some early thoughts, in: H. LECHTMAN and T.S. MERRILL (eds.), *Material culture: style, organization, and dynamics of technology*, St. Paul, 3–20.

LEMOS, R.
2020 Material culture and colonization in ancient Nubia: Evidence from the New Kingdom cemeteries, in: C. SMITH (ed.), *Encyclopedia of Global Archaeology*, Cham, https://doi.org/10.1007/978-3-319-51726-1_3307-1.

LEMOS R. and BUDKA, J.
2021 Alternatives to colonization and marginal identities in New Kingdom colonial Nubia (1550–1070 BCE), *World Archaeology* 53 (3), 401–418.

LUNN-ROCKLIFFE, S., DERBYSHIRE, S. and HICKS, D.
2019 Material culture, analysis of, in: P. ATKINSON, S. DELAMONT, A. CERNAT, J. SHAKSHAUG and R. WILLIAMS (eds.), *SAGE Research Methods Foundations*, https://dx.doi.org/10.4135/9781526421036843497.

MALAFOURIS, L.
2004 The cognitive basis of material engagement: Where brain, body and culture conflate, in: E. DEMARRAIS, C. GOSDEN and C. RENFREW (eds.), *Rethinking Materiality: The Engagement of Mind with the Material World*, Cambridge, 53–62.
2013 *How Things Shape the Mind: A Theory of Material Engagement*, Cambridge.
2019a Thinking as "thinging": Psychology with things, *Current Directions in Psychological Science* 29 (1), 3–8.
2019b Mind and material engagement, *Phenomenology and the Cognitive Sciences* 18, 1–17.

MCCARTHY, C.N.
2022/2023 *Disclosing the Provenance and Production Technology of Meroitic Ceramics from Sedeinga (Northern Sudan)*, Padua Thesis and Dissertation Archive, Padua, https://hdl.handle.net/20.500.12608/54894.

MCFADYEN, L. and HICKS, D.
2020 Introduction: From archaeography to photology, in: D. HICKS and L. MCFADYEN (eds.), *Archaeology and Photography: Time, Objectivity and Archive*, London, 1–20.

OLSEN, B., SHANKS, M., WEBMOOR, T. and WITMORE, C.
2012 *Archaeology: The Discipline of Things*, London.

PITTS, M.
2019 *The Roman Object Revolution. Objectscapes and Intra-Cultural Connectivity in Northwest Europe*, Amsterdam.

PITTS, M. and VERSLUYS, M.J.
2021 Objectscapes: A manifesto for investigating the impacts of object flows on past societies, *Antiquity* 95 (380), 367–381, doi:10.15184/aqy.2020.148.

RENFREW, C.
2004 Towards a theory of material engagement, in: E. DEMARRAIS, C. GOSDEN and C. RENFREW (eds.), *Rethinking Materiality: The Engagement of Mind with the Material World*, Cambridge, 23–32.

ROBERTSON, R.
2017 Globalization thinking and the past, in: T. HODOS, *The Routledge Handbook of Archaeology and Globalization*, Oxon, New York, 54–65.

ROSE, P.
2012 Early 18th Dynasty Nubian pottery from the site of Sesebi, Sudan, in: I. FORSTNER-MÜLLER and

P. Rose (eds.), *Nubian pottery from Egyptian cultural contexts of the middle and early New Kingdom. Proceedings of a workshop held at the Austrian Archaeological Institute at Cairo*, 1–12 December 2010, Ergänzungshefte zu den Jahresheften des Österreichischen Archäologischen Instituts 13, Vienna, 13–30.

2017 Sesebi: Ceramics, chronology and society, in: N. Spencer, A. Stevens and M. Binder (eds.), *Nubia in the New Kingdom. Lived Experience, Pharaonic Control and Indigenous Traditions*, British Museum Publications on Egypt and Sudan 3, Leuven, 465–473.

Roux, V.

2015 Standardization of ceramic assemblages: Transmission mechanisms and diffusion of morpho-functional traits across social boundaries, *Journal of Anthropological Archaeology* 40, 1–9.

2020 Chaîne opératoire, technological networks and sociological interpretations, *Cuadernos de Prehistoria y Arqueología de la Universidad de Granada* 30, 15–34, http://dx.doi.org/10.30827/CPAG.v30i0.15370.

Roux, V., Bril, B., Cauliez, J., Goujon, A.-L., Lara, C., Saulieu De, G. and Zangato, E.

2017 Persisting technological boundaries: Social interactions, cognitive correlations and polarization, *Journal of Anthropological Archaeology* 48, 320–335.

Ruffieux, P.

2016 Pottery of the 18th Dynasty at Dukki Gel (Kerma): Classical repertoire and local style, in: B. Bader, C.M. Knoblauch and E.C. Köhler (eds.), *Vienna 2 – Ancient Egyptian Ceramics in the 21st Century. Proceedings of the International Conference held at the University of Vienna 14th–18th of May, 2012*, Orientalia Lovaniensia Analecta 245, Leuven, 507–525.

2018 *Égyptiens et Nubiens à Kerma: la céramique de Doukki Gel (Soudan) au Nouvel Empire*, unpublished PhD Dissertation, Sorbonne Université, Paris.

Sackett, J.R.

1977 The meaning of style in archaeology: A general model, *American Antiquity* 42 (3), 369–380.

Shriver-Rice, M.

2009 *Materiality, Objects, and Agency: Examples from Archaeology and Anthropology. A Brief Overview for Students*, 1–17. Available at https://www.researchgate.net/publication/312376598_Materiality_Objects_and_Agency_Examples_from_Archaeology_and_Anthropology_A_Brief_Overview, <last accessed 13 June 2022>.

Sillar, B. and Tite, M.S.

2000 The challenge of 'technological choices' for materials science approaches in archaeology, *Archaeometry*, 42 (2), 2–20.

de Souza, A.M.

2020 Melting pots: Entanglement, appropriation, hybridity, and assertive objects between the Pan-Grave and Egyptian ceramic traditions, *Journal of Ancient Egyptian Interconnections* 27, 1–23.

de Souza, A.M. and Ownby, M.

2022 Re-assessing Middle Nubian cultural constructs through ceramic petrography, *African Archaeological Review* 39, 35–58.

Spataro, M., Millet, M. and Spencer N.

2015 The New Kingdom settlement of Amara West (Nubia, Sudan): mineralogical and chemical investigation of the ceramics, *Archaeological and Anthropological Sciences* 7, 399–421.

Sterba, J.H. and D'Ercole, G.

Forthc. Chemical analyses of the pottery corpus from the New Kingdom town of Sai, in: J. Budka, *AcrossBorders 3: Vessels for the Home Away from Egypt. The Pottery Corpus from the New Kingdom Town of Sai Island.* With contributions by Giulia D'Ercole, Johannes Sterba and Philippe Ruffieux, Archaeology of Egypt, Sudan and the Levant, Vienna.

Tilley, C.

2004 *The Materiality of Stone: Explorations in Landscape Phenomenology*, Oxford.

Tsoraki, C., Barton, H., Crellin, R.J. and Harris, O.J.T.

2020 Making marks meaningful: new materialism and the microwear assemblage, *World Archaeology* 52 (3), 493–511.

Versluys, M.J.

2017 Object-scapes. Towards a material constitution of Romaness?, in: A. van Oyen and M. Pitts (eds.), *Materialising Roman Histories*, Oxford, 191–199.

Chapter 11

The provenance of black ritual liquids applied to coffins and cartonnage

Kate Fulcher[1]

Abstract

A black funerary liquid is known from ancient Egypt that was used for mummification and was also poured over the coffin or wrapped body as part of the funerary rites. Analysis of this black material can identify the components used to make it and therefore, to some extent, the geographical origin of its ingredients. Examples of this liquid are known from three sites in Nubia. Analysis of the black liquid from two of these sites indicates similar geographic origins for the materials used, perhaps with the exception of some of the bitumen which may have been obtained more locally. However, the context of the black liquid in Nubia indicates that its use may have differed slightly from its use in Egypt.

Keywords:

Coffin, funeral, resin, bitumen, burial, canopic

There is evidence from ancient Egypt in the form of coffins and cartonnage in museums, and a few archaeological examples, of a funerary ritual involving the pouring of a black liquid over the deceased, probably at the time of burial. The same liquid has been shown to be painted onto funerary statues and shabti boxes, and onto coffins as part of the decorative scheme, and analysis has revealed this black liquid to be the same as that used for mummification.[2] Therefore we have a black liquid that has a predictable list of ingredients, although slightly varying from one example to the next, that was used at several points during the preparation for internment – during the mummification of the body, the production of the coffin and other items for the tomb, and for a ritual during the funeral, perhaps at the point of internment. The time period over which this black liquid was utilised is not entirely clear, but there appears to be an example in the Metropolitan Museum of Art (11.150.15a) from the Middle Kingdom (1961–1878 BC), and it was certainly in use by royalty in the 18th Dynasty, as seen on the death mask of Tjuyu (c. 1375 BC) and covering the inner coffin and mummy of Tutankhamun (1323 BC). The practice is well attested in the Third Intermediate Period (c. 1086–725 BC), but this may be due to the larger number of coffins known from this time, and it continues into the Greco-Roman Period (c. 332 BC–390 AD).

Analysis of the black liquid from mummies and from the surfaces of coffins and cartonnage has shown it to consist of plant oil or animal fat, often mixed with plant resins from conifer or pistacia trees, beeswax, and bitumen.[3] It is very likely that this mixture was heated in order to combine the ingredients and apply them to the coffin or mummy case; in cool temperatures the mixture solidifies, as can be observed in museum collections today, and when heated it becomes a liquid, as attested by Howard Carter in his description of the removal of Tutankhamun's inner coffin from the middle coffin.[4] Oil (from plants) and fat (from animals) were available throughout Egypt and had various uses.[5] Beekeeping is well attested in ancient Egypt,[6] and this is likely the origin of the wax, although plant wax may also have been used.[7]

Neither pistacia nor conifer resin was available in the Nile Valley. Conifer trees would only have grown as far south as Lebanon,[8] so the resin probably would have been imported from somewhere in the eastern Mediterranean. Lebanon is famous for its cedar, and Lebanese cedar was imported into Egypt from the predynastic period onwards for use in coffin manufacture and building.[9] However, distinguishing between conifer genera (pine, cedar, juniper, cypress) is difficult because the biomarkers in various parts of the tree are variable, and common across genera, and can be lost or broken down with time and heating. Therefore, the origin of this resin is generally stated as being from the conifer group of trees.

There are several varieties of pistacia, some of which grow in the Mediterranean and others to the south in Somalia and Eritrea.[10] Resin adhering to

1 British Museum, Department of Scientific Research; kfulcher@britishmuseum.org.

2 Fulcher et al. 2021; Buckley, Clark and Evershed 2004; Łucejko et al. 2017; Serpico and White 2001.

3 Ibid.

4 Carter 2014.

5 Serpico and White 2000a.

6 Hammad 2018.

7 Fulcher et al. 2021.

8 Serpico and White 1998.

9 Gale et al. 2000.

10 Serpico 2000.

Fig. 1 Friable black solid F8623 in Tomb G321, Amara West cemetery D (photo by Amara West Project, Trustees of the British Museum).

multiple sherds of amphorae and incense burners from the site of Amarna in Egypt (1353–1336 BC) have been analysed and shown to be pistacia; the ceramic used to make these amphorae has been shown to originate in the Levant.[11] In support of the evidence of trade in pistacia resin in the eastern Mediterranean, amphorae from the Uluburun shipwreck (c. 1320 BC) off the coast of Turkey were found to contain approximately a ton of pistacia resin.[12] The destination of the cargo is unknown, but the use of pistacia resin in Egypt appears to be extensive, not just as a component of the black funerary liquid, but also for incense and coffin varnish.[13]

Biomarkers can be used to determine the geological origin of any bitumen that may be present, if modern comparisons are available. Most examples from mummy balm and black funerary liquids can be shown to originate from the Dead Sea,[14] and indeed there are Greek

11 Serpico 2003; Serpico and White 2000b.

12 Mills and White 1989. See also Serpico 1998.

13 Serpico and White 2001.

14 Connan and Dessort 1991; Łucejko et al. 2017; Fulcher et al. 2021.

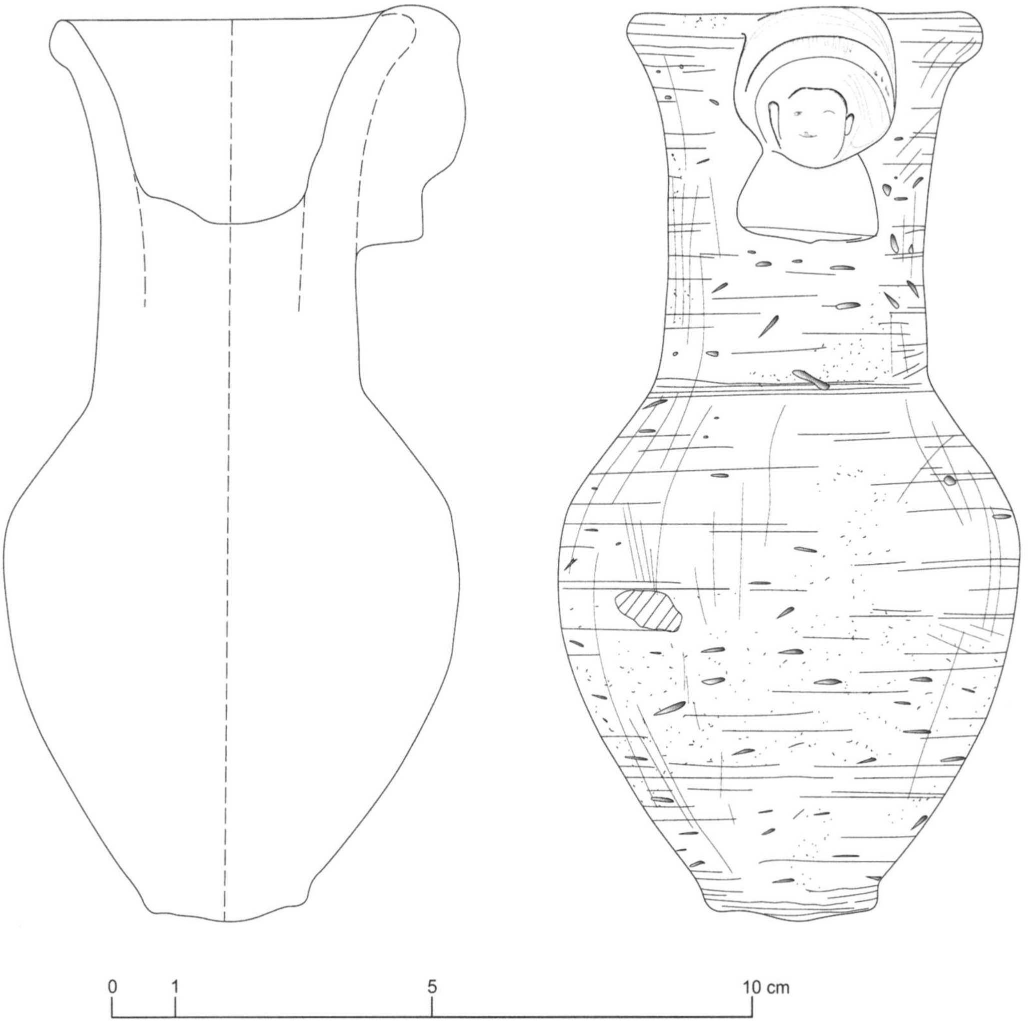

Fig. 2 Vessel SAC5 352/2017 containing bitumen from Tomb 26 on Sai Island (drawing by O.F. Stephan, ©AcrossBorders Project).

accounts of the collection of bitumen from the Dead Sea for trade into Egypt.[15] During periods of tectonic activity, huge lumps of bitumen float to the surface of the lake and can be harvested[16]. There is evidence of the trade of solid bitumen into Egypt from as early as the Naqada Period (c. 3900–3500 BC), when it appears at Maadi in blocks of up to 1 kg.[17]

There is known evidence of the use of black ritual liquids from three sites in Nubia, two of which have been analysed at the British Museum using gas chromatography coupled with mass spectrometry. This article is the first to discuss these Nubian examples as a group.

A friable black solid F8623 was found in Tomb G321 in Cemetery D at Amara West, which was in use from the 20th Dynasty (c. 1190–1086 BC), into the 8th century BC (Fig. 1).[18] The material was fragmented, having been disturbed prior to excavation, but one 2 cm thick layer was preserved over an area approximately 20 cm square next to skeletal remains. The larger chunks retained textile impressions, indicating that it originally adhered to a textile, probably bandages from a body; some pieces were still adhered to fragments of bandages. From the same site, a black layer was found on a painted wooden coffin fragment from Tomb G244 in Cemetery C (19th–20th Dynasties,

15 Hammond 1959.

16 Nissenbaum 1978.

17 Connan, Nissenbaum and Dessort 1992.

18 Fulcher, Stacey and Spencer 2020.

c. 1300–1080 BC). The friable black layer from G321 was found to be made of a fatty substance, wax, pistacia resin, and bitumen. The black layer from the coffin in G244 was found to contain pistacia resin and bitumen. The bitumen biomarkers from both black materials indicate a Dead Sea origin. Therefore, we have evidence for the trade of both pistacia resin and Dead Sea bitumen into Nubia in the late New Kingdom for use in funerary rituals.

A second example of black funerary liquid in Nubia is known from Sai Island.[19] Tomb 26 in cemetery SAC5 (18th Dynasty, c. 1548–1302 BC) contained a jar that was filled to the brim with a black liquid (Fig. 2). This jar was one of a pair placed at the head end of the body of a man; the other was empty. The jars appear to be based on canopic jars, having a similar shape and each with a head modelled on the neck of the jar (rather than a head-shaped lid). Pieces of black material were also found on the body associated with the jars in Tomb 26, suggesting the black liquid may have been applied to the body.[20] The black liquid from the jar was identified as bitumen, no other components could be identified. Unlike the majority of bitumen analysed from Egypt, and the bitumen from Amara West, the biomarkers do not indicate a Dead Sea origin. Other bitumen sources are known to have been exploited in ancient times, including Gebel Zeit near the Red Sea;[21] however, a match for the bitumen from Sai has not yet been identified. Black pigment from a palette from a domestic or small workshop area at Amara West consisted of powdered bitumen; the biomarkers appeared to match the bitumen from the jar at Sai.[22] This may suggest a local or Nubian source of bitumen was being used.

One further example of black liquid has been recorded in Nubia, from an intact chamber at the New Kingdom Tomb S91 at Aniba. Wrappings from two bodies, not mummified, retained black residue, and a stoppered canopic jar had black residue spilling out of it.[23]

Discussion

A black liquid was used in ancient Egypt in a funerary capacity, for mummification, funerary rituals (pouring over the wrapped body or coffin), and covering funerary furniture (e.g. shabti boxes). The date for the use of this black liquid pre-dates the New Kingdom, but certainly becomes much more identifiable in the archaeological record in the New Kingdom and Third Intermediate Period[24].

There appears to be evidence for the use of the funerary black liquid in Nubia in the New Kingdom, similarly consisting of a fatty substance, wax, pistacia resin, and bitumen. However, the use of the black liquid in Nubia cannot be securely linked to a practice of mummification, for which there is almost no evidence in Nubia.[25] Although the black liquid is associated with burials at Amara West, Sai, and Aniba, it does not appear to have formed part of a mummification process, since the bodies themselves are not preserved. Rather, it appears, from current evidence, to have been applied to the exterior of the wrapped body, or to have accompanied the body with an unknown meaning, which may be extrapolated from but different to the uses it had in Egypt. Canopic jars are very rare in Nubia, and as in the case of the jars from Tomb 26 at Sai, they contain no human remains. This may indicate that the funerary role of these objects was also slightly different in Nubia than in Egypt.[26] Therefore it appears that the practice of using the black funerary liquid was transmitted into Nubia, but its exact use in funerary rites developed down its own pathway, distinct from, but not unrelated to, funerary practice in Egypt. This is mirrored in the slightly different uses of canopic jars in Nubia versus in Egypt, and of course the two (black liquid and canopic jars) are closely related, the black liquid often being found within the jars. Additionally, the black liquid from Sai was found to contain only bitumen, no fatty component. The fatty component is always present in black funerary liquids from Egypt,[27] which may again point to a slightly different developmental track for the creation and use of the black liquid in Nubia. Two examples of bitumen from Nubia, a paint palette from Amara West, and the bitumen from the canopic jar in Tomb 26 at Sai, had similar biomarker profiles, with low gammacerane. This may indicate that a new source of bitumen was being exploited by the residents of Nubia during the New Kingdom.

19 Fulcher and Budka 2020.
20 Wohlschlager and Stadlmayr 2021, 166.
21 Harrell and Lewan 2002.
22 Fulcher, Stacey and Spencer 2020.
23 Steindorff 1937; Lemos et al. 2023.
24 Fulcher et al. 2021; Clark, Ikram and Evershed 2016.
25 Lemos 2018. For a general overview of New Kingdom tombs in Nubia see Spence 2019.
26 Lemos 2018; Lemos 2020.
27 Clark 2006.

Acknowledgements

The British Museum Amara West Project was led by Neal Spencer and funded by the Qatar-Sudan Archaeological Project. The AcrossBorders Project on Sai Island led by Julia Budka has received funding by the European Research Council under the European Union's Seventh Framework Programme (FP/2007-2013), ERC Grant Agreement no. 313668. This research would not have been possible without the assistance of the Sudan National Corporation for Antiquities & Museums, who generously allow the export of archaeological samples for scientific research. The analysis was conducted at the British Museum during a PhD funded by the AHRC (Ref. 1350956) and a post-doctoral position funded by the Wellcome Trust (Grant ref: 097365/Z/11/Z).

Bibliography

Buckley, S.A., Clark, K.A. and Evershed, R.P.
2004 Complex organic chemical balms of pharaonic animal mummies, *Nature* 431, 294–99, https://doi.org/10.1038/nature02849.

Carter, H.
2014 *The Tomb of Tutankhamun. Volume 2: The Burial Chamber*, London.

Clark, K.A.
2006 *Tracing the Evolution of Organic Balm Use in Egyptian Mummification via Molecular and Isotopic Signatures*, Unpublished PhD Thesis, University of Bristol.

Clark, K.A., Ikram, S. and Evershed, R.P.
2016 The significance of petroleum bitumen in ancient Egyptian mummies, *Philosophical Transactions of the Royal Society A* 374, 20160229, http://dx.doi.org/10.1098/rsta.2016.0229.

Connan, J. and Dessort, D.
1991 Du bitume dans les baumes de momies égyptiennes (1295 av. J.-C.–300 ap. J.-C.): Détermination de son origine et évaluation de sa quantité, *Comptes Rendus de l'Académie Des Sciences. Série 2, Mécanique, Physique, Chimie, Sciences de l'univers, Sciences de La Terre* 312, 1445–1452.

Connan, J., Nissenbaum, A. and Dessort, D.
1992 Molecular archaeology: Export of Dead Sea asphalt to Canaan and Egypt in the Chalcolithic-Early Bronze Age (4th–3rd Millennium BC), *Geochimica et Cosmochimica Acta* 56, 2743–59, https://doi.org/10.1016/0016-7037(92)90357-O.

Fulcher, K. and Budka, J.
2020 Pigments, incense, and bitumen from the New Kingdom town and cemetery on Sai Island in Nubia, *Journal of Archaeological Science: Reports* 33, 102550, https://doi.org/10.1016/j.jasrep.2020.102550.

Fulcher, K., Serpico, M., Taylor, J.H. and Stacey, R.
2021 Molecular analysis of black coatings and anointing fluids from ancient Egyptian coffins, ummmy cases, and funerary objects, *Proceedings of the National Academy of Sciences of the United States of America* 118, https://doi.org/10.1073/pnas.2100885118.

Fulcher, K., Stacey, R. and Spencer, N.
2020 Bitumen from the Dead Sea in Early Iron Age Nubia, *Nature Scientific Reports* 10, https://doi.org/10.1038/s41598-020-64209-8.

Gale, R., Gasson, P., Hepper, N. and Killen, G.
2000 Wood, in: P. T. Nicholson and I. Shaw (eds.), *Ancient Egyptian Materials and Technology*, Cambridge, 334–371.

Hammad, M.
2018 Bees and beekeeping in ancient Egypt, *Journal of Association of Arab Universities for Tourism and Hospitality* 15, 1–16, https://doi.org/10.21608/jaauth.2018.47990.

Hammond, P.C.
1959 The Nabataean bitumen industry at the Dead Sea, *The Biblical Archaeologist* 22, 40–48.

Harrell, J.A. and Lewan, M.D.
2002 Sources of mummy bitumen in ancient Egypt and Palestine, *Archaeometry* 44, 285–293, https://doi.org/10.1111/1475-4754.t01-1-00060.

Lemos, R.
2018 Materiality and cultural reproduction in non-elite cemeteries, in: É. Maynart, C. Velloza and R. Lemos (eds.), *Perspectives on Materiality in Ancient Egypt – Agency, Cultural Reproduction and Change*, Oxford, 24–34.
2020 Material culture and colonization in ancient Nubia: Evidence from the New Kingdom cemeteries, in: C. Smith (ed.), *Encyclopedia of Global Archaeology*, Cham, https://doi.org/10.1007/978-3-319-51726-1_3307-1.

Lemos, R., Fulcher, K., Abdllatief, I., Werström, L. and Hocker, E.
2023 Reshaping Egyptian funerary ritual in colonized Nubia? Organic characterization of unguents from mortuary contexts of the New Kingdom (c. 1550–1070 BCE), *Archaeological and Anthropological Sciences* 15, 73, https://doi.org/10.1007/s12520-023-01769-6.

Łucejko, J., Connan, J., Orsini, S., Ribechini, E. and Modugno, F.
2017 Chemical analyses of Egyptian mummification balms and organic residues from storage jars dated from the Old Kingdom to the Copto-Byzantine Period, *Journal of Archaeological Science* 85, 1–12, https://doi.org/10.1016/j.jas.2017.06.015.

Mills, J.S. and White, R.
1989 The identity of the resins from the Late Bronze Age shipwreck at Ulu Burur (Kaş), *Archaeometry* 31, 37–44, https://doi.org/10.1111/j.1475-4754.1989.tb01054.x.

Nissenbaum, A.
1978 Dead Sea asphalts – Historical aspects, *The American Association of Petroleum Geologists Bulletin* 62, 837–44, https://doi.org/10.1306/C1EA4E5F-16C9-11D7-8645000102C1865D.

Serpico, M.
1998 Quantifying resin trade in the Eastern Mediterranean during the Late Bronze Age, in: K. Polinger Foster and R. Laffineur (eds.), *Metron. Measuring the Aegean Bronze Age. Proceedings of the 9th International Aegean Conference. Yale University 18-21 April, 2002*, Aegaeum 24, Liège, 223–230.
2000 Resins, amber and bitumen, in: P.T. Nicholson and I. Shaw (eds.), *Ancient Egyptian Materials and Technology*, Cambridge, 430–74.

SERPICO, M. and WHITE, R.
1998 Chemical analysis of coniferous resins from ancient Egypt, in: C.J. EYRE (ed.), *Proceedings of the Seventh International Congress of Egyptologists, Cambridge, 3–9 September 1995*, Orientalia Lovaniensia Analecta 82, Leuven, 1037–1048.
2000a Oil, fat and wax, in: P. T. NICHOLSON and I. SHAW (eds.), *Ancient Egyptian Materials and Technology*, Cambridge, 390–429.
2000b The botanical identity and transport of incense during the Egyptian New Kingdom, *Anti quity* 74, 884–897, https://doi.org/10.1017/S0003598X00060531.
2001 The use and identification of varnish on New Kingdom funerary equipment, in: W.V. DAVIES (ed.) *Colour and Painting in Ancient Egypt*, London, 33–38.

SPENCE, K.
2019 New Kingdom tombs in Lower and Upper Nubia, in: D. RAUE (ed.), *Handbook of Ancient Nubia, Vol. 1*, Berlin; Boston, 541–566.

STEINDORFF, G.
1937 *Aniba. Zweiter Band*, Service des Antiquités de l'Egypte. Mission archéologique de Nubie 1929–1934, Glückstadt.

WOHLSCHLAGER, M. and STADLMAYR, A.
2021 Chapter 6: Anthropological report of human remains recovered from Tomb 26, in: J. BUDKA, *Tomb 26 on Sai Island: A New Kingdom Elite Tomb and Its Relevance for Sai and Beyond*, Leiden, 137–200.

Fig. 1 Map showing the location of H25 in the Middle Nile region and of other sites mentioned in the chapter (L. Kilroe).

Chapter 12

Local agency and foreign products. H25: A potential indigenous distribution site in the northern Dongola Reach

Loretta Kilroe[1]

Abstract

Ideas around Middle Nile distribution processes during the New Kingdom have historically had a strong Egyptological bias, reflecting the adoption of Egyptian-style material culture across the region. An archaeological focus on elite contexts such as temple towns and associated cemeteries only supported ideas around the hegemony of Egyptian socio-economic systems and the vanishing of indigenous practices at this time. However, modern fieldwork has begun to reassess systems of perceived Egyptianisation and to highlight the diversity of interactions across the vast Middle Nile. The site of H25 near the Third Cataract provides a potential window into the socio-economic systems in practice in rural New Kingdom Nubia, outside of the temple towns that, as seats of Egyptian colonial administration, will naturally have followed familiar Egyptian practices. This may represent a space where alternative Middle Nile interactions took place, outside of the more urban temple town environment. Material culture at the site suggests that the excavated structures date primarily to the later New Kingdom. However, over 50% of the material was indigenous, with Egyptian-style pottery predominantly storage containers.[2] This suggests that H25 represents a different social space from temple towns, and can give us an alternate perspective on the variety of exchange systems across Nubia at this time. Excavation of such sites can broaden our understanding of the administration of Nubia under Egyptian occupation, highlighting the multiplicities of practice across this landscape, particularly on the fringes of Egyptian control.

Keywords:

New Kingdom, Colonisation, circulation of goods, H25

Introduction to the site

H25, known locally as el-Eided Mohamadein, was first identified in the Northern Dongola Reach Survey[3] and is located 6 km north-east of the village of el-Ugal and 3.4 km north-west of Barquat Kuluf, on the south bank of the now extant Alfreda Nile palaeochannel in the Wadi Khowi (Fig. 1). This palaeochannel supported a large number of sites in the Kerma Period, before becoming a seasonal channel in the New Kingdom and finally drying out in the Medieval Period.[4]

The first survey recorded the settlement as encompassing a 230 m x 136 m occupation mound measuring 4.72 m high, containing over 34 structures, including tumuli, stone structures, burnt mounds and ovens, below a rocky gebel.[5] The site was then excavated by the British Museum within a Sudan Archaeological Research Society concession, funded by the Qatar-Sudan Archaeological Project, for three seasons.[6] Fieldwork points to a broad *Kerma Moyen* to early Kushite occupation, with ephemeral later use. However excavated structures have so far only revealed New Kingdom stratified deposits within mudbrick remains. These structures were rectilinear and roughly aligned north-south, pointing to organised construction. We find both smaller domestic structures and larger well-constructed buildings that were likely more elite and possibly linked to administration. These evolved over time, reflecting changing use (Fig. 2).

Building 18, for example, was a mudbrick construction made up of five rooms as well as two courtyards containing another room each. Later extensions saw the construction of another courtyard containing a large room, which itself was subsequently divided into three.[7] Storage jars were buried to the sides of its front room and heavy ash deposits were present in a smaller back room, pointing to food storage and cooking. Building 4 was of similar construction, with both located to the south-east of the site. Pottery dated these sites to the later New Kingdom.

Storage facilities were also present, including numerous underground storage ‘cellars’ in Building 5 and potentially a storage structure in Building 3, formed of a rectangular shape divided in two with its floor

1 British Museum, Department of Egypt and Sudan; LKilroe@britishmuseum.org.

2 This varied by season; in the first season, it was c. 50% by weight but 70% by sherd count (Thomas 2014, 65).

3 Welsby 2001, fig. 3.28.

4 Macklin et al. 2013, fig. 2.

5 Welsby 2001, 54–55.

6 Thomas 2014; Kilroe 2019a; Porter 2019.

7 Porter 2019, 77–79.

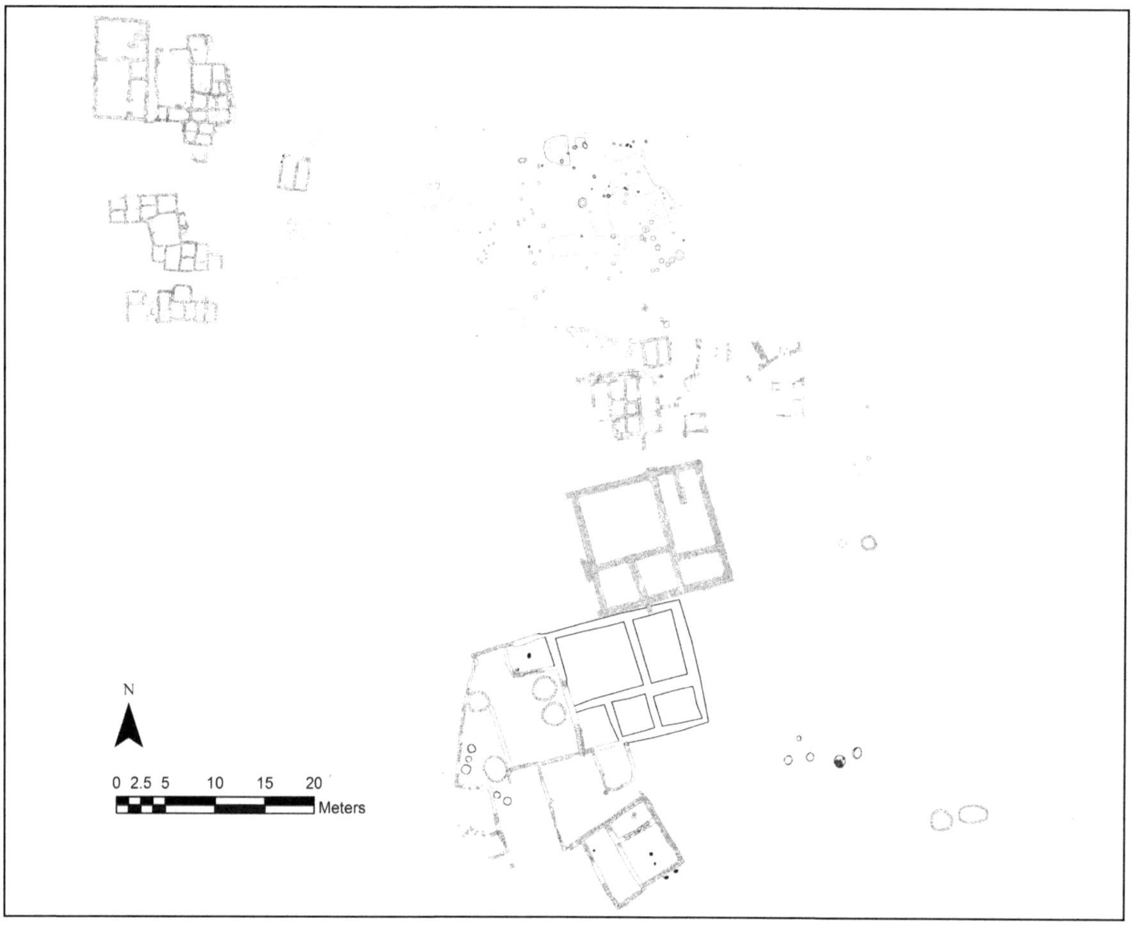

Fig. 2 Map of H25 (drawing by S. Porter and R.I. Thomas).

paved with large flat stones. No temple or any stone structures outside of Building 3 flooring were identified. To the north of the site, postholes indicated the presence of more ephemeral structures that likely reflect later use of the site, preserved at this higher level where erosion was more limited. High levels of organic matter within these small round structures suggest these were animal pens. No manufacturing areas were found.

Indigenous pottery

Pottery made up the vast majority of finds at H25, with the repertoire pointing to activities including cooking, consumption and storage at the site, as well as an interest in display. However, the types and fabrics point to a preference for indigenous material as well as the site's important positioning within exchange systems within Nubia.

The repertoire was not typical of a temple town; over 50% of the pottery was indigenous, while among the Egyptian- style material there was a clear preference for Egyptian-style storage vessels over tableware (Fig. 3).[8] This is much higher than other New Kingdom sites – at New Kingdom Sai, Nubian pottery was present in all sectors in considerable numbers but lower than the Egyptian material,[9] while at Sesebi it made up between 12-30% in each context.[10] In New Kingdom levels at Askut, it was 9.6%, with 83.1% of this cooking pots.[11] The same is true of more rural sites – at AtW 001 in Attab West, Nubian pottery numbered 20% of the total ceramic repertoire.[12] The indigenous pottery at H25 was diverse and comprised both cooking and finer bowls, beakers, and storage vessels. Some fragments of fine Kerma beakers were found on the surface suggesting occupational continuity at the site from the Kerma to the New Kingdom.[13] Bowls ranged in diameter, suggesting diverse usage around cooking and consumption.

Egyptian-style pottery included a variety of storage items as well as tableware bowls and a small number of beer jars and finer wares (Fig. 4). Finer wares included three small ovoid jars decorated with black painted geometric decoration, which were found inside or in the

8 Kilroe 2019a.

9 Budka 2018, 151; Budka 2020, 202.

10 Spence and Rose 2014, 412.

11 Smith 2003, Table 5.3.

12 Budka, Rose and Ward 2023, 28.

13 Thomas 2014, 66.

Fig. 3 Composite of indigenous wares: a. 7119y; b. 7128y; c. 7176y; d. xX; e. 7114y; f. 7585x (photographs by L. Kilroe).

Fig. 4 Composite of storage jars: a: 7476x; b: 7520x; c: 7562x (photographs by L. Kilroe).

vicinity of administrative Building 4[14] and may have had a particularly restricted availability. A variety of both neckless and short-necked storage vessels were the predominant Egyptian-style forms, with and without handles. These were usually in Nile silt with Marl generally rare across the site.[15] Some were very large, for example 7520x (Fig. 5) with a diameter of 25 cm and a height of 49 cm. These were found

14 7091x F9-21 north-east of Building 4; 7369x G8-4 Building 4 Room 2; 7519x G8-4 Building 4.

15 Four Marl or Marl/Nile mixes and three Marl fabrics. In the 2015 season, for example, Marl clay made up 2.3% of the total repertoire.

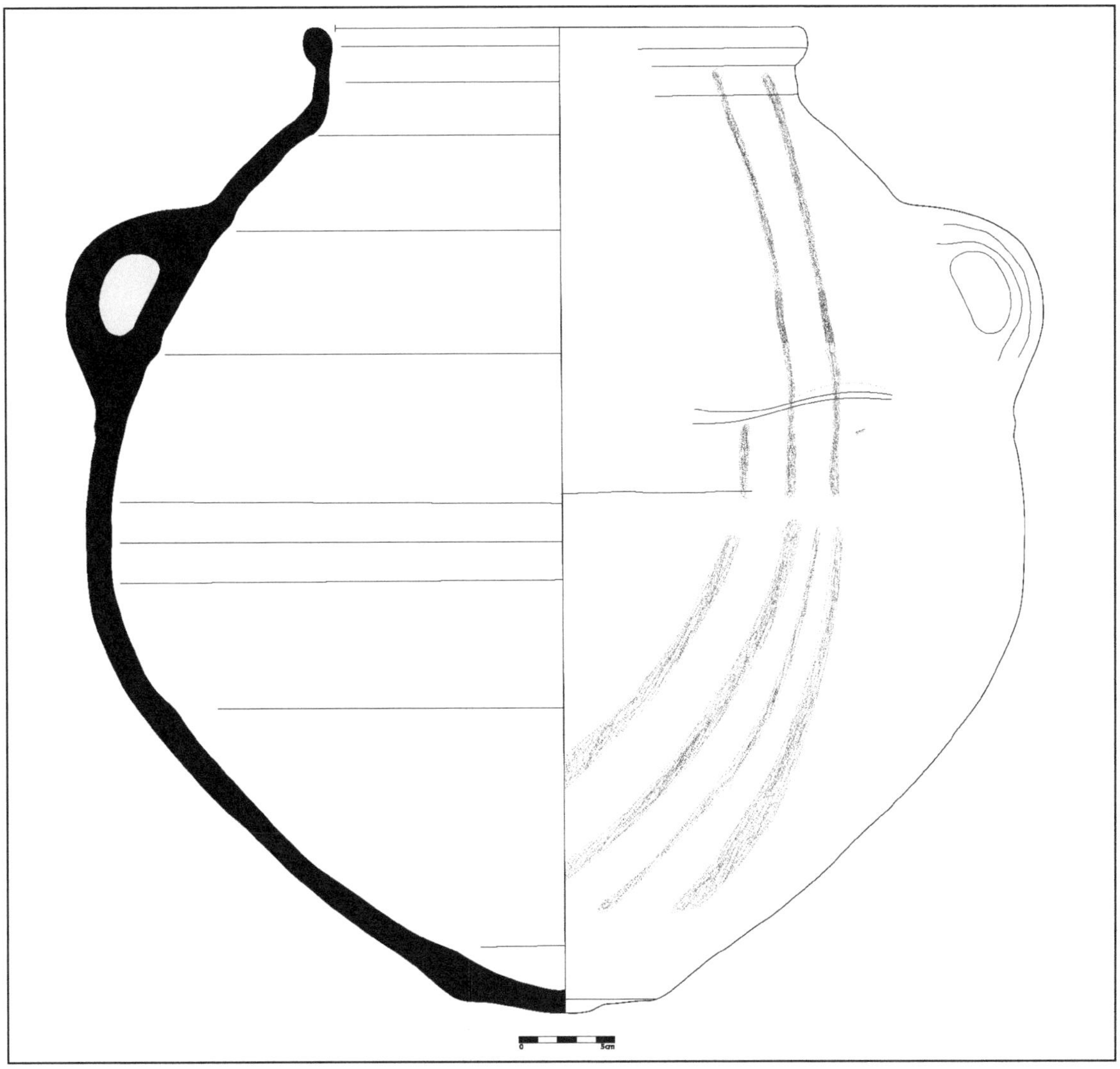

Fig. 5 Drawing of storage jar 7520x (drawing by L. Kilroe).

buried within structures in the settlement, often still covered by stone lids or with traces of matt covers inside, but also as fragments, suggesting a wider use than for domestic alone. Other typical New Kingdom Egyptian wares, such as beer jars, were uncommon. This high quantity of storage jars at H25 can be compared with sites such as Sesebi, where in contrast storage jars were rare and Egyptian-style pottery was predominantly made up of bowls, with a high number of bread cones.[16] The different repertoires observed across New Kingdom sites suggest to different regional practices and activities, pointing to different types of settlement across Nubia.

The preference for storage vessels also suggests that foodstuffs were coming into H25 from at least the wider region, as no manufacturing area was found at the site. While it is difficult to identify exactly where Nile silt vessels were produced along the Nile Valley by macroscopic analysis alone, there are clearly distinct Nile silt fabrics at the site and some were highly micaceous, which may point to a particular source area in Nubia. The presence of Marl and Marl/Nile silt mixes is clear evidence some pottery was certainly coming from Egypt, while fragments of fabrics from the Levant, possibly the Oasis regions, and other unidentified fabrics, although unfortunately too fragmentary to allow identification of a form, attest to wider networks coming into H25.[17] The integration of H25 into wider Late Bronze Age exchange networks is not unique – Mycenaean stirrup jars, for example, were found across Nubia,[18] including at the indigenous settlement of Gism el

16 Rose 2017, 468.

17 One fabric identified as Levantine, two Levantine or Oasis, and seven from an unknown source, Valentina Gasperini, pers. comm. 2016.

18 Schiller 2018.

Fig. 6 Pilgrim flask (reconstructed), 7549x (photographs by L. Kilroe).

Arba[19] and Tombos,[20] while Marl, Canaanite and Mycenaean wares were found at Amara West,[21] Sai,[22] and AtW 001 at Attab West.[23] Focal points for this exchange have generally thought to be restricted to Egyptian sites and temple towns, but the repertoire from H25 and other rural sites such as AtW 001 and Gism el Arba is striking and may suggest a greater indigenous role in these systems than often considered. Furthermore, at least 12 pilgrim flasks have been found across the site (Fig. 6). This was unexpected given the supposed rural nature of H25 and the small area thus far excavated. Two Nile silt pilgrim flasks, 7173x and 7174x, were found inside the western room of the building, while other fragments made from Egyptian marl clay were found across the site, including the well-made 7549x, which had a diameter of 12 cm and was covered with a thick red slip. Pilgrim flasks are common in New Kingdom Nubian sites[24] and their frequent presence here appears to have been a key part of exchange patterns into the area.

Although handmade wares remain difficult to date, their presence in contexts with the wheel-made Egyptian-style material made it clear these were contemporaneous. Its frequent presence points to different living practices around the site than seen in temple town environments – Egyptian pottery was clearly available, but the indigenous material seems to have either been more valued or simply more accessible here than in sites such as Amara West. It is unlikely this was unique; as we explore more settlements outside of temple towns, more regional practices will likely become evident.

A rural distribution node?

The ceramic remains at the site suggest H25 was a part of trading networks in Egyptian Nubia, while not being particularly 'Egyptianised'. The architecture at the site further supports this. The large, well-built structures of Building 4 and Building 18 to the south-east of the site were constructed of three or four row mudbrick walls surviving to three courses. Their presence here may be linked to administration during the New Kingdom, perhaps as living quarters for officials, since evidence for cooking and domestic pottery was found inside alongside fine wares and storage containers still buried in the floor. The small vases decorated with black painted linear decoration were all associated with this area as was Egyptian tableware, although indigenous material appeared alongside. Interestingly, a cow horn was found buried inside the entrance of Building 18, perhaps placed here as a ritual deposit[25] and indicating the ongoing importance of cattle as seen earlier in C-Group and Kerma contexts.[26]

The architecture appears distinct from the urban systems seen in temple towns, unsurprising given the site's more rural location. It is difficult to identify what 'typical' rural architecture was at this time, and how H25 may fit into a broader picture, but the town seems to have been a large centre linked to a wider network of sites along the palaeochannel. Rectilinear architecture was in use by indigenous groups during

19 Miellé 2016, 431, pl. I.
20 Smith 2007, 4, pl. 3.
21 Spencer 2012, 25; Spataro et al. 2014, 400; Gasperini 2023, 20, table 1.
22 Budka 2020, 202.
23 Budka 2022, 48.
24 Kilroe 2019b.
25 Personal observation.
26 Chaix and Grant 1992; Hafsaas 2020, 159–160.

Fig. 7 Building 3 (photograph by R.I. Thomas).

the Kerma Period,[27] although structures generally exhibit different floorplans to that at H25. Rectilinear architecture was also present in Settlement 2 at Gism el-Arba, which was in use for a short time during the 18th Dynasty and represented a move from and new construction to the nearby Kerman Settlement 1.[28] Larger settlements such as Kerma and Tabo seem to have supported Gism el-Arba,[29] and H25 may have served a similar purpose within the string of settlements along the Alfreda. Another site that may have relied upon a larger distribution site is AtW 001 at Attab West, which contained both indigenous and Egyptian pottery but lacked significant architectural remains.[30] However in other respects these sites are distinct from H25 – at Gism el Arba, one structure was built in ferruginous sandstone plastered with mud, and others such as Building 27 in a dual room copying earlier Kerma styles.[31] In addition, Gism el-Arba primarily contained Egyptian material, in common with the temple towns,[32] as well as dozens of animal figurines[33] and so their repertoires are different. AtW 001, while containing 20% Nubian pottery, was still predominantly filled with Egyptian-style material.

Another rural site, Hbb0017 at Habarab, was similarly located on a palaeochannel close to the Third Cataract.[34] This settlement was occupied slightly earlier than the stratified contexts at H25, between the Classic Kerma and early 18th Dynasty. Again, this settlement was architecturally distinct from H25, with rounded stone structures encompassing three large enclosures and 12 homesteads. However, the prolificity of similar handmade matt-impressed pottery and the location of the site within a wider context of other settlements, workshops and cemeteries echoes the situation of H25 within a broader use of the landscape.

Several structures at H25 appear to be linked to storage. Multiple small cells within Building 5 and Building 6 may be underground storage cellars,[35] perhaps with a hardened mud flooring to deter pests. Mudbrick flooring was used in the northern magazines at Amara West, covered with white plaster,[36] presumably for this purpose. Other small pits to the east of Buildings 4 and 18 were lined with mudbrick and given a compacted cobbled floor[37] for storing smaller quantities of goods, which were in a later phase of the site reused as rubbish dumps for large amounts of burnt 18th and 19th Dynasty pottery. Building 3 may be a specifically constructed storage structure (Fig. 7). This building was rectilinear, with a

27 See Gratien 1999; Gratien et al. 2003, fig. 2.
28 Miellé 2016, 423.
29 Miellé 2016, 431.
30 Budka, Rose and Ward 2023, 30.
31 Gratien 1999, 11.
32 Miellé 2016, 431.
33 Gratien 1999, fig. 2.
34 Gobeil and Boonstra 2019.
35 Thomas 2014, fig. 4.
36 Spencer, P. 1997, 56.
37 Porter 2019, 79.

Fig. 8 Mud stores (G10)12 and (G10)13 (photograph by S. Porter).

paved surface constructed of large flat slabs of varying coloured sandstone.

White mortar was found crumbled on the floor and was perhaps used for the walls, while a post hole was also found. This is the only place that stone has been found at the site thus far. Magazines with schist flooring were found at Amara West[38] and Sai.[39] This may be a deliberate choice reflecting a use for specific contents. A pot was buried in the ground and a pilgrim flask was found propped up in Building 3 upon excavation, perhaps relating to this use as a small magazine.[40] Its similarity to a structure that is part of Building 8 in the southern part of the site may point to different types of structure for different goods across the site (Fig. 8). A wooden seal was found in Building 8, unfortunately eroded but showing a rectangular symbol on the underside and perhaps indicating the building was linked to administrative activities (Fig. 9).[41]

Much evidence points to agriculture being the key priority at the site, with vast numbers of quernstones and rubbers and hammers/pounders suggesting the processing of large quantities of grain (Fig. 10). Multiple ovens in open courtyards and open spaces within the town may be communal facilities for its transformation into bread, although interestingly, bread moulds were not found. Several houses were also associated with animal pens. Limited other small finds were recovered, including a small number of scarabs, beads made of ostrich eggshell, carnelian and faience, and small fragments of copper alloy as well as copper alloy tools that are perhaps for kohl application,[42] suggesting these were not a priority for the area. The copious storage jars are evidence for the trade in large commodity vessels,[43] perhaps used to move grain and other more exotic foodstuffs into H25 and through into the other settlements along the Alfreda, with the site being used as a centralised produce centre for collection and redistribution.[44]

Local innovation

In addition to both Nubian and Egyptian-style pottery at H25, the site also contained examples of local developments. These situate H25 as part of a broader trend of indigenous communities adjusting Egyptian imported material for local activities.

Several large Nile silt storage jars were decorated with an unusual spaced vertical burnishing that does not occur in contemporary sites in Nubia or Egypt. This may point to the development of local practices around

38 Spencer 2015, fig. 8.12; Dalton 2017, 360.
39 Budka 2020, 97.
40 3.10 m x 2.8 m, Ashley Thomas, pers. comm.
41 Thomas 2014, pl. 6d.
42 Porter 2019, pls. 6 and 7.
43 Rose 2017, 471.
44 Porter 2019, 77.

Fig. 9 Administrative seal (photograph by R.I. Thomas).

Fig. 10 Quernstone SF 1156 and pounder SF 1238 (not a pair) (photographs by G. Bettinson).

Fig. 11 Photograph of a hybrid Egyptian/Nubian bowl 7391x (photograph by L. Kilroe).

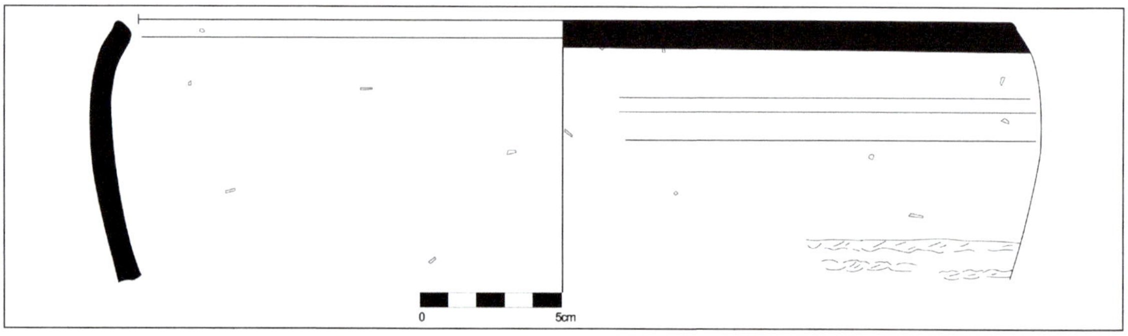

Fig. 12 Drawing of a hybrid Egyptian/Nubian bowl 7391x (drawing by L. Kilroe).

Egyptian-style pottery in New Kingdom communities. Similarly, hybrid jars and cooking pots have been found at Sai Island,[45] modelled on Egyptian types but with a Nubian influence, as well as at Gism el-Arba[46] and Sesebi,[47] so this is part of a broader phenomenon with communities adapting Egyptian styles to better suit their needs/visual preferences.

Hybrid bowls were also found at H25 (Figs. 11–12). These showed a mixture of traditionally 'Egyptian' and 'Nubian' manufacturing and decorative practices: handmade bowls produced from a traditionally Nubian fabric and fired in a reduced atmosphere resulting in a thick black core, covered with a beige slip and given a red painted rim to mimic contemporary Egyptian-style bowls. Similar hybrid bowls have been identified at the New Kingdom temple town of Amara West,[48] while

45 Budka 2020, 203, 225.
46 Miellé 2016, 431.
47 Rose 2017, 466, figs. 1.6, 2.

48 Gasperini 2023, 119.

other types of hybrid wares occurred at Sai Island[49] and AtW 001 in Attab West (see also above, Introduction to Part III).[50] Hybrid vessels are also known from a slightly earlier period at Elephantine, where inversely we see wheel-made imitations of Nubian vessels, as well as further north at Tell Edfu.[51]

The presence of these hybrids across colonial Nubia not only points to creative engagement with Egyptian material culture, but in the case of the bowls also suggests an ongoing commitment across the Third Cataract to indigenous manufacturing practices, even when a strong wheel-made industry was present. This further suggests that the pottery industry – and practices showing Egyptianisation of the area – were much more flexible than traditional models allow. H25 was part of a wider circulation of shared manufacturing practices around the Third Cataract area, telling us that not just goods but ideas were also being distributed during the New Kingdom and that they were relevant to disparate communities in both urban and rural areas.

Conclusion

Excavation of rural sites such as H25 is key for understanding the broader administrative and living situation across Nubia in the New Kingdom, as settlements outside of temple towns are still poorly understood. The material remains at H25 point to links with contemporary Egypt and certainly show some Egyptian influence in architecture, pottery, and small finds. However, this is much less than that observed at many other sites in Nubia, and as such does not seem to point to an Egyptian presence or high levels of 'Egyptianisation'. Instead, evidence seems to suggest the site was an indigenous collection and distribution node for agricultural material, likely for the surrounding settlements along the Alfreda channel. This area seems to have been important in the Kerma Period, with large numbers of settlements scattered along the riverbank.[52] This is accompanied by only a small number of cemeteries, perhaps linked to different burial practices within these communities than in Egyptian spaces, where groups over a large area shared burial spaces, as seen earlier in the Kerma Period.[53] This may have been linked to shared identities that are now invisible in the archaeological record.

Site-specific regionalities that are reflected in different quantities of types of material culture are becoming increasingly evident across New Kingdom Nubia, attesting to a much more diverse engagement with Egyptian imposed structures around the Third Cataract. Rural sites such as H25 broaden our understanding of the Egyptian administration of Nubia during Egyptian occupation, pointing to an ongoing indigenous involvement in the redistribution of commodities across this period.

Acknowledgements

We are grateful to the National Corporation for Antiquities and Museums Sudan for providing the Sudan Archaeological Research Society the concession and permission to work at H25. Thanks are given to Dr Derek Welsby and the Sudan Archaeological Research Society for inviting me to work at H25. This article would not have been possible without the help and advice of Dr Ross Thomas, who worked at H25 in 2016 and remained deeply interested in the site, and Stephen Porter, current director of the site.

49 Budka 2020, 225.
50 Budka 2023, 89; Budka, Rose and Ward 2023, fig. 16.
51 Raue 2017; de Souza 2020, 316–317.
52 Welsby 2001, fig. 2.1.
53 Osman and Edwards 2012, 62; Welsby 2001, 120.

Bibliography

BUDKA, J.

2018 Pots and people: Ceramics from Sai Island and Elephantine, in: J. BUDKA and J. AUENMÜLLER (eds.), *From Microcosm to Macrocosm. Individual Houses and Cities in Ancient Egypt and Nubia*, Leiden, 147–170.

2020 The material remains from the New Kingdom town, in: J. BUDKA, *AcrossBorders 2: Living in New Kingdom Sai,* Archaeology of Egypt, Sudan and the Levant 1, Vienna, 183–270.

2022 Early New Kingdom settlement activities in the periphery of Sai Island: towards a contextualisation of fresh evidence from Attab West, *Der antike Sudan. Mitteilungen der Sudanarchäologischen Gesellschaft zu Berlin e.V* 33, 45–62.

2023 Cultural diversity in the Attab to Ferka region in Sudan: the 2023 season of the DiverseNile Project, *The Project Repository Journal* 18, 86–89.

BUDKA, J., ROSE, K. and WARD, C.

2023 Cultural diversity in the Bronze Age in the Attab to Ferka region: new results based on excavations in 2023, *Der antike Sudan. Mitteilungen der Sudanarchäologischen Gesellschaft zu Berlin e.V.* 34, 19–35.

CHAIX, L. and GRANT, A.

1992 Cattle in ancient Nubia, *Anthropozoologica* 16, 61–66.

DALTON, M.

2017 Reconstructing lived experiences of domestic space at Amara West, in: N. SPENCER, A. STEVENS and M. BINDER (eds), *Nubia in the New Kingdom. Lived Experience, Pharaonic Control and Indigenous Traditions*, British Museum Publications on Egypt and Sudan 3, Leuven, 357–388.

GASPERINI, V.

2023 *Amara West: The Pottery from Cemeteries C and D*, Amara West Research Project Publications 2, British Museum Publications on Egypt and Sudan 17, Leuven.

GOBEIL, C. and BOONSTRA, S.

2019 New investigations on the Third Cataract in Sudan, *Egyptian Archaeology* 55, 1–8.

GRATIEN, B.

1999 Some rural settlements at Gism el-Arba in the Northern Dongola Reach, *Sudan & Nubia* 3, 10–12.

GRATIEN, B., MARCHI, S., THURIOT, O. and WILLOT, J.-M.

2003 Gism el-Arba, habitat 2. Rapport préliminaire sur un centre de stockage Kerma au bord du Nil, *Cahiers de Recherches de l'Institut de Papyrologie et d'Egyptologie de Lille* 23, 29–43.

HAFSAAS, H.

2020 The C-Group People in Lower Nubia: Cattle pastoralists on the frontier between Egypt and Kush, in: G.EMBERLING and B.B. WILLIAMS (eds.), *The Oxford Handbook of Ancient Nubia*, Oxford, 157–178.

KILROE, L.

2019a H25 2019 – the ceramics, *Sudan & Nubia* 23, 80–82.

2019b *Pilgrim flasks: Chronological and cultural transformations in Nubia from the New Kingdom to the Napatan Period,* PhD Thesis, University of Oxford.

MACKLIN, M., WOODWARD, J., WELSBY, D., DULLER, G., WILLIAMS, F. and MARTIN, M.

2013 Reach-scale river dynamics moderate the impact of rapid Holocene climate change on floodwater farming in the desert Nile, *Geology* 41(6), 695–698.

MIELLÉ, L.

2016 18th Dynasty pottery from Gism el-Arba (Sudanese Nubia), in: B. BADER, C.M. KNOBLAUCH and E.C. KÖHLER (eds.), *Vienna 2. Ancient Egyptian Ceramics in the 21st Century. Proceedings of the International Conference Held at the University of Vienna, 14th-18th of May 2012*, Orientalia Lovaniensia Analecta 245, Leuven, 423–435.

OSMAN, A. and EDWARDS, D.N.

2012 *The Archaeology of a Nubian Frontier. Survey on the Third Nile Cataract, Sudan,* Leicester.

PORTER, S.

2019 Excavations at H25 in the northern Dongola Reach, *Sudan & Nubia* 23, 77–80.

RAUE, D.

2017 Nubian pottery on Elephantine Island in the New Kingdom, in: N. SPENCER, A. STEVENS and M. BINDER (eds.), *Nubia in the New Kingdom. Lived Experience, Pharaonic Control and Indigenous Traditions*, British Museum Publications on Egypt and Sudan 3, Leuven, 525–536.

ROSE, P.

2017 Sesebi: ceramics, chronology and society, in: N. SPENCER, A. STEVENS and M. BINDER (eds.), *Nubia in the New Kingdom. Lived Experience, Pharaonic Control and Indigenous Traditions*, British Museum Publications on Egypt and Sudan 3, Leuven, 465–473.

SCHILLER, B.

2018 Aegean pottery in Nubia: imports and imitations, *Cahiers de la Céramique Égyptienne* 11, 91–106.

SMITH, S.T.

2003 *Wretched Kush. Ethnic Identities and Boundaries in Egypt's Nubian Empire*, London.

2007 Death at Tombos: Pyramids, iron and the rise of the Napatan Dynasty, *Sudan & Nubia* 11, 2–14.

DE SOUZA, A

2020 Pots, gold, and viceroys: shifting dynamics of Egyptian-Nubian relations at the transition to the New Kingdom, from the viewpoint of Middle Nubian pottery at Tell Edfu, *Ägypten & Levante* 30, 313–343.

SPATARO, M., MILLET, M. and SPENCER, N.

2014 The New Kingdom settlement of Amara West (Nubia, Sudan): mineralogical and chemical investigation of the ceramics, *Archaeological and Anthropological Sciences* 7, 399–421.

Spence, K. and Rose, P.
2014 Fieldwork at Sesebi 2010, in: J.R. Anderson and D.A. Welsby (eds.), *The Fourth Cataract and Beyond. Proceedings of the 12th International Conference for Nubian Studies*, British Museum Publications on Egypt and Sudan 1, Leuven, 409–415.

Spencer, N.
2012 Insights into life in occupied Kush during the New Kingdom: new research at Amara West, *Der antike Sudan. Mitteilungen der Sudanarchäologischen Gesellschaft zu Berlin e.V.* 23, 21–28.
2015 Creating a neighborhood within a changing town: Household and other agencies at Amara West in Nubia, in: M. Müller (ed.), *Household Studies in Complex Societies: (Micro)archaeological and Textual Approaches*, Oriental Institute Seminars 10, Chicago, 169–210.

Spencer, P.
1997 *Amara West I. The Architectural Report*, Egypt Exploration Society, Excavation Memoir 63, London.

Thomas, R.I.
2014 El-Eided Mohamadein (H25): a Kerma, New Kingdom and Napatan settlement on the Alfreda Nile, *Sudan & Nubia* 18, 58–68.

Welsby, D.
2001 *Life on the Desert Edge. Seven Thousand Years of Settlement in the Northern Dongola Reach, Sudan*, Sudan Archaeological Research Society Publication 7, London.

Contributions to the Archaeology of Egypt, Nubia and the Levant

Vol. 1 **A. Lohwasser**
Aspekte der napatanischen Gesellschaft. Archäologisches Inventar und funeräre Praxis im Friedhof von Sanam – Perspektiven einer kulturhistorischen Interpretation, Vienna 2012.

Vol. 2 **I. Gamer-Wallert**
Die Wandreliefs des Zweiten Lichthofes im Grab des Monthemhat (TT 34). Versuch einer zeichnerischen Rekonstruktion (mit Beiträgen von E. Schindler von Wallenstein und S. Hermann), Vienna 2013.

Vol. 3 **I. Adenstedt**
Reconstructing Pharaonic Architecture in Nubia. The Case Study of SAV 1, Sai Island, Vienna 2017.

Vol. 4 **J. Budka (ed.)**
AcrossBorders I. The New Kingdom Town of Sai Island, Sector SAV1 North, Vienna 2017.

Vol. 5 **M. Bietak and S. Prell (eds.)**
Ancient Egyptian and Ancient Near Eastern Palaces Volume I. Proceedings of the Conference on Palaces in Ancient Egypt, held in London 12th–14th June 2013, Vienna 2018.

Vol. 6 **A. Kahlbacher and E. Priglinger (eds.)**
Tradition and Transformation in Ancient Egypt. Proceedings of the Fifth International Congress for Young Egyptologists 15–19 September 2015, Vienna 2018.

Vol. 7 **C. Sauvage and Ch. Lorre**
Á la decouverte du royaume d'Ougarit (Syrie du IIe millénaire. Les fouilles de C.F.A- Schaeffer à Minet el-Beida et Ras-Shamra (1929–1937), Vienna 2023.

Vol. 8 **M. Bietak, P. Matthiae and S. Prell (eds.)**
Ancient Egyptian and Ancient Near Eastern Palaces Volume II. Proceedings of a Workshop on Palaces in the Near East and Egypt, held during the 10th ICAANE in Vienna 25th–26th June 2016, Wiesbaden 2019.

Vol. 9 **M. Bietak and S. Prell (eds.)**
The Enigma of the Hyksos Volume I. ASOR Conference Boston 2017 – ICAANE Conference Munich 2018 – Collected Papers, Wiesbaden 2019.

Vol. 10 **A.-L. Mourad**
The Enigma of the Hyksos Volume II. Transforming Egypt into the New Kingdom. The Impact of the Hyksos and Egyptian-Near Eastern Relations, Wiesbaden 2021.

Vol. 11 **S. Prell**
The Enigma of the Hyksos Volume III. Vorderasiatische Bestattungssitten im ägyptischen Ostdelta – eine Spurensuche, Wiesbaden 2021.

Vol. 12 **M. Bietak and S. Prell (eds.)**
The Enigma of the Hyksos Volume IV. Changing Clusters and Migration in the Near Eastern Bronze Age. Collected Papers of a Workshop held in Vienna 4th–6th of December 2019, Wiesbaden 2021.

Vol. 13 **E. Priglinger**
The Enigma of the Hyksos Volume V. Zwischen den Zeiten. Überlegungen zum Ende der drei Reiche im alten Ägypten, Wiesbaden 2021.

Vol. 14 **S. Vilain**
The Enigma of the Hyksos Volume VI. Crises et échanges pendant la Deuxième Période Intermédiaire: Tell el-Dab'a, entre Méditerranée orientale et vallée du Nil, Wiesbaden 2023.

Vol. 15 **M. Bietak**
The Enigma of the Hyksos Volume VII. Near Eastern Temples and the Spiritual Background of the Hyksos and their Predecessors, Wiesbaden, forthcoming.

Vol. 16 **A. Ilin-Tomich**
Egyptian Name Scarabs from the 12th to the 15th Dynasty: Geography and Chronology of Production, Wiesbaden 2023.

Vol. 17 **J. Budka and R. Lemos (eds.)**
Landscape and Resource Management in Bronze Age Nubia: Archaeological Perspectives on the Exploitation of Natural Resources and the Circulation of Commodities in the Middle Nile, Wiesbaden, 2024.